Black Powder Guide

Second Edition

On the cover:

Top: The U.S.-marked French Charleville M1763 flintlock musket, .69 caliber, and all the accouterments are from the collection of Vincent A. Pestilli of Whitman, Massachusetts. (The first U.S. M1795 Springfield musket was a copy of the 1763 Charleville Pattern.)

Center: The U.S. M1808 Navy Model percussion-conversion pistol, .64 caliber, made by Simeon North of Berlin, Connecticut, was lent by the town of Whitman, Massachusetts, Bicentennial Collection.

Bottom: The French M1777 flintlock pistol, .69 caliber, is from the collection of Robert W. Meier of Whitman, Massachusetts. This gun was used as a model for the first U.S. government contract pistol made by North and Cheney of Berlin, Connecticut.

Black Powder Guide
Second Edition

George C. Nonte, Jr.

Stoeger Publishing Company

Published by the Stoeger Publishing Company
55 Ruta Court, South Hackensack, New Jersey 07606

Sixth printing, June 1984

ISBN: 0-88317-069-8

Manufactured in the United States of America

Distributed to the book trade and to the sporting goods trade by Stoeger Industries, 55 Ruta Court, South Hackensack, N.J. 07606

In Canada, distributed to the book trade and to the sporting goods trade by Stoeger Canada, Ltd., 169 Idema Road, Markham, Ontario L3R 1A9

Contents

Foreword

There may be people in whom atavistic urges do not surface with a fair degree of regularity—but if there are, I don't know any of them. We all have feelings from and for the past. Perhaps we may not all think of them as "The Good Old Days" in the classic sense, but we do have a love for items out of the past; usually we prefer items associated with our ancestors or with pioneer figures we admire.

While many people satisfy these urges by collecting antiques, *doing* something with old things is far more satisfying than mere ownership. This is especially true with tools of *action,* and nothing connotes vigorous action on the far-flung frontiers than guns of the past. After all, our nation was born in billowing white clouds of powder smoke as musket and rifle fire reverberated from Concord to Fallen Timbers to King's Mountain and beyond. In this, the time of the Bicentennial, no tool from the past is more conspicuous than the arms that fought (and defeated) British, French, Spanish and Mexican armies, and which pushed our frontiers to the Pacific, carving out the great fur-trade and mining industries on the way.

Our frontiers expanded behind a curtain of powder smoke created by the rebels, the adventurers, the wanderers, who must ever enter the wilderness and attain the other side of the mountain. Many of us feel kinship with the mountain man, who froze, rifle in hand, during a Bitterroot blizzard or the dust-grimed, carbine-jingling dragoons following Marcy across the desert. We may even wonder how we'd have performed in their circumstances with their equipment. Civilization prevents us from attempting to duplicate their adventures, but today there are modern copies of their weapons. With these guns, we can do some of the things they did and we can learn how we measure up. When hunting or shooting on the range with the guns of our forefathers—real or imagined—we can relate to those pioneers and fighters better than by other means.

What may have been an exasperating chore for great-great grandfather as he struggled to get a second shot off, takes on the aspect of pleasant recreation for his descendants. Accustomed as we are to totally reliable guns and ammunition that shoot faster, farther and harder than ever before, it can be a pleasant change to work out with a twin of the muzzle loader which some ancestor could have carried at the Battle of Vera Cruz or the Fetterman Massacre.

Acknowledgment

It should be evident that a book of this sort simply couldn't have been put together without the help of a lot of people. The test shooting alone, involving a couple of dozen guns, hundreds of shots and black powder by the bucketful, took many willing hands. When 200-grain powder charges are being fired by the score, no single shoulder holds up under that beating for long, and I can't express enough appreciation for the enthusiasm of the fellows—gals, too—who came on with a "grin and bear it" attitude. Their bruises and the ringing in their ears are testimony to their enthusiasm for black powder shooting.

However, without a broad range of guns and equipment, all that shooting would never have been possible. While nearly all manufacturers and importers made items available for tests, I am especially grateful to Val Forgett, president of the Navy Arms/Service Armament group. Val not only supplied much equipment, he gave freely of advice, time and effort throughout the preparation of the material for this book. Val is one of the few men of this century who have successfully hunted African elephant with a muzzle loader; he is obviously a confirmed, lifetime black powder and muzzle-loading buff.

And so, special thanks are due Val Forgett and Navy Arms, without whose assistance this book would be less than it is.

The old-timers who could tell us how they really loaded and handled a prize "Kentucky" squirrel rifle or Enfield Minie rifle are dead and gone. Some of them put their experiences in writing, but most took their knowledge with them. I have gone through their writings and skimmed off what appears to be useful in shooting today's muzzle loaders, and I have added the shared knowledge developed by the burgeoning groups that have been shooting the old guns since before most of us were born. This has all been put together in this volume for those of you who have succumbed or will succumb to the urge to shoot with black powder, caps and all the other romantic paraphernalia.

This book, then, is for the user, the *doer;* not the gatherer or collector, but the person who for whatever reason seeks to emulate our ancestors' use of firearms in sport or war.

In this volume, I have tried to put together virtually all the information one needs at least to begin to follow any one of several branches of a most fascinating game—black powder shooting.

The glossary of muzzle-loading terms is included through the courtesy of Maj. R.O. Ackerman of Albuquerque, New Mexico.

—Maj. George C. Nonte, Jr.
Peoria, Illinois, U.S.A.
February 1976

1/History of Black Powder

The term "black powder" is relatively new, and did not come into use until the latter half of the 19th century. Tremendous strides were then made in the development of more modern and efficient, so-called "smokeless" explosives and propellants such as gun cotton, cordite, and single and double base nitrocellulose powders. Prior to that time, there was only one propellant suitable for use in small arms and artillery, simply called "gunpowder." It was essentially identical to what we call black powder today, so designated only to differentiate it from the more modern "smokeless powder," which is not really smokeless at all, in spite of the name. It produces much less smoke than black powder, but still smokes.

The origins of gunpowder are, if not lost, certainly shrouded in legend, half-truths, and vague claims and statements. Students of the subject will give you an assortment of answers to the question of just when, where, how and by whom gunpower was invented. While two of the principal ingredients—charcoal and sulphur—were known in antiquity, the third essential ingredient—saltpeter—was not. Consequently, we can safely assume that gunpowder did not exist until all three of its principal ingredients became known, reasonably common and available in quantity.

Saltpeter does not exist as a natural mineral product, but is produced by the slow oxidation by atmospheric oxygen of organic matter containing nitrogen in the presence of basic substances. Microorganisms bring about this oxidation, and it is carried out artificially and commercially in niter-beds, made of manure or urine to supply the organic nitrogen. The raw product must then be carefully purified, and any calcium nitrate in it must be converted into potassium nitrate. This, of course, is the primitive method of producing saltpeter and is seldom encountered today except in areas of India and in some of the more primitive parts of the world.

As a matter of interest, the Confederacy was severely short of powder during the Civil War. Ribald comments were generated by an appeal to southern ladies to save the contents of their families' chamber pots for use in making the saltpeter needed for powder mills.

Modern production of saltpeter is accomplished by a highly efficient process in which native sodium nitrate (Chile saltpeter) is converted on a large scale directly to potassium nitrate.

Indications are that saltpeter became known in Europe about 1250, when it is mentioned in the works of Roger Bacon and Albertus Magnus. Their knowledge of this compound and its properties was probably obtained from Latin translations of various Arabic works. A Latin work called *The Book of Fire (Liber Ignium)* alleged to have been written by Marcus Graecus (Mark the Greek) describes both saltpeter and gunpowder. J. R. Partington, Emeritus Professor of Chemistry at the University of London, stated that this work is a translation not from the Greek, but from an Arabic work dating around the middle of the 13th century. It is probable that scholars such as Bacon and Magnus would have had knowledge of it.

The Book of Fire gives recipes both for incendiary compositions (which were known long before gunpowder) and for basic gunpowder in its most rudimentary form. It also distinguishes between the burning of various compounds for propulsion, as in a rocket, and explosive burning, as in a gun.

It has often been suggested that gunpowder was invented by Roger Bacon. In his *Opus Majus* of 1268, he did describe the explosion of gunpowder and a year or two later gave its composition. Bacon was apparently quite impressed with the explosive force of gunpowder, and conceived of it as a destructive device but it seems unlikely that he invented it.

Other Arabic works of the early 14th century describe gunpowder in detail, while those of 1225 or thereabouts refer only to incendiary compositions. Then, too, cannons were known in Europe as early as 1326 (the date of one manuscript describing them). Obviously, the cannon could not exist without gunpowder, so we can assume that it too was well known by that time.

One Berthold Schwartz (sometimes referred to as "Black Berthold") has frequently been credited with the invention of gunpowder in the middle 14th century. This legend doesn't stand up when we consider that Roger Bacon described it, its effects and its manufacture a century earlier. Then there are oriental manuscripts of earlier times that describe a number of fireworks and incendiary compounds. Often these are mistaken for gunpowder, but evidence that any of them were used to propel a projectile from a closed tube (other than fireworks of the Roman candle type) is significantly lacking.

While it is quite likely that scholars will continue to argue vigorously supporting various sources and dates for the invention of gunpowder, the best educated guess would seem to place it in Europe between 1225 and 1250. The exact date will probably never be known, and isn't really essential to our purposes here. It is sufficient for us to know that gunpowder dates back at least seven centuries.

In its earliest form, gunpowder differed considerably from the black powder we know today. It consisted of a *mechanical* mixture of charcoal, sulphur and saltpeter. The three ingredients were ground separately to a fine powder and then stirred together. This form had several disadvantages. For one, it tended to absorb large quantities of moisture from the air—particularly important where sea-borne weapons were involved—and formed rock-hard lumps and cakes that couldn't be placed in a gun barrel. In addition, the various constituents of the powder tended to become separated if the material was much agitated, as it would be in transportation on a supply wagon or a pitching, rolling ship. Ignition of this fine, mechanically mixed powder could also present a problem if it were packed tightly in the gun, leaving insufficient space between the particles to admit the ignition flame.

Numerous methods were explored to overcome some of these disadvantages. Careful storage, frequent turning of containers, adding powdered quicklime to the mix, even on-site mixing of the three basic ingredients were all tried with varying success.

Eventually it was discovered that by forming the powder into grains or granules (corning) the powder's absorption of moisture could be greatly reduced. Each granule thus formed contained the proper proportions of all the ingredients so separation could not occur. Corned powder is thought to have been invented in the 15th century. Whether it was the result of direct effort or simply observation of the behavior of lumpy powder is not known.

There is evidence that some attempts to reduce the moisture-absorbing characteristics were made by heating the powder until the sulphur therein melted, forming lumps. This could hardly have been considered a very safe treatment for even a crude, rather weak explosive mixture.

Corned powder produced greater explosive force than the powdered mixture. It not only reduced the amount of moisture absorbed, it eliminated any separation of ingredients and provided easier and more uniform ignition. Because of its greater force, guns had to be cast of better materials and in a more perfect manner to withstand the force of the explosion. We really don't know which came first—corned powder, making better guns necessary; or better guns, making the use of corned powder possible.

By the early 19th century, it had been discovered that larger powder granules were more suitable for artillery use. Likewise, it was discovered that small granules burned faster than large. Consequently, the mixture was formed under pressure into hexagonal prisms of different sizes, according to the bore of the cannon in which they were to be used. Some experiments were conducted with large cakes of powder that closely fitted the bore of the weapon. Powder composition was also varied somewhat for artillery use, "brown" powder being made from charcoal not quite completely carbonized. Powders of this type remained standard for artillery use until the advent of smokeless powders at the end of the 19th century.

Early gunpowder consisted of widely varying formulas. Some, particularly oriental mixtures, contained the basic ingredients of charcoal, sulphur and saltpeter—but included all manner of other ingredients according to the temperament of the maker. A fair amount of wizardry or witchcraft was associated with gunpowder in its earliest days, and one recipe suggests, "It is useful to add a spider skin." Roger Bacon's formula of about 1260 was saltpeter, sulphur and charcoal in the proportions 7/5/5. By 1350 the English formula was 6/1/2. At about the same time the Germans used 4/1/1. In 1774, the Prussian mix was 8/1/1, but shortly after 1800 the various formulas tended toward a fairly standard 7.5/1/1.5 or 7.5/1.5/1. During the early 19th century England used the same formula for powder for all types of arms, while some other countries varied the composition slightly between sporting and military small arms, and artillery usage.

Gunpowder is still manufactured in substantial quantities today using essentially the same formulas that were in use during the 19th century.

The black powder of today is manufactured in much the same fashion as it was after corned powder became standard. The three major ingredients are chosen for their purity and are then ground separately into a fine powder. Originally the grinding was done in water-powered stamp mills, but today more sophisticated and efficient means of grinding are used.

When properly pulverized, the ingredients are mixed together in the desired proportions with water and alcohol. The mix is thoroughly incorporated in a mechanical mixer, care being taken to ensure that the proper moisture content is maintained. Should the moisture content be allowed to get too low, an explosion becomes likely. Early powder mills were considered somewhat expendable because of the danger of explosion and were quite lightly and cheaply constructed for that reason. Buildings were framed with heavy, sturdy timbers, but covered with loosely attached light boards; an explosion would blow off the boards without serious damage to the frame or the heavy equipment inside. One can only wonder about the worker's fate.

After being thoroughly mixed, the wet powder is compressed into solid cakes. These cakes are then torn apart by wooden or non-sparking metal tools. In some processes, the fragments are again compressed into cakes. Following this, they are broken into smaller chunks and granules by rollers. Eventually they are broken down into relatively small granules and dried. The batch is not dried to the point where absolutely no water remains, but down to a specified point where the moisture content can be held reasonably stable.

At this point, the powder is glazed. This is accomplished by tumbling the powder in a large drum in which has been placed a small amount of graphite. The graphite serves several purposes: it prevents the discharge of static electricity which might ignite the powder mass; it causes the granules to flow smoothly and easily through measuring and packaging equipment; and by coating the grains, it reduces the formation of dust. When the glazing operation is completed, the granules have lost part of their jagged, irregular look, and are somewhat polished and rounded, though still irregular in shape.

The considerable amount of dust generated by the tumbling/glazing operation is then removed. Following this, the powder is screened to separate it into the four most common granulations—Fg (largest), FFg, FFFg, and FFFFg. This is done by running the powder over successively finer-mesh vibrating screens. Powder that will pass through the Fg screen but will not pass through the FFg screen is channeled off and packaged and sold as Fg granulation. The same procedure is followed for the other sizes. Powder too fine even for use as FFFFg is salvaged, while that too large for Fg may be further broken down and re-screened; or it may be sized for particular special purposes, such as use in loading blank cartridges for artillery pieces or for use in muzzle-loading cannon.

Gunpowder manufacture in America dates back less than 300 years. In 1675, a small powder mill is known to have been at the town of Milton, near Boston. Prior to the existence of this mill, the colonists were dependent entirely upon powder brought from Europe, primarily England, and exposed for weeks to the deteriorating effects of the sea. Though its output of powder was undoubtedly small, the Milton mill quite likely can be credited with reducing the effect of the Wampanoag Indian attack on New England. In 1675, King Phillip, chief of the Wampanoags, launched an all-out attack against New England that resulted in the destruction of thirteen Colonial towns. Without an adequate local supply of powder, it is conceivable that the colonists might have been wiped out completely.

With characteristic thoroughness, England had restricted powder manufacture by the colonies and apparently took care that no great store of British powder was accumulated in New England. These factors combined with the obviously superior quality of English powder (most colonists preferred it) assured that the colonies began the Revolutionary War without any powder industry to speak of. As if this was not enough, sulphur could be obtained only from Europe, and domestic production of saltpeter was small. Of the basic ingredients for gunpowder, the colonies were able to supply only charcoal in adequate quantity. On one occasion at the beginning of the war, General George Washington said, "Our situation in the article of powder is much more alarming than I had the most distinct idea of."

This appalling state of affairs could not be allowed to exist if the war were to be fought to a successful conclusion. Yankee ingenuity proved itself equal to the task. Small powder mills sprang up all through the forests while manure piles became niter-beds to supply the very necessary saltpeter.

One such mill was hidden in the woods near Morristown, New Jersey, while another—operated by a woman no less, Mary Patton—was situated in Tennessee. The latter mill figured decisively in the defeat of Colonel Patrick Ferguson at Sycamore Shoals. Five hundred pounds of powder from that mill were distributed *free* to colonial troops opposing Ferguson when it became known that they were short of powder.

Many of the smaller mills disappeared with the end of the Revolutionary War, and undoubtedly some of them were destroyed by accidental explosions. Even so, enough survived that in the last decade of the 18th century, the bulk of the newly created states' gunpowder needs could be supplied by domestic manufacture. European and British powders continued to be considerably superior to the domestic product, primarily because the powder industries there had become highly developed with many years' experience in manufacture. While no doubt the New Englanders would have preferred to use the better imported powders, the domestic product was sufficiently cheap that few of them did so. At this point, enter one Irénée Du Pont. This young gentleman was in America for the purpose of promoting the creation of a French colony in Virginia. However, it is alleged that he became very dissatisfied with the quality of American powder he was forced to buy while on a hunting trip. Having worked in French powder mills and laboratories, he was qualified to judge the quality of this powder and also to know that if better powder were produced in America, its maker could expect to prosper. He reasoned that a powder industry would be more productive than a new colony.

Suiting thought to action, the first Du Pont powder was produced near Wilmington, Delaware, at Eleutherian Mills, on the Brandywine River, in 1804. The competition notwithstanding, E. I. Du Pont de Nemours and Co. had become the leading American gunpowder producer by 1810.

Older mills fell to the superiority of Du Pont powder, and some disappeared in thunderous explosions. Eventually three companies, Du Pont, Laflin & Rand and the Hazard Powder Company became the "Big Three," dominating the American powder industry. When the Civil War came along, the North was plentifully supplied with powder and the facilities for its manufacture. Following the Civil War, American powder was of such good quality and in such plentiful supply that it began to be exported to Europe, reversing the situation of only a few years earlier.

The Confederacy, however, was not so well supplied with facilities for the manufacture of powder. The Sycamore Powder Mills near Nashville, Tennessee, later taken over by Du Pont, supplied much powder to the Confederacy. The only other mill south of the Mason-Dixon Line apparently made no significant contribution to the cause.

As the war progressed, the "Confederate Gun Powder Factory" was established and operated at Augusta, Georgia, by a West Point graduate, Colonel George W. Rains. Though never plentifully supplied with gunpowder, the Confederacy did manage to produce a great deal during the war. This was not accomplished easily since saltpeter was in short supply.

Little known today is the California Powder Works, which was established as the result of a federal prohibition on powder shipments by sea to the West Coast. The danger of capture by prowling Confederate warships hungry for just such a prize made the risk too great. Since it was absolutely essential that powder be available in California, entrepreneurs there formed the California Powder Works, to be operated primarily by cheap Chinese labor and to use saltpeter imported from India. This plant did not produce its first powder until 1864, but continued in operation for many years afterwards. In fact, the first smokeless powder accepted for use by the United States Army was developed there by W. C. Peyton. "Peyton" powder, as it became known, was a composition of nitroglycerin, nitrocellulose and ammonium picrate.

Even though smokeless powder began replacing "gunpowder" in the last decade of the 19th century, demand for black powder continued quite strong through the first decade of the present century. Still, black powder did not disappear entirely from the scene.

The various sporting arms designed and manufactured during the "black powder period" required supplies of the proper ammunition. In addition, in many parts of the world black powder arms were the only ones allowed by law or the only ones economically feasible for the inhabitants. These markets required a constant supply of black powder.

At no time, even today, has the demand for black powder dropped so low as to justify its discontinuance entirely. Where literally dozens of makes were once available, only one survives. The long-familiar red, white and black Du Pont label passed from the American scene in a thunderous explosion that destroyed the plant founded by Irénée Du Pont nearly two centuries ago. This plant was destroyed in the early 1970's and the Du Pont corporation determined that it no longer wished to be in the black powder business—at least not commercially. Though the plant was sufficiently restored to meet necessary U. S. Government powder requirements, none was produced for the large muzzle-loading market of this country. Instead, the industrial giant Gearhart-Owen purchased the entire Du Pont operation and production continues under a new red, white and black G-O label. Powder now being produced is *not* identical in performance to the old Du Pont product, and the differences will be discussed in detail later in this book.

At the present time, Gearhart-Owen is the only active domestic manufacturer of black powder—however, there are reports of at least one or two other companies preparing to enter the field. In the immediate future, there is also the distinct possibility of a modern substitute for black powder. A propellant called "Pyrodex" has been developed, duplicating all the desirable characteristics of black powder, but eliminating many of its hazards. It will eventually be manufactured in this country and is covered in detail elsewhere in this volume.

Although Gearhart-Owen is currently the only black powder manufacturer in this country, supplies from both Scotland and Canada are plentiful under a variety of labels, the best known being Curtis & Harvey.

And so, nearly seven and a quarter centuries after Bacon described his new compound which "thunders and lightens," it is still available and contributing in a small way to man's enjoyment of life.

2/Yesterday's Guns for Today

It hasn't been so long ago that our great-grandfathers, even grandfathers, depended upon the black powder muzzle-loading gun for food, war and sport. Many's the grizzled oldster who regaled my generation (in its younger days, of course) with assorted and wondrous tales of the front loader's accuracy and efficiency. In the peaceful years after the Civil War, there was shooting aplenty west of the Mississippi. There were lots of spirited lads long used to the ways of war and eager to search out hostile and forbidding territory. And there were considerable hard cases who felt the world was their oyster and they needed only an opening to get at the meat. If they opened it a bit roughly and lawful citizens responded with irritated gunfire, the muzzle loaders were likely to get quite a workout.

Contrary to what screen, television and novel writers would have us believe, the westward migrants weren't armed with braces of Colt single-action cartridge revolvers and 1873 Winchester repeaters. The muzzle loader, be it pistol, rifle or scattergun, was the dominant arm in the frontier country for quite a few years after the Civil War. Most men walked away from the war with their guns, and only a very small percentage of the arms issued on both sides deviated from the standard caplock form. Men used the guns they had—usually a rifled musket and/or a revolver, both of caplock percussion and loaded from the front. In the late 1860's and early 1870's, there were far more muzzle than breech loaders in the hands of western settlers.

With this background, it isn't hard to understand why today's affluence and leisure time has prompted great interest in muzzle-loading shooting over the past decade or so. Of course, the interest hasn't risen just in that period of time. A small group of hobbyists has been shooting muzzle loaders by preference even from the very beginning of the cartridge era. During the pre-World War II period, there was a fair number of black powder fanciers who held regular shoots around the country. At that time, there still were quite a few old-time gun makers, who produced fine rifles in small shops throughout the South. Most of them operated with traditional tools and methods, even to rifling barrels completely by hand and casting their own stock furniture. Some refused to use any store-bought components and even fabricated their own locks from steel stock. Each maker produced only a few guns per year and to try to rush one on an order was to (probably) make certain your gun *wouldn't* be the next one finished. These fine old gentlemen almost invariably turned out "Kentucky" rifles, along with a few heavy bench-rest guns. There simply wasn't a demand for handguns or scatterguns.

The guns produced in those golden years weren't replicas or reproductions as we use these terms today. They were the real thing, authentic and original in every respect. They were handmade with tools that had actually been used to produce identical guns before the time of the cartridge. To call one a *copy* would be to risk getting a rifle barrel bent over your head. Each smith built his "Hawg Rifles" exactly like his daddy and granddaddy had done on the same tools and in the same little lean-to shack.

By the end of World War II, not many of those oldsters were still with us. And by the end of the Korean War, virtually none of the old-timers were left. Fortunately, a few younger fellows took up the trade, some using more modern methods and equipment. Others, though, went all the way back copying late 18th century tools, shops and methods.

Others may rightly claim some of the credit, and I don't really know who took the first steps. But in the middle 1950's, William B. Edwards, then editor of *Guns Magazine,* convinced a few people that modern-production percussion revolvers would sell well enough to make a tidy profit. He organized a group of gun dealers and enthusiasts for a European tour to visit many of the old makers there.

An outgrowth of this tour was eventually seen in the formation of Navy Arms Company and Centennial Arms Corporation. Navy Arms, under the guidance of lifelong muzzle-loading buff Val Forgett, started with the basic Remington percussion revolver design manufactured in Italy. Centennial Arms, somewhat later, had the Colt 1860 .44 Army design produced in Belgium. Oddly enough, the firm producing Centennial guns had once been licensed by Colt to produce percussion revolvers.

Actually, it didn't happen that quickly, as anyone ever involved with offshore manufacturing knows. There were lots of preproduction headaches and as it turned out, Navy Arms' first guns weren't even made by a gun manufacturer.

Both firms were almost instantly able to sell more guns than could be obtained from the fabricators, a condition that continues to exist even today. Even though production capacity was continually increased, the demand for new straight-shooting copies of original percussion revolvers far exceeded Edwards' estimates. Both firms soon followed with additional models, significant among them being Navy's Italian-built reproduction of the Remington .58 caliber "Zouave" rifled musket of the Civil War. It has since become the most widely sold replica percussion long gun of all and has been followed by Springfield M1861 and "Mississippi" reproductions that have also become quite popular.

Eventually, several other firms entered the replica business. With the exception of a few small shops specializing in a limited output of higher-than-average quality work, all replicas were, for a number of years, manufactured in Europe, principally in Italy and Belgium. Since then, however, as European costs went up and the dollar devalued, production of some models has moved to Spain, Japan, and if rumors are correct, even Korea.

In the beginning there was considerable objection to the sale of replica arms. This was generated primarily by collectors' concern that unscrupulous individuals and dealers might use the economically priced replicas as the basis for faking rare, costly guns. Insofar as I have been able to determine, these fears were groundless. At first the replica companies specified certain deviations from the original guns being copied. Rifling, for instance, is quite different in most cases from that originally used. Finishes are different, as are materials. Production methods and tools also differ. Consequently, reworking, for example, a Centennial M1960 Army sufficiently to fool a collector into believing he is getting an original *Colt 1860,* would involve more work than could be justified by the potential return. The following would have to be accomplished: replace barrel with an exact Colt copy; remove tool marks and duplicate original marks; completely refinish, duplicating Colt methods; remove replica markings and replace with correct ones; renumber in proper series. All of this would cost more than could be gained by a fraudulent sale. And even then, the altered gun could still be identified as spurious by a serious Colt student.

Essentially the same may be said for virtually all of the production-model replica guns being sold today. For all practical purposes, the replica muzzle-loading gun has not been responsible for any significant increase in the faking of true collectors' items. If anything, faking of American guns seems less today than it was 20 years ago—but that isn't necessarily because of replicas.

With better than a half-dozen firms engaged *primarily* in the production and importation of new percussion and flintlock guns, it can be honestly said that we have a "replica industry." The availability of such guns has been responsible for vastly increased muzzle-loading activity—and the demand so generated has resulted in more and better guns.

Following this paragraph you will find listed and pictured the principal models produced and sold by the major firms involved. This does not purport to be an absolutely complete list of either models, makers or sellers, but it is as nearly current as circumstances will allow. Note that not all of the guns mentioned are actually replicas of any particular make or model. They are simply functional muzzle loaders of the various basic types and bear some resemblance to certain early arms. All of the firms listed have catalogs and/or brochures available upon request and their addresses are listed in the Directory in Appendix 8.

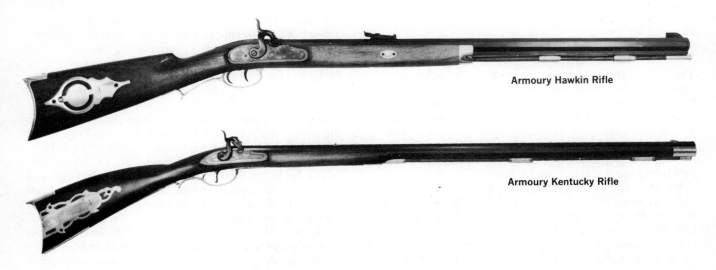

Armoury Hawkin Rifle

Armoury Kentucky Rifle

THE ARMOURY, INCORPORATED

This is a fairly new company formed to import and distribute muzzle-loading guns. Like most of the others, it does no manufacturing of its own, but has its guns made abroad. Many of them are virtually identical to guns sold by other major importers; however, its line is larger than several others. The current Armoury catalog shows 20 handguns and over a dozen long guns as well as kits in both areas.

Navy 1851 Revolver: A brass-frame copy of the basic M1851 Colt .36 caliber. 7 1/2-inch barrel, blue finish, smooth one-piece grips. Also offered in the following variations:

Confederate Revolver—same, but round barrel
Sheriff Revolver—same, but with 5-inch barrel
Navy .44—same, but .44 caliber with rebated cylinder
Sheriff .44 Revolver—same as preceding, but 5-inch barrel.

Navy 1851 Revolver (NS): A steel-frame Colt copy; otherwise same as above. Also offered in .44 caliber with rebated cylinder. Several variations are also offered with fluted cylinder in .36 caliber.

Army 1860 Revolver

Army 1860 Revolver: A copy of the Colt M1860 .44 Army with 8-inch barrel, brass guard, one-piece grips, blue finish and color-hardened frame.

New Model Army Revolver: A copy of the basic M1858 Remington .44 Army. 8-inch barrel, blue finish, brass guard, two-piece smooth grips. Also offered as "Navy Model" in .36 caliber with 6 1/2-inch barrel; and as "New Model Army Target" with adjustable target-type sights.

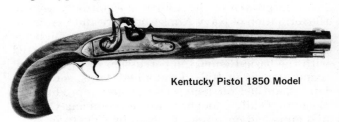

Kentucky Pistol 1850 Model

Kentucky Pistol 1850 Model: A Kentucky-style percussion pistol in .45 caliber with walnut stock and brass furniture. Also offered as "1830 Model" in flintlock form.

Armoury also offers five models of two basic Kentucky rifles in both flint and percussion, .45 caliber. Zouave, Brown Bess and "Hawkin" rifles round out the line.

CENTENNIAL ARMS

One of the first companies into modern muzzle loading, this firm was formed in the late 1950's, specifically to market replica percussion revolvers. Its first product was a reproduction of the Colt M1860 .44 Army revolver which was produced by Centaure in Belgium; Centaure had been one of the few companies originally licensed by Colt to produce the same gun in the 1860's. Centennial's present line comes from other manufacturers and includes both short and long guns. This company is also known for commissioning the

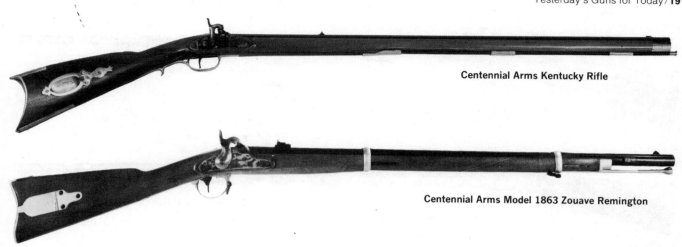

Centennial Arms Kentucky Rifle

Centennial Arms Model 1863 Zouave Remington

manufacture of genuine Colt Single-Action Army "Sheriffs Model" .45 caliber revolvers in 1960–61.

New Model 1960 .44 Army: An accurate copy of the original Colt 1860 Army. Eight-inch barrel; hammer, frame and rammer case–hardened in colors; cylinder, barrel and back strap blued; guard silver plated; round rebated cylinder, engraved scene; one-piece smooth walnut grips.

Remington New Model Army: An excellent copy of the original 1858 Remington in .44 caliber with 8-inch barrel. Six shot with blue finish, brass trigger guard and smooth two-piece walnut grips.

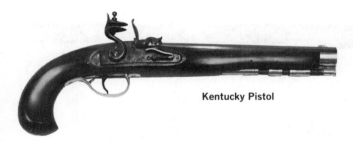

Kentucky Pistol

Kentucky Pistol: Offered in flint or percussion. This is of typical Kentucky style and design, but not a specific copy. In .44 caliber, blue octagonal barrel, color-hardened lock, polished brass furniture.

Model 1863 Zouave Remington: A close 33-inch barrel copy of the original Zouave in .58 caliber. Blue finish with color-hardened lock and brass furniture, including patch box with steel ramrod.

Kentucky Rifle: A .44 caliber rifle in typical Kentucky style, offered in flint or percussion with 36-inch octagonal barrel. Light engraving on lock plate and patch box, blue barrel, color-hardened lock, brass furniture.

Centennial also offers Colt, Navy, Remington Army and Kentucky pistol kits and an extensive line of accessories and flasks.

CENTURY ARMS

This company has long been quite active in military surplus arms and ammunition but added a variety of muzzle-loading guns nearly a decade ago. Generally, Century muzzle loaders are not specific copies and represent basic types rather than makes and models. They are usually relatively inexpensive.

Charleville Flintlock Musket: A rather loose copy of the 18th century French musket smoothbore .69 caliber, 45 1/2-inch barrel. Guard and the three bands are polished brass; balance is polished steel in the white.

Tower Flintlock Musket: A smoothbore .69 caliber musket typical of the British Brown Bess. Pin-fastened barrel, finished in the white.

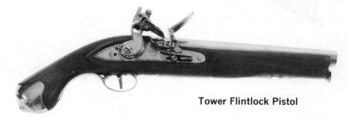

Tower Flintlock Pistol

Tower Flintlock Pistol: A nicely finished, low-cost companion piece to the Tower Musket. Smooth-bored, white finish, Tower markings.

Military-Type Percussion Musket: A very basic .69 caliber smoothbore musket with back-action lock, typical of early 19th century European guns converted to percussion. Steel furniture, finished in the white.

Military-Type Flintlock Musket: Quite similar

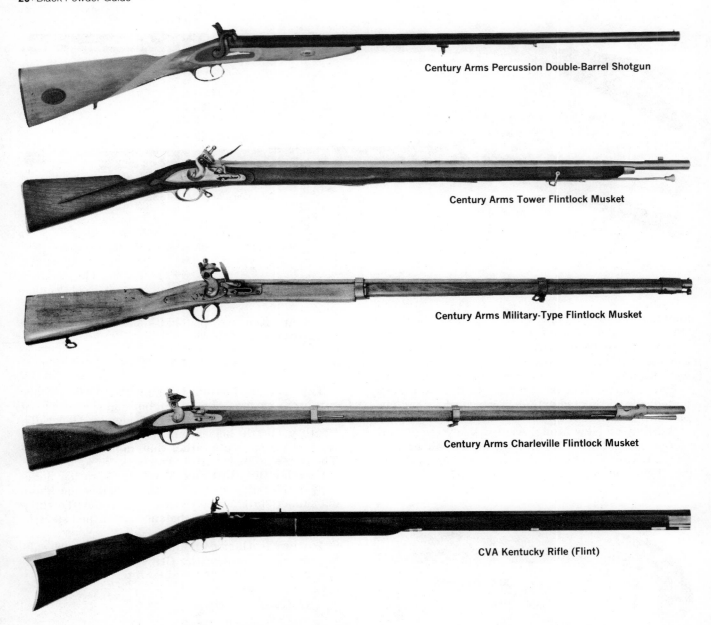

Century Arms Percussion Double-Barrel Shotgun

Century Arms Tower Flintlock Musket

Century Arms Military-Type Flintlock Musket

Century Arms Charleville Flintlock Musket

CVA Kentucky Rifle (Flint)

to the percussion musket, but in .56 caliber with 36-inch barrel.

Percussion Double-Barrel Shotgun: A typical 20-gauge side-by-side double, with 28-inch cylinder-bored barrels and checkered hardwood stock. Bar locks, blue finish, matted rib, small cap box in right side of buttstock.

Century also offers several smallbore single-barrel shotguns of 24 gauge and smaller.

CVA (CONNECTICUT VALLEY ARMS)

CVA didn't exist when the first edition of this book went to press. It came into being in 1971. Dave Silk, a

long-time member of the domestic arms industry, had studied the European scene extensively in his travels there. The result was CVA and what is now an extensive line of replica guns made to order in various European plants. CVA items are moderate in cost and the line includes most typical flint and percussion items but without the Colt revolver profusion of most other companies in the field. There is an extensive line of kits and accessories, part of the latter of domestic manufacture, as well as shooting kits which make it simpler and more economical for the neophyte to equip himself. During a recent interview with Mr. Silk, he indicated there will be continuous expansion of the CVA line.

It is interesting to note that while the other replica companies began very small and grew over a long period of time, CVA has risen to prominence in the field in a mere three to four years.

CVA .44 New Model Army: A replica of the Remington .44 Army of the 1860's. Caliber .44 (.451-inch ball), 8-inch octagonal barrel with cold forged rifling. Weight is 46 ounces, finish is bright blue with polished brass trigger guard, varnished two-piece walnut grips.

CVA Philadelphia Derringer: A typical copy of the basic percussion Derringer in .45 caliber with 3 1/8-inch rifled barrel. Both lock and barrel are color hardened with polished, brass furniture, walnut-finished stock. Lock is of modern, coil-spring, internal design, but traditional externally with some engraving.

CVA Kentucky Pistol: Available in flint or percussion ignition with 10 1/2-inch rifled, octagonal barrel, .45 caliber (.451-inch bore) and weighing 40 ounces. Barrel is blued, lock is color hardened, furniture is polished brass.

CVA English Flint Belt Pistol

CVA English Flint Belt Pistol: A .45 caliber (.451-inch bore) pistol of typical British 19th century style. Light at 30 ounces with 7-inch rifled octagonal barrel and walnut-finished stock. Color-hardened lock, blued barrel, and polished brass furniture, steel ramrod. Ornate lock plate with cast-in decoration. Also available in percussion form.

CVA Tower Pistol: A large flintlock pistol typical of British military style in the late 18th century. Smoothbore, with 8 1/4-inch round barrel, no sights. Caliber is .45; barrel is blued; lock is color hardened. Walnut-finished stock carries polished brass furniture including a very massive butt cap. Weight is 39 ounces. A percussion version is available.

CVA Kentucky Rifle: A full-stock .45 caliber (.451-inch bore) rifle available with either flint or percussion ignition. Barrel is octagonal, 34 1/2-inch long and blued. Stock is walnut-finished with brass hardware (no patch box) and wood ramrod. Lock is color-hardened and engraved.

CVA Kits: A wide variety of kits is offered, ranging from a derringer up to a full-length Kentucky rifle.

COLT

Colt, the company that made practical revolvers possible, stopped making percussion sixguns in the 1870's; then nearly a century later it re-entered the field with the same guns. Early in this decade Colt announced that it would again produce the original M1851 .36 caliber Navy revolver. In the beginning Colt insisted that this was *not a replica,* and serial numbers began where they stopped in 1873. However, there *are* differences between the new Navy and those of the last century, so the gun is generally considered a replica by the industry and the public, if not by Colt.

Then in 1975, Colt delivered the first of its new Third Model Dragoon, again beginning serial numbers where they ended for the original series in 1860.

Both Colt percussion revolvers are fitted and finished at the Colt plant but, at least in the beginning, were not manufactured there entirely. The result is guns of better quality than generally seen among other replicas. This is reflected—as would be expected—in the prices which run about 50 percent higher than comparable models of other names.

Colt 1851 Navy: This was the first 20th century Colt percussion revolver, listed in factory data sheets as "Type: C Frame Single Action Revolver." Of .35 caliber (.375-inch ball) with 7 1/2-inch barrel, weighing 40-1/2 ounces unloaded. Octagonal barrel with 7 grooves, RH twist, one turn in 38 inches. Varnished, smooth walnut stocks with trigger guard and back strap silver plated, square-back guard. Frame, hammer and loading lever are color-hardened, barrel and cylinder blued, engraved cylinder. Serial numbers from the original series forward.

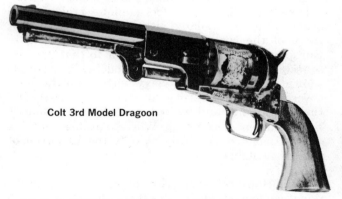

Colt 3rd Model Dragoon

Colt 3rd Model Dragoon: The ultimate development of the Walker, replaced in 1860 by the .44 Army. A very massive gun weighing 50 ounces with 7 1/2-inch round barrel, 7 groove rifling, .44 caliber for .457-inch ball. Blued barrel and cylinder; color-hardened frame, hammer and rammer; polished brass trigger guard and back strap. Smooth, varnished walnut grips. In its original form, this was the sidearm of the U.S. Mounted Rifles until 1860. Serial numbers from 20,901 forward.

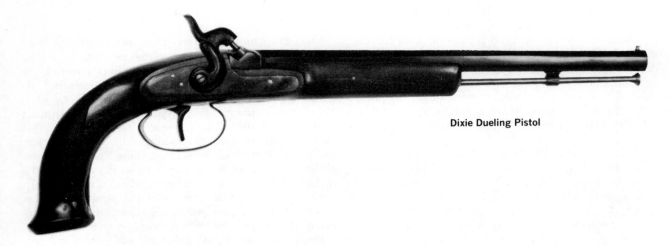

Dixie Dueling Pistol

DIXIE GUN WORKS

In reality, Dixie Gun Works was the first company in the replica industry. After originating with Turner Kirkland as an antique-gun and obsolete-parts supply house, Dixie offered the first *production* replica in 1955. This was a typical Kentucky rifle manufactured to Kirkland's specifications in Belgium. With hardly any change, that same rifle, in both flint and percussion, is still made and sold. Tens of thousands of them have been sold all over the world by DGW. Since then DGW has grown to be the largest single supplier of muzzle-loading items and related equipment in the world. Dixie originated gun kits and even though the kits have been copied by many, Dixie remains the largest source of kits for all types of muzzle loaders.

Dixie Gun Works also offers a unique service in gold ornamentation, available either on its own guns or those of the customer. This is the application, in Europe, of fine gold overlay similar to that done on some original Colt presentation models. The example shown here is an M1851 Navy with complete floral coverage in two shades of gold. This work is costly and time consuming, and limited examples are available.

The current Dixie Gun Works' catalog contains over 400 pages, so I can list here only a small portion of what is available.

Dixie Squirrel Rifle: New manufacture in traditional caplock style. In .40 caliber, 40-inch barrel, 6 grooves, 1-48 twist; brass furniture and patch box; lock case-hardened in colors; maple stock; weight, 10 pounds.

Dixie Kentucky Flintlock: Virtually identical to the Squirrel Rifle above, but flintlock percussion.

Dixie Deluxe Pennsylvania Rifle: In both flint and percussion lock, these guns use the same metal parts as the Squirrel Rifle. The stock is Pennsylvania style and fitted with large ornate brass patch box.

Dixie Halfstock Target Rifle: A modern percus-

sion rifle with 32-inch .40 caliber barrel. Half-stock, shotgun-style butt, checkered grip and forend; steel furniture; weight, 7-1/2 pounds.

Dixie Buffalo Hunter: Percussion. A short-barreled hunting rifle built around the reproduction .58 caliber Zouave rifle described elsewhere. Half-stock with brass furniture; 22-inch barrel; lock color-hardened, rest of metal blued.

Dixie Dueling Pistol: Percussion; 10-inch smoothbore barrel varying from .44 to .50 caliber; maple stock, checkered grip.

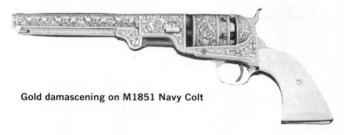

Gold damascening on M1851 Navy Colt

Dixie .36 Target Pistol: Quite similar to the Dueling Pistol, but with .36 caliber rifled barrel 11 inches long, 3/4 inch across the flats.

Dixie Percussion Derringer: A .41 caliber; one-piece cast brass frame and barrel; center-hung hammer; smoothbore; smooth polished grips.

Wheel lock Courier Pistol: An English-made, pocket-sized wheel lock pistol with 4-inch barrel, typical of about 1580. Bore is smooth, slightly flared at the muzzle. Brass frame, steel barrel, all metal, 7-inches long, complete with spanner. This was undoubtedly (in original form) the earliest concealable pistol; all earlier pistols were matchlocks.

Dixie Rifle Kit: Complete kit for assembling a rifle identical to the Squirrel Rifle. In percussion or flint.

Dixie Deluxe Rifle Kit: As above for the Deluxe Rifle.

Dixie Percussion Pistol Kit: Complete kit for

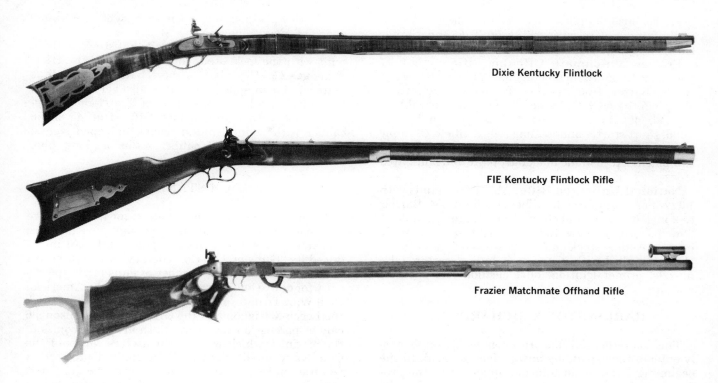

Dixie Kentucky Flintlock

FIE Kentucky Flintlock Rifle

Frazier Matchmate Offhand Rifle

assembling a .40 caliber 9-inch barrel Kentucky-style pistol.

Numerous other kits are available.

FIREARMS IMPORT & EXPORT

This is a Miami-based importing and distribution operation that first handled low-cost cartridge guns, and then went into muzzle loaders a few years ago. At present its line consists of several handguns and one long gun. Except for minor differences, these guns are essentially the same basic models offered under other names.

Kentucky Flintlock Rifle: A basic full-stock .45 caliber Kentucky-style rifle with a 35-inch octagonal barrel. Stock is walnut-finished hardwood with brass furniture, including a simple patch box. Single trigger, open sights, blue finish.

Baby Dragoon: A brass-frame copy of the .31 caliber Colt with brass square-back guard and smooth one-piece grips. Barrel and cylinder are blued, cylinder roll-engraved. Both 4-inch or 6-inch barrel lengths offered.

1851 Model Navy .36: A copy of the basic Colt .36 Navy but with polished brass frame. Smooth one-piece grips, rounded guard, 7 1/2-inch octagonal barrel; color-hardened rammer. Barrel and cylinder blued. Also offered in .44 caliber as "1851 Model Navy .44" with larger rebated cylinder and frame cut to match.

New Army Remington: A copy of the 1858 Remington .44 Army but with a polished brass frame. Smooth two-piece walnut grips, 7 3/4-inch barrel, weight 42 ounces.

FIE also markets a good line of accessories which are manufactured in its own plant in Miami.

CLARK FRAZIER

Frazier is a custom gunsmith making fine muzzle-loading target rifles on a semi-production basis but is included here for the uniqueness of design and quality of work. His "Matchmate" rifle is expensive but represents a high degree of modernization of the M-L rifle for optimum accuracy.

The basic design consists of a large rectangular receiver housing, double-set triggers and a speed-action underhammer lock with the nipple seated directly in the barrel and shielded by stainless steel. Triggers are Anschutz-Mauser, and the coil mainspring is adjustable. The buttstock is laminated and fitted for weights; the hook butt plate is adjustable vertically and for cant. The receiver contains an integral base for the Redfield Olympic sight and the barrel carries a base for compatible front sights. The barrel is fitted with a bullet starter and weight attachment points are provided. A variety of options, including special barrels are available, with a base price in the $650 range.

Frazier also supplies an excellent adapter for installing modern receiver sights on T/C and similar Hawken-style rifles.

Frazier Matchmate Offhand Rifle: About 11 pounds with 15/16-inch octagonal 32-inch .45 caliber barrel. Barrels from 13/16-inch to 1-1/8 inch available, lengths from 26 inches to 38 inches in calibers .32, .36, .40, .45, .50 or .54. Furnished with Lyman mold, short starter and loading rod. Redfield Olympic rear sight and detachable globe front are standard equipment. Adjustable hook butt plate and laminated stock.

National Unlimited Rifle: About 25 pounds with 1 1/2-inch round barrel, caliber .45, .50 or .54. Barrels to 2-inch diameter and 38-inch length are available. A 2-inch .58 caliber barrel brings weight up to about 40 pounds. Action, stock and sights are as for the Offhand Rifle. Supplied with piston-type bullet starter; false muzzle, primer ignition, butt cushion and case are options.

HARRINGTON & RICHARDSON

This is another old-line arms company that recently entered the expanding muzzle-loading field. In the beginning, it chose an unusual approach to the production of a low-cost, functional gun without the usual regard for traditional style and design. To do this, H&R engineers took the basic "Topper" exposed-hammer, breakopen action previously used for both shotguns and rifles. A plug containing a central nipple was placed inside the barrel breech (where the chamber would normally be) and then the firing pin was enlarged and flattened at the tip to meet the nipple. None of these changes are visible when the action is closed; the closing of the action completely encloses the cap and nipple, thus no cap fragment, gas or powder particles can strike the shooter, as often occurs with conventional, exposed-nipple percussion guns. The closure further protects the cap from weather, dirt and impact, as well as from loss when pushing through brush. Thus, in use, the gun is loaded conventionally from the muzzle, broken open and capped, and then closed. The unusual breech plug is also removable to allow full-length cleaning of the bore—an added advantage. This design is called "Huntsman." Later, when production of its 1873 Trapdoor Springfield replica was under way, its lock and some other parts were used in the design of the H&R "Springfield Stalker," a more conventional halfstock percussion carbine.

Huntsman: An unusual, modern M-L design built on the Topper single-shot action. Removable breech plug and fully enclosed ignition with exposed rebounding hammer. Made as a rifle in .45 or .58 caliber and as a shotgun in 12 gauge. Barrel lengths 28-inches, 30-inches, 32-inches; shotgun weight 6-1/4 pounds, .58 rifle 7-1/4 pounds, .45 8 pounds. Walnut-finish hard-

wood stock; adjustable, open rear sight; color-hardened receiver; blue finish.

Springfield Stalker: A basic halfstock carbine built with the lock, stock and furniture of the H&R Trapdoor Cavalry Carbine breech loader and thus quite similar in appearance. It is also very similar to the muzzle-loading conversions of Trapdoor Springfields done with Numrich kits. Offered in .45 or .58 caliber with 28-inch round barrel and open sights; weight, 8 pounds in .45 caliber; 43 inches long, blue finish throughout.

HIGH STANDARD

An old-line company best known for its .22 rimfire autoloading pistols but also for shotguns in more recent times. A few years ago High Standard introduced its "Guns of The Confederacy" series intended to include replicas of a number of guns made specifically for or by Confederate forces during the American Civil War. To date, only two models have been offered, the Leech & Rigdon and the Griswold & Gunnison .36 caliber percussion revolvers. Both are close copies of the originals which were in themselves copies of the Colt Navy modified to suit the limited production facilities and materials available within the Confederacy. Both were offered first as commemorative models, then as standard replicas at a lower price.

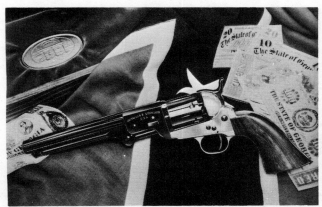

Griswold & Gunnison: Six-shot .36 caliber, 7 1/2-inch barrel, 40 ounces weight, smooth one-piece walnut grips. Polished brass frame and trigger guard, balance blued.

Leech & Rigdon: Identical in appearance and dimensions to Griswold & Gunnison except for brass backstrap and nickeled steel frame.

HOPKINS & ALLEN (NUMRICH ARMS)

The Hopkins & Allen name dates back well into the last century when it was known as a producer of good quality long and short guns at moderate prices. Although the company had a long and successful history, it passed from the active list before World

H&R Huntsman

Hopkins & Allen Over/Under Rifle

Hopkins & Allen Heritage Model

Hopkins & Allen .45 Target

Hopkins & Allen Minuteman

Hopkins & Allen Buggy Rifle

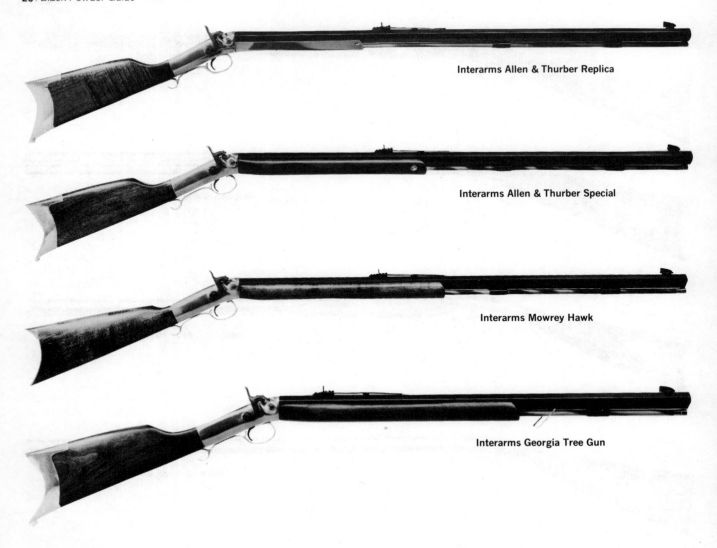

Interarms Allen & Thurber Replica

Interarms Allen & Thurber Special

Interarms Mowrey Hawk

Interarms Georgia Tree Gun

War II. Eventually the name and assets were purchased by Numrich Arms Corporation of West Hurley, New York.

Beginning some years ago, Numrich began producing a basic underhammer percussion rifle under the H&A name. It was not intended to be a replica but rather a genuine shooting arm. The success of that item spawned an extensive line of underhammer guns based on the same design, as well as traditional long muzzle loaders and a comprehensive line of accessories.

Of special interest are the muzzle-loader barrels and breech plugs offered at most reasonable prices. Also, I believe H&A was the first to offer "Instant Muzzleloader" kits. They consist of a caplock barrel that drops directly into the stock to replace the barrel and breech of the Springfield Trapdoor .50 and .45 caliber rifles. An old trapdoor can be converted into an excellent muzzle loader in just a few minutes. Bullet molds, sights, powder horns, nipple wrenches and

ready-to-fit patch boxes round out the H&A line.

Heritage Model: Top of the H&A underhammer gun line, fitted with walnut forend and brass butt plate and patch box. Barrel is 15/16 inches across the flats, 32-inches long, available in .36 or .45 caliber, uniform or gain twist rifling. Hooded aperture front sight, elevator leaf rear and long-range aperture tang sight. Weight, 8-1/4 pounds in .36 caliber; 8 pounds in .45.

Offhand Deluxe: Same barrel and action as above, but without brass fittings and long-range sight. A good hunting rifle.

Buggy Rifle: Virtually identical to the Offhand Deluxe, but with short 20-inch barrel for close quarters use in brush or timber. Weight, 5-3/4 pounds in .36 caliber; 5-1/2 pounds in .45.

.45 Target: Heavy target barrel, 1 1/8-inch across the flats. No forend or ramrod fittings, action and stock same as above guns. In .45 caliber only, 56-inch twist. Open rear sight, hooded aperture front. This gun has frequently outshot custom-made rifles costing many times as much.

Over/Under Rifle: This is a basic percussion-lock turnbarrel design. Two barrels are joined, one above the other, each with its own nipple and set of sights. At the rear, the barrels assemble to the lock frame by a horizontal pivot axis so as to rotate with respect to the frame. A two-position spring detent is provided to hold either barrel in the uppermost position, where the single hammer can fire it. After firing the first (upper) barrel, the barrel unit can be rotated 180 degrees, allowing the second barrel to be fired quickly without reloading. Blue finish, back-action lock, brass butt plate and patch box.

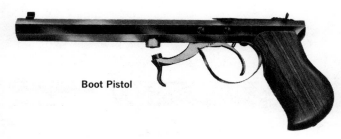

Boot Pistol

Boot Pistol: Probably the simplest and most durable percussion pistol on the market today, representing an unusual design approach. A single octagonal steel bar is machined at one end to accept the standard H&A underhammer lock parts and a one-piece walnut grip. The other end is bored and rifled to .36 or .45 caliber. Open sights are fitted and finish is blue. Overall length, 13 inches; barrel length, 6 inches. An exceptionally accurate pistol for the price.

Minuteman: A traditional style pinned-barrel flintlock Kentucky rifle but not an exact copy of any make. Barrel is 39 inches long, 15/16 inches across the flats, available in .36 or .45 caliber with uniform or gain twist. Silver blade front sight, low notched rear. Maple full stock with brass butt plate, patch box and furniture. Weight in .36 caliber, 9-1/2 pounds; .45 caliber, 9 pounds.

The Minuteman is also available in percussion lock form, all other specifications remaining the same. Interestingly, this gun uses the Minuteman flintlock converted to percussion, just as it was done many years ago.

Conversions: The .58 caliber unit consists of a new chrome-moly steel barrel fitted with breech plug, bolster and musket nipple, in the white, without sights. Barrel is 40-inches long; 1 1/4-inch diameter at breech; .775 inches at muzzle with 8-groove rifling; .575-inch bore diameter; 1 turn in 72 inches. This unit can replace the barrel on all U.S. M1855 through M1864 Springfield Muskets. Can also replace breech and barrel of Trapdoor .50 caliber Springfields up to 1870.

The "Instant Muzzle Loader" consists of a 39-inch-long barrel, breech plug and nipple unit that replaces the breech and barrel of all Trapdoor Springfields in .50-70 or .45-70 caliber after 1870. Polished and blued, dovetailed for standard H&A sights. In .45 caliber only, 8-groove rifling with .445-inch bore diameter, 1 turn in 56 inches.

The "Zouave" barrel is fitted with breech plug and nipple and replaces the original barrel of M1841 Mississippi and Remington .58 caliber rifled muskets. Bore diameter .575 inches, 8-groove rifling, 1 turn in 72 inches, 33 1/2-inches long. Polished and blued, fitted with front sight, drilled and tapped for rear sight.

INTERARMS

Interarms is the American retail/wholesale outlet of the widely known International Armament Corporation established after World War II by Sam Cummings. The parent company maintains massive stocks of all sorts of military arms and deals primarily with governments through its world-wide offices and agents. The name became best known in this country from its vast sales of low-cost military surplus rifles, handguns and ammunition, mainly through its Hunter's Lodge outlet.

In 1974, Interarms added muzzle-loading guns to its extensive line. It is the exclusive distributor for the Allen & Thurber-style brass-frame box lock rifles and shotguns manufactured by Mowery in Texas. While basically copied from the Allen & Thurber, these are not exact replicas; instead they represent adaptations of the original for today.

Allen & Thurber Replica: An unusual piece copying very closely the original A&T rifle with its massive solid-brass forend polished brightly to match the brass receiver. All lock parts are inside the receiver with only the blued hammer exposed. Butt plate is of brass and very massive in semi-schuetzen style. Barrel is 32 inches long and available in .45, .50, .54 and .58 calibers; weight is 10-1/4 pounds.

Allen & Thurber Special: Essentially the same as the A&T Replica, but with wood instead of brass forend, so weight is reduced to 10 pounds.

Mowrey Hawk: The basic A&T rifle restyled by the new maker with a lighter butt plate and wood forend. Weight is 9-1/2 pounds.

Mowrey Shotgun: The basic A&T design fitted with an octagonal 12-gauge smoothbore barrel 32 inches long. Maple buttstock and forend. Weighs 7-1/2 pounds.

Georgia Tree Gun: Identical with the A&T Special except for a shorter 22-inch barrel, making it a 7 1/4-pound carbine.

JANA INTERNATIONAL

Jana International is an arms importing and distributing company located in Denver. Originally it

Jana Gallager Carbine

Jana P-H Long Enfield

Jana P-H Enfield Musketoon

Lyman Plains Rifle

Lyman Brown Bess

Markwell Super Hawken Rifle

offered mainly British Parker-Hale cartridge rifles. However, eventually the old-line Parker-Hale firm was persuaded to manufacture the original Enfield Rifle Musket as adopted by the British armed forces in the early 1850's, and supplied to both Confederate and Union forces during the American Civil War.

Now offered in both short and long form, the Parker-Hale Enfield represents the maximum level of quality to be found in new rifled muskets. These guns are, in fact, manufactured to original Tower-approved patterns and gauges used for original Enfields in the 1850's and 1860's.

P-H Long Enfield: An exact copy of the M1858 Naval Pattern Enfield Arsenal rifled musket. Caliber is .577 (.58), 33-inch barrel. This is commonly called the "two-band" Enfield, there being two barrel bands. Rifling is 5 groove, gain twist, and the entire gun is made to original British government patterns and gauges. Weight is 8-1/2 pounds, length 48-1/2 inches.

P-H Enfield Musketoon: Identical with the above long Enfield except shortened for mounted troop use with 24-inch barrel, weighing 7-1/2 pounds. Copied after the British M1861 musketoon.

Jana Gallager Carbine: The original Gallager carbine was one of the more successful transition-period breech loaders. Designed as a breech loader to use separate-ignition foil cartridges, it could also be muzzle loaded if cartridges weren't available. Ignition was by the conventional musket-sized percussion cap through a nipple and vent in the standing breech.

Jana's Gallager replica is made by Erma in West Germany and shows excellent workmanship. It is supplied with brass gas seals for use in lieu of the original foil cartridge. Powder and ball may be pre-loaded in the seal/cartridge-case unit and then breech loaded; alternatively, the uncharged seal may be placed in the breech and the gun muzzle loaded. In addition, the gun may be muzzle loaded without the seal. The latter method may allow some gas escape at the breech, but if this occurs the barrel shroud directs the gas forward so there is no hazard to the shooter.

Caliber is .54; 22 1/3-inch round barrel; 39 inches overall length; weight 7-1/4 pounds. Supplied with breech seals, piston, nipple wrench and cleaning kit.

LYMAN PRODUCTS FOR SHOOTERS

This is the old-line Lyman Company that has been making reloading gear and sights for nearly a century. Some years ago Lyman got into the muzzle-loading field with Remington percussion revolvers and has since expanded its line to include Colt, long guns and accessories. Lyman has also long been the principal supplier of bullet molds for all types of muzzle-loading shooting.

Brown Bess: A copy of the 42-inch barrel "New Land Pattern" British .75 caliber smoothbore flint-lock musket of the American Revolutionary period.

Meets specifications for the "Brigade of the American Revolution." Bright finish throughout, with brass furniture and steel ramrod. Lock engraved with "Tower" and crown.

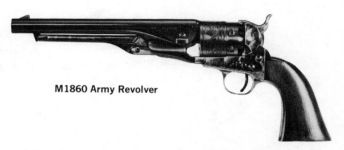

M1860 Army Revolver

M1860 Army Revolver: A good copy of the basic .44 caliber 8-inch barrel 6-shot Colt with blue finish, color-hardened frame and roll-engraved cylinder; four-screw frame and smooth one-piece grips.

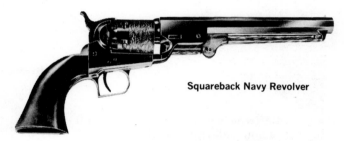

Squareback Navy Revolver

Squareback Navy Revolver: A copy of the M1851 .36 caliber Colt with dragoon-style square-back trigger guard. Backstrap and guard are silver plated, frame and lever are color-hardened, balance of finish is blue.

Plains Rifle: Not a specific copy, but a new gun in the style and image of the 1840-ish plains or mountain rifles made by S. Hawken and others of the period. In .45 caliber with 28-inch, 48-inch twist octagonal barrel. Hook breech design, weight 8-3/4 pounds, double-set triggers, brass furniture. Sights are modernized and adjustable for windage and elevation. European walnut stock with large brass patch box, wedge-fastened.

Lyman also offers accessories, as well as a shooting kit to go with each model.

MARKWELL ARMS

Markwell Arms, division of Ram Merch Corporation, is a newcomer to the replica industry. It was formed for the sole purpose of importing and distributing complete muzzle-loading guns and kits for them. Markwell items are all priced relatively low and in some instances are obvious imitations of basic models that have already proved to be popular under other names. An example of this is the Super Hawken Rifle, which appears to be a dead ringer for the Lyman

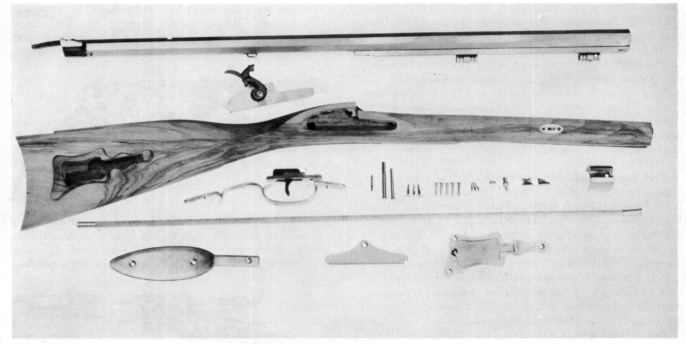

Hawken Rifle Kit

Plains Rifle (which in turn differs exceedingly little from the Thompson/Center Hawken) and sells for substantially less. The line includes derringer pistols, Kentucky pistols, Hawken-style rifles, a blunderbuss and a "Colonial" pistol, as well as a Remington revolver kit.

Philadelphia Derringer

Philadelphia Derringer: A .41 caliber, smooth-bore percussion pistol in the classic Deringer image. Plain finish, 3 1/8-inch octagonal barrel, 7 inches long, weighing 10-3/4 ounces, walnut stock, brass furniture. Rear notch and barleycorn front sight.

Hawken Rifle Kit: Assembles into Markwell's Hawken Rifle; 45 caliber, 28-inch octagonal barrel, open sights, walnut stock. All individual components are assembled, ready for polishing and fastening together; fully assembled patch box; rib and ramrod pipes attached to barrel; all dovetails cut.

Super Hawken Rifle: A heavier plains-style rifle in .45 or .50 caliber with 28-inch barrel, weighing 8-1/2 pounds. It features hook-breech design and a modern adjustable rear sight as well as double-set triggers. Percussion ignition with walnut stock, brass furniture and large brass patch box.

Remington Revolver Kit

Remington Revolver Kit: Actually just an unfinished gun, this kit requires only polishing, bluing and assembly. Everything has already been preassembled and fitted, so the buyer isn't concerned with timing, barrel/cylinder gap and the like. This is the basic Remington in .44 caliber with brass frame.

NAVY ARMS

Navy Arms was formed by Valmore Forgett, Jr., during the 1950's to import and distribute replica percussion revolvers manufactured for it in Italy. At the time, Forgett had already steered Service Ar-

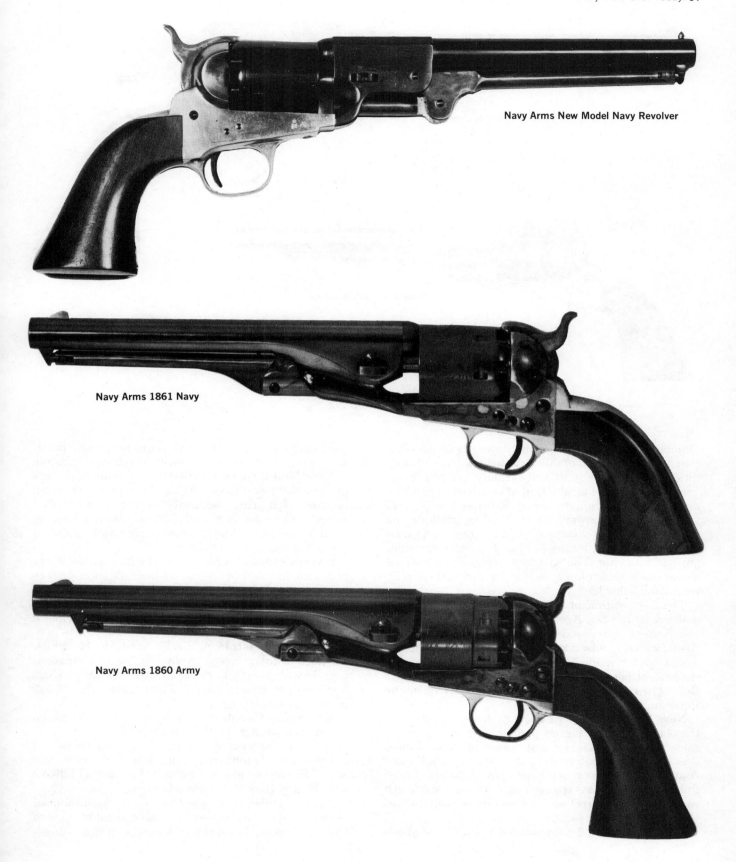

Navy Arms New Model Navy Revolver

Navy Arms 1861 Navy

Navy Arms 1860 Army

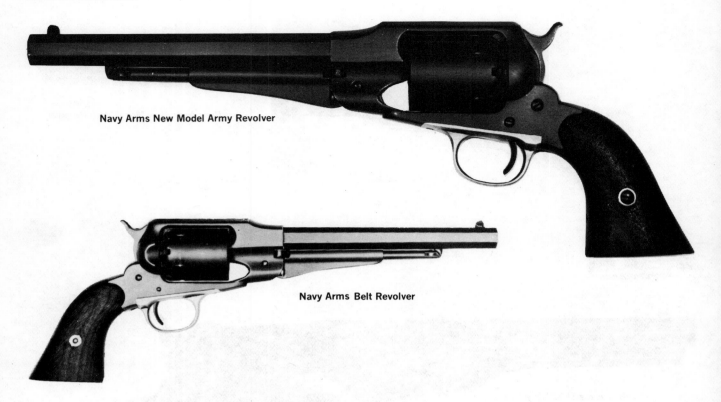

Navy Arms New Model Army Revolver

Navy Arms Belt Revolver

mament to success by engaging primarily in importation and distribution of military surplus arms, ammunition and equipment, as well as many sporting items.

From the initial production of revolvers, for which demand has continually increased over the past 15 years, Navy Arms went on to develop, produce and market the most extensive line of replica muzzle loaders, and later, replicas of black powder cartridge guns of all types. The cartridge replicas are covered elsewhere in this volume, so this discussion deals only with muzzle loaders.

The first edition of this book contained a section devoted to Replica Arms, Incorporated. A few years ago Forgett purchased the entire assets of Replica Arms which is now a division of Service Armament. This addition made Navy/Replica the largest single supplier of percussion revolvers, including the entire Colt series (minus the 1855 Root Model) from the Paterson onward.

New Model Army Revolver: A reproduction of the .44 caliber Remington percussion revolver of the same name. I've used several examples of this model over the years and find it the simplest and most convenient to shoot of those offered today. Blued finish, polished brass trigger guard, two-piece smooth walnut grips. A target-sighted version is available for the more serious shooter.

Belt Revolver: A .36 caliber version of the above

gun, shortened and lightened somewhat. Quite popular among serious shooters because of its lighter recoil.

New Model Navy Revolver: A line-for-line copy of the well-known Colt 1851 .36 Navy Revolver which enjoyed such great popularity during the Civil War period. Frame, hammer and rammer case-hardened in color, barrel and cylinder blued, trigger guard polished brass. One-piece walnut grips.

Sheriff's Model: Identical to the New Model Navy but with shorter 4-inch barrel-rammer shortened to match, .36 caliber.

The above three guns are also available in presentation grades with hand engraving and precious metal inlays.

Kentucky Pistol: A nicely finished .44 caliber flintlock pistol of classic "Kentucky" style. Octagonal barrel, walnut stock, brass furniture, lock is case-hardened in colors, barrel blued. Measures 15-1/2 inches in overall length.

Revolving Carbine: This is the basic mechanism of the New Model .44 Army revolver fitted with a 16- or 18-inch barrel and the frame altered to permit permanent attachment of a walnut carbine-type stock. Brass butt plate, six-shot, .44 caliber. (I killed a wild boar with one of these a few years ago.)

Zouave Rifle: A copy of the Remington-produced version of the U.S. M1863 .58 caliber rifled musket of the Civil War. Walnut stock, steel ramrod, brass

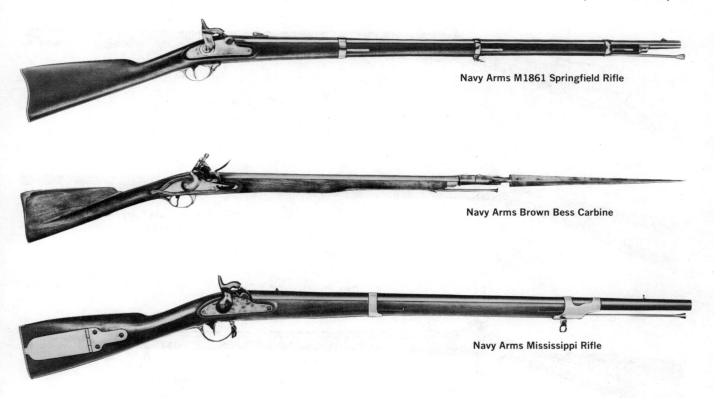

Navy Arms M1861 Springfield Rifle

Navy Arms Brown Bess Carbine

Navy Arms Mississippi Rifle

bands, nose cap, butt plate and patch box. Lock plate color-hardened, barrel and guard blued. Elevating musket rear sight, blade front. Detachable hooded crosswire "sniper" front sight available at extra cost. Uses standard .58 caliber Minie bullets and up to 60 grains of black powder. Authorized by the North-South Skirmish Association for rifled musket competition.

Zouave Carbine: Identical to Zouave rifle above, but with 22-inch barrel and carbine-style stock. Iden-

clean action. Takes No. 10 or No. 11 caps. Five shots. Furnished with 6-, 7 1/2- or 9-inch barrel.

Walker .44: Fine copy of the famous Walker Colt of 1847. Oval cylinder stops; weight, 4-3/4 pounds; 15-3/4 inches overall with 9-inch barrel; one-piece grips; brass guard; blued barrel and cylinder; case-hardened hammer rammer and frame. A nice piece that will take up to 60 grains of FFg powder with a .452-inch round ball. Uses Size 13 caps. Engraved cylinder.

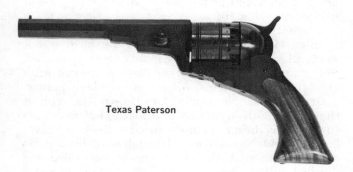

Texas Paterson

Second Model Dragoon

tified mainly as the "Buffalo Hunter" and very popular for hunting of all types.

Texas Paterson: Excellent copy of the original Colt in .36 caliber, highly polished and nicely blued, hammer and frame case-hardened in colors. Crisp,

Second Model Dragoon: An accurate copy of the Colt Second Model Dragoon .44 Revolver. One-piece grips; hammer, frame and rammer case-hardened; barrel and cylinder blued. Engraved cylinder. Also available with 16-inch barrel as a stocked carbine.

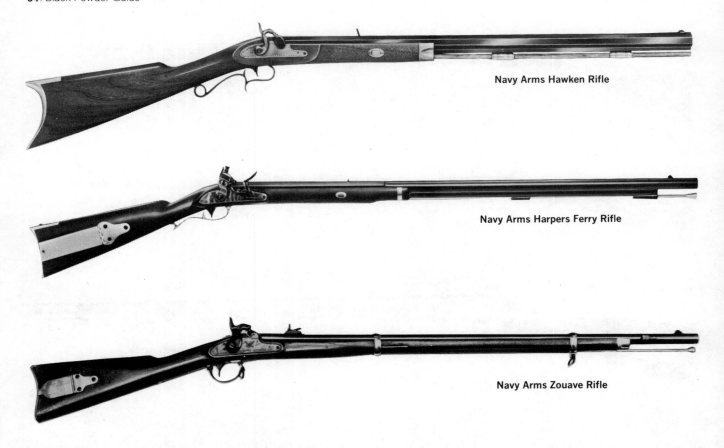

Navy Arms Hawken Rifle

Navy Arms Harpers Ferry Rifle

Navy Arms Zouave Rifle

Baby Dragoon/Wells Fargo

Baby Dragoon/Wells Fargo: Copy of the .31 caliber Colt M1848. Six-inch barrel, 10-3/8 inch overall, weighing 25 ounces. Hammer, frame and rammer case-hardened in colors; polished brass guard and backstrap, rest blued. One-piece walnut grips. Octagon barrel, five-shot, takes Size 9 or 10 caps. Available in 4-, 5- and 6-inch barrel with rammer as Baby Dragoon; 3-, 4-, 5- and 6-inch without rammer as Wells Fargo. Engraved cylinder.

1860 Army: Excellent copy of the original .44 caliber Colt Army revolver. An 8-inch barrel, 13-5/8 inches overall, weighing 38 ounces. Six-shot, uses .452- to 454-inch round balls, Size 9 or 10 caps. Frame, hammer and rammer case-hardened in color. Polished

brass guard, one-piece grips; barrel, cylinder and backstrap blued. Engraved cylinder. Cut for shoulder stock.

1861 Navy: Identical with Army above but in .36 caliber, with lighter 7 1/2-inch barrel and straight cylinder. Very comfortable to shoot with 000 buckshot and 16 grains of FFFg powder. Available with brass or iron strap and guard.

In addition, Navy Arms offers excellent reproductions of .44 Army shoulder stocks, Paterson chargers, loading levers and accessories, molds, nipple wrenches. Soft or hardwood and leather cases patterned after the original Colt items. All are of excellent quality.

Brown Bess: Navy offers two Brown Bess replicas that differ both in quality and method of manufacture. First is the gun manufactured in the Navy plant in Ridgefield, New Jersey. Although some basic parts are subcontracted, the entire gun is assembled and finished entirely by hand. A small staff of old-world master gunsmiths carefully fit and finish all parts by traditional hand methods. The gun is, therefore, a bit costly and output is quite limited. This model is considered the "piece de resistance" of musket replicas and is always in short supply. The second Navy

Navy Arms Brown Bess

Brown Bess is a conventional production copy made abroad and priced accordingly. Functionally, it performs the same as the handmade gun, but esthetically it is inferior. Both guns are .75 caliber, finished white, with brass furniture and walnut stock. A 30 1/2-inch barrel carbine version of the better gun is also offered.

M1861 Springfield Rifle: This gun is comparable to the contemporary Zouave and is copied from the standard Civil War rifle musket of the Union Army. It is of .58 caliber with 3-groove rifling and 40-inch barrel. All metal is finished bright and furniture is steel; stock is solid walnut.

Hawken Rifle: A heavy hunting rifle made in the style and image of the early 1840's plains or mountain rifle—big bore, short, thick barrel and thick sturdy stock. Caliber .58 (also .45 and .50), 9-3/4 pounds, 26-inch octagonal barrel—rifled for extra-heavy Minie bullets with maximum powder charges of up to 200 grains. Musket-sized nipples are standard to improve ignition of large powder charges. Open sights, blue finish, color-hardened lock, brass furniture, walnut stock, steel ramrod.

A lighter version is offered as the Hawken Hurricane in .45 and .50 caliber.

Harpers Ferry Rifle: A close reproduction of the first U.S. standard rifle made at Harpers Ferry in flintlock in the early 1800's. This copy has a 36 inch, 1/3 octagon barrel in .58 caliber (rather than the original .54) with under rib and walnut halfstock. Furniture is brass, including a large patch box, and ramrod is steel. Barrel is blued, lock is color-hardened.

Mississippi Rifle: A copy of the two-band .58 caliber musket used by the Confederacy, combining both Springfield and Enfield features and similar to the U.S. Model 1841.

STURM, RUGER

William Ruger launched this company right after World War II to produce advanced-design, reasonably-priced modern cartridge handguns. The company was remarkably successful with .22 rimfire autoloaders and single-action revolvers; then with big-bore centerfire revolvers of both single- and dou-

ble-action persuasion; then later with rifles. A few years ago Ruger adapted his well-known and highly regarded Black Hawk SA revolver to percussion ignition. The result was the *only* modern-design percussion revolver in existence. The design is basically Black Hawk with percussion ignition and a loading lever added. Overall appearance greatly resembles that of the Remington M1858 Army revolver. This new "Old Army" revolver is far superior in strength, and also mechanically, to *all* original-design replicas being made today.

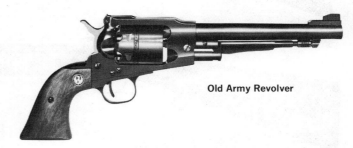

Old Army Revolver

Old Army Revolver: Six-shot percussion revolver, 7 1/2-inch barrel, weighing 46 ounces. Blue finish; smooth two-piece wood grips; unusual loading lever latch which uses inertia during recoil to prevent unlatching. Micrometer-adjustable rear sight housed in frame boss; ramp front sight. Also offered in stainless-steel construction with natural brushed finish. This is the only stainless black powder gun currently available.

TRAIL GUNS ARMORY

This is a small company which at present offers only American-made muzzle loaders. Its main item as this is written is the *Texas Carbine*, a .58 caliber 24-inch barrel short rifle built on the brass Allen & Thurber box lock action. The barrel is one inch across the flats, rifled with four grooves and carries an adjustable elevator-type open sight. All furniture is brass and the butt plate is old-carbine style, complemented by a sling bar and ring on the left side of the receiver. The

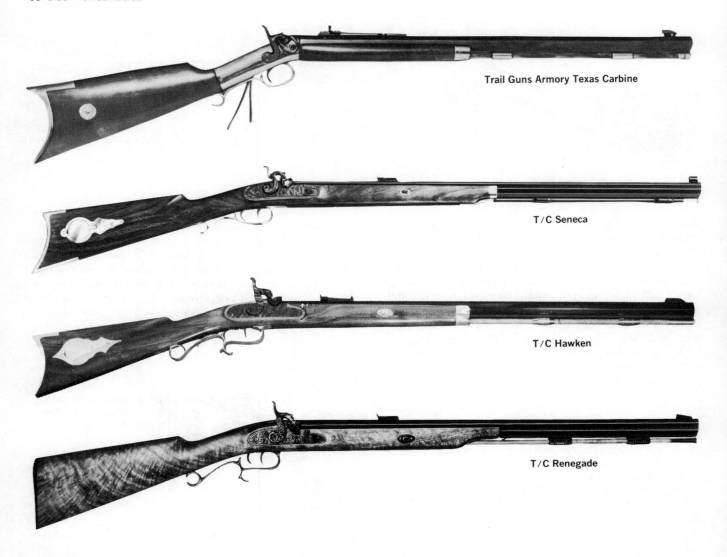

Trail Guns Armory Texas Carbine

T/C Seneca

T/C Hawken

T/C Renegade

gun weighs a little over 7 pounds. A "commemorative" flask featuring the Arms of Texas is offered with the rifle, serial numbered to match.

In addition, Trail Guns Armory is introducing a new side-by-side percussion double rifle which is not illustrated. This gun is to be in .58, .50, or .50/12 gauge combination with 28-inch browned barrels. Weight is about 8 pounds and sights are adjustable. Stock is of English style, joined to the barrels by a hook breech. To date there have been no new double rifles, so this will be a most welcome addition.

THOMPSON/CENTER

At the time this book was first written, Thompson/Center was not publicly in the shooting business. It was an investment-casting firm of considerable repute in the process of developing its first firearm—what we now know as the Contender interchangeable

barrel single-shot pistol. Following that item's success, the company designed and produced its first muzzle loader, the T/C Hawken Rifle, utilizing its in-house casting expertise to the fullest. As a result, the Hawken contains a maximum of precision-cast parts. T/C was determined to maintain traditional appearance along with improving internal design where possible. This resulted in the first production coil-spring lock, now standard on all T/C guns and available separately.

Since the excellent initial success of the T/C Hawken, several other models have been added to the line and all are produced in their entirety in the Thompson/Center plant.

T/C Hawken: A .50 or .45 caliber rifle in "plains-rifle" style with 28-inch octagonal barrel measuring 15/16-inches across the flats with hook breech. Sights are modernized, fully adjustable and fit into the basic style. Offered in percussion or flint style with modern coil-spring lock and decorative engraving on lock plate and hammer. Half-stock style with polished brass furniture, patch box and ramrod pipes. Comes with double-set trigger and weighs 8-1/2 pounds.

T/C Seneca: Named after the famed Seneca match of the NMLRA, this is a light half-stock percussion hunting rifle in .36 or .45 caliber. The octagonal barrel is 27-inches long and 13/16-inches across the flats; sights are as for the Hawken. Furniture is polished brass and is less massive than on the Hawken. Weight is 6 pounds, making it a nice light hunting rifle.

T/C Renegade: This is a plain half-stock rifle in .54 caliber, priced a good deal less than the Hawken and Seneca. Barrel is octagonal, 26-inches long and 1-inch across the flats. Triggers are double set; stock is plain without furniture.

T/C Patriot

T/C Patriot: A percussion pistol seeming a cross in style between the Kentucky and a dueler, .45 caliber with 9-inch barrel, 13/16-inches across the flats. Adjustable sights, ebony ramrod and double-set trigger; stock is walnut modified saw-handle style.

T/C offers complete shooting kits for all its guns, containing all the essential supplies and accessories except powder and caps.

3/Lock Types and Ignition Systems

As will become apparent in this book, the caplock gun is by far the most popular of all front loaders among shooters today. This certainly doesn't mean that good work can't be done with the earlier ignition systems, or that even today there aren't many people who prefer to use them.

A review of the several ignition methods is in order, along with coverage of the various lock types, so that their origins and differences can be understood.

The first "gonnes" were muzzle loaders, and the first muzzle loaders were fired by simply shoving a lighted slow match, hot coal or red-hot wire into a powder-filled flash hole (vent) which communicated directly with the propelling powder charge. This type is called cannon lock. Probably the earliest surviving example is the "Tannenburger Buchse." It is known to date from *before* 1399, having been excavated from the ruins of a German robber baron's fortress that was completely razed in that year. The Tannenburger Buchse is a simple tapered iron tube formed at the breech end into a socket to accept a pike-pole "stock" which was held under the shooter's arm. It was fired in this position by directing it with one hand while the other applied a slow match to powder exposed in the vent. Guns of this type were also called "hand cannon," and sometimes "petronel." One contemporary illustration shows this type resting in a fork attached to a cavalryman's saddlehorn.

The cannon lock could hardly be considered a reliable means of ignition; but I must admit it possessed the virtue of simplicity and, after all, everything must start somewhere.

It might seem that today's shooters would have no interest at all in the cannon lock, but that's not quite true. A small but avid group prefers to shoot muzzle-loading cannons. Most of their guns use cannon-lock ignition, though varied in that a fuse is inserted beforehand into the vent instead of applying the flame by hand. Then, too, reproduction hand cannons have been known to show up for firing on black powder ranges.

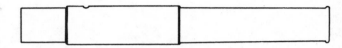

Cannon lock, without pike-like stock pole, as typified by the Tannenburg Buchse.

Following the cannon lock, the matchlock—a vast improvement—made its appearance. Matchlock guns used the same open vent and match, but were fitted with a pivoted, C-shaped metal arm which carried the smoldering slow match. In the earliest form, this match arm could be moved by a finger to bring the burning match into contact with powder in a small flash pan next to the vent. For the first time, both hands could be used to aim and fire the gun. Since the gunner didn't have to watch the match to ensure its reaching the powder, he could keep his eyes on the target and aim, after a fashion. However, the match moved to the *rear* to engage the vent—and that hot ember approaching one's eyes might have been somewhat disconcerting.

The first positive record of the matchlock appears in Codex 3069 at Vienna and is authenticated at the year 1411. By 1471, the mechanism had been greatly improved. The match arm became S-shaped and was called the "Serpentine." It was moved to contact the powder by a spring or linkage when a rudimentary trigger was pressed. This marks the first use of the finger-actuated trigger to bring about ignition. As in the earlier form, the match moved toward the shooter's eye. It is likely many arquebusiers' eyes were closed at the instant of firing.

In 1475, there was published a description of a vastly improved lock in which the match moved *away* from the eye to contact the powder. It also contained a lock plate, springs, levers and the first sear. Thus began the true lock we use today. Incidentally, matchlock revolver-type repeating arms were made in Germany at about this time, nearly 400 years before the revolver became a practical reality.

The matchlock continued to be made in numerous variations until the coming of the wheel lock. Johann Kiefuss is given credit for the wheel lock's invention at either Vienna or Nuremberg in 1517. This system derives its name from a roughened metal wheel spun rapidly against a piece of flint or iron pyrites to throw a shower of sparks into a pan containing fine priming powder.

The pyrites (most commonly used) were held in the jaws of a "cock" resembling today's familiar flintlock hammer. The cock was spring-detented in two positions—clear of the wheel and down against it. To fire, one first "spanned" the wheel with a wrench or "spanner" provided for the purpose. As the wheel was thus rotated, a chain was wound upon its shaft, tensioning a heavy leaf spring. A sear engaged the wheel to hold it in this position. The cock was then lowered, placing the pyrites in contact with the wheel's grooved rim. Pulling the trigger released the wheel which was spun violently against the pyrites by the spring and chain, throwing off a shower of sparks which ignited the powder.

Incidentally, the wheel lock, to be safe from accidental discharge, characteristically had a very heavy trigger pull, the result of a large sear engagement. This led to the development of the "set" trigger, whose weight of pull was not related to the load placed on the sear.

Compared to its predecessor, the wheel lock was quite reliable, particularly in bad weather, and the

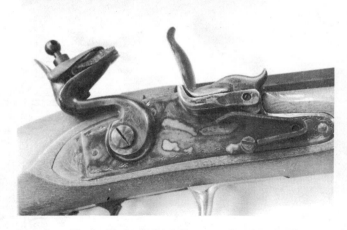

A modern flintlock of relatively low cost but has good durability and reliability. Most parts are made by the investment casting process; yet original style, appearance and functioning are retained.

arquebusier was not clearly revealed at night to the enemy by a glowing match. However, its manufacture required much greater skill and better materials—and it cost many times more than a matchlock. For these reasons, it never entirely displaced the matchlock.

Following on the heels of the wheel lock came the "snapping (snap) lock," or "snaphance." Here, the pivoted cock was spring-powered and carried in its jaws a flint which was struck downward across a rough, hardened "steel" or anvil to throw sparks into the priming powder.

The snaphance seems to have appeared around 1525 and was in fairly wide use by 1550 in various European and Scandinavian countries. No individual or country can positively be credited with its invention.

While internal variations were many, the snaphance principle consisted of the powered cock, movable spring-loaded anvil and *separate* manually operated flash pan cover. It was cheaper and more reliable than the wheel lock and thus more suited to military use. Sporting wheel locks could be afforded only by the wealthy, but those of more modest means could aspire to snaphance ownership.

The true "flintlock" evolved from the snaphance as really a single improvement. The pan cover was combined with the steel into what is called the "batterie" or "frizzen" (also once known as the "hammer"). This formed an efficient cover for the flash pan which automatically opened as the cock struck, exposing the priming to a shower of sparks. As the flint struck the curved face of the frizzen, it cammed that surface up and forward, carrying with it the integral right-angle pan cover. Coincidentally, this *upward* movement of the frizzen as the flint moved *downward* increased the relative velocity of the two, improving the shower of sparks.

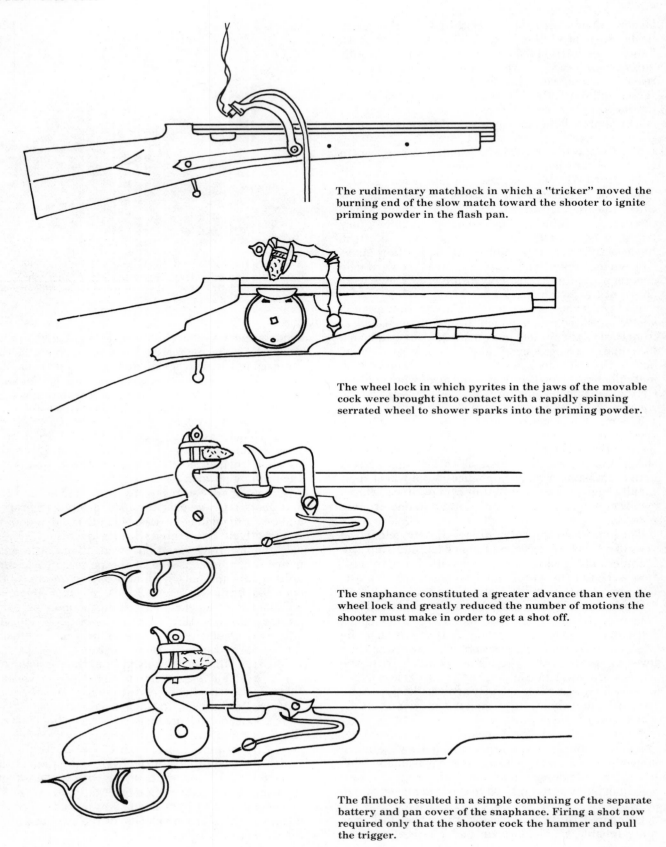

The rudimentary matchlock in which a "tricker" moved the burning end of the slow match toward the shooter to ignite priming powder in the flash pan.

The wheel lock in which pyrites in the jaws of the movable cock were brought into contact with a rapidly spinning serrated wheel to shower sparks into the priming powder.

The snaphance constituted a greater advance than even the wheel lock and greatly reduced the number of motions the shooter must make in order to get a shot off.

The flintlock resulted in a simple combining of the separate battery and pan cover of the snaphance. Firing a shot now required only that the shooter cock the hammer and pull the trigger.

A modern flintlock, frizzen open, showing the interior of the flash pan, the fence to the rear of it and the hardened frizzen face against which the flint strikes to produce sparks; note the mottling on the frizzen face left by the hardening process.

Typical flints available today (these in musket size) from Brandon, England. These are of English type and are "black" flints as opposed to the yellowish type sometimes encountered. At bottom is the flat underside, and directly above it the beveled upper side.

Whereas the snaphance pan cover had to be opened at least several seconds before the flint struck, the flintlock priming powder was exposed to the elements only at the instant sparks were already flying toward it. The advantage in rain, snow and wind is obvious. Improvements such as fences and drain grooves made the flintlock more reliable than its predecessors in rain and snow, but it was never truly waterproof.

The name "flintlock" appeared first in "Pallas Armata" in 1683, but the actual origin of the type is shrouded in the mists of history. The flintlock's salient features are known to have been combined in a single mechanism and used in France before 1615. One specimen exists by maker Jean C. Bourgeoys, who died in that year.

The flintlock caught on slowly and did not become widely distributed until after 1640. In 1690, it was officially adopted by the British Army, long after its acceptance by the French. Actually, the geometry and dynamics of the flintlock are complex and were not widely understood at the time.

Development stagnated with the flintlock. For example, the British used it with little variation from 1690 until 1840. France's Army used a single basic model flintlock Charleville musket until 1842. For very nearly a full century no notable improvement took place.

Little record remains of the firearms used in the earliest days in America. In 1628, the Massachusetts Bay Company was known to have imported snaphances for use by its mercenary troops. Wheel lock fragments and spanners have been unearthed at some

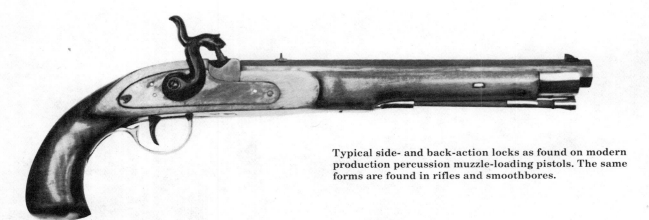

Typical side- and back-action locks as found on modern production percussion muzzle-loading pistols. The same forms are found in rifles and smoothbores.

colonial sites. Considering the circumstances under which the first colonists arrived on these shores, it is likely that the bulk of their arms would have been the cheap though obsolete matchlock. The few wealthy administrators and adventurers were probably carrying wheel locks, but these expensive and complicated arms would have been beyond the average colonist's means. Then, too, few colonial groups contained anyone skilled enough to repair a wheel lock.

Arms making per se, as opposed to repair and overhaul, no doubt began in America with flintlock arms of the German gunsmiths who settled in Pennsylvania. Their products eventually evolved into the flintlock Kentucky rifle and descended directly from the heavy Swiss and German Jaeger rifles brought from their native lands.

The ultimate in muzzle-loading arms ignition was achieved in the percussion lock. It represented little mechanical change, but rather an adaptation of the existing flintlock to the use of the percussion cap that will be covered in detail later. The cap made it possible to do away with the heavy double-jawed cock and flint, as well as the flash pan and frizzen, with their related parts. Their places were taken by a simple one-piece hammer, nipple and bolster screwed directly into the gun barrel. Internally, the flintlock mechanism needed no change—and none took place, other than evolutionary simplification.

Freed from the encumbrance of flash pan and frizzen, the percussion lock developed into smaller and more pleasing forms. The familiar lock configuration with its mainspring ahead of the hammer predominated and became known simply as the "side lock" or "bar lock." The back-action lock was developed with the mainspring behind the hammer. This eliminated need for extensive weakening of the stock forward of the hammer. The back-action lock was inletted into the wrist of the stock, permitting a more graceful overall stock shape, but weakened the stock at that point.

The box lock also became more prominent in per-

cussion form, though it existed earlier in flintlock form. The hammer was placed *inside* the lock plate, thus rendering it less likely to snag on brush or on clothing and equipment. It was often used on small pistols of pocket or muff type, where the hammer was situated on the center line of the bore. It was a salient feature of the first U. S. military breech loader, the Hall.

The percussion cap made possible the "under-striker" or "under-hammer" lock—something not possible as a practical matter so long as loose priming powder was used. Simplicity and low cost were major virtues of the under-striker. The percussion nipple was placed on the underside of the barrel and a conventional but upward-striking hammer hung centrally to its rear. In its simplest form only two other parts were required—the mainspring which did double duty as the trigger guard and a trigger. There was no complicated and costly arrangement of sear, tumbler, stirrup, lock plate, etc. It possessed other virtues as well: cap fragments and vented gases are directed away from the shooter's face, nipple and cap are somewhat protected from rain and snow by being beneath the

The box lock, with most of the hammer enclosed, became popular for small concealable pistols such as this brass-barrel spur-trigger derringer.

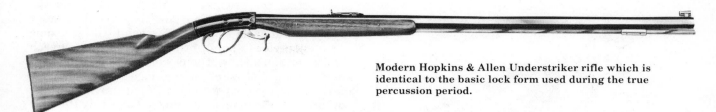

Modern Hopkins & Allen Understriker rifle which is identical to the basic lock form used during the true percussion period.

barrel, and nothing protrudes upward to interfere with sighting.

It is interesting that an under-striker caplock muzzle-loading rifle is produced in quantity today—the Hopkins & Allen by Numrich Arms—for the same reasons that the design was originally developed. This gun is available in several models priced as low as $100. Many modern-day percussion target rifles are built around under-striker locks that have been highly refined to produce minimum lock time and maximum uniformity of ignition.

Also an off-beat product of the practical percussion cap was the "mule-ear" lock. This type has the nipple placed horizontally on the *side* of the barrel. The hammer is a simple lever or bar that swings horizontally to strike and detonate the cap. The mule-ear possesses most of the advantages of the under-striker, except that it is neither cheap nor simple. If anything, it is more complicated than a conventional side lock. It does have the virtue that the hammer(s) lay very close to the barrel(s); thus making for a very compact and streamlined arm, advantageous for a superposed two-barrel gun.

For all practical purposes, percussion lock development ceased with the introduction of breech-loading arms. In recent years, however, black powder target shooters (primarily) have sought more uniform ignition in muzzle loaders. Since the modern center-fire primer is more uniform and reliable than the percussion cap, attempts have been made to utilize it in place of the latter. The result is called the "primer lock" for want of a better name.

Primer locks are almost invariably custom-made by the shooter or his gunsmith, and they take several forms. The most basic is a modification of a conventional percussion lock. The nipple or nipple and bolster is replaced by a block containing a recess for a standard pistol primer and a vent into the barrel. On top of the primer is screwed or otherwise detented a closing block containing a short firing pin. The original hammer may be altered slightly to strike the firing pin and detonate the primer. This type retains several disadvantages of the original caplock—long, slow hammer fall and a right-angle turn the primer flash must traverse—so it is not particularly common or popular.

The under-striker form seems most common, with mule-ear and center-hung box lock following in that order. All three utilize a single straight vent leading directly from the primer to the propelling charge.

A boss or bolster is secured to the barrel, counterbored and threaded for a housing containing the primer and firing pin. Since this housing must be removed to replace the fired primer, interrupted threads and even handles may be used. Some are constructed so that the primer may be precrushed—seated under a specified, uniform load—to increase its sensitivity.

Hammers and internal lockwork are almost invariably designed to function in the quickest possible time—producing minimum lock time. This allows less chance of throwing a shot off in that fraction of a second after the sear releases but before the bullet departs the muzzle. Such units are invariably custom-built to widely varying designs and may be seen at almost any major muzzle-loading bench-rest match.

Though the primer lock is a far cry from the traditional percussion lock, it has evolved directly from the latter to meet a specific need. As such, it cannot be ignored. In fact, it was in limited use, for the

A typical modern flintlock made in Italy for Dixie Gun Works. Note the profusion of parts protruding inward from the lock plate for which clearance in the stock must be made. Modern percussion locks are identical internally.

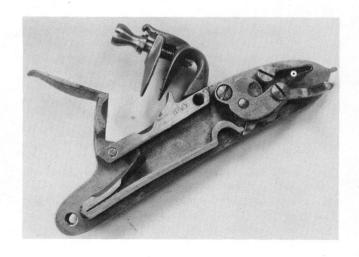

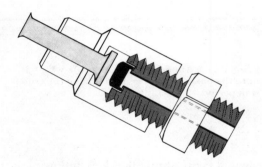

In the primer lock, the nipple is replaced by the device above. A primer is placed in the shallow recess; then the cap containing the striker or firing pin is screwed over it snugly. A typical percussion hammer then strikes the firing pin to explode the primer. Some designs use a swinging or hinged piece carrying the firing pin rather than the threaded cap shown.

same reasons as now, by match shooters of the late 19th century.

Several other modern percussion–lock types exist and deserve some mention. They are conversions of early breech loaders backward in time to furnish cheap muzzle loaders for fun shooting.

One such conversion was carried out on large-caliber Remington rolling-block rifles. The firing pin is removed from the breech block which is then fitted with either a conventional nipple or some form of primer lock. The hammer face is then altered to suit either cap or primer.

With this accomplished, a decapped fired cartridge case fitting the original chamber is seated and the breech block closed. The gun may be fired as a percussion muzzle loader at this point, though some shooters prefer to pin or otherwise secure the breech block permanently in the closed position to prevent inadvertent removal of the cartridge case. This case is essential to the conversion because it provides proper obturation. Cleaning is simplified if an easily (but not accidentally) removable split pin is used to secure the breech block shut. The action may then be opened to allow cleaning from the breech and also to draw the charge when that becomes necessary or desirable.

Given this discussion of lock types and ignition systems, you may wonder just how many of them are actually used by black powder buffs today. Well, I'd say all of them are, with the possible exception of the wheel lock. The latter is left out primarily because originals are too scarce and valuable, and new ones are too costly and difficult to make. I know only one man who has shot a wheel lock, and he did it in order to write a story about it.

Cannon locks are seen at every artillery shoot. Oriental matchlocks aren't too hard to come by in shooting shape. And if you can't find an original, one is quite simple to make, especially since Turner Kirkland sells new locks of this type.

Snaphances show up occasionally. But, again, Kirkland will sell you an original lock and a new barrel if you just can't get along without one and are willing to expend time and effort to assemble them into a complete gun.

Flint and percussion arms are seen in profusion at every shoot. A wide variety of new guns, complete kits,

The two forms of percussion caps; at left is the common rifle and pistol cap available in slight variations of the size shown and used on almost all civilian-type guns; at right is the typical musket or "top-hat" cap with its large, split flange and substantially greater content of detonating compound.

In the early 1800's Ethan Allen devised this boxlock action with a heavy, cast-brass receiver housing all the moving parts and the hammer situated externally. The nipple is threaded into a bolster integral with the receiver, and the barrel is screwed into the receiver rather than fitted with a breech plug.

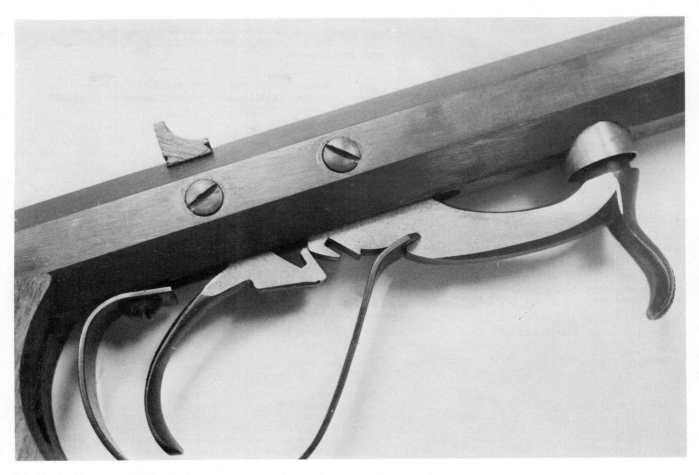

Principal advantage of the underhammer action is its extremely small number of parts;
all can be seen here in this Hopkins & Allen Boot pistol except the trigger return spring which
is hidden. Note also how simple it is to completely shield the nipple with this type action.

and both new and original parts are available from several sources.

In short, virtually every basic type of muzzle loader ever made—and that takes us back roughly seven centuries—is still shot for fun.

Flintlock shooting isn't as popular among black powder buffs today as is the more reliable and convenient percussion ignition system. Even so, lots of people lean toward the flint Kentucky rifle and pistol. In recognition of such taste, some competitions allow only flintlocks to be used.

The history of the flint itself—thumbnail-size pieces of stone that for centuries sparked the entire firing cycle—is more than a little interesting. Wheel lock arms didn't use flint. Iron pyrites provided the spark. Being rather friable (easily crumbled), a single piece could last for only relatively few shots at best, and might fall to pieces on the very first.

The snaphance was the first firearms ignition mechanism to use flint as a producer of heat. Since it was invented sometime in the 16th century, flints (more properly called gunflints,) became indispensable to arms users the world over—and remained so for about 250 years. As such, gunflints became an important item of commerce—more so than guns themselves, for in its lifetime a gun might consume thousands of flints. Anyone with skill in metals could produce a gun from readily available raw materials, but good supplies of the proper type of flint were rare, being found as natural deposits in only a few places in the world. There were only a few families and groups with sufficient rare skill in "knapping" the big nodules into usable gunflints. These people were concentrated at the sites of commercially profitable flint deposits and the skill was passed from father to son for many generations.

No one knows just where or how the first flints were produced, but undoubtedly some residual knowledge of stone tool-making figured in shaping the first ones. In fact, the first "flints" may well have been made from *chert* nodules. Chert is quite similar to flint and occurs in the same form and under much the same

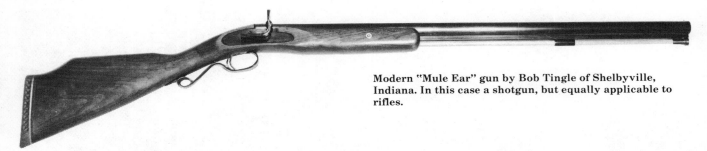

Modern "Mule Ear" gun by Bob Tingle of Shelbyville, Indiana. In this case a shotgun, but equally applicable to rifles.

conditions. It was often used in lieu of flint for tools in stone-age times.

Flint occurs in irregular, rounded nodules weighing up to 40 pounds or more. Relatively large deposits existed as float, apparently resulting from the great glaciers of northern Europe eons ago. Major sources were found near Brandon, Mindenhall, Savenham and Tudenham in England and at Yonne, Loire et Cher and Indre, France. Fairly extensive deposits also existed in Russia and Asia, but little is known of them.

In any event, historians and arms students agree that by 1650 a characteristic form of gunflint had developed and was fairly well standardized. Some prefer to call this form a "gunspall," rather than a gunflint—this for the reason that a single "spall" (chip) was struck from the prepared surface of a relatively small, rounded flint nodule. This was done by striking the surface sharply with a pick-like hammer which concentrated great force (in terms of pounds per square inch) in a small area. A skillful knapper could produce reasonably uniform spalls quite rapidly in this fashion, holding the nodule in a leather apron between his knees with one hand and working around it with his hammer.

This spall came from the nodule in the shape shown, and was then trimmed or "gnawed." Light hammer taps chipped away the excess to produce a usable flint of the desired size. Alternatively, each spall would be trimmed as quickly as possible without regard to size—leaving sorting and grading to someone whose time was less valuable than the knapper's.

The gnawed heel thus produced is characteristic of later French flints, and it is often assumed that the process developed first in the French flint quarries. No documentary evidence exists to back this up, so it may well have happened another way. I can't think of any valid reason to suppose the English, Prussian or even Russian knappers may not have originated the gnawed heel. In any event, the gnawed flint became known as the "French" type, while the squarish, untrimmed variety became known as the "English" type.

The spall-type flint worked well enough but took more time to produce than was desirable. In addition, its working edge is thinner and more likely to wear or chip away rapidly than later types.

During the early 18th century a new method of producing flints was developed. Whether this was the result of deliberate effort or simply an accidental rediscovery of cave-man techniques is hard to say. Neolithic man had mastered the art of striking long, sharp blades (strips) of flint from prepared nodules. From these several-inch-long blades, he fashioned knives, lance points, and other piercing and cutting tools.

The knapper wasn't interested in stone knives, much preferring iron and steel, but rather in those long flint blades of the proper cross section to make strong, durable gunflints. A properly struck blade could be broken across at intervals to produce as

Small natural flint nodules as they come from the pits. The nodules shown are purposely small and are sold as curiosities by Dixie Gun Works. Those from which the knappers shape gunflints weigh 20 pounds or more. Above photo on one-inch grid to show size.

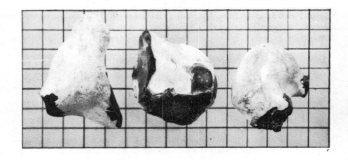

many as a half-dozen flints in less time than was required to trim one or two spalls to shape and size.

By the middle of the 18th century, this technique had been well developed, resulting in the conventional "standard" gunflint forms still familiar to us today— British and French. The former consisted of the blade segment untrimmed, and either end could be expected to strike an ample shower of sparks. With care, it could be reversed in the cock to provide a second striking edge when the first wore out. The French type had one end trimmed and rounded in gunspall fashion. This produced a sturdier, neater flint, but consumed more time and left only one striking edge.

As the flintlock became universally accepted for

both military and sporting use, demand for flints ballooned. Dependable supplies were a must. The common soldier was usually issued flints in the proportion of 1 per 20 rounds of powder and ball—even though contemporary writings state that "a good flint will last for more than fifty fires." "Large," "medium" and "small" flint sizes evolved. Muskets took the largest, about one-inch wide, while the 3/4-inch wide medium size sufficed for shotguns and some rifles. Small flints measured about 5/8-inch wide and fitted most sporting rifles and pistols. (Generally, the flint should be as wide as the widest part of the cock jaws.)

The British and French areas already mentioned became centers of organized flint mining (from open pits) and knapping.

Actually, both sites are reported to have been operating in a well-organized manner before 1700. Russia is reported to have obtained its flint from Podolia, in Poland, but whether as nodules or finished gunflints is unknown. Other countries with any significant deposits of suitable flint are certain to have developed and exploited them for their own use, but French and British flints became, for all practical purposes, the world's source. They were shipped in barrels to wherever firearms were in use and were as essential to war (ever a popular pastime in those days, as now) as powder and lead. Reference is often found in the writings of the 18th century campaigners to either a shortage or plenty of flints and the effect it had upon their actions. A soldier down to his last flint, even if it was fresh and unused, might be reluctant to fire his musket.

If that last flint failed, his Brown Bess or Charleville became nothing more than poor club and a worse pike.

In 1789, France is reported to have had over 30 million flints in stock, while Russian production was at the meager rate of 45,000 per month. France was more active than England in the world flint trade, supplying that country, as well as Spain, Holland, the newly freed American States and other lucrative markets.

It is interesting to note that British and American troops faced each other during the Revolutionary War—both with gnawed-heel, yellow French flints in their musket cocks. Excavations of battle sites show the French type outnumbering the angular, black British flints 9 to 1.

There is documentary evidence that France dominated the world flint trade through 1800, after which canny British merchants began to get their share. Historians and archaeologists have found that in the War of 1812, only half of the flints used by British troops came from France—the rest being the domestic product. Then by the close of the flintlock period around 1850, virtually all flints used in the Americas came from the hands of British knappers.

Though the flintlock era may be said to have ended

Small pieces of iron pyrites which were used in wheel locks before gunflints came into being. These pieces would have to be carefully shaped before use.

by the middle of the 19th century, demand for gunflints by no means died out entirely or even quickly. Military demand by the major powers did cease during the period armies were re-equipped or converted to percussion ignition. But a smaller flintlock market continued and was exploited extensively. Even today flintlock arms will be found in use by many primitive tribes. British knappers enjoyed reasonable prosperity until roughly the period of the First World War and then their fortunes declined rapidly.

Today knapping isn't entirely a lost art, but few practice it. Virtually all the world's supply of natural gunflints comes from a handful of English knappers near Brandon. There they still strike razor-edged blades from blackish flint nodules, then break them into usable flints. They work squatting on the chip-covered ground, resting a nodule on a stake and steadying it between leather-aproned knees while plying the knapper's hammer with precision and regularity.

Although some flints are used by gun buffs on the Continent, the bulk of Brandon's output is shipped to the United States and Africa, with a sprinkling going elsewhere.

The true traditionalist—the fellow who tans and sews his own buckskins and smokes willowbark in his hand-made pipe—will insist on natural flints for his present-day shooting. However, if the small supply ever completely disappears, modern technology has provided ready substitutes. In fact, some substitute flints (if we may call them that) produce a better and hotter spark and will last many times longer than the original. They are saw cut to precise shape and can be had to fit almost any size and type of flintlock.

Some are made from Montana agate, which is a very hard, dense stone, somewhat less brittle than flint. Doubtless, there are other materials that would be suitable, but many flintlock shooters say agate is the best they've tried thus far. Shooters have reported a life in excess of 200 fires, with virtually no misfires due to poor sparking. Though ignition time hasn't been checked with sophisticated instruments, many say it seems faster than with natural flints.

When properly seated in the cock, an agate flint simply wears down without significant chipping of the edge. When wear has progressed to the point that not enough sparks are produced, an agate flint may be restored to usefulness by "sharpening" the edge on a power grinder. A fine-grit wet wheel is used, with plenty of cooling water. Otherwise, heat and pressure will crack the agate.

As natural flints become harder to get, it seems logical to use agate for regular shooting while hoarding a good supply of fine black English Brandons for whatever the future might hold and for showing off occasionally.

No doubt some of the ceramic materials produced today would make ideal flint substitutes. It only remains for some black powder buff familiar with these materials to do a little research. I'll wager someone will come up with a cheap, easily produced "flint" for the day when the last Brandon knapper lays down his hammer.

Percussion ignition changed firearms history and development virtually overnight, comparatively speaking. Flint ignition had reigned supreme for over two and a half centuries; for all practical purposes, gun development had stagnated within that system's considerable limitations.

Then in the first decade of the 19th century (1807), a reasonably safe and reliable percussion ignition system appeared. By the early 1820's, the percussion cap had been patented and placed in production. The passage of another score of years saw the percussion cap eclipse the flint entirely. Thus, in less than 40 years, a new system wiped out one which had endured for some 250 years. Considering the resistance to change which was typical of the early 19th century, this is a most remarkable accomplishment. Actually, that resistance to change, particularly among military minds, prevented the changeover from coming at least a decade earlier.

Today when "percussion" ignition is mentioned, we tend to think only of the small, shiny copper percussion cap with which we prime our muzzle loaders. However, the cap was preceded by other forms of percussion ignition, and they should at least be examined briefly. In reality, even today's superb metallic cartridges use the percussion ignition system.

By definition, "percussion" (from the Latin "percutere") means to strike smartly or violently. Anything used or caused to function by being struck, such as drums, cymbals, etc., is a percussion instrument or mechanism. Consequently, any ignition system depending upon a sharp blow to initiate an explosion which then fires the propelling charge belongs, at least technically, in the "percussion ignition" family. The flint system may seem to fit this definition—but does not. Ignition in that system is produced by sparks struck when the flint *slides* or skids along a roughened

British flint knapper Ray Ward demonstrates here the manner in which he breaks the long, razor-edged flint *flakes* to proper size and shape to form functional gun flints. Note that while the individual flakes on his work table are similar, they are by no means identical in either size or shape, so each requires individual attention to obtain from it the maximum number of serviceable flints. Obviously some flakes are suitable for large musket-sized flints, while others serve only for the smaller sizes.
Russ Carpenter

steel surface. There, friction, not percussion, does the work.

Alexander John Forsyth, a Scotsman from Aberdeenshire, was an ardent sportsman frustrated by wild-fowling misses he attributed to the inefficiencies of flintlock ignition. A minister of the Gospel, he was also accomplished in chemistry and mechanical arts and skills, a well informed and inquiring person not averse to probing the unknown. He began experiments with highly sensitive fulminates which had been reported upon earlier by Edward Howard.

He obtained sufficient political support to be allowed by the British Master General of Ordnance, Lord Moira, to conduct secret experiments in the Tower of London. Beginning there in 1806, he had by

1807 developed a magazine device that placed small quantities of fulminate adjacent to the arm's touch-hole, there to be struck by the hammer to fire the piece. The fulminate magazine resembled the bottles of scent or perfume used by the bathless ladies of the day to improve their downwind impression. Forsyth's invention is called the "scent bottle lock" for that very reason.

Forsyth patented this system of percussion ignition and formed Alexander Forsyth and Company, 10 Piccadilly, London, to produce guns utilizing it for general sale. Though far from perfect, this was the first percussion ignition system of any practical value. Others attempted to copy and improve upon it but were prevented, or at least seriously hindered, by Forsyth patents. Unfortunately, wear or corrosion or a slight defect in parts fit could cause the entire mechanism to explode violently when a shot was fired.

Forsyth's work launched the percussion ignition system. Others saw the scent bottle's shortcomings, and the "patch lock" developed. It utilized small quantities of fulminates made into discs or cakes and sealed between layers of waterproof paper. Placed next to the touch hole or over a short perforated nipple and struck by the hammer, these patches gave reliable ignition and were waterproof—an area in which Forsyth's system was grievously deficient.

After the British army switched to percussion ignition some years later, Forsyth was belatedly granted credit for inventing the system, though he and his "rubbish" had been ejected from the Tower by Lord Moira's successor, John Pitt, Second Earl of Chatham. In 1839, the House of Commons awarded Forsyth £200 in recognition of his pioneer work that resulted in the development of a reliable percussion ignition system. After his death, that same august body, evidently suffering pangs of conscience, awarded an additional £1000 to surviving relatives. As is the usual case, true recognition and appreciation of his accomplishments came too late to do him any personal good.

The patchlock primer was further developed in metallic form to become the Lawrence disc primer and, when made in a long paper or metal-foil strip containing multiple spots of fulminate, the Maynard tape primer. Both saw considerable use in the Civil War. The latter survives today in the rolls of paper noise-making "caps" used in toy "cap pistols."

Contemporary with the patchlock was the pellet lock, sometimes called "pill lock", and the two are much alike. Wet fulminate was rolled into small spherical or egg-shaped pellets. They were then coated with wax, varnish or even foil to waterproof them. These pellet primers were then placed individually over the touch hole in a fairly close-fitting depression. The depression might be in a nipple, or simply sunk into the barrel over the chamber. The hammer nose was shaped to crush the pellet in the depression to detonate it.

The pellet lock made revolving repeating arms

A closeup of a flint lump from which flakes have been struck, showing the smooth cleavage lines left as the flakes split away.
Russ Carpenter

To produce those razor-edged flakes which break into flints, the prepared nodule is held in the gloved hand and rested to some extent on a thick leather pad over the knapper's leg. The hammer is then applied with the delicacy of experience at exactly the right point around the rim to split off the desired flakes.
Russ Carpenter

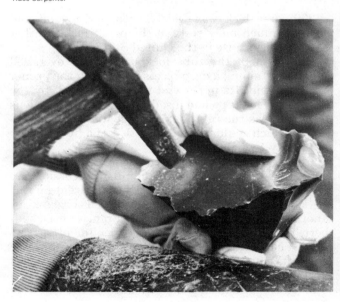

practical. The pellet could be stuck firmly in its depression with pitch or wax rubbed over it, yet this did not interfere with its proper functioning. This feature also added to the reliability of any arm; wind, rain or rough handling was unlikely to dislodge the primer as often happened with loose or patched fulminate. Significant among pellet locks was the Joseph Manton patent of 1816.

But the pellet lock was short-lived. Manton soon placed the fulminate loosely in a thin, short tube of soft metal (usually pure copper) closed and water-proofed at the ends. Called the "tube lock," this primer was laid in a trough or notch over the flash hole. Struck at mid-point by the hammer nose, it detonated, the tube burst and flame flashed through to ignite the propelling charge. This design gave certain ignition under all conditions. The Manton version (others soon produced similar primers) was appproximately 1/16 inch in diameter and a bit less than one inch in length.

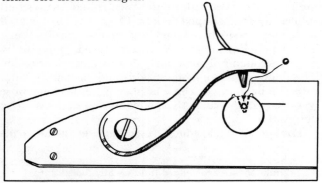

The pill lock or pellet lock utilized a cone-shaped hammer nose to crush a pellet of fulminate that was placed in a recess in barrel or bolster.

The tube lock was widely used in England and Europe, much more so than the pellet lock. Neither saw significant use in the United States.

One form of the tube lock utilized an oversized nipple containing a deep recess into which the primer fitted on end. Its upper end was then struck by the hammer. This type had disadvantages—most obvious of which was the fulminate residue and copper fragments which could prevent insertion of a fresh primer after only a single firing.

Percussion ignition achieved its most practical form for non-cartridge arms in the familiar percussion cap as we know it today. In 1819, a French patent on this device was issued to someone named Prelate. In another form, it was patented in France by Deboubert. These patents covered a copper (or other soft metal) cup containing a layer or wafer of fulminate inside its closed end. This cup was inverted and placed over a perforated nipple or cone, confining the fulminate over the flash hole. The walls of the cup were

springy, tough and sized so as to grip the nipple tightly enough to prevent movement or loss during rough handling of the arm. The hammer struck the closed end of the cup, detonating the fulminate inside to flash through and ignite the propelling charge in the barrel. In a very short time, this "percussion cap" was to prove to be the greatest single development in the history of firearms until the advent of the self-contained metallic cartridge.

Unfortunately, the two French patentees have received very little credit for their work. In the United States, Joshua Shaw, British-born artist and dentist, was granted a percussion cap patent in 1822—this, despite the fact that the French patents of nearly two years earlier were not unknown here. In addition, there is considerable evidence that a form of percussion cap had also been developed in England. Egg, Purdey, Hawkes and others of that country are known to have done work on caps, and all hotly denied that Shaw's cap preceded theirs.

Shaw was granted an award by Congress in the amount of $18,000 as full compensation for all U.S. Government use of his invention. The amount of this award was left to the discretion of the Secretary of War, W. L. Marcy, who unaccountably raised the amount from the $12,500 recommended by the Ordnance Office. The full $18,000 was paid May 4, 1847.

Reportedly, the award was granted on the basis of a report made to Congress by F. W. Risque that no American or European percussion cap patents existed before 1822. This was completely erroneous and causes one to wonder just how Risque could possibly have overlooked two French patents and evidence of English developments. Apparently, Risque either did not bother to investigate or else deliberately ignored the existence of the earlier patents.

It is known that Shaw did do considerable work on the percussion cap in the United States. For a time, he

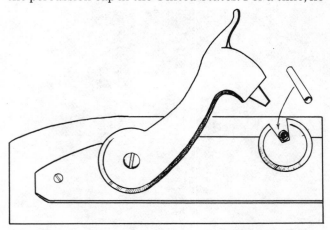

The tube lock was contemporary to the pill lock. Though perhaps superior in waterproofness and ease of handling, it was more costly and didn't represent much of an advantage over pills or pellets.

was employed at Frankford Arsenal in production and further development of the cap.

The percussion cap had developed into two basic forms by the 1840's. Large sizes for military use were called musket caps and had an outward flange at the open end. The flange was solid on some, split into three or four segments on others. Small sizes for pistol and sporting rifle use had no flange, being simple open cups.

Some were smooth, others ribbed. In the latter, the walls of the cup contained shallow, accordion-style

The percussion cap of today differs little mechanically from those in use a hundred or more years ago. It is just a simple soft metal cup containing a layer of detonating compound to be crushed against the nipple and ignited.

vertical folds. This design accommodated worn or odd-size nipples the best. It could be made slightly undersized, yet expand easily to pass over nipples of varying size and still stay securely in place. Smooth caps had to be rather carefully matched to nipple diameter to avoid looseness or splitting when pressed in place.

In production, open cups were stamped from thin sheet or strip copper in a single operation on a punch press. After cleaning and pickling, the cups were held mouth-up and a small amount of wet fulminate paste pressed against the inside of the closed end. Over this was pressed a disc of foil or waterproof paper which could then be sealed with a drop of varnish or lacquer. This produced a completely waterproof cap that would fire reliably under all weather conditions.

The percussion caps used today differ only in that they are made faster on more modern automatic machinery and that pure fulminates are replaced by modern, non-corrosive detonating compounds. Physically, however, a cap made today is indistinguishable from one turned out at the Frankford Arsenal 140 years ago.

Regardless of who is given credit for its development, the percussion cap made reliable repeating arms possible. The Colt revolver and its many imitators depended upon caps almost entirely for its reliability, rapidity of fire and speed of reloading. Revolvers had been designed around nearly every earlier ignition system, and yet none of them had been even remotely acceptable for field use. But in the proving ground of the Civil War—the bloodiest war in history—the percussion cap clearly established its supremacy.

Oddly enough, man's ingenuity was accelerating, and the percussion cap was eclipsed almost in the hour of its glory. The first metallic cartridge began with the Swiss Johannes Samuel Pauley's centerfire obturating brass-case cartridge of 1812. It reached practical acceptability with the Smith & Wesson and Henry rimfire cartridge of the late 1850s, and by the end of the Civil War had completely outclassed and made obsolete the percussion cap.

4/Selection, Repair and Maintenance

The care and maintenance of muzzle-loading guns presents a number of problems that will not be encountered in the modern centerfire breech loader. Not only does one have to maintain guns in safe operating condition, but also guard against deterioration that will reduce their accuracy. Modern guns don't suffer from corrosion as a direct result of firing, but muzzle loaders do. The copious black powder fouling causes serious rust that can weaken the gun if not thoroughly removed.

On top of this, when starting with a used or original gun, one must be absolutely certain that it is safe for use. While both old and modern muzzle loaders have an ample mechanical safety factor designed and built into them, they are made from relatively soft metals and possess inherent characteristics that make frequent maintenance and occasional repairs essential.

Since modern muzzle loaders are in plentiful supply and quite reasonably priced, let's first take a look at what might transpire after you walk out of the store as the proud possessor of a new front loader.

The majority of modern muzzle loaders are manufactured in foreign countries that have quite rigid proof laws. These laws require that every firearm, regardless of type, must be test-fired with heavier-than-normal charges and survive that firing undamaged before it can be offered for sale. In addition, guns that do pass this proof firing are required to be stamped with a symbol indicating that they have been so fired and inspected afterward and determined to be in safe, undamaged condition. All guns offered today by reputable importers and distributors have been proved by the manufacturer or by the official government proof house of the country in which they were made. However, occasionally low-priced muzzle loaders that have not been proofed will show up on the market. The more reputable importers and dealers will make this known when they offer such guns for sale, but this practice is not entirely universal.

Unless a gun displays what are called "proof marks," it ordinarily has not been proofed—unless manufactured in the U.S.A. where no proof laws exist. Such marks are usually stylized symbols of some sort. There are no rules governing their design, and they may appear as letters or numbers or something resembling a combination of a cattle brand and a royal crest.

A knowledgeable and reputable dealer will be able to show you the proof marks on any gun—if they exist. On new guns this presents no problem for if there is a proof mark it will be stamped clearly somewhere on the surface of the barrel near the breech. On the other hand, guns that are old, heavily used, neglected, or perhaps repaired or refinished may have the proof marks obliterated.

A listing of proof marks found on modern muzzle

loaders has been prepared in tabular form. It will not only help determine whether a gun you're considering is properly proofed, but will also make it possible to easily determine *where* it was proofed. This is probably where it was manufactured, or at least where it was assembled and inspected. Though modern muzzle loaders are usually made entirely in one country— if not all in the same plant—barrels and locks are sometimes obtained from one country and assembled into complete guns in another.

Consequently, if the purchase is your first, and you do not *know* that the gun has been proofed, prudence dictates that you should attend to this detail yourself.

This is not difficult to do. Generally speaking, some load recommendation will be supplied with the gun. By simply increasing the recommended powder charge by 25% you will have assembled a workable proof load. In the case of revolvers or screw-barrel pistols, where limited powder space is available, simply use all of the powder that can be accommodated in the chamber without excessive crushing. If no standard charge data for your particular gun are supplied, then use the data in the chart. There is no need to exceed the 25% increase mentioned; it is entirely adequate. Seeking to make your gun "safer" by using an excessive proof load is to run a much greater risk of damaging a gun that might very well have passed the 125% proof.

For basic proofing, however, this table should be sufficient. Use round balls.

PROOF CHARGES FOR RIFLES, MUSKETS AND HANDGUNS

Gun	Caliber	Weight of Black Powder	Powder Granulation
Kentucky Rifle or Pistol	.28	35 grs.	FFFg
Kentucky Rifle or Pistol	.44	60 grs.	FFg
Rifle-Musket	.58	75 grs.	FFg
Smooth bore Musket	.69	85 grs.	FFg
Smooth bore Pistol	.54	45 grs.	FFg
Revolvers	Use the maximum amount of FFg the chamber will accommodate with a round ball seated flush with the chamber mouth.		

Proof firing must never be done from the hand or shoulder. Should a weak gun let go, serious injury to the shooter might very well result. The gun must always be fired by remote control from some form of rest. Considerable time and money can be spent to construct a very nice fixture for this purpose. However, it will not likely serve the purpose any better than an old auto tire to which the gun is lashed firmly.

Lay the tire on the ground, and insert the butt of the gun into the casing with the forend or barrel resting over the tire carcass opposite this point. A few

PROOF LOADS FOR MUZZLE-LOADING SHOTGUNS

Gauge Bore	Diameter (inches)	Powder Charge (drams)*	Shot Charge (ozs.)
10	.775	5½	1½
12	.729	4	1¼
14	.693	3¾	1⅛
16	.662	3½	1
20	.615	3¼	⅞
28	.550	2¾	¾
32	.526	2¼	⅝
.410	.410	2	⅝

*FFg black powder. Some shooters prefer Fg powder for 10-ga. Patterning is generally better with light loads. One dram equals 27.5 grains of powder.

turns of clothesline or heavy cord will secure the gun upright in place. Before placing it in the tire, load, but do not cap or prime the gun. Once it's lashed down, attach a long cord or wire to the trigger and string out to a safe distance or to a position behind some sort of nearby barricade. Only after all this has been accomplished is it safe to cap or prime the gun, making certain no one is likely to pull the string.

Retire to the end of your cord, and give it a twitch to pull the trigger. If the gun misfires, stay right where you are for a full minute. An apparent misfire often turns out to be only a hangfire. And, if you are leaning over the gun to check it at the time the hangfire lets go, the consequences could be dangerous, especially if the gun does prove to be defective and blows up.

If the gun has more than one barrel or chamber, only one should be loaded and fired at a time. In other words, don't try to prove both barrels of a double, or all six chambers of a revolver by loading them all at the beginning and firing in rapid succession. If a defect does exist, firing one chamber can set all the rest off, creating a dangerous explosion.

After proving, first examine all parts of the gun very carefully. Take particular pains to determine if there are any bulges in the barrel or any evidence of gas leakage at any point. If it is a caplock, check the position of the hammer immediately after firing. It should be fully down on the nipple. If it has been blown back to half-cock or full-cock, the nipple passage is surely oversized, and the mainspring may also be too weak.

After this visual examination, clean the gun thoroughly and disassemble it completely. Examine every part as closely as possible. Pay particular attention to the junction of breech plug and barrel, bolster and barrel, nipple and bolster—looking for any evidence of escaping gas. Should a small amount of gas be escaping, it might not be immediately dangerous in itself, but will certainly erode the metal to the point that the leak *will* become dangerous. Be on the lookout for any bulges or cracks that were covered by the stock.

The cheapest and simplest method of tying a gun down for proof firing is to place it in an old automobile tire like this; then fire by means of a long cord or wire tied to the trigger. This old 12-bore double took the heavy charge in stride.

Cracks in the metal can be particularly difficult to locate. They can exist, yet be closed tightly enough that no gas escapes through them. Under these circumstances, they cannot be seen except under fairly high magnification. Should you be fortunate enough to have access to electromagnetic metal flaw detection equipment (Magnaflux) or die penetrant (Zyglo) equipment, by all means use it. Either will disclose flaws not visible to the naked eye. Lacking access to such services, stand the barrel upright and fill it with a highly efficient penetrant such as "Mistic Metal Mover." The penetrant will find its way through cracks too small to be visible. The process may be speeded up by lightly tapping at random points on the barrel or by applying slight pressure to the penetrant at the muzzle. Applying a few pounds of air pressure using an expanding neoprene nipple clamped to the muzzle is about the only practical way of accomplishing this.

In any event, continuous examination of the entire barrel and breech plug surface for evidence of the penetrant leaking through is desirable.

Most penetrants are highly volatile and therefore will evaporate very rapidly. Since only a very small amount will seep through the cracks, it may easily evaporate before you see it if you allow 15 or 30 minutes to pass between examinations. Any leakage of penetrant through the barrel walls is reason for scrapping that barrel immediately. Some seepage around the breech plug is acceptable if the plug is secure. Of course, it goes without saying that the nipple or flash hole has to be securely plugged for a penetrant test. Incidentally, when the penetrant is poured out of the barrel, it's a good idea to clean the bore thoroughly with solvent and oil it lightly. Some

penetrants leave a protective coating; others do not—rust can develop rather rapidly in the case of the latter.

The old-timers' favorite barrel-testing procedure consisted of hanging the tube by a string and striking it sharply with a small hammer or knife butt. According to the story, if the barrel gave off a dead, thud-like sound, it was flawed. On the other hand, if a clear, bell-like ring resulted, the barrel was sound and in perfect order. This *is not* a valid test. Sound barrels *will* ring clearly, but so will some that are badly flawed or cracked. The dead sound does indicate a bad barrel—but the ringing *does not* necessarily indicate a good barrel. You can demonstrate this little trick to amuse your friends if you like, but don't use it to check out a barrel you intend to shoot.

After all of the metal parts have been checked thoroughly, take a close look at the stock. Check carefully for any splitting or chipping in the area contacted by the breech plug. The breech plug and rear surface of the barrel transfer the bulk of the recoil loads, and if not perfectly fitted to wood may split the stock. The combination of a heavy load and damaged stock *could* cause the barrel to jump out under recoil and gouge the shooter.

Chipping and splitting do not require scrapping of the stock. Stocks may be easily repaired as outlined elsewhere, and this should be done immediately before any further shooting is undertaken. The lock recesses should also be inspected carefully for damage. If after all this your gun shows no defects resulting from the proving, you can be assured that it is safe for normal powder charges and bullet weights.

But let us suppose that the gun you are using is an original that's been around 75 or 100 years. Or that it is a modern gun, but well used and worn. Proofing and examination procedures will remain the same as those just outlined. However, the gun should first be completely disassembled and carefully inspected for any visible defects of wood or metal. Any necessary repairs should be accomplished *before* proving. This applies particularly to nipple, breech plugs or bolsters in badly eroded condition. Proving may well blow a loose nipple sky-high. Or if the passage is badly eroded and considerably oversized, back pressure may blow the hammer upward so violently as to damage the lock. You may be reluctant to spend much time in repairs before proving, but such repairs are essential if the gun is to pass proof. It should hardly be necessary to add that a thorough cleaning should accompany the pre-proving inspection and that all rust and other debris should be removed from the bore.

Speaking of bore debris, a surprising number of old guns remain loaded. Because of the difficulty of withdrawing the charge, it was not uncommon for a muzzle loader to be put away containing powder charge and bullet or shot. Eventually, as such guns passed from frequent usage, they remained loaded.

Many a gun carried home from the Civil War has been discovered to be fully loaded in recent years except for a cap on the nipple. Several accidental firings and some injuries have been attributed to such long-ago-loaded guns. One flintlock fuzee came into my hands a few years ago to be used onstage in a television show. It turned out to be loaded. Drawing the charge produced wadding in the form of fragments of a French newspaper bearing a date in 1848. It would seem to have been loaded for over a hundred years.

It is easy to determine whether a gun is loaded. Simply take the ramrod (or in its absence, an adequate length of dowel or rod that will go easily into the bore) and drop it into the bore until it comes to rest against whatever may be at the breech. Make a mark on the rod at the muzzle, withdraw the rod and measure its length from mark to tip alongside the barrel. If the rod extends down to nipple or flash hole, the arm is unloaded. If it does not reach this far, the gun is either loaded or clogged with debris of some sort, more likely than not the former. However, mud-dauber nests, lost marbles and even hidden greenbacks have been found in barrels more often than you might think.

Soldiers of the percussion and flintlock era used another method for determining whether their muskets were loaded, called "springing" the rammer. The gun was held vertically and the steel or iron ramrod was dropped freely into the muzzle. If it struck the bare face of the breech plug, it gave off a clear, sharp sound of uncushioned metal-to-metal contact. If, on the other hand, the rammer struck a bullet or powder charge, its impact was cushioned and only a dull thud would be heard.

When a new acquisition is found to be loaded, or for that matter, any time one of your guns is loaded and it shouldn't be, the charge must be "drawn." The traditional tool for this purpose is a "worm." It normally takes the form of a sort of double corkscrew attachment which screws onto the end of the ramrod. The ramrod, with the worm in place, is dropped down the barrel and rotated clockwise while being held tightly against the bullet. This causes the points of the worm to dig into the soft lead of the projectile. Once a good purchase is obtained, you simply pull out the bullet by drawing out the ramrod. In the case of a gun that has not been loaded for a long period of time and whose barrel is reasonably clean, drawing the charge with a worm is, if not easy, at least possible without too much trouble. However, if the bore was badly fouled when that particular bullet was rammed or if the load has been in place any great length of time, I do not use the worm.

It isn't that the worm won't get a good grip on the bullet, but that the end of the ramrod does not offer sufficient purchase to apply the power necessary to draw out a badly stuck ball. A transverse hole drilled through the rammer head to allow a stiff piece of drill rod to be inserted offers a much improved grip, not only for drawing out the ball, but for twisting the worm into the ball. Even with this added help, it becomes a difficult two-man job to get the ball out. Instead of the worm, some shooters use a ball screw. This consists of a wood screw soldered to a bushing that screws to the end of the ramrod. The ramrod is bounced hard against the ball several times, causing the screw point to start a hole, and then rotated clockwise while under pressure to turn the screw into the ball. While this does obtain a much tighter grip on the ball, it also results in the ball being expanded tightly against the interior of the bore. This creates no particular problems in the case of a reasonably clean, smooth bore with a fresh load; otherwise, it simply makes the ball grip the bore more tightly than ever.

Often a stubborn ball can be drawn more easily if penetrating oil, light oil or even water is poured into the bore to provide lubrication. With an old gun or a particularly stubborn ball, considerable time and profanity can usually be saved by dismantling the gun, unscrewing the breech plug, pouring out the powder charge, then driving the ball out the breech by means of a long bore-sized rod inserted through the muzzle. Old powder may be caked solid—if so, play it safe and soak in water to soften; then dig it out with a non-sparking tool.

This method is absolutely certain to work, no matter how tightly the ball may be stuck. In the case of an old neglected gun, removal of the breech plug might present a problem, but we'll get to that shortly. Charges may be drawn from revolvers through the barrel by use of the worm, but this is really doing it the hard way. Simply remove the cylinder by whatever method the gun design dictates, and unscrew the nipple(s) from the offending chamber(s). Loosen the

Worms and ball screws take many forms. These are just a few of those available from Dixie Gun Works and other sources.

powder charge with a nipple prick or piece of wire, and pour it out through the nipple opening. After this, insert a piece of brass rod that will just pass through the threaded nipple hole, and use it as a punch to drive the ball forward out of the chamber. Take care *not* to damage the nipple-seat threads with the rod. With some makes of revolvers, the cylinder need not even be removed. The nipple can be unscrewed and the rod inserted following the capping groove or clearance cut.

Drawing the charge from a muzzle-loading shotgun normally presents no problem whatsoever. Even in a much-abused long-loaded gun, the overshot wadding is easily penetrated by a worm or screw. The wad may be rusted tightly to the bore, but can be broken up sufficiently to get the shot out without difficulty. The same can be said of the filler and over-powder wads, though their greater combined thicknesses make it a bit more difficult to break them up if they will not slide freely in the bore. Of course, once the charge is completely removed, fragments of wads clinging to the bore walls must be scraped out if the next round is to be more than indifferently loaded. Firing two or three rounds will often clean out the residue of the original lodged wads.

Whether it is old or modern, the first step in determining that a gun is safe and shootable, or making it that way (after visual inspection and ascertaining it isn't loaded), consists of complete disassembly. Quite often it is very difficult to disassemble such guns without damaging them. Age alone has little bearing on this difficulty.

One frequently encounters Civil War-era guns that have been kept clean and well lubricated for their entire life. Consequently, they can be separated part from part with little more difficulty, if any, than a gun fresh from the factory. On the other hand, I've encountered modern percussion revolvers a few years old that were so clogged by rust and abuse that their disassembly was a major operation.

Since muzzle-loading guns are identical in design and configuration to those of a century or more ago, there is no point in differentiating between them with regard to disassembly instructions. We'll start from scratch—long guns and single-shot pistols first—then revolvers.

A careful visual inspection is first in order. Make certain that you know which parts must be removed first (an exploded view of the type can be a big help—one source is the book *Exploded Firearms Drawings),* or you may very well damage some irreplaceable component. For example, I have known Kentucky rifle stocks to be broken in attempts to remove the barrel simply because a single barrel pin had been overlooked.

A clean gun will be easier to disassemble, so scrub the grime and the accumulated grease and oil off all external surfaces, both wood and metal, with a small, stiff bristle brush and mild soap. Don't let the wood soak up water—wet the brush, stir up an ample dryish lather on its bristles and use this to do the scrubbing. Clean the bore as well as its condition will allow. Utilize scrapers filed from brass to very carefully clean all debris and rust out of screw–head slots. Any attempt to loosen a stuck screw is certain to produce damage unless the slot for the screwdriver can be used to its full depth.

With everything cleaned, take screwdrivers that fit the screw slots perfectly and make a tentative try at loosening the individual screws. Unless they break loose with relative ease, go no further or you'll ruin the heads. Apply a good grade of penetrating oil or rust-freeing penetrant such as "Liquid Wrench" or "Mistic Metal Mover." If both ends of the screw are accessible, apply it to both places generously. Next, take a brass drift and rap the head of each screw smartly two or three times to aid the penetrant. Let them sit for an hour or so, and try the screws again. If they still don't move freely, repeat the penetrant and rapping treatment. Several days of this treatment, frequently repeated, is sometimes necessary to loosen the screws. Don't be in a rush. It is far more practical to take several days in freeing a screw than to break it off and have to drill it out and replace it.

If after a reasonable period of time this treatment fails, insert the screwdriver bit in the slot and strike the driver sharply with a small hammer several times. Generally, this treatment will loosen all but the most stubborn screws, providing sufficient slot remains with which to turn them. In the event you encounter a screw whose slot is so badly chewed up as to be unusable or one whose head was filed smooth in assembly thereby destroying the slot, use a hand grinder (such as the Dremel Moto-Tool) with a small metal-cutting slitting saw or abrasive cut-off disc to cut a new slot or clean up the old one. If all else fails, chuck a screwdriver bit in a drill press with the gun clamped to the press table. While applying downward pressure on the driver with the press spindle, rotate the chuck by hand to break the screw loose.

If a screwhead breaks or the shank twists in half, a drilling job is called for. Carefully centerpunch the remains and drill through with a bit whose diameter is about half that of the screw shank. Go slowly and carefully. Open this hole up with successively larger drills until the screw remnants can be picked out. Do not use a drill large enough to spoil the threads into which the screw is turned. By going up in small increments, a point can be reached where the bit just touches the threads without harming them. If screw fragments can't then be picked out of the threads, chase them out with a tap of the correct size.

Once the screws have been loosened, don't get carried away and take them all out. When you have succeeded in loosening each of the exposed screws 1/4 to 1/2 turn, give them another shot of penetrating oil and turn them back in finger-tight.

Now (or during the period of time you were waiting for the screws to soak loose) locate all barrel-retaining devices—pins, wedges, keys and/or bands. Pins are simply driven straight out with a punch of slightly smaller diameter than their own. Keys and wedges must be examined very carefully to make sure no hidden retaining device is sheared off in driving them out. When made of iron or steel, keys and wedges are often rusted in position and must be given the penetrating oil/tapping treatment to break them loose. Bands are usually retained by a spring catch or pin. The pin may be driven out easily enough. Spring catches often cannot be depressed far enough to allow the band to be moved because of debris filling the clearance cut under them. This debris usually consists of dust and dirt mixed with oxidized oil and grease and can be dissolved or softened by repeated applications of carbon tetrachloride or other solvent. I find carbon tetrachloride best, and it may be applied with considerable pressure by means of a syringe and hypodermic needle. By squirting a jet of carbon tet under the band spring, the accumulated debris of years can be dissolved and washed out, allowing the spring to be depressed. Keep in mind, though, that carbon tet vapors are toxic and the effect is cumulative—keep it off your skin, and *don't* breathe the fumes.

At this point, you may discover—in a sporting arm—that your gun has a "patent breech." This means simply that it is fitted with a hook-shaped breech plug which engages under a separate tang. If so, the barrel may be lifted free of the stock. Elevate the muzzle, and the breech plug will disengage from the tang and the entire barrel may be lifted out of the stock. If the barrel resists being lifted at the muzzle, then it is either fitted with a solid breech plug/tang or is rusted tightly to the stock. In either case, *do not force it.* The next step is to free the tang from the stock. The tang screw must be turned out of its engagement with the trigger plate and drawn clear, freeing the tang. Try again, lifting the barrel muzzle. If the barrel and/or tang still appear to be stuck tightly to the wood, take out the lock-plate screw. In some guns, this screw passes through a reinforced portion of the tang or breech plug, further securing it to the stock. Usually it enters from the off side of the stock, but not always. With it removed, try again. As the barrel lifts from the stock, be very careful that it does not peel out large splinters of wood that are adhering tightly to the metal. If any splitting starts, work carefully with a thin, sharp-pointed knife blade to separate wood from metal. If pieces of wood unavoidably come out with the barrel and tang, save them for gluing carefully back into place later.

Lay the barrel and tang aside. If the metal is heavily rusted where covered by wood, douse it with light oil that can be working while you proceed with further disassembly. Also run penetrating oil down the barrel where it can work internally on the breech plug threads, and also apply some to the external junction of plug and barrel. A few sharp raps on the plug with a brass hammer will assist the oil in penetrating the joint.

Removal of the lock is next. In most instances, only the lock-plate screw already mentioned holds the lock in place. However, you may occasionally encounter a reinforcing screw or bolt inserted from either side. If either is present, turn it out. Additional screws may also be found securing the side plate opposite the lock. The lock quite likely will be stuck tightly in its mortise. Tap very gently around its edges to break it loose—being careful to avoid bruising the wood. Turn the gun lock-down, and rap on the opposite side of the stock with the heel of your hand. Often this is sufficient to free the lock and cause it to drop out. If not, insert the lock screw from the left and turn it into the lock only one or two threads. Gently tap the protruding head of the lock screw with a brass hammer to start the lock from its recess. Watch carefully to ensure that the edges of the mortise in the stock are not being splintered. The lock must come out squarely, or some splintering will surely take place. Once the lock has started moving, the lock screw may be turned in from the right side and used as a handle in conjunction with the hammer to gently work the lock clear of the stock. At this point, the best treatment for the lock is to drop it into a container of solvent where for the next few days the many years' accumulation of oil, grease and dirt can be soaking loose.

Locate the pins securing the trigger guard to the stock. In addition to or in place of pins, you may find wood screws entering vertically from beneath. Remove them and lift out the trigger guard. Often the trigger plate will have been secured in place only by the tang screw, but there may be another wood screw or a pin or two as well. Whichever the case, remove

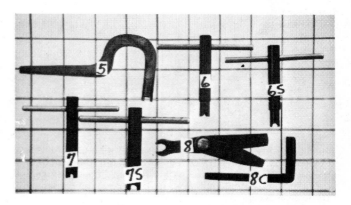

Nipple wrenches will be found in a wide variety of forms, but the T-Handle type shown here is the most common of modern production. It works well if properly made, dimensioned and hardened, but some of the older types like No. 5 above give more leverage for loosening rusted nipples.

the trigger plate.

At this point, set the stock aside. We'll cover its rejuvenation and/or repair a little later. One word of caution—*don't* lean it against the wall or stand it in the corner, particularly if the humidity is high in your area. The long, slender forend may warp badly from its own weight, having been deprived of support of the stiff barrel. Your best bet is to tie a cord around the forend tip and hang it somewhere.

Now we can get back to the barrel group. If the gun has seen much use, the nipple very likely will require replacement. Make certain you have a nipple wrench that fits the nipple properly. More nipples are ruined by improper wrenches than by any other single cause. If you do not have a wrench that fits correctly, clean up the opposing flats on the nipple with a small file. Then clamp a small adjustable (crescent) wrench tightly on these flats and unscrew the nipple. Nipples often require lots of penetrant before they will break loose. Even if the nipple looks "good enough," it should be replaced with a new one made from an alloy that will not corrode as rapidly as the older types. Use a stainless steel or an "Ampco" nipple that is known for its long life. Check the condition of the nipple threads in the bolster. If they are clean, sharp and full, simply order a replacement nipple to fit. If the threads are badly rusted or chewed up, order the next larger size nipple and a tap with which to "chase" new threads to fit. The bolster will probably be fitted with a "clean-out" screw running in from the right side. This should be turned out and the condition of the threads checked. If they are badly worn or chewed up, they should also be recut and a larger screw fitted. At this time, the interior of the bolster should be cleaned and checked to ensure that it offers free passage for the cap flash from the nipple and directly into the bore.

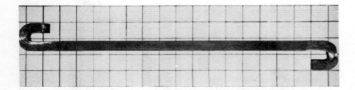

One of the simplest forms of a breech plug wrench. A bar of steel is simply forged around a form and then filed to fit the tang closely. A close fit is necessary to avoid damage to the plug. With torch, hammer and anvil you can make one of these in 20 minutes. They are available ready-made from Dixie Gun Works.

The bolster itself may be either welded, brazed or threaded to the barrel. Generally speaking, if there are opposed flats on its outer end to fit a wrench, it is threaded in place. If so, it too should be turned out and the condition of the threads checked carefully. These threads should also be refurbished, if necessary, but this will necessitate fitting a new bolster. Fortunately, they are available in many sizes and styles from the Dixie Gun Works.

The breech plugs of many older rifles are seemingly immovably rusted in place. The secret of their removal lies in having the barrel securely clamped in a heavy-duty vise, using a carefully fitted wrench on the plug, and breaking the plug loose by impact, rather than steady pressure. Clamp the barrel tightly between copper-faced vise jaws. Make sure the breech of the barrel overhangs the bench sufficiently so that the wrench used on the plug can be rotated through a full circle. If the sides of the breech plug are parallel and flat, a large, old-time monkey wrench or a large adjustable crescent wrench can be fitted tightly and will do a good job. If, however, there is vertical and/or longitudinal taper to the plug and tang, then you'll have to file and hacksaw a close-fitting opening in the end of a 12-inch or 18-inch bar of 1/2-inch x 1-inch steel. A poorly fitted wrench is bound to damage the plug and may not start it properly from its seat.

With the barrel tied down solidly, strike the end of the wrench handle a light, exploratory blow with a heavy (2-pound) hammer, driving it counter-clockwise. Often only a single moderate blow will readily break loose a plug that resisted the full weight of steady pressure. If the first blow doesn't do the job, a second or third heavier one will invariably suffice.

Clean and inspect the threads of both barrel and plug. The same criteria already described apply here. If the threads need restoration, have a lathe operator recut the existing thread in the barrel, increasing its diameter only as much as is necessary to clean it up. He can then thread a new blank breech plug (available from the Dixie Gun Works) to fit. However, if in the interest of maintaining originality you should prefer to use the original plug, simply have a welder build up the threaded shank and cut new threads on it.

While the miscellaneous parts are removed from the barrel, this is the time to do whatever work you intend or is necessary to do on the bore. If rifled and in reasonably good condition, I recommend nothing more than a vigorous cleaning at this time. Of course, if the rifling has been ruined, it will have to be recut or relined before you can expect anything like decent accuracy. If the barrel is a smooth-bore, it can be polished with strips of fine abrasive cloth placed in the end of a slotted rod and spun by a portable electric drill as it is passed back and forth through the barrel. For my part, I'd prefer the barrel to be used as is unless it is completely ruined.

Now is also the time for external refinishing of the barrel, while all of the protuberances are removed. This procedure is described elsewhere in this volume, so I will pass over it for now.

Assuming that you have everything about the barrel properly cleaned and rethreaded where necessary, return all the parts to their respective places. Take care to maintain the original alignment of drum, nipple and breech plug. If the parts screw in past their original stopping point, either peen the mating shoulders out slightly or use thin *steel* shim stock for spacers so that they will draw up tightly and stop in the right position.

If the gun you've been working on is a flintlock,

check the diameter of the flash hole. If it is over 3/32 inch and appears roughened and eroded, it requires repair. A stainless-steel insert makes by far the best replacement vent. The old vent can be drilled out and tapped 1/4 x 28 threads per inch, after which the replacement stainless vent sold by the Dixie Gun Works can be screwed in tightly. Of course, you can make a vent insert from a stainless-steel screw or threaded rod stock, but with the DGW inserts available at less than a dollar each, it hardly pays to do so. So much for the vent.

By now the lock should have soaked well enough in solvent so that it can be cleaned fairly well by scrubbing with an old toothbrush. Careful brush work will clean most locks well enough so that they will function reliably without requiring detailed disassembly. Today, small ultrasonic cleaning units are available at low cost. Using a detergent solution and high-frequency sound waves, they do the best and simplest cleaning job on dirty locks and other small parts. However, I prefer to take these completely apart. One item is absolutely essential for proper dismantling—a spring vise. This is available from most dealers in muzzle-loading equipment and supplies; however, you can make one quite simply from a pair of cheap pliers. Grind or file the jaws of the pliers so that they will reach in and fit around the two arms of the mainspring which can then be compressed by squeezing the handles. Then drill and tap the handles of the pliers so that a long stove bolt can be inserted and turned up to close the handles and lock them in any position. With this tool, compress the mainspring sufficiently so that it can be lifted out of engagement with the lock plate and the stirrup. Unless reassembly is to take place within a relatively short period of time, release the spring vise and let the spring relax.

Turn out the hammer screw. Check to make certain that the hammer is snug upon the tumbler axle. Even the smallest amount of play will increase very rapidly as the gun is fired. This condition can be corrected only by welding the square hole in the hammer and then carefully filing it to a very snug fit on the tumbler. It would seem easier to weld and reshape the tumbler. This would destroy the heat treatment of the sear notches essential to maintaining a safe trigger pull. If the hammer does not lift easily off the tumbler, turn the lock plate over, hammer-down, and rap on the bridle with a block of wood or a plastic hammer. If this doesn't loosen the hammer so that it can be lifted off, then make two narrow metal wedges (preferably of brass) and tap them gently between hammer and lock plate from opposite sides in line with the tumbler. Tap them in equally so that pressure applied to the hammer is in line with the tumbler. Pressure applied only to one side of the hammer will simply cause it to bind even more tightly on the tumbler. Examine the hammer screw carefully, and if it is not a good snug fit in the tumbler or if its driver slot is badly chewed up,

replace it with a new hardened screw. Check the face of the hammer. If it shows evidence of uneven bearing of the nipple, wait and correct this after the gun is completely assembled. If the hammer face is pitted and rough, grind or polish it smooth with a stone mounted in a hand grinder. Do not destroy the lip around the hammer face, since this helps protect the shooter's face from cap fragments.

Next, turn out the bridle screws and lift the bridle off, thus also freeing the sear. Turn out the sear spring screw and remove the spring.

Only the tumbler remains to be removed from the lock plate. If it cannot be drawn out from the inside of the plate with the fingers, turn the plate over and drive it out with a soft drift. Drive out the small pin retaining the stirrup, and the percussion lock disassembly is complete.

Disassembly of a flintlock is virtually identical to the foregoing except that the frizzen spring must be compressed and removed, and the frizzen screw turned out to free that part. Then, the top jaw and screw of the cock (hammer) must be removed.

The average black powder buff won't be able to do a great deal to the internal lock parts except to clean off rust carefully and replace ill-fitting screws or broken parts. Burrs may be found on the moving parts, and these should be carefully removed with hard Arkansas stones. The sear nose and sear notches in the tumbler can be polished to improve trigger pull, but under no circumstances should the angles or depth of engagement be changed. Occasionally screw-hole threads in the lock plate will be stripped or badly worn. About the only cure for this is to chase the hole out to the next larger size thread that will produce a full-depth thread. Once this is done, a special screw must be made and the related holes in other parts enlarged to fit. Usually no great amount of enlargement is possible because of the small size of parts such as the bridle, sear and sear spring. An alternative is to rethread the lock-plate hole and then screw into it a threaded stud over which the internal parts will fit without enlargement of their holes. The protruding end of the stud may then either be tapped for a retaining screw or threaded for a lock nut. As a last resort, the holes in the lock plate may be welded up and redrilled, but this may warp the plate and is a job for an *expert* welder.

A common repair required to place a flintlock in service is resurfacing and rehardening the face of the frizzen. While this can be done at home, the results are often far from satisfactory. Most gunsmiths who do muzzle-loading work will reface and harden a frizzen for a very nominal cost. The best solution is to let one of these experts do the job. The frizzen requires resurfacing and hardening if it shows deep scratches and gouges from contact with the flint and if it does not produce a good shower of sparks from a new flint set properly in the jaws of the cock.

After all of this (and unless you are very fast and

eager, it will have taken a good many evenings), reassemble the lock and place it and the trigger and trigger plate back in the stock. Check to make certain that the trigger position allows full engagement of the sear at both half- and full-cock. At the same time, ensure that there is not excessive free travel of the trigger before it contacts the sear arm. The trigger should just barely touch the sear arm with the hammer at full cock and the sear fully seated in the notch. Any trigger play that does exist can be taken up in one of two ways. Simplest and quickest is to inlet the trigger plate slightly deeper into the stock. Alternatively, the rear of the trigger can be built up by welding or brazing, then filed down. If the trigger bears too much on the sear, it may be filed down or a shim placed under the trigger plate in the stock.

This completes the essential metal work in thoroughly checking and repairing a well-used muzzle-loading shoulder arm. Refinishing of the metal and the stock are covered elsewhere in this book. Consequently, all you need to get the gun talking again is to clean out dirt and grease from the inletting cuts in the stock with a good solvent and place all of the metal parts back into the wood.

This may seem like an inordinate amount of work to do on a gun that looks pretty good from the outside. However, unless you do all this work, you won't really know whether the gun is safe—no matter how good it looks.

Percussion revolvers are a somewhat different breed of cat and carry with them a somewhat different set of problems. The Colt design usually gives the most trouble, so we'll take a look at it first.

Complete disassembly and *thorough* cleaning is the first order of business. Remove the barrel wedge, first turning out its screw on the left side of the barrel, then depressing the catch on its right end and tapping it clear of the barrel to the left. If luck is with you, the barrel may be drawn off the base pin. However, if it resists hand pressure, place the hammer at half cock and rotate the cylinder so the solid metal between chambers falls directly under the end of the rammer. Unlatch the rammer arm and bring it down so that the rammer contacts the cylinder solidly. Pressure on the rammer arm will jack the barrel free of the base pin if it is not stuck too tightly. Only hand pressure should be applied to the rammer arm. After all, it was designed merely to seat bullets and will bend if overloaded. Never strike it with a hammer in an attempt to break the barrel loose from the base pin.

If the foregoing fails, apply penetrating oil generously through the wedge hole and where the base pin enters the rear of the barrel. With a fiber hammer, tap vigorously over the portion of the barrel through which the base pin passes to assist the penetrating oil in working its way through. Wait an hour or so and try the rammer again. Repeat this treatment at frequent intervals until either the barrel comes free or you give

up. If this fails, complete the other stripping and then clamp the frame tightly in protected vise jaws and place a solid wood rest under the barrel. Next, take a brass or aluminum drift and place it solidly against the rear of the barrel where it meets the cylinder. Strike the drift sharply with an 8-ounce hammer; this is reasonably certain to break the barrel loose from the base pin. It is also quite likely to make a dent or two at the rear of the barrel, but this is better than having to drill out the base pin which is the only alternative.

If the hammer and drift method fails, and it seldom will except with a very badly rusted gun, the head of the base pin should be carefully centerpunched where it appears in the hammer recess at the rear of the frame. It can then be drilled out, using successively larger drills so as not to damage the threads in the frame. Base pin and barrel can then be punched out from the rear of the frame, after which the barrel can be clamped in a vise and the ruined base pin twisted to break it loose from the barrel. The remnants of the old base pin must next be chased out of the threads in the frame and a replacement pin carefully fitted. This is a job for an expert, and I do not recommend that the average home mechanic attempt it—even though new replacement pins are available from at least a couple of sources.

Back to the beginning and assuming that you got the barrel off easily, remove the rammer screw and disassemble that unit from the barrel. Scrub the bore and the base-pin recess and clean all dirt out of the wedge recess. Check the muzzle for burrs that intrude into the bore and carefully remove them with a countersink if they exist. Rammer screws and catches are often badly worn; fortunately, replacement parts are readily available.

Slide the cylinder off the base pin, and with a nipple wrench remove all nipples. They will probably require replacement if the gun has seen much use. If you anticipate any significant amount of shooting, it is best to install all new Ampco nipples, as already described. Scrub the chambers thoroughly, removing rust with steel wool or fine abrasive cloth in a slotted rod spun by a portable electric drill. Since there is very little metal between chambers, be very careful not to remove any more metal than is absolutely necessary to clean out rust. Before doing this, check carefully for outside dents which bulge into the chamber. Any deep dent of this sort will result in a very thin spot in the chamber wall after the chamber is polished. This can be avoided by using a shortened version of a shotgun dent remover to force the metal back where it belongs.

Check the chamber mouths for burrs and carefully file or stone off any that are found. Lay the cylinder aside.

Turn out the two screws flanking the hammer that hold the backstrap in place and also the single screw at the lower forward corner of the grip. These screws naturally get the same treatment already described for recalcitrant fastenings. Pull the back strap off and the one-piece grip can then be slid off the trigger guard to the rear. Observe where the tip of the mainspring engages the hammer, depress it and rotate the spring sideward to clear the hammer. Turn out the mainspring screw and lay both units aside. Turn out the three screws holding the trigger guard in place and lay those pieces aside.

Turn out the bolt spring screw and remove the spring. Remove the bolt screw and the bolt will drop out. Remove the trigger screw and the trigger will drop out. Turn out the hammer screw and carefully slide the hammer down so as not to lose the hand.

Toss all the small parts and screws in a container of solvent to soak. Screwheads are usually pretty badly battered, but since replacement screws are readily available at low cost, it's best to go ahead and get a complete new set.

Scrub all of the dirt and debris out of all the frame recesses. Remember the ultrasonic cleaner mentioned earlier. Clean off any burrs that intrude into any of the recesses.

The base pin is the heart of the Colt design, so check carefully to make sure it is tight in the frame. If there is any wobble whatsoever, the gun will shoot loose in short order. If it is loose, a temporary fix can be accomplished by centerpunching around the perimeter of the pin where it is exposed in the hammer recess at the rear of the frame, staking it solidly in place.

If the base pin is solid, place the cylinder on it and determine whether excessive cylinder play exists. There is no specified tolerance for this fit; the cylinder should simply fit as snugly as possible and still rotate freely. Looseness can be corrected within the cylinder in either of two ways. The simplest consists of counterboring the front and rear end of the base-pin hole, pressing in bushings, then machining the bushings to a slip fit on base pin. The alternative is to bore out the hole its full length, then press in a full-length sleeve which is then reamed to a slip fit on the base pin. Both of these methods are beyond the capabilities of the average black powder shooter. Any competent gunsmith or machinist can do the job without much difficulty, but the job won't be cheap.

If the base pin itself must be replaced, then the cylinder should be sent with the frame to the smith doing the job. He can then utilize an oversized base pin and fit the cylinder correctly to it.

After the base pin/cylinder relationship has been taken care of, replace the barrel on the base pin and tap the wedge in place. The barrel should be snug without binding on the base pin, but without any play whatsoever. In addition, it should be drawn up snugly against the frame, with the alignment pins at the forward end of the frame seating fully in their respective recesses in the barrel lug and preventing any sideward rotation. The cylinder should rotate freely without dragging on the rear face of the barrel. On the

other hand, the gap between barrel and cylinder, with the cylinder as far forward as it will go, should not be more than .006″.

Correcting an excessive gap here is rather difficult. It can only be done by partially welding the front of the wedge cut in the base pin or the rear of the wedge cut in the barrel, and then filing the hole to size and removing a comparable amount of metal from the barrel lug where it contacts the forward end of the frame. In this manner, the entire barrel can be drawn farther to the rear. Generally speaking, the saving of a few feet per second in velocity that can be achieved by closing up the barrel/cylinder gap in this manner is not really worth the trouble and expense of the job. Accuracy does not suffer significantly from an oversized gap, but velocity does drop off. However, a slight increase in powder charge can compensate for this.

With barrel and cylinder matched back to the frame, check the hammer, hand, trigger, bolt and bolt spring. If these parts all appear serviceable and function well enough to index and lock the cylinder positively when the hammer is brought to full-cock, don't concern yourself with them at this time.

Reassemble the gun completely and refer to other chapters concerning refinishing and the like.

The Remington design has a solid frame and fixed barrel. Consequently, one simply removes the rammer screw and draws out the rammer, which then allows the cylinder base pin to be removed. Next, the cylinder can be lifted free of the frame. Removing a single grip screw allows the grips to be taken off and provides access to the mainspring for its removal. Take out the single screw at the forward end of the trigger guard, and the guard lifts off, making way for the action parts to be removed after their screws are turned out.

The barrel, frame and cylinder should be given the same general treatment as already outlined for the Colt. Tightening the cylinder on the base pin is relatively simple. Any machinist can either bush the cylinder or very quickly turn out an oversized replacement base pin.

The Remington action functions essentially in the same manner as the Colt, though the bolt is pivoted to the trigger, rather than separately.

Aside from these differences, albeit with considerably less time and effort involved, the Remington Percussion Revolver can be treated as the Colt.

Refurbishing an old or well-used modern percussion revolver does involve the expenditure of time and effort. However, if you want a gun that is accurate, reliable and safe, the essential operations must be carried out. If you haven't the time or inclination to take care of these details, then you will be far better off by beginning with a new, modern copy of the original item. It may not be as romantic as shooting a gun that might have been used in the Civil War or one of the Indian campaigns, but it is certainly more practical.

5/Shooting the Caplock Rifled Musket

The sporting guns are nice to shoot. They have grace and beauty found in few mechanisms—a fine Kentucky is a delight to all the senses and comes to shoulder with the ease of a zephyr-wafted feather. More man-hours have been spent on beautifying some fine sporting muzzle loaders than it takes to build a Cadillac. To see a fine Whitmore or similar example of the gunmaker's art is much like viewing an old master or the Parthenon.

Target rifles will lie there and punch neat holes in 40-rod paper all day long. They satisfy our urge to seek perfection of performance at any cost. They are fun to shoot, too, but are practical for little else than paper-punching. We like them, of course, and to see them perform on the line at Friendship can stretch one's credulity. But there is one truly utilitarian front loader that can be shot reasonably well by anyone—it doesn't cost a fortune, and it doesn't have to be custom-made. You can buy one off the counter with little or no difficulty for less than your wife will pay for a new spring outfit.

It's the caplock rifled musket, manufactured in uncounted millions the world over during the middle third of the last century. With few exceptions they are sturdy, rugged guns with all the grace and aesthetic appeal of a wagon tongue. They are heavy, bulky and come to shoulder like a cedar post. Nevertheless, the rifled musket has tremendous appeal all its own.

For one thing, there's hardly one among us who can't claim some near or distant relative who struggled through Chickamauga, Gettysburg or some similar bloodletting with an Enfield or Springfield "Minie Gun" in hand. With an original or reproduction of that arm, one's mind slips so easily into imagined scenes of blue and grey uniforms appearing wraithlike through billows of white, pungent black powder smoke. As you stand there, the faint sounds of long-dead drums and bugles can be heard, along with the crash of caisson and carriage wheels, the scream of horses and the hoarse, inarticulate cries of valiant men lunging toward an implacable destiny.

In short, the rifled musket creates a feeling that can never be produced by the most beautiful Kentucky or most accurate 40-rod gun ever built. With it, we can relive history that is still close enough to have real meaning.

Seemingly, from what we've heard and seen, the military arm of the Civil War is by far more popular among black powder shooters than any other type. I like *all* the caplock guns, but as I write this, a Navy Arms "Zouave" copy of the Remington M1863 .58 caliber U. S. rifle leans against my desk. It's as faithful a copy of the original as one could want.

To shoot one must have a safe and serviceable gun,

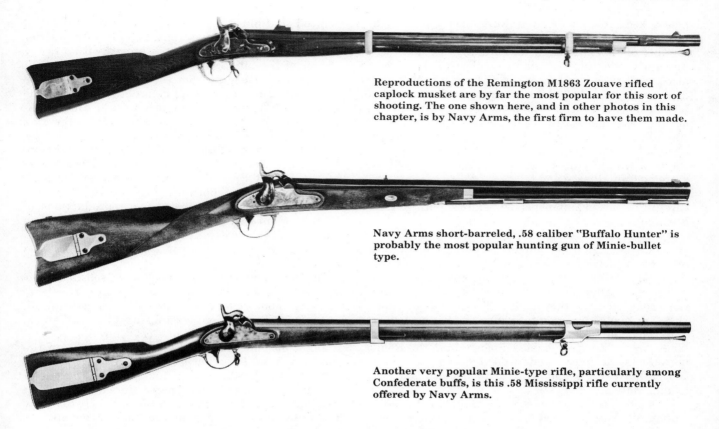

Reproductions of the Remington M1863 Zouave rifled caplock musket are by far the most popular for this sort of shooting. The one shown here, and in other photos in this chapter, is by Navy Arms, the first firm to have them made.

Navy Arms short-barreled, .58 caliber "Buffalo Hunter" is probably the most popular hunting gun of Minie-bullet type.

Another very popular Minie-type rifle, particularly among Confederate buffs, is this .58 Mississippi rifle currently offered by Navy Arms.

so let's take a look at what's available. The days when "war surplus" British, U. S. or other nationality caplock rifles could be picked up for a couple of bucks have long since passed. Drool all you want over Bannerman's old catalog, but bargains like that just aren't to be had anymore. Even so, quite a few of the hundreds of thousands of rifled muskets left over from the Civil War are still around. And occasionally a small lot of recently discovered foreign military guns will show up in the hands of surplus dealers. Some of these have turned out to be superb arms, virtually equal in quality and accuracy to top-grade commercial models of the same period.

The basic Union arm of the Civil War was the M1861 .58 caliber rifled musket. Produced extensively at the Springfield Armory, it was procured by the hundreds of thousands from commercial sources—some good, some bad. Consequently, it is the most common today and, when in good mechanical condition, an excellent shooting arm. One of this model in fine shooting condition may be encountered today for up to $300—a pretty good piece of change for most of us. A specimen that can be put into even reasonably good shootable condition will easily bring half that much, even though it may look rather rough.

The later M1863 rifled musket is also not difficult to

find and at about the same price; it is thought of highly by shooters.

The second most common surviving caplock military rifle is the ubiquitous .577 caliber British Enfield of which several hundred thousand were procured by both the North and the South. The entire British small arms industry grouped loosely around Birmingham seems to have enjoyed unusual prosperity while producing Enfields for *both* sides in the Civil War. In his *Civil War Guns,* W. B. Edwards says that over 700,000 arms were exported from there in 1861 alone. Of course, not all of them were the Enfield rifled musket, but a substantial portion were.

The Enfields probably shoot just as well as the M1861 and M1863 rifles, but are usually picked as a second choice by hard-to-please shooters. In today's market, the Enfield is just as costly as the original Springfield M1861 or M1863, so there is really nothing to be gained by shopping specifically for it.

Of course, there are dozens of other different makes and models suitable for shooting. Generally, they did not survive in sufficient numbers to be easily come by now. Collectors have priced them out of the shooter's reach. Rifled British Tower muskets in .69 caliber show up now and then—and they don't shoot badly.

If you do decide to use an original gun for shooting,

please keep in mind that it won't last forever. An average-condition specimen may be shot a reasonable number of times—if cared for carefully—without significantly affecting its value to collectors. However, any *visible* deterioration resulting from shooting will depreciate its value. And shooting *will* cause deterioration, even with the greatest of care; it cannot be avoided. A gun in really fine original condition simply shouldn't be shot—too few have survived this long to be able to justify reducing their number any further. As for a "mint" gun—to shoot it would be an act of extreme folly. Please don't.

Original guns must be *completely* disassembled and carefully checked and inspected before shooting. This is explained in detail elsewhere in this book.

By far the most economical and practical approach to acquiring a shooting rifled musket is to buy a new one. Yes, a new one! Very fine reproductions of the basic M1863 rifle are produced in Europe and sold here at prices ranging up to $125. While these reproductions may lack the fine hand finish of the old guns, they are made to closer tolerances and from better materials. Outstanding in this group at $125 is the Navy Arms, "Zouave," copied directly from the Remington contract piece made from 1863 onward. Over 100,000 have been sold to date to modern muzzle-loading buffs.

This model follows the contours of the original very closely. With its polished brass furniture, bright steel

ramrod and blued barrel, it is a most colorful sight, well made of modern materials and certainly superior in strength to the original. It is proved with a heavy charge of special "proof" black powder by its manufacturer. As it comes from the box, it need only be degreased and checked over before it is ready for the range. Certainly this is far less trouble than completely overhauling an original gun. And in the long run, it will be far less costly.

Since the first edition of this book was written, Navy Arms has introduced other fine modern replicas of the M1861 Springfield and the earlier Harper's Ferry rifled musket, both in .58 caliber.

Other firms offer less expensive reproductions of Civil War vintage rifled muskets, their quality ranging from acceptable to excellent. As with most things, you get what you pay for—so I suggest buying the best you can afford.

In any event, let's assume you've selected your gun—old or new—and that it is now in perfect mechanical condition. Also, that it is in essentially as-issued configuration, with open sights, full stock, and equipped with an iron or steel ramrod.

What else do you need? First, ammunition in the form of musket ("top-hat") caps; a can of FFg or FFFg granulation black powder; and a supply of *pure lead* .58 caliber Minie bullets properly lubricated.

If you are casting your own bullets, be sure to follow the procedures outlined in the chapter devoted to

Charge your piece! After bore is clean and dry and nipple has been cleared, pour the proper powder charge down the muzzle.

Properly greased Minie bullet (Lyman's No. 57730, weighing 570 grains) should be started straight and as far into the muzzle as possible with the fingers. Note that no part of the hand is actually directly over the muzzle.

Fourth from left is the traditional form of Minie bullet; all others shown are attempts (sometimes successful) at improving upon its performance by changing profile and lubricant groove shapes and dimensions.

various projectiles, their fabrication and preparation for shooting. I prefer that all grease grooves be completely filled though some shooters obtain good results without too much concern for this detail.

In addition, you should have a nipple prick, nipple wrench, and both worm and cleaning heads for the ramrod (or separate cleaning rod if you prefer) and a charge cup or adjustable measure-flask. These and other accessories serving the same purposes are described fully in another chapter.

Prepare the gun for firing by wiping all oil and grease from the bore with a patch dipped in solvent or lighter fluid. Pour a small amount of solvent into the upright barrel and let it run out through the nipple (hammer at half cock) to clear oil from the vent hole. A piece of flexible tubing slipped over the nipple will keep solvent from soaking into the stock. If solvent doesn't get through, use the nipple prick to get it started. Next, blow through the nipple to dry up any residual solvent.

With the hammer at half cock, place a cap on the nipple. Ear the hammer to full cock and fire the cap making certain the muzzle is pointed down range or in a safe direction. Some smoke should issue from the muzzle, indicating all passages are clear. The cap flame will burn moisture out of the nipple and drum passages. Firing a few more caps will make doubly certain everything is clear and is normal practice. Soldiers were regularly issued extra caps for this purpose.

Assuming you'll begin with loose powder and bullet, lower the hammer full upon the nipple. With rifle butt near your feet, lean the muzzle out at arm's length, thus making certain that any accidental discharge will be directed up and away from you and anyone else

in the area, no matter how remote the possibility might seem.

Pour a charge of 50-grains (weight) of powder down into the muzzle. While doing this, avoid placing any part of the hand directly over the bore. If you haven't cleaned all oil and grease out of the bore, it will catch and hold powder. Take the lubricated bullet between thumb and finger and start it base first into the muzzle. Do *not* use the fist or palm to drive in the bullet. Held between thumb and finger as shown, the bullet will not do any damage in the event of an accidental firing while your hand is there. Muzzle flash may scorch your digits a bit, but the bullet will pass safely between them.

Draw the ramrod from its seat in the stock. Holding it between thumb and forefinger, reverse it and use the cupped end to force the bullet home on the powder. A

Smallest to largest of the currently available Minie bullets—.45, .58, and .69.

In returning the ramrod to its seat in the stock, use the tip of a finger so as to keep all parts of the hand clear of the bullet's path in the event of an accidental discharge.

single, smooth movement ending with the bullet solidly on the powder is best. Bullet should be seated with uniform force, but never ram it really *hard,* and never "bounce" or "throw" the ramrod against the bullet as depicted in some television and movie sequences. To do so will seriously deform the bullet and crush the powder granules, resulting in a very inaccurate shot.

After firing several shots—perhaps 15 or 20 but often fewer—ramming will become difficult. When it reaches the point that the thumb and finger won't do the job, clean the bore—don't start trying to *drive* the bullet down the barrel. This will only deform it and ruin accuracy. A clean barrel and proper sized bullets will always produce smooth, easy ramming and best accuracy.

Return the ramrod to its seat, pushing it into place with the tip of a finger so as to avoid passing any part of the hand over the line of the bore. In the case of a rapid-fire match, you'll probably just stick the ramrod upright in the ground at your feet; some shooters stick it in their belt.

Assuming you intend to fire immediately, point the musket down-range, cradled in the left arm (for a right-hander). Ear the hammer back to half cock, making certain the trigger is not even *touched* during the process. Any trigger movement can result in improper engagement of sear in the half-cock notch, setting the stage for just a slight jar of the gun to cause an accidental firing. This precarious engagement is sometimes called "false cock."

With the hammer properly at half cock, place a cap over the nipple, pressing it solidly home with the ball of the thumb. A capper may be used if desired, but even then, seating should be verified by thumb pressure. The cap should be snug on the nipple, but should not require great pressure for seating.

"Ready on the right—ready on the left—ready on the firing line!" Pull the hammer to full cock, aim, finger on trigger—"Commence firing!" Settle the bull on the front sight, press the trigger and as that broad butt shoves ponderously back into your shoulder, orange flame and white smoke blossom from the cavernous muzzle. A 500-grain slug as big as your thumb arcs toward the target, just as thousands of them did on battlefields more than a century ago all over the world.

Simple, wasn't it? Fun, too! No modern, high-velocity, smallbore rifle can match the atavistic thrill to be had from the big military charcoal-burners of yesteryear.

Hurry—load her up again and let's have another go at it! That's probably your very next thought.

Stop right there. The infantry private in the line at First Manassas had to hurry loading or take a bayonet in the throat—he *had* to risk things like poor accuracy, a misfire, or an accidental firing. There wasn't any other way with a forest of glittering bayonets rushing toward him. You don't have that problem—but you *will* have problems if you get in a bodacious hurry for that next shot and do something stupid.

First, if you upend that musket immediately after firing and dump a fresh powder charge down the barrel, there just *might* be a spark or ember down in there. If so, it *might* ignite the powder with one hell of a bang, perhaps causing the flask (if you're using one) to explode.

There *could* be a half-dead ember in the vent hole. If so, nothing might happen until the bullet is rammed home at which time air being forced out through the hole could fan the spark to ignite the propelling charge. If that happened, both bullet *and* ramrod would be shot out, quite possibly making a mess of your hand or anything else in line with the muzzle.

After the bullet is rammed, seat cap on nipple solidly.

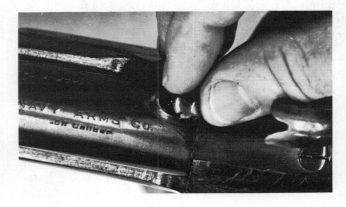

This is another reason for careful handling of the ramrod as already described.

This sort of thing is easily prevented. Just don't be in a big rush to reload. Second, before reloading, lower the hammer full down on the nipple, preferably sandwiching a small piece of leather between the two. This will prevent the rush of air that might fan a near-dead ember to life. Some shooters affix a short leather strap to the hammer for this purpose, swinging it aside for shooting. Usually, leaving the hammer down on the spent cap is adequate, but the leather is more certain.

So, take your time reloading. In too big a rush, you might even ram a bullet *without* any powder under it. Don't laugh; it's happened to many an experienced shooter, this writer included, and can be most embarrassing. Another rather interesting result of too much haste occurred to a friend of mine. He hurriedly charged, rammed, capped, and fired to watch in open-mouthed dismay as his four-foot long ramrod

Lyman No. 575213 Minie is of traditional shape with deep conical base hollow, weighing 460 grains. At right is No. 57730, 570 grains, with larger cylindrical base cavity and a good bit more bearing surface for more accurate alignment in bore during ramming and seating.

The final and most enjoyable step is the shooting. Navy Arms .58 caliber Zouave is a man's gun and feels really good when it spouts flame, smoke and lead.

At left is one of the several hollow-based Minie bullets available; at right is the Thompson/Center "Maxi-ball" which utilizes solid-base construction.

The thin skirts of the traditional Minie-bullet distort and cause poor accuracy when excessive powder charges are used. This type is shown on the left; at the right is a more modern Minie with much thicker skirts, designed specifically for use with very heavy powder charges.

sailed end over end toward the target. In the rush, he'd forgotten only one thing—to take the ramrod out of the barrel! Only a *little* mistake, but . . .

All this is intended to convince you to take it easy in the beginning, not to make muzzle loaders sound dangerous; they aren't, if you treat them right.

Shooting *can* be safely made faster and more convenient. The first step in this direction is to place premeasured powder charges in plastic containers to simplify handling. Plastic tubes which are a snug fit on the bullet may be obtained in various calibers. Powder is placed in the tube which is then stoppered

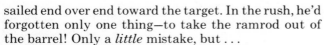

Although the .58 rifled musket (other calibers as well) is generally thought of for use only with the Minie bullet, it performs quite well with the round ball at left when patched and loaded as for the traditional round-ball.

with the bullet. In use, one simply plucks the bullet from the tube, pours the charge into the barrel, and immediately starts the bullet in the muzzle. North-South Skirmishers often grab the bullet in their teeth and twist the tube off.

Also a considerable convenience is the prepared paper cartridge described in detail elsewhere in this volume. Since its use is fairly well restricted to the rifled musket, we'll dwell on it here at some length.

The envelope or tube contains the powder charge and is tied or cemented securely to the bullet. Either the base may be torn open or the end containing the bullet may be torn off to expose the powder. In either case, the powder is poured down the barrel. Then the bullet and whatever paper remains attached to it is rammed home. The paper may be torn in almost any manner, so long as the powder isn't spilled, but the soldier armed with the rifled front-loader grabbed the bullet in his teeth and ripped away, often spitting the bullet into the muzzle as he reached for his ramrod after pouring in the powder. Or, if he were more fastidious, he might hold the bullet in his hand and bite off the base of the cartridge.

In either case, good teeth were essential. Interestingly enough, the army's rigid dental standards stemmed from this need. Only in the past few years have those old cartridge-biting tooth standards been relaxed.

Paper cartridges of this type are *not* nitrated, so the paper is blown clear of the barrel without being consumed. This increases the possibility of a live ember being left in the bore and also of range fires due to smoldering wadding.

Combustible cartridges may also be used. They, too, are covered in detail in another chapter. This type is inserted whole into the muzzle and rammed as a unit. The tapered nitrated paper case ruptures when rammed solidly, exposing raw powder to the cap's

At left is the conventional, hollow-based Minie bullet which depends upon expansion of the hollow base to engage the rifling; at right is the Thompson/Center solid-based "Maxi-ball," which when upset under initial powder-gas acceleration is depended upon to engage the rifling.

Largest to smallest in hollow-based Minies: left, .45; center, .58; and right, .69 calibers.

flash. However, even if the nitrated paper blocks off the vent hole, the cap flash will ignite and pierce it to fire the propelling charge. The paper is consumed by the burning powder, but there is still the possibility that an ember will linger in the chamber depths to scare the hell out of you if proper charging precautions aren't taken. Nitrated combustible cartridges are far more fragile than the plain type and must be handled carefully.

The original issue powder charge for the U.S. .58 caliber rifled musket was *60* grains of black powder, Fg granulation. It produced 934 fps with the *500*-grain Minie bullet from the 33-inch barrel. That load is too hefty for comfortable range work. And, in fact, it is often considerably less accurate than lighter charges. Charges in the vicinity of 50 grains of FFg or FFFg usually give much better accuracy than the issue load, and produce much less recoil as well. Particularly pleasant to shoot is 35-40 grains of FFFg which produces excellent accuracy at 50 yards, the range at which most rifled musket competitions are held.

Since individual rifles will behave differently, the charge should be varied until maximum accuracy is obtained from your particular gun. To be competitive in official North-South Skirmish matches, a gun must be able to group its shots into slightly less than three inches.

Although Lyman Bullet 575213 normally shoots quite well in .577 and .58 caliber rifled muskets, it will be well worth your while to try 575213 O.S. (oversize), 575494 and the new 57730. The latter has a very blunt nose, which shifts the center of gravity well forward, and has been producing very fine accuracy.

Perhaps I've been remiss here in referring only to .58 caliber guns. Actually, rifled muskets will be encountered in .54 and .69 caliber with some frequency. An occasional European arm of the type will also show up in some other caliber. Also, most mold makers now offer Minie-style bullets in .45 and .50 calibers for other modern muzzle loaders. Procedures are the same with all of them. Smaller calibers work best with less powder, the bigger ones with more. Lyman makes molds suitable for about any bore size you might encounter, so no problems there.

Seldom is much thought given to shooting anything but Minie-type bullets in the rifled musket. However, patched round balls can also be used with a fair degree of success. Simply load them as for a conventional round-ball rifle, with ticking patches. Keep powder charges light to start, beginning at about 30-35 grains and working up only to the point where acceptable accuracy is produced. The heavy charges often used in round-ball rifles are a bit much for the relatively thin-walled barrels of some reproduction muskets and are definitely too much for original guns, so don't try them. Round balls often won't do as well as the Minie, but they are fun for plinking and short-range work.

Hunting with the rifled musket can be a most rewarding experience. A gun and load tuned to produce the three-inch groups at 50 yards already mentioned are easily capable of taking deer and black bear at ranges up to 100 yards—and most of those animals are shot a lot closer than that.

As for power, don't fret. On paper that big Minie develops less than 1000 fps of energy at the muzzle. But its performance is much more impressive than that figure suggests. It hits like the flat of an axe swung by a lumberjack. Any deer hit squarely with it will either plow dirt with his nose or die of pneumonia from the wind going through that huge hole in his hide.

The rifled musket was all things to all men in war. And it can be many things to you—serious competition in the skirmish tradition, plinking along the creek bank, or putting winter meat in the smokehouse. It can do them all—just take the time to do your part.

6/Shooting the Caplock Round Ball Rifle

Of all the sporting and target muzzle loaders, I believe the caplock rifle with patched round ball is shot more than any other today. Of course, the slug guns have their following, as do the picket ball guns. The scattergunners have their day as well, along with those optimistic fellows who bang away with smoothbore "rifles," wishing all sorts of projectiles toward the target.

The round-ball rifle, hereafter called simply a rifle, has earned its popularity. As a flintlock, it's the form in which the rifles of Rogers' Rangers, Marion's Swamp Foxes and similar bands of patriots decimated Redcoat ranks in the forest battles of the Revolution. It's the gun upon which the trappers and mountain men staked their lives as they explored the vast unknown domain west of the original thirteen newly independent states. It's the gun upon which the golden era of the fabulously wealthy fur trade was built. It's the Kentucky rifle, descended from heavy, stubby Jaeger rifles of Europe that generated the legend of the 18th century in America.

The rifle comes in many forms. It may be the incredibly slender .30 or .28 caliber "pea rifle" used for small game; the short, robust .45 to .55 caliber "plains rifle" intended for bear and Indians west of the Father of Waters; the light, short "buggy rifle" of the settled areas; or even the 20- or 30-pound target rifle intended

for showing off one's skill in the peaceful times. Big or little, heavy or light, short or long, playful or deadly serious—the round–ball rifle may be any of these. There's one to suit everyone's taste, either original guns or those of modern production following the old designs.

Round balls are the easiest of all bullets to cast or to buy already made. They require a minimum of lead and are economical. They can be bought dirt cheap in many calibers by the bagful; as stated elsewhere, the factory-swaged variety will often shoot better than the ones you carefully make yourself. These factors all contribute to the rifle's popularity among today's black powder shooters.

If you don't already have a front-loading rifle for the coming season's activities, start looking. What's best? That depends on what you want to do. If you plan a journey backward in time to include a fall elk or bear hunt with round ball, you'll need something on the order of a plains rifle, shooting a ball of around 40 to the pound (.49-.50 caliber)—but preferably of even larger bore.

If you simply want to shoot, a slender Kentucky of around .32 or .36 caliber is best, though the latter is easier to load for top accuracy.

If you want to do some serious target work, then the thing to get is a heavy target rifle of at least .45 caliber, and it won't be light enough to take to the field.

Original guns of any type have become too precious and rare to be spoiled by shooting. Money isn't the real problem since many of us spend as much on a custom-built *new* rifle as a fine original is worth. But once the original is worn out or damaged, the entire supply of a very important historical item is reduced by one—it can never be replaced. The modern gun is easily replaced, without loss to posterity.

So heed the pleas of collectors and historians, and confine your shooting to modern rifles. There are plenty available, ranging from the Hopkins & Allen .40 or .45 caliber under-striker at about $90, upward to as much as you want to pay a custom maker. Examples are the Dixie Plainsman rifle at $175, the Dixie Deluxe Kentucky at $200 and others in the $200-$300 range. You can even buy parts or kits and build your own, as detailed elsewhere in this volume. That will not only save you money, but add to your education as well.

In any event, get the catalogs of the outfits supplying such guns (listed in the directory at the end of this book) and decide what you want and what you can afford. Get the gun, and then we'll take it from there.

You'll need round balls of the proper size, usually specified by the maker of the gun. Generally, though, the ball should be about .005-inch under bore (land-to-land) diameter. Patching cloth can be unbleached muslin sheeting or striped bedticking or more expensive linen, thoroughly washed twice to remove all the sizing. The gun maker will normally recommend patch material thickness, and several supply it in a shooting kit you may buy with the rifle. From there it's just a matter of carrying a micrometer and shopping. When you find some that's right, buy enough for a season's shooting—at least a couple of yards.

Get caps as specified by the gun maker and some FFFg powder. Check caps for proper fit on the nipple—tight enough not to fall off but large enough to be seated by easy thumb pressure. You'll also need a patch knife, patch cutter or patch lubricant.

The usual shooting kit is essential: nipple prick; nipple wrench; screwdrivers; worm; cleaning supplies; powder horn, flask or measure; and so forth. This outfit is described in detail elsewhere and is pretty much the same for use with any muzzle-loading arm.

With all the gear together, perhaps you're beginning to wonder just what kind of ballistic performance can be gotten from the rifle. Probably better than you think.

The round-ball rifle drives its bullet faster than any other muzzle loader and uses considerable powder to do so. A Hawken .52 or .53 caliber might well consider 200 grains of FFg or FFFg powder a perfectly normal full-charge diet. A .40 caliber rifle with 40-inch barrel can produce well over 2400 fps with its 95-97 grain patched ball, using 120 grains of FFFg powder. I've set

up a chronograph at matches and recorded velocities even higher from small-bore long-barreled rifles charged to the hilt. Extensive velocity tests have been conducted with a variety of modern rifles. The results are contained in the appendixes to this volume, and reading them can be a revelation to those who think in terms of "low-velocity" muzzle loaders. Even the 20-inch barrel produced over 1400 fps with a light powder charge and nearly 2000 fps with a full charge.

Of course, since the round ball is a poor ballistic shape, it loses velocity at a rapid rate. Trajectory is likewise high when compared to that of heavier, conical projectiles of the same diameter. Even so, there are many contemporary accounts of men and game being killed consistently at ranges of over 200 yards in the late 18th century. During the Revolution, Tim Murphy is credited with a single-shot kill on a British officer at over 300 yards.

You don't have to load for maximum velocity. In fact, accuracy will often suffer if you do, just as in modern, smokeless powder breech loaders. Shoot for comfort and accuracy, not just for speed and noise. After all, this is supposed to be a "fun" game.

On the range with all your gear, start by wiping the bore clean and dry and clearing the nipple by firing a cap or two. Set the hammer down on the nipple, preferably with a piece of leather between them, and prepare to charge with powder.

How much powder?

The old-timers had rules to go by, and the one most

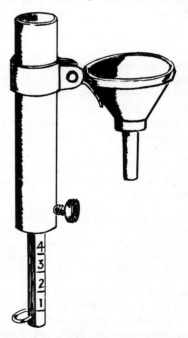

Especially handy when working up a load or varying powder charges is this simple combination adjustable powder measure and loading funnel. By recording the settings, a single measure like this can be reset for use with more than one gun.

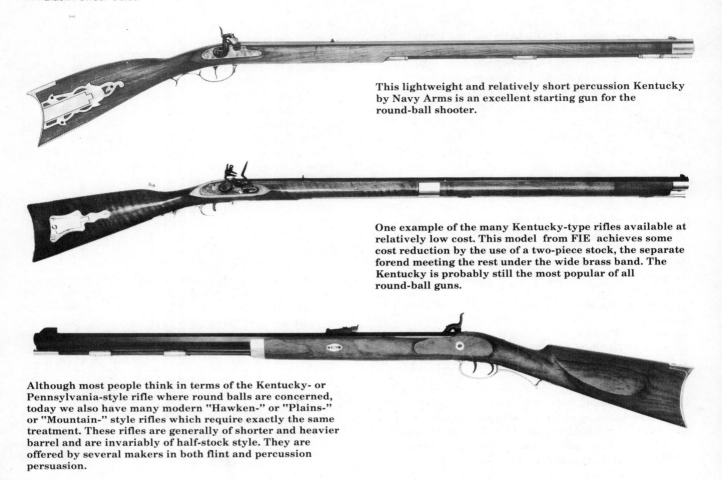

This lightweight and relatively short percussion Kentucky by Navy Arms is an excellent starting gun for the round-ball shooter.

One example of the many Kentucky-type rifles available at relatively low cost. This model from FIE achieves some cost reduction by the use of a two-piece stock, the separate forend meeting the rest under the wide brass band. The Kentucky is probably still the most popular of all round-ball guns.

Although most people think in terms of the Kentucky- or Pennsylvania-style rifle where round balls are concerned, today we also have many modern "Hawken-" or "Plains-" or "Mountain-" style rifles which require exactly the same treatment. These rifles are generally of shorter and heavier barrel and are invariably of half-stock style. They are offered by several makers in both flint and percussion persuasion.

often cited consisted of placing the ball in the palm of the hand and pouring out enough powder to cover it. Once this was done for a new rifle, a cup-type measure of horn or similar material was made to hold that much powder. The actual weight of the charge didn't really matter. It was results that counted, and the average rifleman couldn't tell you what his charge weighed. In *The Muzzle-Loading Cap Lock Rifle,* Roberts states that this method results in the following average charges:

Caliber	Weight	Powder
.31 cal. (150 per lb.)	(47 gr. ball)	25 grains
.36 cal. (100 per lb.)	(70 gr. ball)	40 grains
.44 cal. (56 per lb.)	(116 gr. ball)	60 grains
.60 cal. (18 per lb.)	(388 gr. ball)	85 grains

You can easily interpolate between these four examples for other calibers. The charges given are moderate—far from maximum—and all that you will need in the beginning. Additional "standard" charges for all types of guns will be found in the appendix.

With further shooting, you'll develop a charge that performs best with your particular rifle and ball/patch combination and can then make up a

charger or measure a supply of the starting charge into plastic bottles.

Pour the powder into the barrel. Lubricate a corner of the patch material by rubbing in enough Crisco or prepared lube to fill the weave. Lay the lubed patching across the muzzle, and center a smooth ball in the muzzle. Make certain the sprue is uppermost and centered, and then press the ball into the muzzle as far as possible with your thumb.

Take the short ball starter and with a single blow of the heel of the hand, seat the ball the depth of the short leg of the starter. Take your patch knife and while gathering up all excess patching with the other hand, trim the patch flush with the muzzle. This must be done cleanly and the knife must be very sharp. A ragged trimming job will reduce accuracy. Next, repeat the starting operation with the *long* leg of the starter thrusting the ball three to four inches into the bore.

Take the ramrod; seat it on the ball and with a single smooth motion, thrust the ball down firmly on the powder. Don't pound the ball or bounce the ramrod. The ball should be seated tightly enough to compress the powder only slightly. More pressure will deform the ball and interfere with uniform powder ignition. Contrary to popular belief, flattening the front face of the ball with the ramrod won't have a great effect on accuracy.

Withdraw the ramrod. No, that piece of instruction isn't superfluous. Many a man, including the old-timer who lived by his front loader, has shot out his ramrod. Loading routine should become so fixed in one's mind that no matter what interruptions occur, the proper steps will *all* be taken.

Ear back the hammer to half-cock and place a cap on the nipple.

Cock and shoot! It is best to do all your first work with a new gun from bench rest. Lacking a *solid* bench, use a bedroll or roll of blankets and shoot from the prone position. In checking accuracy initially, don't hesitate to get a local expert to shoot for you if you lack the requisite skill or if you lack confidence in the skill you do have.

Assuming the ball went on the paper, proceed to shoot a 5-shot group. Load the second and subsequent rounds exactly as the first. Clean the bore thoroughly after each group before trying another. The more uniform your balls, patching and the loading operations, the better the accuracy that will be produced. Observe all the loading precautions outlined in the

Hodgdon's squeeze-bottle "Spit Patch" is a very effective and easily applied patch lubricant for round-ball rifles. It also seems to work quite well on Minie bullets.

Recovered patches should look as in "D." "A" means fit in bore is too tight; "B" too loose; and "C" muzzle has cut through patch in loading.

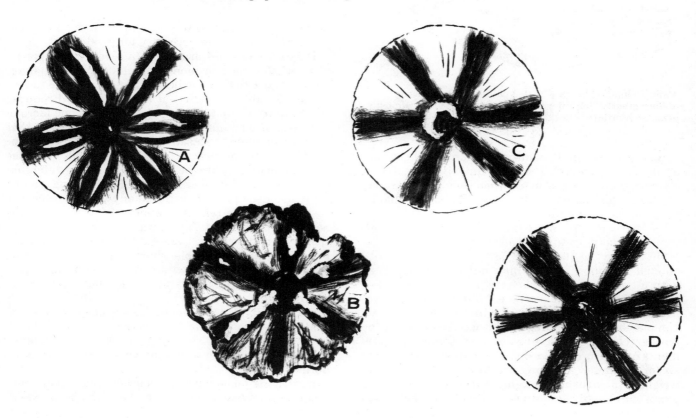

chapter on the rifled musket. Powder charges *have* been ignited by an ember as they were poured down the barrel. Bullets and ramrods *have* been fired right through a shooter's hand during loading. As in driving a car, muzzle-loading shooting is as safe as you, the shooter, make it—for both you and others nearby.

As shooting progresses, watch the pressure required to ram the ball. If it increases significantly, the bore is becoming too heavily fouled and needs cleaning.

Look in front of the muzzle a few yards for patches that have fallen off balls. All *must* fall off, or the ball's flight will be erratic. Inspect recovered patches carefully. The drawings on page 73 show you clearly what to look for. Patches cut as in (a) indicate either too-thick patch material or too large a ball so tight in the bore that the lands cut through the fabric. If the patch is scorched by blow-by gas (windage) as in (b), the patch is too thin or the ball is too small. Annular cuts as in (c) are made by the sharp bore edge at the muzzle. If not accompanied by other cuts as in (a) the muzzle edge is too sharp and should be lightly chamfered. This is best done in a lathe, but with care a 45-degree countersink reamer will do an acceptable job.

A simple loading block whittled out of a piece of scrap lumber greatly simplifies reloading in a hurry. It's almost a must for hunting.

Any of these patch conditions mean you'll get poor accuracy, so correct them as quickly as possible. Patches should look as in (d) when they are recovered.

After adjusting patch thickness and/or ball diameter, you should obtain several groups of about the same size. If not, most likely your loading isn't uniform, and more attention to detail is needed.

Or, it may be that your new barrel isn't smooth enough. A rough surface may not wipe clean, even with a tight patch. In that case, it may be lapped or polished as outlined elsewhere. More thorough cleaning after each group may well cure this problem also. Having checked the foregoing, proceed to varying the powder charge. Work upward first, going in increments of two or three grains for small calibers, five or six for the larger. Top limit for thick barrels is powder weight equal to ball weight, but best accuracy is almost invariably found below that level. Don't ex-

While a powder horn and separate measure makes for a more impressive costume and is certainly more in keeping with the frontier image, a measure-type flask is far more practical.

pect a single group to tell you much at each charge level. At least five are necessary for a valid test.

If heavier charges aren't the answer, work downward in the same fashion from the starting charge. Don't expect to find the best charge in a single range session. In all probability, at least a hundred rounds will have to be fired just to determine this one factor.

Having ironed out these first problems, you might then try changing to a saliva, or "spit," patch. It may produce better accuracy than a greased patch. Some improvement may also be obtained by trying different patch lubricants such as Vaseline. For hunting, you'll want to use greased patches anyway to prevent rusting of the barrel. All manner of lubricants have been used on patches. Tallow was once popular, as was sperm oil and bear oil. I've used both petroleum jelly (Vaseline) and vegetable shortening (Crisco) with good results. Some shooters soften beeswax with Vaseline and dip patches in this melted mixture. If you're striving for perfection, try them all.

Occasional "flyers"—single shots wide of the rest of the group—may be due to defective balls containing voids or air bubbles. This can be avoided by weighing balls and discarding any that vary much from the norm.

In striving for maximum accuracy, remember that you'll never know the cause of the effect if you vary

Precut round patches speed up loading for hunting, particularly when they are carried dry, and wet with saliva as needed.

When bullet and patch are properly fitted to a *smooth*, clean bore, ramming the ball home normally requires only one hand.

more than one factor at a time. For example, when switching to a thicker patch, don't change anything else.

You may find that accuracy improves unaccountably over a period of time. This can happen as a result of the bore being slowly but surely polished by each shot, or it might be simply the result of *your* increased skill. Conversely, if through neglect you allow the bore to become rust pitted (no matter how slightly), accuracy may deteriorate.

Slow and careful shooting with plenty of attention to cause and effect will enable you to extract all the accuracy possible from your round ball rifle.

Eventually, you'll want some plain fun shooting, perhaps even some hunting and probably some competition. Where speed in reloading is required, a loading block is essential. It's simply a block of hardwood with a row of three or four holes drilled in it. The holes are a snug fit for a patched ball and balls are seated in it exactly as in the rifle muzzle. Attached to the block by a thong is a starter with stem long enough to push the ball through the block and into the bore where the ramrod can take over. The ball is seated in much less time than otherwise. Since the ball must be centered over the bore, a muzzle-fitting counterbore in the bottom of the block around each hole is a decided improvement.

When hunting and rain or moisture is a problem, drip melted beeswax or candle wax around the seated cap to keep water from working in through the vent to kill the powder charge.

So far, we've talked only about the sporting or hunting round ball rifle. There are, however, quite a few shooters who fancy this type in bench rest form—heavy guns not suited for any other purpose. The basic rules are the same, with added emphasis on uniformity of loading and of components. Such guns are more temperamental and careful load development is required. These guns are fitted with false muzzles and mechanical ball starters. Essentially, they must be treated as outlined in the chapter on slug rifles, allowing for the difference in bullet type and patching material and method.

Round ball heavy target rifles are capable of superb accuracy, significantly better than hunting rifles. Nevertheless, they are a lot more trouble to shoot, and significantly more costly.

Aside from plinking and shooting on the range, the round ball rifle is the basis of nearly all of those shooting games muzzle-loading fans talk about—the woods walk, the rendezvous, the famous "Seneca" match, the squirrel hunt and many others. It's the real backbone of the sport and can open up a whole new world of fun for you.

7/Shooting the Caplock Revolver

Whether it is an ingrained urge to emulate our great grandfathers or simply a desire to try a different form of shooting, the muzzle-loading black powder percussion revolver enjoys greater sales and popularity today than at any time since the advent of the cartridge handgun. Original arms of this type are by no means scarce; in anything like safe shooting condition, they come very dear, indeed. The tremendous upsurge in the collecting of percussion revolvers has driven prices out of sight of the casual shooter. Then, too, shooting an original Colt or Remington will cause some mechanical deterioration, accompanied by a depreciation in value. The answer is quite simple—don't shoot original percussion revolvers. There's no need to, really, for a new modern percussion revolver can be had for hardly a fraction of the price of a shootable original—and it will shoot better and be safer as well.

To use the word "modern" in describing today's percussion handguns is perhaps not entirely correct. A large assortment of newly manufactured guns is available. Though manufacture and materials are modern, design is little (if at all) changed from Civil War days. In fact, with one single exception—the Ruger "Old Army" .44 revolver—all are merely copies of original guns. Reproductions of Remington and Colt revolvers, circa 1860, are sold under a number of brand names, including Navy Arms Company, Cen-

tennial Arms Corporation and Replica Arms, to name some principal suppliers. Centennial guns were produced in Belgium by a firm that once manufactured the same design under Colt license but are now produced elsewhere. Both Replica and Navy guns are manufactured mostly in Italy. In addition, *single-shot* pistols—including an underhammer "boot" pistol—are offered by Numrich Arms, Tingle, Replica, Navy and others.

The safety margin of the imported replica revolvers is undoubtedly greater than that of the originals. I have yet to encounter a single instance of a "blow-up" that could be traced to defective materials when only black powder was used. While current production guns lack the fine finish and bright blue of the original models, they appear to be produced to closer tolerances, and are certainly made from better materials than were available in the 1860's. Consequently, so long as only black powder and proper bullets are used, modern percussion revolvers are as mechanically safe as a gun can be. In fact, it is impossible to generate excessive pressures with any amount of black powder than can be loaded into the individual chambers behind a proper bullet. In the discussion of shooting techniques which follows, I will concentrate on revolvers. Single-shot pistols are less complicated, and require techniques virtually identical to those used with rifles, covered elsewhere.

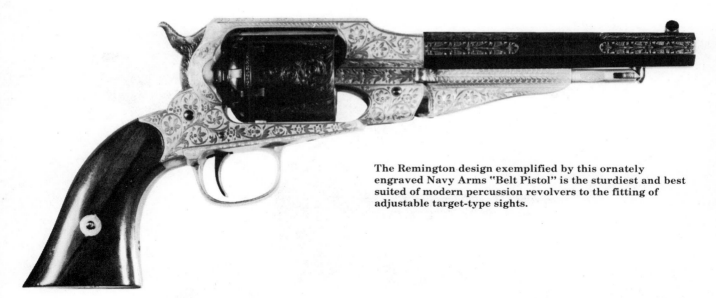

The Remington design exemplified by this ornately engraved Navy Arms "Belt Pistol" is the sturdiest and best suited of modern percussion revolvers to the fitting of adjustable target-type sights.

Caplock handguns are available from a number of sources. Navy Arms offers replicas of the Colt and Remington revolvers. Both are available in either .36 or .44 calibers. Centennial Arms features replicas of the Colt 1860. Replica Arms (a division of Service Armament) has the Remington and a most complete line of Colt revolvers—from the Paterson, Walker and the 1860 Army down to the diminutive Wells Fargo. They also offer a single-shot target pistol. Numrich Arms offers their Hopkins & Allen Boot Pistol in .36 or .45 caliber. Tingle makes a single-shot target pistol. The Dixie Gun Works has a low priced "Navy" revolver and several models of single-shot caplock pistols. Incidentally, the Dixie catalog is a treasure chest of black powder shooting information. It should be a must for every black powder shooter. In addition to these, several other firms offer single-shot caplock pistols. All are listed in the directory section of this book.

Accessories are generally available from any of the above, including round ball molds, caps, powder flasks, etc. In addition, there are swaged .44 caliber balls, and buckshot for the other calibers, ready to shoot. The well-known Lyman Company offers popular molds in round ball sizes to fit every black powder caliber, as does RCBS and Lee.

In the revolvers, the Colt design with its open-top frame and wedge-fastened barrel is quite simple to disassemble for cleaning.

This is absolutely essential after every shooting session. The Remington design with its solid frame completely encircling the cylinder, and its screwed-in barrel is inherently a stronger design than the other; it also has far fewer screws and parts to become lost or damaged and is generally more durable. Both are entirely satisfactory; aside from sights, a choice between the two should be made on the basis of personal preference. The Remington is far more suited to sight improvement and fitting of modern target sights.

Unless you are completely familiar with single-action revolver mechanisms, the newly-purchased gun should be completely disassembled and studied until you know it well enough to tear it down and put it back together properly with a minimum of effort. Don't forget the value of an exploded drawing. This can be combined with an initial disassembly and cleaning of the gun to remove all preservative grease before the first shooting session.

Wash all the component parts in non-flammable solvent or in gasoline, if nothing else is available. If the latter, be certain you do it outdoors.

During reassembly, coat the base pin (upon which the cylinder revolves) liberally with heavy grease. Apply a good grade of lubricant to all pivoting and sliding parts, and some lubricant at the sear notch, mainspring bearing, and bolt cam. A drop of oil on each screw will also facilitate later disassembly. If you want to be real classy, use a molybdenum disulphide base grease, such as "Moly Dee." Molybdenum disulphide lubricants are by far the best. If shooting is to commence within a day or two, do not oil or grease the inside of the chambers or the nipples.

In shooting the caplock muzzle-loading revolver, all normal firearms safety precautions *must* be observed. In addition, others are necessary. These will be pointed out as we go along.

To prepare for shooting, assemble the following items and materials: a can of FFFg black powder; caps of proper size to fit nipples of your particular gun (No. 11 fits some, but is a bit too large for others, which require No. 10); pure lead round balls, which may either be cast or swaged (.44's require .452″ balls; .36's, .375″; and .31's, .320″); a small tin or wide-mouthed bottle of soft grease or kitchen shortening such as

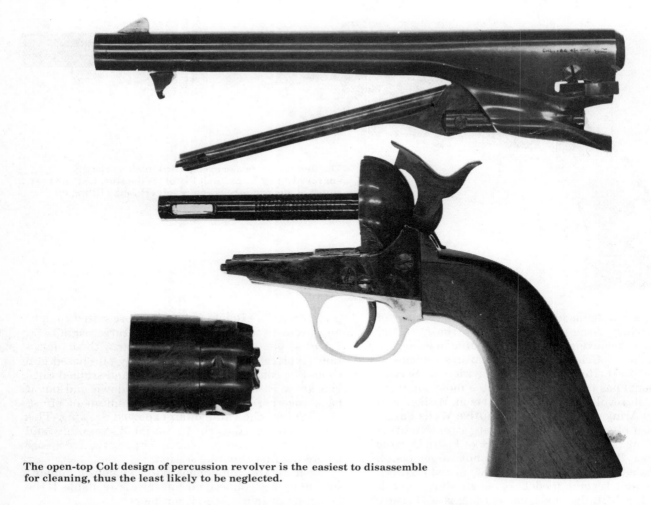

The open-top Colt design of percussion revolver is the easiest to disassemble for cleaning, thus the least likely to be neglected.

Crisco; a powder flask with spout of proper size to throw the correct charge for your particular gun, or a charge cup. A .38 Special fired case works well in .44 caliber, the same case shortened 1/4 inch for .36 caliber.

For a trouble-shooting kit, you might add a nipple prick; a nipple wrench; screwdrivers to fit all screws; and a cleaning rod and patches, preferably a slotted-tip rod. And, if you don't want your wife objecting too loudly to dirty clothing, a wiping cloth, and, if you are truly fastidious, a carpenter's canvas apron.

Swab all oil and grease out of the individual chambers with solvent, and allow some to run through the nipples, clearing grease from them. Wipe the bore out also. These functions can be performed before leaving home.

To make absolutely certain the nipples are clear and the gun will fire, it is standard practice to explode a cap on each nipple before loading. Personally, I make it a practice to explode *two* caps on each nipple. Set the hammer at half cock and make certain the cylinder rotates freely. Turn the cylinder by hand so a nipple lines up with the capping cut in the right side of

the recoil shield. With your thumb, press a cap firmly on the nipple. This is most easily done by holding the gun on its left side, muzzle angled downward, then thumbing the cap firmly onto the nipple. The cap should be snug enough on the nipple that it cannot be shaken off if the gun is held vertically. Yet it must not be so tight that any great effort is required to force it on, or that it stretches or splits in being seated. Actually, a straight-line capper makes the job much easier, for there really isn't much finger room. The cap must go fully down on the nipple and not drag against the face of the recoil shield as the cylinder is rotated. Never let the muzzle point at your own body or at anyone else during this operation.

All six nipples should be capped in this fashion, then the hammer drawn to full cock and each cap exploded. Smoke issuing from the barrel as the cap explodes indicates the nipple vent or flash hole is clear. If no smoke issues, check that particular nipple by running the nipple prick through it, or looking through it at the sky to make sure light can be seen. Most of the time, firing a second cap will clear a clogged nipple.

To load, make certain no *unfired* caps are inadver-

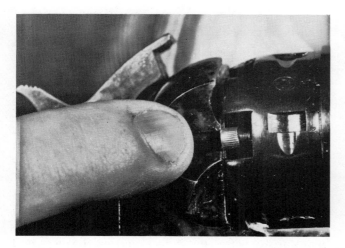

Caps must be seated snugly and firmly on the nipples. Cap shown here is not fully seated and must be pushed down until it rests solidly on the nipple face. Use correct size or cap will either split in seating or fall off.

Gun should be held muzzle-up and powder charge carefully poured into chamber. A charge cup is adequate, but a flask is more convenient and rapid.

tently left on the nipples. Set hammer at half cock. Hold the gun muzzle-up, right side toward you and, with charge cup or flask, pour the proper amount of powder into the chamber nearest the loading cutout. Take a ball and seat it on the mouth of the chamber. It will be large enough that it will not enter. If cast balls are used, orient them carefully so the sprue cut is upward and centered. Now rotate the cylinder so that the ball comes directly under the rammer plunger. Unlatch the rammer lever and with smooth, even pressure, seat the ball firmly on the powder. A thin ring of lead will normally be sheared off by the mouth of the chamber, and the ball can be felt grating against the powder as it seats. Use just enough pressure to compact the powder slightly and to seat the ball at least 1/16-inch below the chamber mouth. Too much pressure will deform the ball and reduce accuracy. Continue placing powder and ball in the remaining chambers, striving for uniformity of powder charge and of ball-seating pressure. For informal or competitive shooting, only five chambers of a six-shot gun are normally loaded. The hammer is rested on the nipple of the unloaded chamber.

Get out your grease or shortening, and use it to fill the chamber over and around each ball using a knife blade or wood spatula to keep the mess off your hands. The grease should fill the chamber flush with its mouth.

Grease thus applied serves two purposes. It prevents flame from the chamber being fired from flashing over and firing adjoining charges. Though this possibility may seem remote, it can happen if an effective means is not used to seal each chamber. The grease also serves to lubricate the bore and ball and keep the abundant black powder fouling moist and soft. If kept moist, fouling from each shot will be wiped out by the

After each chamber is charged, carefully center ball in chamber mouth with sprue upwards, and then seat with a single, smooth stroke of the rammer lever. Don't crush powder excessively, and don't leave space between ball and powder. Ball snug on powder works best.

When ball diameter is correctly matched to chamber, a thin ring of lead will be sheared off as the ball is seated.

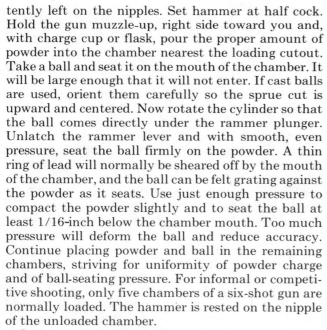

next, increasing the number of rounds that can be fired between cleanings.

If applying grease in this fashion is too messy for you, use grease-soaked felt wads under the ball instead. Prepare them by cutting wads about 1/32-inch larger in diameter than the chamber, then soaking them in melted grease or tallow. Place one in each chamber over the powder and seat the ball on top of it. With powder, ball, and grease in place, cap each nipple as outlined before. Unless shooting is to begin immediately, carefully set the hammer down so that the small safety pins protruding from the cylinder between nipples of Colt-type guns enter the slot on the hammer face. If your gun lacks these pins or the pins will not prevent inadvertent cylinder rotation, then your only safe choice is to leave a chamber unloaded and let the hammer down on its nipple. Personally, I prefer the Remington-type gun here because of the deep safety notches between nipples. The hammer nose is lowered into these notches and is made more secure than by pins. If at the time you are loading you know that firing will not take place immediately, simply do not cap the nipples until you are ready to shoot.

Actual shooting of the caplock revolver is no different from that of any other single-action handgun. Pull the hammer to full cock, align the sights carefully, and then hold and squeeze. Sights on these modern

The old-timers had trouble with multiple discharges when flame from one shot ignited powder in adjacent chambers. Filling mouth of chamber over ball with grease or shortening prevents this and also serves to keep powder fouling soft and easily removable. Helps prevent bore leading, too.

guns are copied directly from the original. Consequently, they are not particularly conducive to fine shooting. Certainly they handicap the inherent accuracy of a properly loaded gun. Considerable improvement can be achieved on the Remington-type guns by filing the rear sight notch to a neat, square form, after which a flat-face blade can be attached in lieu of the original front sight. The Colt-type guns present another problem in that the original sight is simply a very small V-notch in the hammer nose. Deepening and widening this notch will help some, but the sideplay in the hammer limits accuracy.

Modern adjustable target sights may be fitted to any one of the reproduction caplocks, but this is outside the scope of this book. Personally, I prefer to shoot these guns with the original sights. This may handicap my scores, but it does increase the pleasure I receive from the shooting.

If your caplock has been properly prepared—chambers free of grease and nipples properly cleared—and properly loaded, misfires will be conspicuous by their absence. However, as fouling builds up from successive firing, you may eventually pull the trigger to be greeted only by the slight "crack" of the cap—the charge and bullet remaining right where you loaded them.

When that happens, more often than not exploding a second or third cap on the offending chamber will ignite the charge. If it does not, additional measures are in order.

Take the nipple prick and thrust it through the vent into the main charge. Wiggle it around to make certain that the passage is completely free into the chamber and that some loosening of the powder has taken place. Then, holding the gun muzzle down, dribble fine granules of powder into the vent. Fill the vent full, but do not attempt to tamp the powder down. Place a fresh cap on the nipple and attempt to fire. In my experience, this action has fired the charge almost every time.

If it does not, remove the cylinder from the gun and use your nipple wrench to unscrew the nipple. Clean it thoroughly and set it aside. Take your nipple prick and work through the nipple hole to break up and remove a portion of the rear of the powder charge. Pour fresh powder into the base of the nipple hole, and reinstall the nipple. Fill the vent with powder granules as outlined above; then replace the cylinder and cap, and fire. I have yet to encounter an instance where this action would not clear the chamber. However, should you be so unfortunate as to have a misfire that does not respond to these treatments, simply ignore that chamber until you get home. Then remove the nipple, flush out the powder and push the ball out *forward* with a brass rod through the nipple hole.

One other malfunction may occur, though rarely. If only a small portion of the powder charge burns, perhaps due to the balance of it being contaminated

The complete lineup of percussion revolver calibers—.31 round ball, .36 round ball, .44 round ball, and .44 Lee conical bullet. Note the .31 and .36 balls are of the commercial, swaged variety, while the .44 ball is cast. The difference in appearance between swaged and cast balls is clearly evident.

by oil or grease, the ball *may* come to rest somewhere inside the barrel. By far the safest way to remove the ball is with a stiff cleaning rod. My shooting kit contains a dowel as large as can be accommodated by the bore and this is used to force the ball out from the muzzle after removing the cylinder. In Colt-type guns, the barrel is usually removed and the ball forced out from the rear. Never try to remove a stuck ball by shooting. More likely than not, such an attempt will at least result in a ringed or bulged barrel.

Normally, a properly loaded gun may be fired many times before becoming too fouled for proper functioning. However, if you anticipate a great deal of shooting, it is a good idea to carry cleaning gear along to the range. Complete disassembly and cleaning isn't usually necessary to restore reliability. Remove barrel and cylinder (cylinder only in the case of Remington types) and wipe all exposed surfaces free of fouling and/or unburned powder. Swab the barrel with a wet bristle brush until clean and then dry with clean patches. Clean the chambers in the same way, taking special care to get all fouling out of the nipples. Put a little fresh grease on the base pin if necessary, wipe the rest down with an oily cloth, and reassemble. The gun will again be ready to go.

Except in extremely dry climates, black powder fouling may promote rust in a matter of hours. The higher the humidity, the quicker rust will develop. Because of this, the gun should always be cleaned almost immediately. There are solutions offered for sale which are alleged to prevent rusting if sluiced liberally over all fouled areas. This may be true, but if you are too lazy to clean the gun the same day you shoot it, you deserve all the rust you get.

Cleaning must be complete and thorough. Completely disassemble the gun, putting all pins, screws, and small parts in a wide-mouth container several inches deep. I find a pint Mason jar ideal. Wipe off the grips (stocks) and set them aside. Put all other parts in a basin of hot water, add any good detergent, and scrub off all fouling. Take particular care with the bore, chambers, nipples, and frame recesses. Put a small amount of detergent into the small-parts jar, fill it half full of hot water, put on a lid, and shake vigorously a few times. Remove lid and run in hot tap water until all residue and suds are gone.

Rinse all parts in the hottest water you've got. Drain by dumping the parts into a large metal colander or strainer, and then put the whole thing in the kitchen oven with the temperature control set

A variety of muzzle-loading revolver bullets, all .44 caliber—left to right: round ball; modern conical bullet by Lee; hollow-based, Minie-style; and the base of the foregoing bullet. Of the lot, this author's best results have been obtained with the Lee bullet.

Neither rifle nor pistol by the usual definition, this Remington-style revolving percussion carbine by Navy Arms offers six fast shots in a shoulder arm; unfortunately, it is limited to the power of revolver loads that can be housed in the cylinder.

about 200°-250° F. Most of the water will evaporate quickly from the heat of the parts; however, there will be pockets and screwholes that remain wet for hours unless given the oven treatment. After 20 or 30 minutes in the oven, all metal will be absolutely dry. Then, while parts are still hot, spray with your favorite gun oil. When cool, wipe and reassemble.

This method of cleaning takes far less time and effort than one might imagine. I do not find it inconvenient nor particularly demanding—it absolutely guarantees that no rust will develop for many weeks, even though the gun may be completely ignored in the meantime.

So much for the bare mechanics of loading and shooting. But there are other factors to consider. First, the question of bullets. The round ball has proven in most instances to provide better accuracy than the conical bullet. Conical bullets were supplied in the prepared cartridges used during percussion days, and essentially the same forms (and molds for them) are available today. I suspect that their relatively poor accuracy is due primarily to the fact that because of their shape they are often canted in seating and that they are likely to enter the bore at somewhat of an angle. The spherical bullet, on the other hand, is relatively free of this trouble. Pure lead bullets have always given better accuracy than those made from harder alloys.

A more modern conical bullet which ensures proper alignment is made by Lee. It has a guiding section at the base to center it properly in the chamber, then an enlarged portion to seal the chamber and secure the bullet in place. It performs very nicely and is easy to load.

Cast balls are often carefully trimmed so the sprue matches the curvature of the surrounding area. As long as the sprue is centered as described earlier, I cannot see that such careful pruning serves any useful purpose. It has been recommended that balls be rolled between glass or steel plates to improve accuracy. I have not found this necessary or even desirable. In fact, it can actually cause wide variation in diameter and roundness.

Swaged lead balls are available in .44 caliber (.452-inch diameter), and the various sizes of swaged buckshot serve for the smaller bores. These balls look rough—they have been tumbled loosely together in packaging and shipping and are coated with graphite.

They don't *look* as if they would shoot as well as a smooth gleaming cast ball. However, they run more uniform in diameter, weight and density than the *average* cast ball. Not only does their use eliminate the job of casting, which can be irritating and time consuming, but in my experience, they generally produce slightly better accuracy.

The question of powder charge is always good for an argument. Quite light charges are preferred by many for target shooting to 25 yards, with a heavier charge used beyond that range. The full charge for which the gun was originally designed is seldom used except for hunting or "showing off." Taking averages of the guns in my rack, full charges with round ball are generally 27 grains in .36, and 38 in .44 except the Dragoons and Walkers, which hold as much as 50 and 60 grains respectively. The following table shows the velocities produced by these charges:

BLACK POWDER LOADS AND BALLISTICS

Caliber	Bullet	Granulation	Charge	Velocity	Remarks
.36	RB	FFFg	25 gr.	1005 fps	Full Charge
.36	RB	FFFg	16 gr.	—	Target
.36	CB	FFFg	15 gr.	700 fps	Full Charge
.36	CB	FFFg	12 gr.	—	Plinking
.44	RB	FFFg	38 gr.	990 fps	Full Charge
.44	RB	FFFg	22 gr.	—	Target
.44	CB	FFFg	26 gr.	820 fps	Full Charge
.44	CB	FFFg	18 gr.	—	Plinking
.44	#454424	FFFg	30 gr.	800 fps	Full Charge

For paper punching and general plinking at ranges up to 25 yards, I have found 10 grains best in .31 caliber, 16 in .36, and 22 in .44.

Lesser charges have been recommended by some; however, they leave a great deal of air space under a properly seated ball. Seating the ball deeper isn't a good idea. Most chambers are not particularly smoothly bored and the ball suffers additional mutilation in being shoved deeply into them. Also, the deeper the ball is seated in the chamber the farther it must travel before engaging the rifling. Long travel here is not particularly conducive to good accuracy.

Deeply seated balls also make it difficult to apply grease properly except by filling the chamber to its mouth. And half a chamber of grease makes for messy shooting. Instead, use a measured charge of corn meal or similar inert filler between powder and ball. It should be large enough to be slightly compressed by the ball, thereby placing the powder under pressure.

Some shooters also prefer to use different powder granulations in various calibers. One shooter of my acquaintance insists on FFFg in his .36's and loads the big .44's with FFg. For years I have used FFFg in all calibers, and can detect no improvement with the other granulations.

A powder flask with spout filed to correct length to throw the desired charge is the simplest method of getting powder into the chambers. Some shooters who are particularly concerned with maximum uniformity of powder charge carry adjustable volumetric measures to the range. Others premeasure or preweigh charges at home and carry them to the range in small plastic or glass vials. I have found that by careful and uniform use of a flask I can throw charges that vary no more than one grain. Charges carefully weighed to plus or minus 0.2 grain have not produced any measurable increase in accuracy. Therefore, I see no point in complicating a pleasant pastime with additional accessories and work.

If there are varmints or small game within several hundred miles, you'll eventually want to use your front-loading revolver on them. Because of the conditions often encountered—especially rain and snow—loading for the field requires a somewhat different technique than for paper punching. In spite of the claims made for it in its heyday, the percussion ignition system is far from waterproof. If you're hunting in Arizona, this may not be of any concern to you, but where I live showers come up fast. Though the caps themselves are waterproof, I need a way of waterproofing the joint between cap and nipple—otherwise water can seep in under the cap and through the vent to kill the main powder charge. The old-timers sealed this gap by rubbing beeswax or tallow over it after seating the caps. That method works, but it is difficult to seal the area between the nipple and the bottom of its cutout in the cylinder. I have found it far simpler to first make certain the area is dry, then run melted beeswax completely around the nipple. Melted candle wax should serve just as well.

The grease applied around the balls for target shooting will also keep moisture out, but it collects dirt and debris and may also run in hot weather, making a mess of holster or pocket. It will also come out in big gobs from the impact when you jump off a cutbank or across a creek. The best solution is a greased felt wad under the ball, combined with melted wax around the ball to further seal any gaps.

Carefully loaded in the above manner, a percussion revolver can be carried for hours in the rain, even

Constant reference is made to the use of the hinged, loading lever for seating balls in percussion revolvers. However, there are a few guns which do not possess an attched lever. Our example here is the Navy Arms replica of the Colt Baby Dragoon in .31 caliber, but there are also short-barreled variations of the Colt .36 and .44 revolvers which are not fitted with an attached rammer. Some have a hole through the barrel lug so that a short loading rod may be used; others do not, and it is therefore necessary to remove the cylinder and load it separately with a short hand rammer.

immersed in water, and still fire reliably.

If you are expecting damp weather and want to get more than five or six shots off before coming home again, invest in a spare cylinder or two. Load the spares in exactly the same manner as above, and then place each in its own well-padded cloth or leather bag and carry them in separate pockets. If two are in the same pocket and bang together, there is the possibility of rupturing the wax seal around the nipples or even firing a cap and shooting yourself. Cylinder changes are made quickly and easily on the Remington type, though the Colt type requires the butt of your knife or some similar instrument to tap the wedge loose, and the use of the loading lever bearing on the cylinder between chambers to jack the barrel free of the base pin.

Once you've become familiar with the caplock black-powder revolver, you'll have a new respect for it. Properly loaded and cared for it is both powerful and accurate. With a little attention to detail, it is also extremely reliable under severe weather conditions. With a pair of them riding loaded in saddle or belt holsters, the cavalryman of the 1860's wasn't too badly off—he had 10 or 12 powerful accurate shots that could be delivered as fast as with the finest modern single-action revolver. His sustained fire power may not have been great by today's standards, but for the first round of the festivities he was a formidable opponent.

8/Shooting the Slug Gun

In every field there is one particular item or piece of equipment that has a reputation for producing the finest results, yet being the most expensive, temperamental and hard to please. Its brothers do a good job, but it does the same thing infinitely better—albeit requiring as much careful handling as a new bride.

In our game, the slug gun is the one I am talking about. It's the Ferrari of muzzle loaders. It was the elite of muzzle loading nearly a century ago, and it still is.

If the slug gun has any outstanding physical characteristics, they are size and weight. A middling gun will have a barrel well over an inch in diameter and will weigh close to 20 pounds. A *big* one will have a barrel as big around as your wrist, and go as much as 40 pounds. Some guns top that considerably and 50- to 60-pounders are not particularly rare.

Slug gun bullets aren't small, either. A .50 is more common than scarce, and those big slugs may weigh up to an ounce and a half. The average .45 caliber slug will go 500 to 550 grains.

The heart of the slug gun is its massive barrel and carefully mated false muzzle. While original guns are normally finely finished all over, the modern tube may be (and often is) externally only a roughly planed octagon without any polish or finish. (The boys spend their money on performance, not looks.) Inside, it's another matter. The bore is meticulously rifled and

polished to produce a glass-smooth surface and just the right amount of choke (inward taper) toward the muzzle. In all likelihood, the false muzzle will have been cut from the same steel bar and carefully fitted and doweled in place before final reaming and rifling. This is to ensure that lands and grooves of barrel and false muzzle are in absolutely perfect register. One of the characteristics of the slug gun is the perfection with which the bullet is engraved (forced into the rifling) and centered in the bore during muzzle loading. A perfectly aligned false muzzle is essential to this.

The rifling is of the shallow, wide-groove type with narrow lands that has proven best with paper-patched bullets. It may be cut with either uniform twist or "gain" (rate of twist increasing toward the muzzle) twist. Some shooters swear fervently that uniform twist produces maximum accuracy, while others are equally adamant that *only* gain twist can do the job properly. I doubt there is any difference, all other factors being equal. Both have won matches and set records—now and 100 years ago.

Of course, the slug gun is normally of percussion lock design, though primer locks appear to be becoming more and more popular on modern guns. The understriker lock is most often seen among new guns, mostly because it leaves the top completely clear for installation of a large target-type scope sight. Guns so

Although one may choose from a wide variety of low-cost, single-barrel percussion shotguns, the side-by-side double is by far the most practical as a hunting gun. Several are available, prominent among them being this Navy Arms gun made in Italy. When properly loaded with modern components, it performs surprisingly well on both game and clay targets.

equipped don't often have forends, just buttstocks. A forend only gets in the way on a rest gun, anyway.

Since the slug gun is shot only from bench rest, the barrel is usually fitted with a solidly attached muzzle rest. This is of metal, sometimes aluminum, and flat across the bottom to rest on the bench or a shelf thereon. The rest prevents any canting whatsoever, which is of special value with guns producing relatively low velocity. The muzzle rest may be screwed or pinned to the barrel, or merely clamped around it. Some have even been formed integrally with the barrel.

The slug gun is shot with a large-caliber *swaged* lead bullet of relatively long length and cylindro-conoidal form with blunt nose. Bullets are smooth surfaced, and are not grooved or lubricated. Instead, they are encased during loading with a bond paper patch that is often oiled.

Recently, patches have been made of Teflon-coated paper and other exotic materials that would make the old-timers shake their heads.

Each individual bullet is carefully made by hand. Nothing less than perfect bullets will produce the accuracy for which the slug gun is known. Two types of bullets are used. The solid or one-piece design is swaged from a single piece of pure lead that might be cast first into rough form and trimmed to precise weight. The "composite" or two-piece bullet has the bearing surface portion cast from pure lead. The nose is cast separately from *hardened* lead and assembled to the body. A cavity in the front of the body accepts a tenon on the rear of nose, (or vice-versa) and swaging locks the two parts securely together. The hard nose of the composite bullet is intended to avoid deformation that might be produced on soft bullets by starter or ramrod. Pure lead is used for the body because it receives the rifling freely and more perfectly than any harder alloy. And, experience has proven that it usually produces the best accuracy. Slug gun fans may not know why, but they do know what performs best.

Whether solid or composite, the slug gun bullet is always swaged. This serves two purposes—bringing

the bullet to proper shape and size more precisely than it can be cast and compressing the lead to eliminate any voids or air pockets such as occasionally occur in even the most carefully cast bullets. Swaging must be done uniformly; the same amount of pressure applied to every bullet produces uniform lead density, weight, and length. Top shooters always check finished bullets for uniformity. Weighing each one separately may be best, but careful measuring their length is equally effective in weeding out those that are too light or too heavy. Length varies directly with weight, and measuring is much faster and easier to accomplish. (The swaging and casting of proper bullets are covered in the chapter dealing with bullets and molds.)

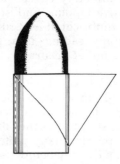

Typical slug gun bullet is long and heavy, swaged from soft lead and wrapped carefully in a paper patch.

Slug gun barrels are rifled with wide, shallow, slow-twist grooves to produce the best accuracy with the bullet enclosed in a paper patch. Such patches are usually cut from a high grade of 100% rag content bond paper. Most often the patch takes the form of two (sometimes three) separate strips of paper crossed to form an "X." Some shooters prefer to cut the "X" in one piece as a matter of loading convenience. The 2-or 3-strip patch is considered better, though, since strips can be cut with the grain of the paper. And it is agreed that having the paper grain parallel with the bullet axis produces best accuracy. The patch is dimensioned so that when the bullet is centered on it and forced

Here we see a fairly conventional bench-rest rifle with underhammer lock and primer ignition, but fitted with a modern 20-power target scope. This gun will undoubtedly weigh 30 pounds or more and is practical only for bench shooting.

into the bore, the strips fold up along the sides. In this manner, they completely cover the bullet's bearing surface without overlapping and isolate the soft lead from the bore. Unlubricated lead rubbing on the bore will produce instant leading—fatal to accuracy. Failure to center the bullet accurately on the patch will also spoil accuracy.

Patches are usually oiled before use. Bear oil was once the preferred lubricant, but few of us have the opportunity to render out much bear fat these days. Neats foot oil, as sold for leather dressing, seems an ideal substitute, though many prefer pure sperm oil. Oiling is best done the day before use. Patches can be dipped or laid in the oil, then taken out and allowed to drain. To remove the excess, place the patches between blotting paper. Some guns prefer oilier patches than others, but a dripping wet patch is no good at all. Only experimental shooting will tell you which is best in a particular barrel. Once this has been determined, you'll know that soaking for 15 minutes, draining for 3 hours, then blotting for a specified time will produce patches perfect for a particular rifle.

Oiling not only lubricates the bullet's passage in ramming and firing through the bore, but makes the patch less likely to tear as the bullet is seated. And a torn patch means a shot out of the group. Some guns have shot well with an unoiled paper patch, but they are few and far between. It won't hurt anything to try dry patches in your gun a time or two to find out what happens.

This is an original, factory-made paper-patch bullet nearly 100 years old. Despite the stains and other evidence of handling over the years, the one-piece patch still clings tightly to the smooth, lead bullet. The end of the patch can barely be seen, running from upper left to lower right.

While the older slug guns generally utilized a conventional side lock, modern guns are likely to be of under-striker type. Even so, the old-timers sometimes used the under-striker. William Billinghurst produced very fine under-striker target rifles, as did several other makers. Early guns nearly always used percussion-cap ignition, but in the constant search for better accuracy, both shotshell and metallic cartridge primers were tried late in the last century. Both Warner and Brockway produced devices to use primers in lieu of caps, and many modern guns are made with variations of those devices. As mentioned elsewhere, the modern primer is more uniform and reliable—being more highly developed than percussion caps ever were or will be. In *The Muzzle-Loading Cap Lock Rifle,* the late Ned Roberts recommended primer ignition for his "ideal" slug gun. I'll go along with that and recommend primer ignition for any new gun you might want to build. Pistol primers, incidentally, possess all the power needed to ignite black powder.

Of course, it goes without saying that whatever the type, the lock and other firing mechanism must be of the best quality and suited to the shooter's tastes. Set triggers are the general rule.

The slug gun will produce the accuracy for which it has become known only if all the components are perfect and the utmost care is exercised in loading.

Base of the same bullet, showing where the excess patch has been twisted while moist and pressed into a cavity in the bullet.

This means perfect bullets, patches, and absolute uniformity in all loading operations.

As with any other muzzle loader, the bore must first be wiped clean and dry of oil or grease, and the nipple passage must be cleared by firing a cap (primer) or two upon it. Some shooters recommend wiping the bore with a dry patch after snapping the cap.

If you are a convenience-minded shooter, you will have placed premeasured powder charges in plastic tubes or bottles before going to the range. Charges should be weighed or very accurately measured. Argument will rage forever as to whether weighing to ± 0.2 grain is really essential to accuracy. However, it certainly can't do any harm. Because of wind and weather, it isn't practical to weigh charges on the range. The scale simply won't function uniformly in any appreciable air current. A good adjustable drum-type powder measure, however, can be used to throw accurate charges directly into the barrel at the range. The measure may simply be held over the muzzle or clamped in a fixture that slips over the muzzle.

With bore clean and dry, the charge can be funneled directly into the muzzle. Little if any of it will cling to the bore if everything is dry and humidity is low. Even a single granule, though, *can* interfere with good accuracy by getting between bullet and bore, cutting the patch or notching the base in seating. This is best avoided by using a long-spouted loading funnel. A bore-sized tube of barrel length is soldered to the funnel to carry powder to the breech without touching the bore. This is the only *sure* way of keeping powder from clinging to the bore walls.

Any new rifle will be furnished with powder charge recommendations, and original or used guns should also be accompanied by some data on what has been used. If you have nothing to go by, there are several old rules of thumb that can be employed. Simplest is the one that goes, "Use 1-1/2 calibers of powder for rifles under 70 gauge (.40 caliber) and 2 calibers for those over that gauge." This means you simply multiply the caliber in hundredths of an inch by 1-1/2 or 2 to get the powder charge weight in grains. Thus, a .50 caliber rifle charge would be 50 x 2 = 100 grains of powder. For .38 caliber, it would be 38 x 1-1/2 = 57 grains. Charges figured by other rules will be fairly close to the above, so I quote only this one rule. Some conservative shooters feel charges figured this way are a bit heavy, preferring to start at a weight equal to the caliber; 40 grains for a .40 caliber barrel. Since this is only a starting point, it doesn't really matter which you use.

Keep in mind that charges so computed are only approximate and that the best accuracy will undoubtedly be produced by a bit more or a bit less powder. Generally speaking, use FFg powder in barrels over .45 caliber, FFFg in those under that. Try both, though, for rifles vary widely in their preferences.

Place the gun upright in the loading rack and check

to make certain the false muzzle is properly seated. Even a single powder granule or piece of dirt between it and the barrel will result in the bullet being seated at a slight angle, reducing its accuracy. Assuming you are using a 2- or 3-strip patch, slide the strips into their respective slots in the face of the false muzzle. They must be precisely centered and not wrinkled or torn. They should also be checked to determine that they are neither too dry nor too oily. If oiled too soon before shooting, they may be too wet; if too long before, too dry. Once the proper degree of oiliness is determined for the best accuracy in a given barrel, observe it strictly. Store ready-oiled patches in air-tight tins or tape-sealed plastic boxes to keep the oil from evaporating.

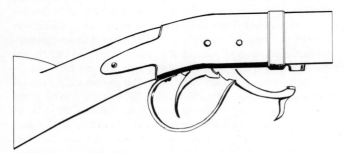

The typical under-striker lock is popular for slug guns because of its simplicity and the fact that it is underneath the breech and out of the way of sights.

Inspect the bullet. It must be free of nicks, scratches or dents, especially at the edges of the base. Any base deformation whatsoever will reduce accuracy. Though a bullet may have been cast and swaged perfectly, it is quite soft and can easily pick up defects before the time comes to load it. Bullets are best kept in a block or compartmented box having a separate space for each individual bullet. Even then, very careful handling is required. The more perfect the bullet, the greater the accuracy to be expected. I've known some shooters to arrive at the range with bullets wrapped in cotton batting. Others do the swaging just before loading to reduce bullet handling.

Center the bullet over the patch and false muzzle and press it in gently with the fingers. Seat the bullet starter on the false muzzle and press it gently down as far as it will go. Note carefully whether the patch strips are folding up evenly. If one leans sideways or wrinkles, that particular bullet won't go as close to point of aim as it should.

Strike the knob of the starter a single, solid blow with the heel of the hand, seating the bullet the full length of the starter. Take the time to learn just how heavy a blow is required, then strive to make it uniform from shot to shot. Even with composite bullets, some point deformation will result if the blow is too heavy. The point will also be deformed if the blow is too light and a second one is necessary to complete the seating operation. As in all other operations, absolute uniformity is the ultimate goal and is essential in producing best accuracy.

Lever-type bullet seaters as encountered on false-muzzle Schuetzen rifles may also be used. Even with them, uniform pressure is required.

With the bullet properly started, remove the starter and insert the ramrod in the barrel, resting it on the bullet. Then, with a single, smooth motion, run the bullet fully down on the powder.

The bullet must be seated firmly on the powder, yet without too much pressure. And it must be seated the same every time. If the powder charge is felt to "give" only a small amount, seating pressure should be just about right. If the ramrod stops part way through the operation and a second stroke is necessary to finish the job, that bullet will be out of the group. Barrels are finished with a slight constriction or choke at the muzzle, and the starter is intended to carry the bullet through this area. Ramming then requires relatively little pressure, since in passing through the choke the bullet has been swaged slightly smaller than the rest of the bore. Most shooters use only enough fingers in gripping the ramrod to ensure single-motion seating of the bullet. This avoids having an excess of strength available which can result in too-hard seating of the bullet. The ramrod must be stiff enough so that it won't bend and rub the bore.

If one just happened to start a bullet *without* cleaning the bore, it may be impossible to start it moving again with the ramrod. This situation may call for disassembly of the gun in order to drive the bullet from the breech.

Make absolutely certain the false muzzle is removed next. Don't laugh. Many a rifleman has fired, only to see the false muzzle go sailing downrange. Most false muzzles have some sort of protrusion that blocks the line of sight. Then any attempt at firing makes it obvious the device is still in place. If your false muzzle isn't so equipped, I recommend you attend to that detail immediately. If you don't, there is bound to come the day when you'll shoot off the muzzle. This is not only highly embarassing, it ruins your score—and can also ruin the false muzzle.

All that remains is to place the cap (or primer) on the nipple, and the gun is ready to cock and fire.

The slug gun demands a perfectly solid and rigid rest. If you don't have a bench that meets these requirements, you'll never know just how well your gun can shoot. You'll never know when the load and loading is exactly right because there will be "bench error" enlarging your groups. The goal of slug gun shooting is maximum gun/load accuracy, and no outside factors should be allowed to influence it.

Rest shooting requires as much uniformity in firing the shot as in loading the gun. It might seem that with so heavy a gun solidly rested, minor shooter inconsistencies will have no effect. T'ain't so. Even shifting your derriere's position on the stool or chair can cause changes in point of impact. You must sit the same; shoulder and cheek the gun the same; press the trigger the same for every shot. The gun may shoot better held lightly or it may prefer to be gripped tightly. It may prefer to recoil fairly freely or to be held up somewhat. Individual guns behave differently. The best approach is to start with good basic benchrest shooting techniques and then vary only one factor at a time until the most accurate combination is found. One well-known shooter says he gets better accuracy shooting while kneeling on the ground instead of sitting on a stool or chair. He must be right, because he wins matches. What works for him is not necessarily best for you and your gun, but try it anyway. Then you'll know.

In any event, get that first shot off carefully, making mental note of just how you performed each function. Everything will have to be the same for each subsequent shot.

Let's assume the first bullet was on target and take it from there.

If it wasn't, you'll have to spend a few rounds zeroing, but that can be combined with learning to load and handle the big gun correctly. After the shot, half cock the hammer and remove any cap fragments or, if a primer lock, remove the fired primer. Set the gun in the loading rack.

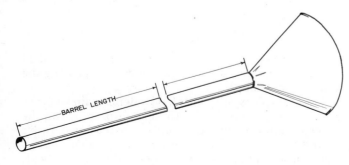

A loading tube made by soldering a funnel to a barrel-length tube is a sure way of getting *all* the powder to the chamber area.

Cleaning the bore after each shot is essential to the production of top accuracy. It is equally essential that the cleaning be performed exactly the same each and every time. A wet bristle brush (not metal bristles) or patch is used first to loosen the fouling, being passed the full length of the bore the same number of times after each shot. Then, a clean dry patch is used to swab out the loosened fouling, followed by a final clean patch to completely dry the bore and pick up any fouling missed by the first. The number of patches and number of passes through the bore is of no great

importance as long as the bore finishes clean and dry and the operation is performed in exactly the same manner each time. Some shooters blow through the nipple or run a pipe cleaner through it to dry it out before the last dry patch is used. Others snap a cap on the nipple after cleaning, but before reloading. Obviously, there must be no water in the nipple when the gun is fired. Shooters have been known to load and fire the next shot into the dirt if a goof was made in cleaning, knowing that bullet might open up the group.

Regardless of exactly how you wind up cleaning the bore between shots, develop a fast, rhythmic routine for it so as to ensure uniformity without waste of time and effort. A hardened steel cleaning rod is best since it will not pick up and hold abrasive fouling or dirt which can eventually wear away the rifling. Wiping the rod clean after each use is a good idea. The rod should be thick and stiff so it won't bend and rub the rifling somewhere inside the bore.

With the gun cleaned, set the hammer at half cock. Note that this is contrary to rules given for loading other guns that are not cleaned after each shot. The water cleaning eliminates any possibility of an ember remaining that might ignite the charge. With the hammer at half cock, air compressed ahead of the bullet during seating can easily escape. If trapped by a tightly-sealed nipple, compressed air might force the bullet up off the powder—producing at best a poor shot, at worst a "ringed" and ruined barrel.

Repeat the complete loading procedure, again with emphasis on uniformity of every component and every action. Concentrate on developing an unbroken loading routine that ensures uniformity.

Do not under any circumstances allow others to interrupt or intrude during loading. Shooting records are full of incidents where a top shooter lost a match because fans interrupted and caused a loading error.

Fire several shots before judging the accuracy of the gun or "going for record." Heavy slug gun barrels must "warm up" (both literally and figuratively) before they shoot their best. Eventually, you'll learn whether three, four, five, or more shots are required to condition your particular barrel for its best ten-shot group. No matter how small and insignificant such factors seem, they *are* important in achieving maximum accuracy.

As shooting progresses and you develop proficiency with the big gun, you'll note many factors affecting its day-to-day accuracy. This necessitates the keeping of a comprehensive score book or log book. This really should be done from the first round fired from a new or newly acquired gun.

Record each group and load, along with temperature, wind direction and velocity, humidity, barometric pressure, etc. If you travel a lot and shoot at places differing considerably in elevation (altitude), record that also. If loading routine is altered, it too should be

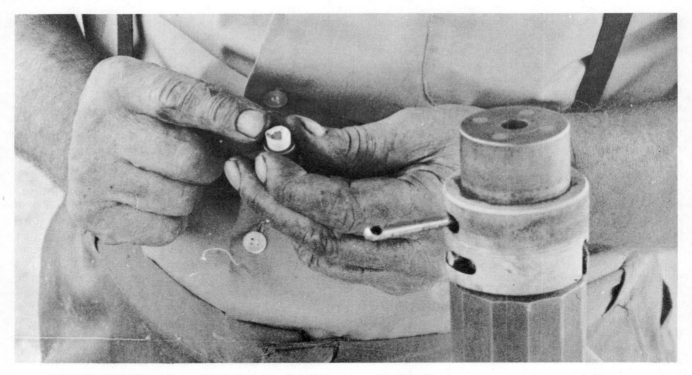

Here a slug gun is being loaded—the powder charge has been poured down the bore; the false muzzle is in place; the shooter has patched his bullet with a wraparound patch, and is carefully folding the patch over the base of the bullet before placing it in the false muzzle for seating.

The paper-patched bullet has been placed in the false muzzle; the piston-type starter has been placed over the false muzzle; the bullet has been forced into the rifling, and now the ramrod is being used through the starter to seat the bullet firmly against the powder.

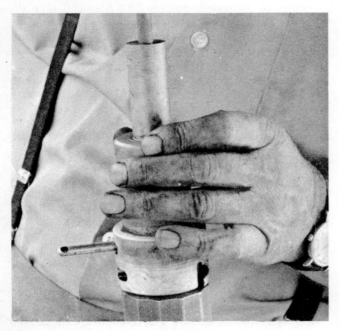

recorded along with any visible effect it produced on target.

If such records are kept assiduously and studied periodically, they will give vital clues to improving the gun's performance.

For example, you'll find that under certain weather conditions groups begin to open up, but can be brought back in by reducing or increasing powder charges. Once this is known for your particular rifle, you can second-guess the weather and load specifically for it.

Another thing you might notice is the effect of hot direct sunlight on center of impact. Years ago U. S. Army tests confirmed that a heavy barrel long exposed to bright sun will shoot *away* from the sun. This is due to expansion and elongation of the side of the barrel facing the sun as it heats up causing the muzzle to move ever so slightly away from the sun as the barrel bends. This is ample reason for never leaving your gun lying in direct sunlight while waiting to shoot. Even though the shaded inside of your car might seem like an oven, the barrel will heat uniformly there and remain straight.

It is interesting to note that a 90mm tank gun tested for the sun's effect in desert-like temperatures walked its center of impact in a U-shaped pattern around the point of aim as the sun moved through the sky. This was with the gun pointed due south.

A slug gun's behavior may change. That is, the load developed today may not shoot as well next week. One set of rules says, "When groups with one-piece bullets open up vertically, add powder; if horizontally, reduce powder. Reverse for two-piece bullet." And, "If one shot is out of the group, decrease powder charge." Then a gun's behavior may change as one season moves into another, being affected by temperature and humidity.

Such rules may apply to your rifle or they may not. You must experiment to find out. When you first encounter vertical or horizontal stringing of the group and are certain it isn't *your* fault, vary the powder charge both ways to determine which is the proper corrective action. Most important of all, keep a record. Again the next time the same thing happens you can correct it immediately and positively instead of fumbling in the dark. A slug gun is somewhat like a lover in that one must know it intimately and treat it correctly in order to get the most out of it.

Because of its temperament, the slug gun must be cared for carefully. The least marring of the muzzle or the false muzzle will be fatal to accuracy. Degrees of other wear and tear that are acceptable in sporting guns can easily result in decreased accuracy. Erosion and enlargement of the nipple vent or uneven hammer/nipple contact can cost you points. Use an Ampco or carbide-lined nipple to avoid this. Loss of mainspring tension can produce non-uniform ignition, even though every cap or primer seems to fire correctly. Tests by Ed Yard proved conclusively that primer energy, consequently ignition, varies directly with hammer or firing-pin energy. While black powder is relatively easy to ignite, variations in ignition can occur, and they affect velocity, which in turn affects vertical dispersion on target.

Probably no other type of shooting requires the minute attention to detail and uniformity demanded by the heavy slug gun. Even the centerfire bench rest shooter is less plagued by minutiae.

He, at least, must concentrate only on shooting, once he's loaded his ten rounds. The slug gun shooter probably expends more physical and mental energy on a single shot than a breech-loading man does on an entire ten-shot string.

The slug gun demands the most from the shooter— but it will return equal measure in accuracy and sense of accomplishment. It represents the epitome of muzzle-loading guns and shooting.

9/Shooting the Scattergun

Once the trailbreakers had passed and cabins and homesteads began to spring up, rather than the rifle, the muzzle-loading shotgun was more likely to be the family defender and provider. More often, it was an old smoothbore musket stripped of its excess weight and hardware and loaded with anything from factory-swaged buckshot to a handful of gravel.

Contrary to popular belief, the gun of the *average* citizen was not a rifle but a smoothbore, which was more versatile and suitable for his varied needs. He wasn't usually a skilled, long-range marksman anyway and did his shooting—at game or Indians—at close range where a smoothbore was quite effective with ball or shot.

Shot, as we know it today, wasn't available on every street corner, and it wasn't unusual for it to be made at home. Large buckshot could be cast like bullets and, of course, the larger balls for "buck and ball" loads were easily molded. "Small shot" was another matter. Obviously, no one could afford to build his own shot tower on the frontier to make spherical shot in the traditional manner. So, as has been done since almost the beginning of firearms, shot was often *cut* from sheet lead. Thin sheets of lead had long been an item of trade because in that form it was more easily handled and parceled out than clumsy, heavy ingots. Lead sheets even served as money at times. One simply hauled out his Bowie, Green River or butcher

knife and peeled a narrow strip from one edge of the sheet, then chopped it roughly into cubes. Many a man alive yet today remembers cutting shot as a boy. With a supply of sheet lead at hand, a man could make shot, or cast balls or conical bullets as desired, and the cost was less than for store-bought "dropped" shot, when it was available.

Square or cubical shot may not sound like much today, conditioned as we are to 80% and 90% patterns from commercial loads. Yet, it seems the pioneers managed to kill enough game with it to feed their families; on the frontier, this assumed more importance than paper pattern density. Consider also that square shot is still sometimes used in European factory-loaded shotshells when wider patterns are desired.

Most original muzzle-loading shotguns were cylinder bored—without a choke. Lots of guns are shot today without a choke, but more and more shooters are having their guns reworked. Apparently, it was only recently that the choke was considered by modern shooters to be practical in a barrel loaded from the muzzle. That's odd, when old-time market hunters spoke of their choked front loaders and didn't mention any loading problems. Be that as it may, match winners and successful hunters of today do use choked barrels.

A number of gunsmiths are set up to choke cylinder-bored guns. The simplest, quickest and probably least desirable type is the "swaged" choke. A tapered hollow punch is driven over the muzzle, constricting the barrel slightly. It is practical only on single-barrel guns unless it is done before the barrels are soldered together. Next in line is the "jug" or recessed choke. The bore is enlarged behind the muzzle for a few inches, then tapered down toward the muzzle. The best method calls for enlarging all but the last few inches of the bore near the muzzle, working from the breech. A conventional choke is then formed at the muzzle.

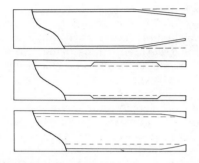

Muzzle-loading shotgun barrels may be choked in one of the above ways. Top consists simply of swaging the muzzle inward on a taper. Middle, a recess is bored in the barrel behind the muzzle; and bottom, the entire barrel is bored out to large diameter, leaving the muzzle constricted to produce the choke. The last two methods require fairly thick barrel—something many of the old-timers don't have.

The last two methods require that the barrels have walls thick enough to stand removal of a significant amount of metal—and many old-time guns don't meet that requirement. For them, the swaged choke is the only solution. For all its theoretical weak points, it seems to do rather well.

Procuring a shootable muzzle-loading shotgun means following the same guidelines set forth with regard to other guns. Make certain you have a *safe* gun before loading up and shooting from the shoulder. Replacement eyes and arms are hard to come by.

You'll need caps, powder, wads, and shot. Caps, of course, must fit the nipples of your gun snugly, and the powder should be FFg granulation. Some shooters recommend Fg in the larger gauges, but I feel that's too coarse. Choice of shot size will depend on what you intend to shoot, and since everyone has his own idea on that, far be it from me to try to change any minds. In any event, buy good shot. Don't try to make it yourself.

Wads are another matter. It will pay you to make your own, especially if your gun's barrel has been polished or freshed out. Barrels vary a great deal in bore diameter. Consequently, standard-sized wads are often too loose or too tight. Even when of standard gauge, muzzle-loading shotguns do not use the same

wads as shells of the same gauge. Generally speaking, a wad one gauge larger than the bore designation is used—that is, a 12-bore front loader requires an 11-gauge wad to insure proper bore fit. Eventually it will be best to make a wad cutter from tubing or pipe of exactly the right diameter for your barrel. Make it as outlined for a patch cutter in the chapter on accessories.

For a starter, though, you can buy wads or cut them with a gauge cutter from the Dixie Gun Works. Use a card wad directly over the powder; it should be tight in the bore. If making your own, use stiff 3/32-inch to 1/8-inch thick sign cardboard. One goes over the powder, followed by a 1/4-inch or thicker filler or cushion wad. Thicker filler wadding will reduce recoil and improve patterns by cushioning the shot during acceleration. The best effect here is obtained with a filler wad column–height equal to bore diameter. Commercially available fibre or composition wads are fine. If making your own, upholsterer's felt is best, though Celotex-type insulating board can be used, also. Another card wad goes over the shot, and it too must also be quite tight in the bore. If it isn't, recoil of the first round in a double gun will loosen the charge in the other barrel. The over-shot wad need not be as thick as the over-powder card; 1/16 inch or less is best, if stiff enough. Very thick O-S wads tend to disrupt the pattern.

Many a shooter has started by using toilet tissue for wadding—three or four sheets tamped down over the powder, one over the shot. Guns so loaded will shoot and kill game, but not as well as when proper wads are used. There is also the possibility of fires being started by smoldering pieces of tissue. Old-timers tell of using newspapers, even cornhusks, for wads—but understand that they did it out of necessity, not preference.

This is all it takes to charge your trusty muzzle-loading fowling piece: cap, powder charge, composition filler wads, shot charge and over-shot wad. Note this wad is home cut with a slightly out-of-round punch but it performs perfectly.

Begin loading by wiping the bore and firing a cap or two to clear the nipple. Working from the charge table given below (which is conservative) or those appearing in Appendix 2, pour the powder down the barrel.

ALL LOADS WITH FRESH POWDER AND CRISCO OVER BULLET.

Gauge	Powder*	Shot
20	2¼ dr.	⅞ oz.
16	2¾ dr.	⅞ oz.
14	3 dr.	1 oz.
12	3¼ dr.	1⅛ oz.
11	3½ dr.	1⅛ oz.
10	3¾ dr.	1¼ oz.

*One dram equals 27½ grains weight

Start the over-powder card wad in the muzzle. If it's not a snug fit, it may fall edgewise on the powder. If that happens, the ramrod may simply shove it into the powder charge or flip it over so that part of the charge is on top of the wad. So make sure the wad is pressed smoothly into the bore and seats squarely on the powder. It doesn't require pounding into position—just solid seating, compressing the powder slightly. All this needs a flat head on the ramrod of just under bore diameter at the muzzle.

Start the cushion wads in the muzzle and give them the same treatment. Cup grease applied to the edge of the wad will keep fouling soft, but makes loading rather messy. One shooter recommends occasional use of two card wads with a layer of grease between them to keep fouling soft. Some shooters substitute additional card wads for the cushion wad, but the latter produces less shot deformation during initial acceleration of the charge.

The best results I've seen with fibre wads, however, were obtained when the wads were dipped in water-soluble oil before loading. The moisture loosened all fouling during ramming and left subsequent fouling soft. Excellent results will also be obtained when fibre wads are waxed by dipping or rolling them across a hot metal plate coated with melted beeswax.

Follow with the shot charge, also given in the foregoing table and in the appendixes. Start the over-shot card wad; then seat it solidly with the ramrod. This wad *must* be tight in the bore. If it feels loose as it seats, don't pound on it in the hope of making it stay in place. Draw it out with your worm

and start over with a tighter wad. Make certain it doesn't tip and scoop part of the shot charge up to lay on top of the wad.

With the hammer at half-cock, cap the nipple and you're ready for the morning flight. Of course, if your gun is a double, both barrels will have to receive the same loading treatment. This brings up a couple of safety precautions that must be taken with doubles. Loading should be very carefully regimented or sooner or later you'll get *two* charges of powder in one barrel and none in the other. A double charge *may* not wreck the gun, but I'll guarantee it won't be good for either your shoulder or peace of mind. Develop a set loading routine, and don't allow it to vary.

Much of your shooting will be single shots. While a well-loaded charge in the off barrel will remain in place against recoil for a shot or two, repeated firing of one barrel eventually *will* loosen the charge in the other. Should you then happen to fire *both* barrels and the one shot charge has moved a few inches, a bulged or burst barrel will result. I prefer to fire both barrels alternately to preclude any such happening. It is good practice, when reloading one barrel of a double, to run the ramrod down into the other, reseating the over-shot wad. If it's loose and you don't want to shoot it out, simply ram a second O-S wad on top of it. Naturally, all the safety precautions already outlined with respect to other long guns must be strictly observed.

The average muzzle-loading shotgun in good condition can be loaded up in the traditional manner, taken afield, and will kill *some* game if you're any sort of a marksman at all. But if you'll take the time to try it at the pattern board and work up the load that produces the best pattern, the odds will grow mightily in your favor. In the process, keep in mind that the shorter the shot column in relation to its height, the better the patterns will be.

That's the way it was until the coming of plastic, one-piece wad columns for modern paper and plastic shotshells. Not too long after that, muzzle-loading scattergun buffs started trying to figure out how they could have some of the advantages plastic wads gave breech loaders. One result was loading methods that allowed the use of the Remington Power Piston and similar one-piece wads in some, if not all, muzzle loaders of standard gauges.

The process is relatively simple, whether the gun is

cylinder bored or choked, although a little work is sometimes necessary on the gun before things go smoothly.

The first step is to make sure that standard wads will fit your particular gun. This is dependent mainly on bore diameter, and the variations we mentioned earlier can cause some trouble. To check, first drop a small powder charge down the bore—only a few grains are needed, just enough to blow the wad out if it sticks tight. Then attempt to finger-start a plastic wad unit in the muzzle. If it goes in easily without too much force and yet without a lot of clearance, you're home free. More likely, however, it will be very tight and will frustrate efforts to get it into the bore with just your fingers. To get around that, make a short starter as for a round-ball rifle—a piece of dowel that will just enter the cup of the wad and set into a wood ball or knob to serve as a handle. The dowel should protrude 1-1/2 inches to 1-3/4 inches. Center the wad on the muzzle; place the dowel in the cup; then strike the knob smartly to drive the wad into the bore. If it goes, fine—but if not, try chamfering the inner edge of the muzzle slightly (about 1/16 inch seems to be plenty); then polish the bevel smooth. Don't cut the chamfer so deep that the outer edge of the muzzle becomes sharp. For this reason, if you are shopping specifically for a gun in which to use plastic wads, always choose one with fairly thick barrel walls at the muzzle. After chamfering and polishing, try again to seat a wad with the short starter. Unless you have an abnormally

tight barrel for its gauge, the wad should go in without too much trouble. If there is still some difficulty, try another make of wad—subtle differences in design and construction can make one wad enter a tight bore easier than another.

Once you've gotten a wad seated, try ramming it—you'll be surprised to find that it goes down with relative ease, even though getting it into the muzzle required a rather hefty smack on the starter knob. Now you know why we said to drop a small powder charge in the bore before beginning—the wad won't come out easily any other way, so cap your fowling piece and shoot it out. Take care, though, for even that dab of powder makes a dangerous missile out of the empty wad.

At this point, if you feel that seating the wad in the muzzle requires a bit more effort than you like, try polishing very smooth the first inch or so of the bore. Sometimes a significant improvement can be had this way, depending on how smooth the bore was in the beginning.

Now, with all the preparatory work done, you're ready not only for better patterns, but smoother and faster reloading. Here is the proper loading procedure: drop the powder charge down the bore, set a plastic wad in the muzzle, use the short starter to seat the wad inside the bore (cut stem to 1-1/2 inches and the wad will stop in the right place as the starter knob strikes the muzzle), pour in the desired shot charge (it should fill the plastic cup brimful or overflow slight-

Shot bags or a shot belt with similar heads are a great convenience for loading scatterguns in the field. This bag is shown with a detachable measure looking much like a small scoop which slides up inside the head. Shown separately is a different type of head which automatically dumps the desired charge of shot when the lever is pressed inward.

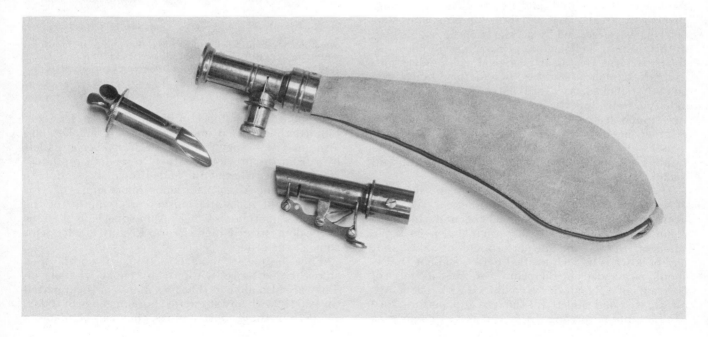

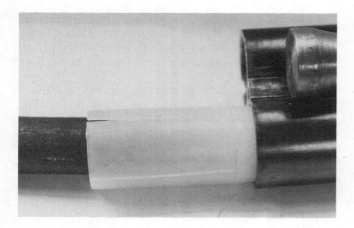

The best method of using plastic wads in a muzzle-loading scattergun is to finger start the wad in the muzzle, then use a short length of dowel set in a ball or knob as a starter, the dowel cut to a length that will seat a wad the desired distance below the muzzle.

ly), thumb a card over-shot wad into the muzzle, take up the ramrod (big, flat head, remember) and run the entire wad/shot package smoothly down against the powder charge. Don't drive it down hard on the powder; just seat it solidly so that you feel the powder give just a bit.

Now you are ready to cap and shoot. The plastic wad has eased loading, and it will also function in a muzzle loader just as it does in a modern breech loader. That is, its flared base will seal in powder gases better than a card, it will isolate shot pellets from the hard bore walls and thus prevent them from being scrubbed out of round, and its excellent cushioning effect will greatly reduce the clumping and shot deformation produced by acceleration forces. Loaded in this fashion, a choked muzzle loader will normally shoot patterns very nearly as good as a modern gun using the same wad and load in a factory shell. If the gun is not choked, it will still pattern better than with old-style wads, but the amount of improvement will vary much from gun to gun. Put another way, a cylinder-bored front loader with plastic wads will usually—not always—shoot at least as well as the same gun *choked* with conventional bulk-wad loading.

The use of plastic wads also opens up another form of scattergunning previously not practical. We've all heard of shooting shot in muskets, and the most common musket today—either original or new—is the *rifled* .58 Minie-gun. The performance of naked shot and bulk wads in such a rifled bore is so poor that it should be avoided entirely. However, when a charge of 50 grains of FFg powder is combined with a 28-gauge plastic wad and shot to fill the wad cup, performance can be quite surprising. In fact, it is just as good as

that of a top-quality, unchoked smoothbore of the same gauge loaded conventionally.

Treated in this fashion, the rifled musket suddenly takes on a new dimension of usefulness—it starts out as a Minie-bullet rifle that also performs quite well with patched round balls, and it also becomes a very worthwhile small-gauge scattergun when loaded with modern plastic wad units.

As for handling, the musket in standard-length barrel is about the same length as a long-barrel shotgun—a bit heavier, to be sure, but not so much so that it doesn't swing rather well on the farther targets. It really comes into its own in the shortened musketoon and buffalo hunter versions. Though still a bit hefty, those models swing as sweetly as a short-tubed quail gun—in fact, it is on quail and other close-in upland game not requiring large charges of shot that they shine when used as a scattergun.

Some muzzle-loading shotguns have sharp muzzle mouths which make it difficult to start plastic wads. This Italian-made double has had a 45-degree chamfer cut at the inner edge to ease wad seating.

While on the subject of *rifled* muskets, I am reminded that a good many *smoothbore* muskets are around. They range from .69 to .75 caliber guns left over from the previous century to modern reproductions of the Charleville and Brown Bess, not to mention some Asian-made smoothbore copies of circa 1850 Enfield rifles and musketoons. Quality of the modern smoothbores ranges from superb, in the case of the domestically-made Brown Bess, to mediocre for some of the others.

These guns all have one thing in common—a smoothbored barrel without any choke whatsoever. They are also alike in that few, if any, of them match up exactly with any standard shotgun gauge of today. Aside from these shortcomings, they can be made to perform as well with small shot as most cylinder-bored shotguns.

The only real problem lies in obtaining wads that fit properly. Begin by checking standard-gauge wads against your gun's bore. If they fit snugly enough, you're in business. If they don't, then try the various muzzle-loading supply houses such as the Dixie Gun Works for odd-sized wads which might fit. When writing about this, always include the *measured* bore diameter at the muzzle, so the supplier will have something more than a trade name to work from. If all else fails, make a wad-cutting hollow punch from a piece of steel tubing. If you aren't a machinist, it might be easier and simpler to buy a punch of the next-smaller standard size, then open it up in steps until it turns out exactly the right size wad for your bore.

Once you have done all that, there is no reason whatsoever that you can't load and shoot your smoothbore musket just as any other front-loading scattergun. Properly prepared, the average smooth-bore musket—assuming the bore suface is really smooth—should shoot just as well as a cylinder-bored scattergun of similar gauge.

Now, back to plastic wad details.

All of the one-piece plastic wad columns are designed for a specific weight of shot charge when used in conventional shotshell cases. This is essential to produce a loaded shell of standard length and to maintain a tight crimp. Such limitations don't pertain in the muzzle loader, thus there is more freedom in shot charge weight. If you wish to use more shot than the cup will hold when it is filled to the brim, simply do so, still taking care to ram the over-shot wad carefully and solidly in place. The amount of the shot charge that extends above the lip of the plastic cup will be in contact with the bore and will be deformed by scrubbing and will cause some deterioration in pattern density and uniformity. However, this involves only a small percentage of the total shot charge, so the effect is relatively small. It's easy to live with this if you require a larger charge of shot.

On the other hand, smaller charges than that for which the wad was intended can be used *only* if the cup is shortened to suit. The cup must be trimmed to a depth that will just accommodate the amount of shot you want to use. If the cup is not completely filled by shot, seating the over-shot wad results in its being supported on the mouth of the cup, leaving the shot rattling around loose beneath it. This not only reduces the resistance of the shot charge to initial powder combustion (necessary), but under the influence of recoil when the adjoining barrel is fired, the shot gets a "running jump" at the over-shot wad and is, therefore, very likely to unseat it. This sets the stage for either losing the shot out of the muzzle and firing a blank or, worse yet, having the shot come to rest several inches down the barrel to cause a burst barrel when fired.

So, when using small charges of shot, always trim the plastic shot cup down so that the charge fills it completely. This is easily done in a V-block fixture made of wood or any other handy material. Lay the wad in the V against the stop, then simply slice off the excess with a razor blade or *very* sharp knife. Be certain, however, that the new cup mouth is square—at right angles to the cup's longitudinal axis. If it isn't, the over-shot wad will be tipped in the bore and therefore less securely seated. The finished cup length should be such that with the shot charge in place and the over-shot wad rammed securely, the shot itself is under compression by the wad. This may take some trial and error, but is well worth the trouble in the end.

Plastic wads also allow the development of fairly good buckshot loads in muzzle loaders—something that isn't too practical with conventional loading methods. To do this, make a shorter-leg wad seater that places the mouth of the shot cup only about 1/32-inch to 1/16-inch below the muzzle. Then it becomes rather simple to place large individual shot in the neat geometric layers necessary to reduce deformation and produce the best patterns. If you like, at the same time you may add granular polyethylene filler material to cushion the lead balls just as is done in the better buckshot shells to produce maximum-density patterns by further reducing shot deformation.

Once the shot (and filler, if used) is in place, thumb the over-shot wad into the muzzle, then again use the short seater to force the entire assembly an inch or so into the muzzle before applying the ramrod for the finishing operation. When this method of loading buckshot—including filler—is used, the muzzle loader will shoot fully as well as a modern breech loader with premium factory-loaded buckshot shells. Now, you really can't ask for more than that from a centuries-old system, even if it has been somewhat modified to take advantage of modern technology.

Varying powder charge, wad column and shot charge all have their effect on patterns. The effect isn't predictable, but it's there. Vary both shot and powder charge both ways and note the effect on patterns. Do the same with wad column, wad material, ramming pressure and shot size. After a few conscientious range sessions devoted to this sort of experimentation, you may easily wind up with as much as 15% to 20% better patterns. And you can be sure that much improvement will put a lot more meat in the pot.

The front-loading scattergun can often be just as effective for one or two shots as the most modern breech loader. A new, properly choked double that is carefully loaded from the muzzle will kill just as far and just as cleanly as any cartridge gun made—it just can't be reloaded quickly. Considering today's bag limits, that isn't as much of a handicap as one might think.

10/Bullets and Bullet Making

Muzzle-loading shooters of yesteryear tried all manner of bullets in developing what we use now. If some of their efforts seem ridiculous today, it's because they were probing an unknown field in attempts to produce accuracy and effectiveness on game and on target. Before you laugh or sneer at old bullets, just remember what the autos and airplanes of a mere 50 years ago looked like. They seem pretty silly, too, but were an essential part of the development of what we have today. Laugh at the deformed, hammered-down, naked lead bullets of the 18th century Jaeger rifle if you will, but remember that they gave birth to the patched ball of the Kentucky rifle and many other developments.

Today we use the following bullet types in muzzle loaders: cloth-patched round ball; grooved, lubricated hollow-based Minie bullet; paper-patched, solid lead, unlubricated bullet; and the naked lead ball or bullet with grease smeared over it in revolvers.

All are customarily cast from the softest and purest lead available, though for casual shooting, many shooters will use anything that resembles lead. It is generally conceded that pure lead gives the best results but the difference is often so small that scrap lead of unknown content is used without the least bit of trouble.

Casting techniques are essentially the same for all types and are the same as those used for cartridge bullets. Equipment can range from a tomato can and spoon used on the kitchen range with an old finger-burning brass mold to a modern thermostatically controlled electric furnace and heavy multiple-cavity molds.

Much has been made of the romantic scene of the frontiersman molding rifle balls over a tiny campfire hidden deep in the forest. No doubt this happened often enough out of necessity, but I suspect more legend than fact is contained in that image. Carrying a melting pot, ladle, mold and bar lead certainly didn't fit in with the mountain man's concept of mobility. Bar or sheet lead was certainly obtainable on trading trips, but it and bullet-making equipment were undoubtedly cached along with other occasionally needed items. Contemporary writings often referred to such caches of lead, powder (sometimes in a lead container) and other necessaries. The cache could be visited when replenishment was necessary. After all, the frontier rifleman didn't shoot for fun except when visiting "civilization." He expended powder and lead only for food and in defense of his scalp and so his consumption of them wasn't great.

With small-caliber round-ball rifles, a horn of good powder would take care of 150 to 200 shots, and an equal number of, say, .36 caliber balls weighing only 1 1/2 pounds or less, could be carried in a bag no larger than your fist. Even a .55 caliber gun gave from 67 to

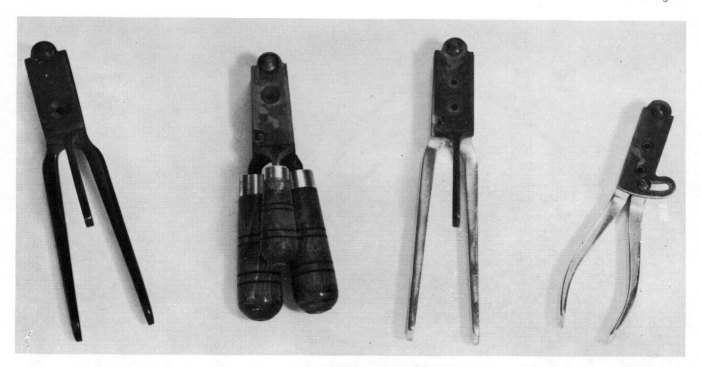

A variety of old-style molds as they are produced today in replica form by, oddly enough, Replica Arms. Those with plain, short metal handles become impossible to use after casting only a few bullets. The second from left, copied after Colt Paterson molds is somewhat better, but still difficult to use because of the extreme shortness of the handles.

70 shots to the pound of powder and about 30 balls to the pound of lead.

Considering that the working rifleman would probably average less than a shot per day, it can be seen that Natty Bumpo didn't have any real reason to cast bullets very often.

The round-ball devotee using arms of .30, .32, .36 and .44 or .45 caliber doesn't even have to concern himself with casting bullets. Commercial swaged buckshot is available in sizes correct for the three smaller calibers. Swaged balls are available in the larger calibers.

Both buckshot and the large balls are formed in automatic "cold-heading" machines from lead wire. Wire is fed directly into these machines, cut to length, and squeezed to spherical shape between two hollow-ended punches—all faster than the eye can follow. The swaging operation closes any voids that may exist, producing round balls of very uniform weight and diameter. Once formed, the balls are tumbled in powdered graphite which gives them their blackened, dirty appearance. The tumbling also produces the numerous flats and dents one sees on the balls' surface. This rough appearance leads many to believe such balls can't possibly shoot as well as one gleaming and freshly cast. But they do. In fact, many guns deliver better accuracy with these commercial balls than with the hand-cast variety. No cast bullet *is as*

uniform as a swaged bullet, and so it is with round balls. Personally, I consider them a blessing and hardly ever cast a ball unless it's a size not available ready-made.

The traditional bullet-casting setup consists of a cast-iron pot (often with a heat shield) intended to be set on an old coal- or wood-burning kitchen range; an iron ladle; a single-cavity brass or bronze mold; and a knife or nippers with which to trim the sprue. The pot and ladle work nicely today—better than before—with gas or electric ranges whose heat can be carefully controlled. Yesterday's mold, though, leaves a lot to be desired. Its short all-metal handles are guaranteed to blister your hands in short order. The small blocks overheat rapidly, and the sprue cutter (if there is one) is too flimsy to do a proper job. If you do plan to use such molds, insulate the handles or attach wood extensions.

Far better are the modern separate-block molds manufactured primarily by the Lyman Company and to a lesser degree by SAECO, RCBS and Hensley & Gibbs. As you get deeper into muzzle-loader shooting, by all means try the old molds. But, in the beginning, use the modern type and far better bullets will certainly result.

In making the foregoing statement, I don't mean to downgrade the very fine old molds furnished with high-grade rifles by makers such as Billinghurst,

Not much is really needed to cast good bullets. The simple layout here is plenty: melting pot; mold; dipper; lead hammer handle for striking the sprue-cutter; and an ingot mold in which to pour leftover lead. The latter isn't at all necessary, but is convenient.

Brockway, Whitmore or Pope. These molds are works of art and easily produce perfect bullets. They resemble modern molds more than the old-timers. But, they represent only a very small percentage of the old molds encountered. They are in themselves collectors' items.

Except for the nose portion of composite slug gun bullets, begin with the purest lead available. The temptation to use everything from auto wheel weights to junk battery plates is great, but it really can't be justified in the end if you want the best accuracy possible. Commercial pig lead can be obtained as this is written from most large plumbing supply shops at 30-35 cents per pound. Since a pound will produce 100 .36 caliber round balls, this isn't at all prohibitive. Scrap lead of unknown composition will cost half to two-thirds as much, and isn't quite as satisfactory. Some saving can be realized by melting up scrap and softening it with pure lead. If you're serious about this, use a SAECO hardness tester to make batches more uniform.

A bullet mold is simply a pair of metal blocks into which has been cut a cavity shaped exactly like the finished bullet. Molten lead is poured into this cavity. After hardening, the blocks are separated and the bullet falls out. Round balls are then ready to shoot, but Minies require lubrication, and slugs require patching. For some purposes the bullet may be forced through a die to size it and make it perfectly round. Nothing to it—or is there?

Let's take handgun bullets first, for the short guns are less critical of minor qualitative and quantitative variations and are far more tolerant than rifles of lead temper (hardness) and bullet shape. And it's easier to cast good ones. In spite of all this built-in "forgiveness," perfect bullets are no less desirable.

Whether you're using a Lyman pot on mom's gas range or one of the big electric outfits, lead must be melted and heated to a temperature at which it will flow as freely as water. As it becomes fluid, dross (dirt, grit and impurities) floats to the top and must be skimmed off.

When the lead is hot enough to char a dry wood splinter without it bursting into flame (or at about 700° F. with a controllable heat pot), you would traditionally drop in a bullet-sized lump of grease. This works well enough some of the time, but more modern fluxes are now available. I've had excellent results from Marvelux.

Grease will boil and bubble, smoke a lot, and stink up the whole house—so don't do this while the lady of the house is entertaining her bridge club. The disruption won't last long, so a fan and an open window will clear things up in a hurry. Or you can carry the pot outdoors for fluxing if you have a tyrannical housemaid. If the kitchen range has an exhaust hood and fan and you can work there, you're in real luck. Most modern chemical fluxes don't smoke or stink.

When dipping from the pot, whether it be the fine thermostatically controlled SAECO unit shown or a tin can set on the kitchen range, submerge the dipper deep into the molten metal; fit its nozzle to the sprue hole while still horizontal, and then turn mold and dipper upright together so that the weight of metal in the dipper will force lead into all corners of the mold.

As soon as the smoke has cleared away and you've assured the hysterical neighbors that there's really no fire, stir the mixture well, wait a few seconds and skim off the dross. An old serving spoon with a few small holes punched or drilled in its bottom works quite well for this. What's left should be reasonably pure lead— just what is needed for good bullets or balls.

While the lead was melting, you should have washed all grease and oil out of your mold. Solvent is okay for this—even gasoline in an emergency—but acetone leaves no residue and has given me perfect results. And, if you had set the mold on the edge of the pot to warm up, you'd be a few minutes ahead of the game. But no matter, it will heat quickly enough as casting progresses.

Next make a last-minute check to ensure that no foreign material is on the block faces, thus keeping them from joining completely together.

Hold the mold in one hand (left, for a right-hander), with cavities *parallel* to the floor, cut-off plate toward the pot. Take the Lyman dipper (the one with the integral pouring spout) and immerse it in the lead for a few seconds to heat up. Unless the dipper is hot, lead will "freeze" in the spout. Lift dipper horizontally and bring its spout into firm contact with the sprue hole in the mold cut-off plate. Holding dipper and mold firmly together, rotate them to an upright position (counterclockwise for a right-hander) and hold steady. The lead will flow from dipper to mold and the excess lead in the dipper will exert pressure on that in the mold, forcing out air and filling all nooks and crannies.

Separate dipper from mold, rolling the two apart so that no lead is spilled. A small puddle of molten lead should remain in the sprue hole, and will harden in two or three seconds. You'll see it rapidly change color and texture, and shrink as it solidifies.

In the event that you are using a bottom-draw electric pot for your first bullets, I'd better cover that somewhat different procedure before continuing. The spout valve on the bottom of such pots is usually opened and closed by a handle connected to a rod dropping down through the molten lead. An adjustable stop controls the amount the handle will move, thus the rate at which lead will flow out the spout.

The spout appears to be made to insert in the sprue hole of the mold and, in truth, that is the way the makers intend it to be used. By all means try it that way, but in my own experience it seldom works well. Better results are often obtained by letting lead run freely into the sprue hole. Build up a support that will

The hardened sprue should look like this. Never use a hammer or other metal object to strike the sprue plate and never strike the mold proper. The plate must be struck in a line parallel to its face—any other angle will eventually bend it, causing uneven bullet bases.

When using a bottom-draw pot such as this Lyman unit, it is sometimes better to have the mold a short distance from the spout. Using the Lyman Mold-Guide shown simplifies this considerably and also makes handling multiple-cavity molds a lot easier.

hold the mold with sprue hole directly under the spout and about a half inch below it. Scrap wood works fine and sometimes so does a common brick. Lyman makes an excellent "Mold Guide" that bolts directly to the furnace for this purpose.

If using wood, wrap a piece of aluminum foil over it to prevent spilled lead (yes, you'll spill some) from adhering to it. Wood has the added advantage in that you can drive a few nails into its top, forming a sort of pocket for the mold, aligning it with the pot spout. This will save a lot of time getting the mold in the right place each time.

Slide the mold under the spout and raise the valve handle very carefully. The stream of lead should enter the sprue hole dead-center. If lead splashes over the side, the stream is too big and must be reduced by cutting down the valve opening. Adjust the valve handle stop.

As soon as lead wells up in the sprue hole, close the valve by letting the handle drop. Fast action is called for here or lead will overflow and freeze on the mold and you'll have to pry it off before the mold can be opened easily. Cutting and prying such spillage off is a chore, so avoid it.

Fast action is called for with the valve handle, and you'll no doubt invent a few new swear words before you've learned to avoid overflow. With practice you can develop a technique whereby exactly the right amount of lead is left in the sprue without spilling a drop.

Now, back to the pot and dipper method. The dipper should be immediately returned to the pot so it will stay hot. When the sprue (that puddle of lead) has hardened, it's time to open the mold. First, the cut-off plate must be swung aside, cutting the sprue from the body of the bullet. This is best done by a sharp, light blow on the cut-off plate arm.

Never use a metal bar or hammer; the plate may be bent or warped. Instead, use a stick of hardwood (an old hickory hammer works well) or a plastic mallet. Never strike up or downward at the plate. This also will deform it so it will not lie flat on top of the mold blocks, causing lead to leak from under it.

With a little practice, you can cut off the sprue and have it fall directly into an old sardine can for eventual return to the pot.

Open the mold by spreading the handles apart. If the bullet doesn't fall out readily, rap the top of the mold hinge joint with the same instrument used on the cut-off plate (never a metal object). This will jar the bullet out. As the bullet comes from the mold, it is still quite hot and soft enough that being dropped on a hard surface will knock it out of shape. Fold an old towel or piece of blanket into a pad on which bullets can be dropped and left until cool.

Man, that first bullet you just cast sure is a mess, isn't it? Full of wrinkles, rounded edges and voids. What's wrong? Nothing. The mold won't make perfect bullets until it has been warmed up. And, if it's a new mold, it may not turn out good ones until it has been broken in by casting a hundred or more slugs.

After becoming hot enough to cause a drop of water to dance and sizzle audibly (the old-timers spit on them to check this), the mold should turn out well-formed bullets. If it doesn't, the lead probably isn't hot enough so turn the heat up a bit, and keep trying. Eventually you'll get good, if not perfect, bullets. It may take a few hours' experimentation with mold handling and lead temperature. Adding more flux will often make the difference between bad and good bullets.

Soon, though, you'll get the hang of it and be able to turn out a pair of bullets per minute, even with only a single cavity mold. You may find that after quite a few have been cast rapidly that they come out of the mold with a frosted appearance and the sprue is taking a longer time to harden. Either the mold or both lead and mold are too hot.

First, try slowing down the casting, and if that doesn't do the trick, turn down the pot heat a little. If this seems to slow production too much, then immerse the mold, *closed with bullet and sprue in place,* in a bucket of lukewarm water for a few seconds. This will cool it off quickly and allow casting to continue faster. Some people I know work so fast they dunk the mold every half dozen bullets.

By now, you should be getting pretty good bullets (or, at least you think you are), and you've decided there really isn't much to this casting bit. But you're wrong; there's a lot more to it. Take a few of those bullets and look them over closely under a magnifying glass. Are the edges of the bands and grooves as sharp and clean as they appear in the mold cavity?

Are the bases clean and square with no "tail" or perhaps a ragged cavity where the sprue was cut away? Do you find any holes when probing with a pin where the sprue was cut? Split a few bullets lengthwise. Do you find air holes and voids? Weigh a dozen bullets carefully. If you don't have an accurate scale, call on your local pharmacist for help. Are they uniform in weight? Borrow a micrometer (you really should have a good one, you know) and check a dozen bullets for diameter. Are they as uniform as you thought?

Left is a properly cast bullet with all areas of the mold fully filled. Center is the first bullet of the day, lead not quite hot enough run into a cold mold. Waiting until the lead became hot enough and preheating the mold on the edge of the pot would have made the effect far less pronounced. Right is a bullet deliberately cast to produce a thick fin on one side. Anything that interferes with complete closing of the mold blocks will produce this same effect to a lesser degree; I deliberately emphasized it here.

Running through this list of tests, you'll find enough wrong with your new bullets to deflate your ego somewhat, maybe even to make you think the equipment isn't any good. But don't throw anything away. That setup will give you perfect bullets virtually every time it's heated up, once you learn the tricks of the trade. Don't be discouraged; there are many things you can do to eliminate the defects you discovered. And when you can do these tricks, you'll make bullets that have a natural "X-ring" tendency.

Wrinkled irregular surface: Check first to make certain that no oil or grease is present in the mold cavity. Check temperature of both mold and bullet metal. If either or both are too cold, this defect will be produced. If you have just begun to cast, continue casting to bring the mold up to proper temperature. If casting 15 or 20 bullets does not produce any significant improvement, increase the temperature of the

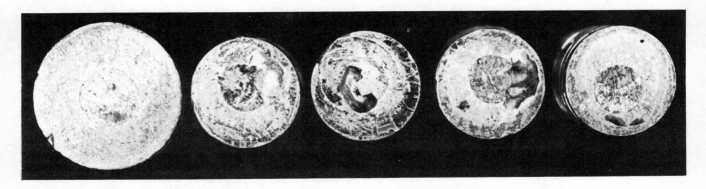

Largest bullet has a correctly cast base. All the others show varying degrees and types of cavities that result from poor casting methods.

lead also. These factors often require considerable juggling.

Bands, lubricating grooves, Minie-bullet bases, and other sharp edges not filled out cleanly in exact duplication of the mold cavity: If using a hand-dipper, keep a larger quantity of lead in it and keep in contact with mold for a longer period of time. The weight of additional metal in the dipper applied for a longer period of time to the fluid metal in the mold will force lead into the mold's nooks and crannies. If using a bottom-discharge furnace, open the valve more and hold it open for a longer period of time.

Next, try additional fluxing of the metal in the pot. Some mixtures may require more frequent fluxing than others to flow well. If the condition persists, try adding a small amount often to the metal. A very small amount of tin will often make the mixture flow

Left bullet has dull, frosty appearance resulting from both mold and lead becoming too hot as work progressed. Right bullet is smooth and glossy, coming from mold and metal of just the right temperature.

better and won't harden the lead enough to cause trouble. Up to 1 part tin in 40 parts of lead will improve casting without impairing accuracy.

If all else has failed, it may be that your bullet metal has been contaminated by zinc, aluminum or one of the other materials that act to greatly increase the surface tension of molten lead alloy. This contamina-

tion can easily exist when scrap lead from the local junk yard is used. Particularly, soldered joints found on some cable sheathing can contain impurities. Once so contaminated, the metal is of no further use for casting "good" bullets. You may as well use it to make vise jaws or door stops.

Air trapped in the mold can also prevent filling out the sharp corners. Modern molds have the blocks machined on their matching faces with a series of regular, shallow grooves which allow air to escape as lead flows in. These grooves can become clogged, trapping air. Cleaning with solvent and an old toothbrush will usually do the trick. *Don't* use steel tools or abrasives.

Older molds were made with smooth faces and often require "venting." This consists of very carefully filing a minute groove from the offending portion of a mold to the edge of the block, thus providing an escape passage for trapped air. I don't recommend attempting to vent a mold yourself—the factory is far more able to do a proper job.

Edge of bullet base not fully filled out (bullet poured from base): This also results from trapped air, and is usually corrected by slightly loosening the cut-off plate screw. The plate must swing freely yet not be held so tightly against the face of the blocks that it prevents the escape of air. Grease and oil between the plate and the blocks can also contribute to the problem.

Holes or cavities in base of bullet: This can be caused by either trapped air, insufficient weight of metal in the dipper (as noted above) or a combination of both. Loosen the cut-off plate and use more lead in the dipper.

Ragged cavity in the base of the bullet where sprue was cut off: Usually caused by striking the cut-off plate before the sprue has fully hardened, and is sometimes accompanied by smearing of lead across the cut-off plate and surface of mold blocks, even being soldered there. Make certain the sprue has really solidified before striking the cut-off plate. Also try touching the underside of the hot cut-off plate with a dab of beeswax.

Wedge-shaped lump left when sprue is cut off: Make certain underside of cut-off plate is perfectly flat and that edges of the sprue hole are clean and sharp. Loosen cut-off plate screw so that plate swings freely, then strike plate sufficiently hard to cut off the sprue in a single movement.

Band appears to be cracked or slightly separated from body of bullet: Caused by dropping the bullet from the mold before it has cooled sufficiently. One-half of the mold pulls free of the bullet cleanly as the mold is opened, but the bullet remains momentarily in the other and tips as it falls clear. Thus, the bands are slightly displaced. Allow a longer cooling period.

Bullets have crystalline, frosty appearance: Either metal, mold or both are too hot. Reduce heat of metal, and slow down casting until bullet appearance is bright and normal. This can be a particular problem with large, heavy bullets in single cavity blocks. The large amount of molten metal heats the blocks very rapidly, even though lead temperature is held to a minimum. If a satisfactory production rate cannot be maintained, cool the mold by dipping it periodically in lukewarm water (with bullet in the cavity) or by using two molds alternately.

Fins appear on bullet at line where blocks meet: Foreign material is holding blocks slightly apart, or guide pin holes are clogged and causing the same thing. It is also possible that you are relaxing your hold on the mold handles at the time the lead is entering the mold, allowing the blocks to be forced slightly apart. Clean mold block faces and guide pins and holes, and make sure you keep a good grip on the handle.

Fins on base of bullet: If fins are uniform around the perimeter of the base, the cut-off plate is too loose. Tighten the screw slightly until fins disappear. If the fin is predominantly on one side of the bullet base, the cut-off plate is probably warped or bent, usually as a result of incorrect striking of the plate. If the deformation is only slight, the cut-off plate may be removed from the mold and polished flat on abrasive cloth stretched tightly across a perfectly flat hard surface. The only other solution is a new plate. Once bent, it cannot be straightened satisfactorily.

Bullets do not drop freely from the mold: Shift the position of the mold as it is opened. If this fails, strike the top of the hinge joint one or two light but firm blows with the stick used on the cut-off plate. If more effort than that is required to jar the bullet free, there are burrs in one of the mold blocks embedded in the surface of the bullet.

With the blocks clean and dry, examine the surface of the cavity under a magnifying glass. Burrs of sufficient size to cause trouble should easily be seen. Usually they are small and fragile, and can be very carefully removed with a pointed scraper. Often they are at the outer edge of a cavity, having been produced by the two blocks banging into each other. This type *may* be safely removed by extremely cautious application of a fine Swiss needle file. Most authorities advise against any such work on a mold, but there is no other way to salvage a mold so damaged. I feel it is better to at least attempt to correct the condition than to discard the mold without trying. After all, what can you lose?

Air holes inside bullet (disclosed by weighing or sectionalizing): Usually the result of inadequate weight of metal when the mold is filled, resulting in excessive shrinkage with nothing to replace it. Also sometimes caused by too-rapid filling of the mold which results in a splashing action that traps bubbles of air. Use more metal in the dipper and fill the mold more slowly.

Irregular, sharply defined small holes in bullet surface: Caused by foreign material or oil in the mold cavity, either falling in from the surface of the mold or being carried in with the molten lead. Keep mold clean inside and out, and flux lead frequently so that all foreign material floats to the surface to be skimmed off.

Careful attention to all details mentioned above is not something that you'll be able to accomplish in the first or perhaps even the tenth casting session. It requires continuous practice and effort over a period of some time. Often you may be casting perfect bullets, then suddenly one or more of the above conditions will crop up for no apparent reason. It's all part of the game. You can be sure that sooner or later it will happen to you. When it does, don't give up in despair; just analyze the defect and take the appropriate corrective action.

Now, casting a bullet that looks perfect, is uniform in weight and possesses no internal or external defects

Most people think round balls are ridiculously easy to cast; they are, if proper attention is paid to the procedures and to the condition of the mold. Note here the torn and excessive sprue on the left ball, also the cavity at its base which will throw the ball out of balance. The right ball is cast well, but its two halves are offset, clearly showing that the mold blocks were badly out of alignment.

still does not accomplish the entire job. The bullet must be cast from an alloy reasonably correct for the job you intend it to do. There are fussy people who keep three, four or even more bullet alloys available and use each one for a specific purpose. I do not find this at all necessary.

Unless you intend making hard-alloy noses for composite slug gun bullets, a single mix containing no more than 1 part tin in 40 parts of lead is all you need. For hard noses, make up a quantity of 1:20 mix.

However, we all eventually find ourselves in possession of bullet metal whose contents are totally unknown. More often than not it will be quite soft. I reserve such windfall metal for use in round-ball guns. Normally, it is melted up in batches of 25 to 30 pounds, fluxed and skimmed to remove impurities. If skimmed several times without stirring, excess tin and antimony will be removed as they float to the surface. Then a few sample bullets are cast from it. If the metal flows well and fills the mold completely, I use it as is. If it gives any casting problems, though, tin is simply added until it flows well enough to produce good bullets. Consequently, I usually have two different bullet alloys on hand—one of more or less unknown content which is soft and used only for round balls, and the other which is of known content and used for more demanding guns.

Round balls are the easiest of all bullet types to cast, though even they aren't as ridiculously easy as some people seem to think. They are *relatively* simple, but require plenty of care and attention to detail—all the rules apply if perfect, smooth, uniform-weight, void-free spheres are expected.

While most Minie bullets are shot as cast, it is sometimes desirable to size them to a specific diameter to suit a particular barrel. This sizing die, available from Dixie Gun Works, is marked with a diameter of .575 inch. Forcing a bullet through a sizing die will not only bring it to diameter, but will iron out any surface irregularities and true up the base.

This is typical of the damage that can be done while casting Minie bullets. This bullet was dropped too soon from the mold onto an unyielding surface and one side of the skirt is badly flattened. The same kind of damage can occur through rough handling.

Next up the ladder come solid-base grooved bullets. Not many are used in muzzle loaders, other than a few conical revolver bullets, the Thompson/Center "Maxi-Ball" and similar Minie substitutes. A mold/alloy/temperature combination that will produce perfect round balls may turn out badly distorted grooved bullets—the base and driving bands can be rounded rather than sharp; there may be internal or base voids; the edges of the base may be irregular.

When this happens after you've cast perfect balls, don't tear your hair out—instead, go back over that check list a few pages back. It will bail you out.

Most difficult to cast of all bullets—whether for muzzle loaders or cartridge guns—is the hollow-base grooved bullet. It's at its sneakiest in the form of the traditional Minie bullet with its wide, deep cavity and resultant thin, weak base. The base is so thin it is usually referred to as a "skirt" rather than a base.

In the past several years, there have been improvements in Minie design. Those which include thickening of the skirt walls by reducing cavity diameter do make casting easier. Mold improvements have also helped a lot.

The traditional Minie mold has the sprue at the bullet nose, and a removable plug fits between the blocks to form the base cavity. Only a narrow space remains between plug and mold cavity wall for the molten lead. If the mold or lead is the least bit too cool, lead will splash and freeze, producing a wrinkled and deformed skirt. Unless this area of the mold is thoroughly vented so that air can escape easily, the base won't fill out properly. If the base plug and its seat are not scrupulously clean, the blocks won't close completely, resulting in an eccentric bullet with fins. The large amount of lead in a big Minie makes it necessary to lay lots of extra lead in the sprue—otherwise shrinkage as the alloy cools will produce a deep cavity in the nose. This will be dramatically illustrated if you fill a Minie mold but leave only a small amount of lead in the sprue. In seconds you'll see the molten metal disappear downward, sucked in by shrinkage, and a hole will grow there, right before your eyes.

The removal of Minies from the mold is also tricky. First, the base plug must be removed, then the blocks opened. If the entire bullet isn't *completely* hard, one side of the skirt may be deformed or cracked loose as the bullet falls out; the result is at best an egg-shaped base which probably won't enter the musket muzzle. Because of the weak skirt and considerable weight, a bullet hard enough to clear the mold okay may well have its skirt bent if dropped on a firm surface. Avoid this by letting the bullet stay in the mold a few extra seconds, then drop it on a well-padded surface with the mold held quite low.

With all these precautions and the rapidity with which large-caliber Minie molds overheat, casting *good* bullets can be a very slow process. Cooling the mold in water helps, but I prefer to alternate with two molds, giving one bullet plenty of time to set up while another is being poured. A spring clamp to hold the blocks tightly together is a big help when using two molds.

Often Minie bases will distort in coming from the mold, in spite of your best efforts. If there are no cracks, the skirts can be trued up by rolling the bullets between two smooth, flat steel bars—or by running them through a sizing die.

Casting Minie bullets has been simplified with improved molds introduced by Shiloh and Lee. These molds have a guide plate fitted over pins in the bottom of the blocks; the base plug (to form the cavity in the bullet base) is attached to this guide. The blocks close

Typical Minie bullets that have been lubricated by smearing grease in their grooves by hand. When sizing isn't required and not too many bullets must be processed, this is a quick and easy way to get the job done.

smoothly around the plug—then when the blocks are opened *both* move away from the plug, leaving it centered between the blocks, with the bullet sitting down over it. Inverting the mold allows the bullet to fall clear. This greatly speeds up handling the mold, but heating still keeps casting slow, in spite of the mechanical improvement. However, the design reduces skirt damage, so it is well worth having. This design uses *straight* angled cam slots in the guide plate to position the base plug. I've found that while this works well most of the time, *curved* cam slots offer a significant improvement in smoothness of operation.

In any event, casting perfect Minie bullets does require lots of practice, more than the other types. But, if you want maximum accuracy, it can be done.

Once cast, a round ball is ready to shoot, but a conical or Minie bullet might not be. The latter often requires two other things: reduction to the diameter correct for your particular barrel, and the application of a suitable lubricant in the grooves to prevent

Typical Minie bullet with its large base hollow which causes the bullet to be expanded by powder gases to engage the rifling, while still being small enough for easy loading through the muzzle.

leading of the barrel. Bringing it to proper diameter and perfect roundness is called "sizing" and is accomplished by forcing the bullet base first through a die made for the purpose. Minie bullets must finish up slightly smaller than bore of the barrel in which they will be used. Patched bullets, regardless of patch type, must be smaller than bore diameter to allow space for the patch, yet large enough to fill the rifling when the patch is in place.

Sizing is required because molds, like all other mechanical contrivances, must be made to certain tolerances. They often cast a bullet somewhat larger than the desired diameter. While it has been said that sizing *always* damages a cast bullet to some degree, damage can be held to a minimum by using the proper type die. Older dies were made with a two-diameter hole—the upper portion to accept the as-cast bullet, the lower of the size to which it was desired to reduce that bullet. These two holes were connected by a sharp shoulder or a sharply tapered area.

Such dies shear metal off one side or the other of the bullet bands, yet do not touch the bottoms of the

The Lee Minie-bullet mold viewed from the front with the blocks open; note that the base punch or pin remains attached to the bracket at the bottom while the blocks move away from it.

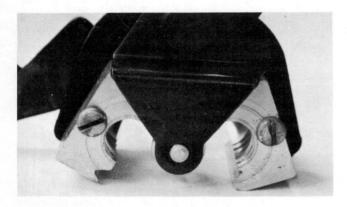

The Lee Minie-bullet mold viewed from the bottom, showing the configuration of the steel plate that supports the base pin and remains midway between the blocks.

grooves. This simply means that a bullet so sized is more often than not thrown out of balance and may not be expected to produce the best accuracy. More recently produced sizing dies connect the two holes of different diameters by a long, very gradual taper. This longer taper does not remove any metal from the bands, but rather compresses the bands in a reasonably concentric manner. Bullets sized in the newer dies are generally more accurate. In any event, the less reduction, the better.

The lubricant may be applied either before or during sizing. Fewer tools are required for the former. Lube may simply be rubbed into the grooves by hand (a time-consuming process) or the bullets may be stood in molten lubricant that is then allowed to harden. After the lubricant is hardened, a fired cartridge case with the head cut off or a length of tubing may be pressed down over the individual bullets to cut them free from the cake of lubricant.

Either way is entirely satisfactory. The lubricator-

sizer tools made for breech-loader bullets seldom work well with muzzle-loading bullets, so are best left alone. Instead, lubricate first and if sizing is necessary, do it in a simple ring die from Shiloh or DGW.

Lubricating and sizing is not so simple that it doesn't require considerable attention to detail. The nose punch which forces the bullet into the die must fit the bullet, and it must also be aligned correctly with the die. If it is not, then the bullet may be forced through the die somewhat canted, resulting in an appearance which is, of course, less than desirable. Such a bullet is sized off-center and along a line not parallel to its longitudinal axis. Consequently, it may be badly out of balance and grossly inaccurate.

Of course, it goes almost without saying that perfect bullets, perfectly sized and lubricated, must be kept undamaged until they are loaded and fired. Minie bullets are especially susceptible to damage because of their thin-walled and weak bases or skirts. If lubricant is allowed to be contaminated with dust and dirt, or grit is allowed to collect on the bearing surfaces of the bullet, less than perfect results can be expected. Also, if the bullet base is damaged in any way, accuracy will be reduced. I find it best to store prepared bullets stacked closely on their bases in covered boxes. This protects them properly until use. Because of its soft nature, a lead bullet must also be seated and rammed carefully in the rifle or it may become damaged in the process. Seating punches should fit the nose correctly, as should the ramrod head.

Bullets are seldom swaged by the shooter except for use in slug guns. Swaging consists of compressing a cast or cut-from-rod or wire slug in a die to eliminate all voids or air spaces and to bring it to a greater perfection of shape and surface finish than can be produced by casting.

The die body contains a polished cylindrical cavity of the exact diameter to which the bullet is to be produced. Close-fitting punches enter the cavity from both ends. One forms the base, which can be flat, rounded or containing a cavity. The other is shaped to form the bullet nose, which is usually gently rounded with a flat tip.

The slug is cast or cut slightly undersized, trimmed to exact weight, lightly lubricated (case resizing lube or lanolin works very nicely) and placed in the swage. Both punches are inserted; and, in normal slug gun practice, the assembly is placed on the bench, base punch down. The nose punch is struck smartly several times with a hammer. This compresses the bullet between the two punches and expands it radially to fill the die cavity perfectly. All surface imperfections are smoothed out and all internal voids eliminated. The result is a perfectly homogeneous bullet. Bullets are forced out of the die by a separate close-fitting punch.

Diameter of bullets so swaged will be uniform, but weight will remain as cast and length will vary in

Front view of the Shiloh Minie-bullet mold with the bracket that holds the base pin in place.

Bottom view of the Shiloh Minie-bullet mold showing the plate to which the base pin is attached, and the cam slots which control movement of both blocks and pin.

relation to weight. By providing a positive, adjustable stop for the nose punch and drilling an escape vent in the die, bullets of surprisingly uniform weight and length can be produced. To do this, bullets are cast very slightly overweight and swaging pressure then "bleeds" excess lead through the vent. When the nose punch strikes its stop, no further pressure is exerted in the bullet and the desired weight and length is produced. The excess lead forced into the vent remains attached but is sheared off as the bullet is forced from the die. Bullets varying no more than ± 0.2 grain in weight can be produced in this manner.

While "hammer-swaging" as outlined above is the most common, the job is simpler in a heavy-duty vise, arbor press or hydraulic press. However, the only method by which the pressure applied can be closely controlled, both in amount and rate of application, is by use of a hydraulic press. Theoretically, this will produce the most uniform bullets. In practice, however, shooters develop an "educated hand" that can turn out surprisingly uniform bullets.

Composite slug gun bullets are generally cast in two parts: a pure lead body, and a hardened alloy nose. I've heard of, but haven't seen, bullets whose two parts were first swaged separately, then joined and swaged together. A tenon on the nose fits into a cavity in the body or vice versa. The parts are pressed loosely together by hand, then swaged as already described.

Some shooters go a step farther in attempting to produce swaged bullets as homogeneous as possible. The cast or cut slug is laid on a clean, smooth steel plate and pounded with a hammer. A roughly cylindrical shape is retained, but the lead is thoroughly pounded to close any voids it might contain. I frankly cannot see any value in this treatment since proper swaging accomplishes the same end—but some match winners swear by it. It's always difficult to argue with success.

Swaged bullets can be produced without casting, and I prefer this method. One obtains extruded lead rod or wire of a diameter small enough to enter the swage body freely. Slugs of the correct length and weight are cut from the rod and placed directly into the swage. It's much simpler than casting the slug. This system has the added advantage of allowing any reasonable variation in weight to be made by changing slug length. When cast slugs are used, one needs a separate mold for every weight. Extruded lead wire or rod, formed under very high pressure, is virtually free of voids, something that can't be said for cast slugs.

Swaging dies are usually furnished by the rifle maker. However, any *competent* gunsmith or machinist can make them without difficulty. Die body and both punches must be very carefully polished to exactly the right diameter, hardened, then lapped to a "slip" fit. If not hardened, the punches will upset and stick tightly in the die. If not fitted very closely, they will allow lead to extrude between them and the die. This is particularly bad at the base of the bullet since it is especially difficult to trim such "fins" off and preserve a perfectly square base. The bullet "knockout" punch must also fit snugly or the same thing will happen.

Obviously, swaging can be applied only to ungrooved bullets. This limits swaging to paper patch-type bullets. In addition to the slug gun, you may have a breech loader chambered for one of the obsolete black powder cartridges that used lead bullets with wraparound paper patches. Exactly the same swage design and operations can be used to produce this type.

As with any rifled firearm, the bullet is the most important component of any shot fired. It is of first importance to accuracy, and that is what the game is all about. Without good bullets, the very finest gun won't shoot worth a damn.

11/Sights

The muzzle loader, aside from the smoothbores, whether common rifled musket or the finest bench-rest slug gun in the country, is no better than its sights. Traditional on the hunting or military rifle is the V-notched open rear sight together with brass blade front sight. And, make no mistake about it, the boys do some really fine shooting with this combination. You'll see more open-sighted guns than any other at muzzle-loading matches around the country. However, that doesn't mean those original sights are the best to be had. In fact, open sights of the black powder era are lousy by current standards.

Needless to say, if you're really interested in shooting, you will want maximum accuracy—and that means modern, efficient sights, at least where match rules don't prohibit them. However, keep in mind that many sight installations will require drilling and tapping or other alteration of the gun. That's okay if a modern muzzle loader is being used, but such shenanigans can greatly lower the value of an original gun.

A look at the original guns first. Hunting models will normally have a simple one-piece rear sight dovetailed laterally into the barrel ahead of the breech. There will be no vertical adjustment, and windage can only be obtained by driving the sight sideward in its dovetail. The sight will be low and have a simple central V-notch filed in its upper edge. Military sights may contain a sliding leaf and elevat-

ing steps, though the steps will usually be of some indeterminate value, even when marked for specific ranges. The front sight will be a one-piece rounded brass or silver blade—the poorest possible shape—also dovetailed into the barrel.

The V-notch and rounded blade may be fine for snap-shooting at close range in darkened primeval forests, but sunlight bouncing off that shiny brass front blade can shift the center of impact several inches *away from the sun* at 50 yards. It is simply impossible for the human eye to obtain a precise image of that sight when light flares off its rounded face in all directions. If you must keep and use the original sights, smoke them dead black with a candle stub or carbide lamp. This will help a lot, even though sight shape is poor. Of course, the soot won't help much in hunting, for it rubs off too easily—for that purpose use a flat brass-blackening finish.

To improve the situation, the original sights may be carefully removed and new ones made to fit the original barrel dovetails. Use a soft drift and light hammer to tap the old sights out from left to right. Take care not to damage either the barrel or sights. Save the sights; then the gun can be restored to original condition and equivalent value whenever you wish.

Because the original dovetails were most likely hand-filed by eye and not to any particular specifica-

Although this rear sight is a bit higher than that found on many original Kentucky-style rifles, it is typical of those found on reproductions. This particular one is on a Dixie gun.

This long, slender, tapered brass front sight is typical of the type found on original guns, usually made of either silver or brass; when silver, usually German silver or coin silver, not the more costly sterling.

tions, they will not accept any standard modern sights. You'll have to whittle new ones to fit from solid stock or from rough-cast blanks available from several suppliers. Use hacksaw and files to cut new units to the shapes shown. Leave the tops well oversized, while fitting the dovetails very carefully. If the sight dovetails are made too large, the barrel dovetails will become enlarged and won't hold the original sights securely when you want to reinstall them at some later date.

After fitting the dovetails, shape the front blade and rear leaf, but leave them higher than you want. Make certain the rear face of the front blade is square and the top of the rear leaf is level. Slanting it rearward a bit will help, too. Align the two sights over the bore centerline as perfectly as possible.

Now you can file the front sight down to approximately the desired height, but don't cut it lower than the rear sight for the time being. Carefully file the square notch centered in the rear sight. Make it just wide enough to allow a thin line of light to be seen on either side of the front sight when the gun is properly mounted. It need not yet be filed to full depth—that can be done in conjunction with zeroing later—just deep enough to line up the front sight with the gun at your shoulder.

A lot of shooting can be avoided if the breech plug is removed and the gun is bore-sighted at this stage. Clamp the barrel in a padded vise, pointed at a target about 100 yards distant. Almost any kind of target—even the top of a fence post—will do. Check horizontal sight alignment on the target. Drive both sights sideward if necessary to obtain perfect lateral alignment with the bore and still have them fairly centered on the barrel.

Now file down the top of the front or rear sight (deepening the rear notch accordingly), until the sights are aligned on target *a few inches lower* than the bore. This difference compensates partially for

bullet drop and simplifies zeroing, even though it can't be calculated precisely. Assemble the gun and shoot it in at the desired range. Fifty yards is a good zero range. Final windage adjustment should be made as you shoot by tapping the rear sight sideward. Make final elevation adjustments by filing down the top of the rear sight to lower the point of impact; raise it by filing down the front sight. Once zeroing has been accomplished to your satisfaction, true up the edges of the sights and clean up the rear-sight notch, making it at least as deep as it is wide. If it needs deepening or widening to suit your particular taste or vision, do that now. Don't make the mistake of making the

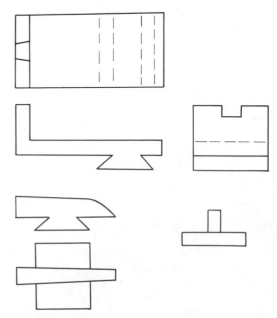

New rear (top) and front sights can be filed to these shapes and fitted into the old dovetails. These particular shapes are considerably better than the originals.

notch too wide, thus allowing too much light to show on either side of the front sight. Tapering the edges of the notch inward toward the rear and the front blade toward the front will reduce reflection and produce a sharper, blacker image.

The completed sights can be removed and blued or browned—or touch-up solution can be used to finish them in place after polishing. Don't leave them bright or they'll rust—and glare will destroy some of their effectiveness. If they are removed, be sure to make index marks first on barrel and sights. If this isn't done you won't get the sights back in the same locations and will have to re-zero. Such sights won't spoil the appearance of an original gun, and they will certainly improve your scores.

Of course, the same procedures can be used on a modern muzzle loader if you aren't satisfied with the sights that come on it. Original sporting and target rifles were often fitted with an aperture rear sight mounted on the tang. The earliest of such sights were usually made adjustable only for elevation by screwing them in and out of a vertical hole in the tang or by sliding the eyepiece up and down a staff. The simplest form of this type of sight is a piece of threaded rod turned vertically into a hole in the tang and containing an aiming aperture in its flattened upper end. A modern muzzle loader can easily be drilled and tapped for such a sight, but to do so on an original gun would not be a good idea.

Later designs used a threaded stem carrying an aperture up a ladder-like frame. A vernier scale and very fine thread was used to allow precise elevation adjustment. A limited amount of windage adjustment was sometimes provided in the base, but more often this was provided in the front sight. Today excellent

The musket sight with its long-range leaf elevated; note aperture for one range, open notch in end of leaf for a greater range.

reproductions of old-style sights are available from several sources.

An alternative to the original-type rear sights exists and it works equally well on old or new guns. It doesn't require that they be permanently altered. The Redfield Gun Sight Company makes a "Muzzle Loading Adapter" to which can be screwed a modern, micrometer-type receiver sight adjustable for both windage and elevation. This soft-steel adapter is attached atop the tang by means of a new, longer tang screw(s) (which must be custom-made). The adapter is drilled and tapped to accept standard receiver sights and may be bent cold to position the sight as desired, as well as to fit the curve of the tang. If the original tang screw is kept, the gun may be restored to original condition at any time. No evidence of the sight adapter will remain. This installation also has the advantage of placing the receiver sight back near the shooter's eye where it is most efficient.

When any form of aperture sight is added to your muzzle loader to improve its accuracy, a new and better front sight is in order. Generally, a higher front sight is required since adjustable rear sights sit higher above the bore than the originals. The simplest form is a plain straight blade fitting the original dovetail. Make it as already outlined, but as high as the rear aperture is above the bore. It can then be filed down for bore sighting and zeroing.

Original top-quality target rifles carried hooded front sights containing pinhead or post-aiming elements. These sights usually incorporated fine windage

A typical rifle-musket rear sight, shown here with its short leg or "battle sight" in position.

Typical musket front sight with its large, squared base which sometimes served as an attaching or latching point for the bayonet.

This sight, shown on a reproduction Gallagher carbine, shows that arms of the transition period used the sights that had been developed for muzzle loaders.

adjustments and sometimes a small spirit level used to avoid cant. They were called "wind gauge" or "spirit-level" sights.

If you're really serious about getting the best target sights to be had, interchangeable-insert target-type front sights are readily available. Of course, they are made for modern cartridge arms, but this doesn't lessen their effectiveness on muzzle loaders. Both Redfield and Lyman make good models. Fitting them requires either a new dovetail in the barrel or a mounting block secured to it. There isn't any way to do the latter except by drilling and tapping holes in the barrel, so think about it before doing it to a good original gun. Such sights can also be fitted to an original gun without altering it by making a split clamp ring to fit the muzzle, then attaching the sight to this ring.

The combination of a Redfield or Lyman receiver sight and target front sight with interchangeable inserts is probably the best to be had for paper punching. It can even be used for hunting if a plain-post front insert is used. It offers the advantage of being readily adjusted to zero for any powder charge or bullet change you might want to make. Fixed open sights force you to take Kentucky windage and elevation when any load changes are made and that's not the best way to shoot "possibles."

Bench-rest guns, whether for slug or round ball, are often fitted with scopes at least for matches where this is allowed. Even some better quality original sporting guns carried scopes. An occasional original example

will be seen with a contemporary scope, but modern instruments of 20X or so are by far the most common on today's target guns. They are usually target-type scopes of highest quality, in adjustable mounts, attached to the rifle barrel by screwed-on longitudinal dovetails. Mounting them correctly is a job for a competent gunsmith. It isn't something to be undertaken with hand tools on the kitchen table.

Now and then we see a muzzle-loading rifle fitted

When Thompson/Center introduced its semi-reproduction muzzle-loading rifles several years ago, it recognized the need for a fully adjustable, open rear sight—this is the result and is standard on many reproduction guns today.

Many of today's guns utilize a rear sight similar to this Thompson/Center variation because it is technically far superior to the original type.

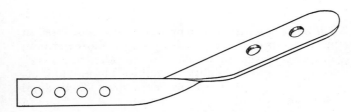

An adapter for modern target sights can be made by selecting a piece of bar stock which is first bent to fit the tang. It is then twisted to form a vertical surface to which the sight can be screwed. Redfield sells such an adapter ready for use.

with a modern scope for hunting. The late Al Goerg, a well-known hunter with muzzle loaders, fitted a regular hunting scope on his Navy Arms Zouave .58 caliber rifled musket and killed a variety of big game with it. In 1975, Val Forgett (President of Navy Arms) and I hunted everything from elephant on down with scoped muzzle loaders in East Africa. The guns were .58 caliber Hawken-style, loaded quite heavily and fitted with low-range Weaver variable scopes in plain mounts.

Any scope can be fitted to a Weaver one-piece mount base attached directly to the barrel ahead of the hammer. The mount base must be chosen to match the barrel radius to obtain a solid installation. Octagonal barrels present no problem at all since most mount producers make flat-bottomed bases. They can be installed with no fitting or filing. Since muzzle-loading barrels are often quite thick-walled, there is plenty of room for this installation. However, don't let the screw holes run into the bore on the thinner barrels. If the mount base is carefully fitted to barrel contour, it can be attached with solder or epoxy cement, thus eliminating the need for screw holes. Personally, I prefer screws and suggest other methods be used in conjunction with rather than instead of them.

Actually, with a little ingenuity you can fit almost any type of modern sights to a muzzle-loading rifle. Standard models aren't made specifically to fit such guns, but by careful selection and slight modification, you can come up with sights that can be made to fit without too much trouble.

Front-loading handguns present no great problem. Single-shot pistols and solid-frame revolvers can be easily fitted with modern target sights. If the barrel and frame are thick enough, dovetails can be cut to accept new sights. If there isn't enough metal to allow a dovetail to be cut safely, then a base block can be

Although this vernier-adjustable tang sight is actually copied from one made for early breech-loading rifles, it may be attached with relative ease to the wrist of a muzzle-loading stock to provide for more precise elevation adjustment in long-range shooting. It should be paired with a globe-type front sight.

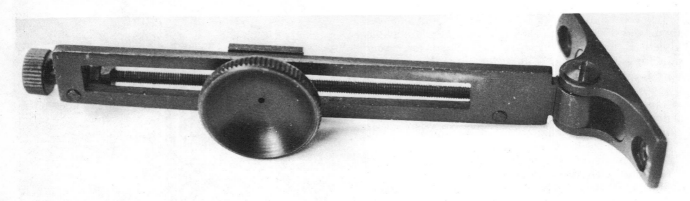

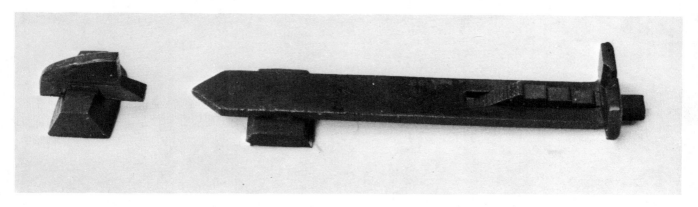

This front and rear sight is typical of what is found on low-cost sporting arms today, yet it is quite useful in updating the sighting equipment of a muzzle loader without, spoiling its appearance.

sweated or screwed in place, and the sight installed upon it. Original sights on single-shot pistols can be given the same treatment outlined earlier for open rifle sights.

Fortunately, we now have available both revolvers and single-shot pistols factory-fitted with excellent target sights. The best of these are the Ruger .44 "Old Army" based on the same company's Super Blackhawk cartridge revolver and the Thompson/Center "Patriot" percussion single shot.

Open-top frames like the Colt percussion revolver leave no proper place to install a target rear sight. I've seen this tackled two different ways. The first consists of simply fitting the rear sight on the breech of the barrel and accepting the loss in efficiency that results from placing it so far forward. The other consists of attaching a bar, like a rib, to the rear of the barrel, extending back over the cylinder. The rear sight is then installed on this bar in the normal relationship to the cylinder. Properly fitted, such a bar does not interfere with functioning or care and maintenance, though it does look a bit odd. A collector will scream and foam at the mouth at the sight of such an installation on an original gun, and I really can't blame him.

The original Colt sights aren't worth much. The V-notch in the hammer nose is better than no sight at all—but not much. It can be improved by reshaping the notch, but is still a wobbly affair that does very little for accuracy. The simplest improvement consists of an L-shaped square-notched rear sight bent from sheet metal and screwed or soldered to the upper rear of the barrel. Dovetailing a similar solid sight in place looks better, but takes a lot more time and effort without producing a corresponding increase in performance.

Solid-frame revolver rear sights can be improved by filing the notch to square shape. Even better is a new sight fitted to the top strap. It may be the type just mentioned or, if you want to go all-out, use a microm-

eter-adjustable target-type sight. Micro makes an excellent flat-based unit which attaches by screws, thus avoiding a dovetail cut which weakens the top strap.

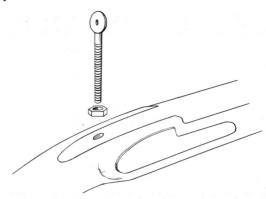

Some early rifles were fitted with a simple tang aperture sight as this. Elevation adjustment is obtained by screwing the threaded stem in or out of the tang and then locking it in place with the jam nut.

Almost any rear-sight improvement requires a new front sight. The cone or pin sights on many caplock revolvers are really not of much value, particularly when they are of shiny brass. Dovetailing a new properly-shaped sight into the barrel is one approach, but there are also good ramp units which can be soldered and/or screwed easily in place. Either should be fitted as outlined for rifles. If an adjustable target rear sight is being installed, by all means include a matching front sight of the same make. My favorite "shooting" Navy Arms Remington .36 replica is fitted with Micro front and rear target sights and will out-perform a good many modern cartridge revolvers when carefully and properly loaded.

In the final analysis, it's the results on target that count—but you need top-notch modern-style sights in order to extract the accuracy built into your barrel.

12/Accessories

Like the cowboy with a ten-dollar horse, fifty-dollar boots and hundred-dollar saddle, the muzzle-loading shooter soon finds himself swamped with accessories.

We all know it's entirely possible to own and shoot a rifle with nothing more than ammunition. But life would be pretty dull and prosaic that way—somewhat like a bar that only served Scotch. Accessories not only make shooting easier, faster and more fun, they give you more room in which to display your initiative and knowledge of the game. Better yet, many of the standard accessories can be made with only hand tools—and what's wrong with something that keeps you off the streets?

Let's take a look at the items you'll eventually collect to go with most sorts of common shooting.

    nipple wrench
    nipple prick
    ball starter
    patch knife
    loading block
    capper
    powder horn
    powder flask
    powder measure
    priming horn
    wiping (cleaning) rod
    breech cover
    nipple protector
    hunting bag
    rifle-loading bracket
    handgun-loading stand
    patch cutter
    gun case
    authentic costume

The list may never be completed because someone will always reinvent an old gadget or think of a new one you just can't afford to be without. But what are they good for? Why do you need them; and, what is more important, how can you make them yourself to avoid borrowing from the grocery money?

Any time you go out to shoot you need, in addition to ammunition and ramrod, a **nipple wrench.** This is one item you won't make on the kitchen table. It's used to unscrew or replace the nipple and must fit that part very closely. It comes in all forms, but most common today is the T-handle type. Of course, you can buy cheap ones, but they'll be soft, indifferently machined and poorly heat treated. They will bend and twist on the first tight-stuck nipple you encounter. In an emergency, you may be able to use a very small adjustable (crescent) wrench on a long gun where there is plenty of clearance, but it's easier to carry the proper wrench—and don't forget spare nipples.

A **nipple prick** is probably the easiest accessory to make. Go to the nearest model or hobby shop and get a short length of piano wire that will just pass through the nipple. For a flintlock, the same instructions apply, but fit it to the flash hole.

Make a comfortable handle of horn or hardwood and drill a tight hole to accept the wire. Force a length of wire into place. Cut it off, leaving about 3/4 inch to 1 inch sticking out and polish the end smooth and round. Nothing more is required. To clear the flash hole, simply run the wire through, pushing out fouling and debris.

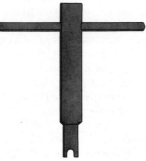

The T-handle nipple wrench will work in the closest quarters but lacks leverage and requires careful heat treatment if it is to hold together on tight nipples. I wouldn't try to make this type.

Any long gun other than the rifled musket and shotgun requires some sort of **bullet starter.** Once the ball is centered on the patch, it must first be pressed just below the muzzle so the patch can be cut off. Then it needs to be shoved several inches into the bore so the ramrod can be used with greater ease and safety. A seater for this purpose is easily made from scrap hardwood. Whittle a rough ball or knob that fits your hand comfortably, then drill two holes in it at right angles. Carve out a pair of short pegs just under bore diameter—or use commercial dowel—and glue them in the holes. Trim one very short, perhaps 1/4-inch to 1/2-inch long, and hollow its end to fit snugly over the ball. Trim the other to 1-1/2 inches or 2 inches and give it the same treatment. Give the completed starter a good coat of oil or stock finish, drill a hole through the ball, and string it on a thong for hanging around your neck or tying to your outfit.

A **patch knife** is essential unless you will *always* use pre-cut patches. And that is not likely. The best knives come with slightly curved blades sharpened on the inside of the curve. The edge is formed by beveling only one side of the blade leaving the other flat so as to slide smoothly across the muzzle.

Actually, any sharp knife will do for cutting patches. Old straight razor blades work very nicely. The accompanying drawing shows a patch knife easily made from a hacksaw blade in a few hours' time. The handle can be of any material, but the horn blanks available from the Dixie Gun Works suit me best.

The rifle can be loaded faster by means of a **loading block** than by any other method. Our drawings show

how simple this gadget is—a flat piece of hardwood (I prefer maple) with a row of drilled holes that fit patched balls snugly. On one side the holes should be concentrically enlarged to fit over the gun's muzzle, centering the patched ball over the bore. Strung on a thong, the loading block can be carried around your neck.

In use, you simply seat patched balls in each hole just as in the rifle muzzle. To load, the block is slipped over the muzzle and the long leg of the starter is used to drive the ball from block into barrel. This can be speeded up by stringing the starter to the block. The loading block may just as easily be of horn, metal, or plastic, but wood to match the gun's stock seems more appropriate.

A **capper** may look like a complicated gadget—more trouble than it's worth. And one that doesn't work will have you cussing a streak. Essentially, it's just a magazine for caps. An opening in one end exposes a single cap. Slip that cap down over the nipple, a twist of the wrist, and drop the capper back in bag or pocket. It's so much less trouble than fumbling in bag or pocket for loose caps, or trying to remove the lid from a tin box. Once you've tried a capper, you'll never want to be without one. They come in a variety of sizes and shapes, and to fit either plain or musket caps.

You *can* make a simple capper. Bend a sheet of thin brass into a square tube just large enough for free passage of the caps you'll be using. Slot and shape one end so that a cap sliding down will be held there, yet can be pulled free after being pressed over the nipple. Place a plastic follower block and *weak* coil spring in the tube and close the other end. I should point out that several suppliers offer good cappers for less than you'd pay for material to make one.

The **powder horn** was in its heyday during the time of the flintlock. When caplocks came into use, however, the patent charger flask became the accepted powder container. Today, many front-loading fans seem to prefer the horn, even though flasks are much simpler to use. The horn adds color, I guess.

Several suppliers offer new horns ready for use, but this is one item many shooters prefer to make them-

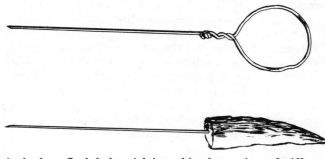

A nipple or flash-hole prick is nothing but a piece of stiff (preferably spring tempered) wire that can be forced through the hole to clear out debris. It can be either plain or fancy, as shown here, but it is quite simple to make in either case.

selves. Raw cowhorns can sometimes be obtained from farmers, ranchers, or slaughterhouses, but it's far simpler to order what you need from a mail-order supplier.

That smelly, rough-looking horn can be turned into as fine a powder carrier as you'd want, but it's going to take some work. First, it must be boiled to loosen the core and soften the shell. Unless you have a very broad-minded wife or housekeeper, do this outside— and downwind from the house. It will stink! After cooking, rap the open end on a hard surface and the core will pop out. With knife or glass, scrape the outer surface of the horn to remove the rough skin. Don't worry about getting it real smooth; just remove the outer layer completely.

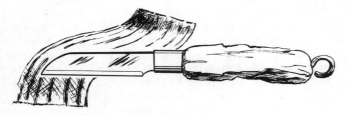

A patch knife is a necessity and blade should be beveled on one side only as shown here. The blade can be ground out of a piece of saw blade with little trouble.

Poke a wire up into the hollow, measuring to its end. Mark the end on the outside of the horn, then saw off the tip about 1/4-or 1/2-inch past that point. Use a fine-tooth hacksaw blade for a smooth cut. Save the cut-off tip. Drill a 1/4-inch or 5/16-inch hole into the hollow, centered in the cut-off face. With a round file and scrapers, taper this hole slightly, then carve a hardwood plug as shown to fit it snugly. The plug can be made perfectly plain, with just a knob or grip, or you can get real fancy. Some shooters prefer to make the plug from horn.

Trim off the large end of the horn squarely. The horn won't be very smooth inside so, if you like, you can now use scrapers, files and knives to clean up the roughness. Don't make the walls too thin near the opening or securing the base plug may be a problem.

Carefully shape a plug to fit the open base. It can be turned on a lathe, but the out-of-round opening may require boiling to soften in order to fit the plug. With the plug in place, secure it by driving in a ring of brass nails or small brass screws. Drill small pilot holes in both horn and plug to prevent splitting. The outside of the horn can now be left plain if you like. If so, carve a shallow groove around the neck and tie a thong there to which the plug can be secured. Then add another long thong or carrying strap at the same place, securing its other end at the base plug.

The cut-off horn tip should now be drilled with a cavity to hold just the proper charge for your favorite

The simplest form of true capper is this square tube fitted with a spring and follower and cut at the end to allow caps to be slipped in and out. Requires rather careful work to make.

rifle. Then drill a cross-hole through its end and loop a thong through. Secure it to the horn-carrying strap.

Much of the charm of older plain horns was due to the fact that they had been scraped almost paper thin, then polished to a high gloss, rendering them somewhat translucent. The powder level could be seen by simply holding them up to the light. This was for practical as well as esthetic reasons, since it made the horn lighter and smaller.

You can achieve the same results by slow, careful scraping and sanding. Care must be taken to keep the wall thickness as uniform as possible. An old plane blade or piece of saw blade makes an excellent scraper, but broken glass will do nicely if handled carefully. When the walls are thin enough to suit you, cross-polish in bootblack fashion with strips of fine abrasive cloth. This will remove all scraper marks. Then wet-sand with the grain of the horn to remove cross-polishing marks. Finish up with the finest grit wet-or-dry paper you can find. Final polishing is best done on a soft muslin wheel, but lacking that, rottenstone and oil rubbed by hand will do the job—it just takes much longer. A felt pad charged with any very fine abrasive also works well.

That's the plain, traditional horn. Maybe you'd like a horn with a charger spout like those on powder flasks. No problem. Simply obtain a flask head from a supplier such as the Dixie Gun Works, and then choose a raw horn that can be cut near its small end to accept the head assembly.

Measure head and horn carefully and saw off the latter squarely at a point where the head can be fitted snugly in place. Actually, the horn walls will be thick enough to allow considerable handfitting. The horn may have to be boiled to soften it, then rounded by driving in a wood plug of the proper diameter. When cold, the horn will hold its new shape and the circular head may be easily fitted.

With the head carefully seated in the horn, drill and tap holes for the securing screws. Use at least four screws or, better yet, six. If you're lazy, use epoxy adhesive. To be really high-class, thread both head and horn, and then screw them together.

Flat pocket horns are sometimes more convenient and aren't difficult to make. Select a horn that curves only in one direction (no twist) and boil until very soft. Place it between two stiff flat boards and compress it in a heavy vise until the horn is as flat as desired. If a big-enough vise isn't available, use large C-clamps or

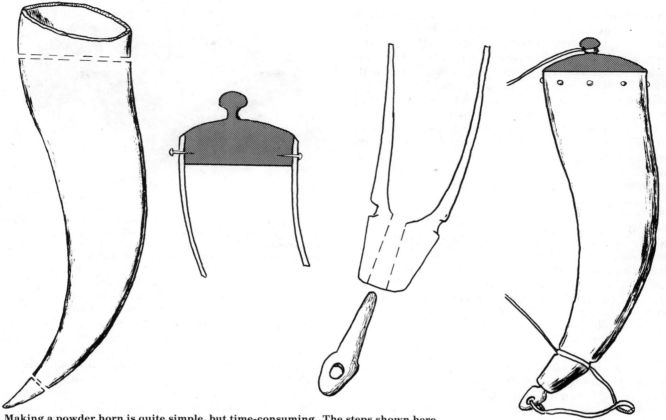

Making a powder horn is quite simple, but time-consuming. The steps shown here (left to right) are all that are needed to turn out a perfectly serviceable horn in a couple of evenings.

weights to apply the pressure.

Leave the horn under pressure until completely cold and *dry*. If taken out too soon, it will assume some of its original shape. Once the flattened shape is achieved, all other steps remain the same. I particularly like a small, pocket-size flat horn for flintlock priming powder. Incidentally, percussion caps were once carried in small horns with a mouth just large enough to let one cap out at a time.

A powder horn can be decorated in a number of ways. The most common is carving or burning one's name or simple designs upon it. We leave this step to your imagination and initiative.

The **powder flask** with charger spout is the most convenient way I know to carry powder ready for use. Both modern designs and reproductions of traditional measures are readily available, but it's fun to make one. If you're really handy and have a well-equipped shop, you can make the whole works. But, I prefer to buy the charger head, then make the body and put everything together.

The simplest design is the tubular or cannister body shown. Get brass or copper tubing of a diameter to fit the head and cut it to length. Solder or rivet in a base disc, then attach the head with screws or solder.

Epoxy cement will do as well, but it may seem too modern to use on a powder flask. Such a flask can be ornamented by cutting designs out of matching or contrasting metal and soldering or riveting them in place. Eagles and bears look good. If tubing of the proper size isn't handy, roll sheet metal into a tube and solder or braze the seam. A carefully-made lap joint can be "feathered" with a file so as not to break the smooth radius of the tube.

Other flask shapes can be made, but require more patience than I possess. A female die of the shape you want can be carved in a hardwood block. Very soft, rather thick copper sheet can then be carefully pounded into the shape of the die. Two halves are produced this way, then trimmed and soldered together to form the body. I haven't done it, but this is what I'm told by fellows who have.

Some sort of **measure** is necessary to get the right powder charge into your gun. Naturally you can't just pour from the horn and get the same charge twice. One of the simplest measures is a large-caliber center-fire cartridge case shortened to hold the right amount. More in keeping with tradition is the cowhorn tip hollowed out as previously described. A simple adjustable measure can be made from any convenient piece of tubing. A sliding plug is made to fit inside it and is held in place by a setscrew. Ideal are the adjustable metering chambers furnished with the Belding & Mull and Redding-Hunter standard powder measures. They are sturdy tubes fitted with threaded plugs and jam nuts. Several sources also offer adjustable brass measures combining a funnel to simplify pouring the charge into the muzzle.

Good muzzle-loader **cleaning rods**—wiping sticks—aren't easy to find. I prefer a very stiff, sturdy rod of hardened steel. Traditional wood rods and light metal ones pick up grit and dirt and often bend enough to rub on the bore. Soft iron barrels of some guns can be badly worn in this way.

The best rod is a length of hardened, ground drill rod, drilled and tapped at one end to accept standard accessory tips. The other end should be fitted with a ball-bearing swivel handle. An old roller skate wheel makes a good handle. Thread the end of the rod and run a lock nut on it. Add the wheel, then another lock nut, and clamp the inner portion of the wheel tightly between the nuts. This leaves the rim of the wheel free to rotate independently of the rod. The handle may be used as is, but is improved by addition of a hand loop bent from 1/4 inch or heavier rod. It can either be welded or threaded in place. I'll admit that modern fiberglas rods are quite good, and you won't go wrong using them; but, personally, I still like steel.

A **breech cover** isn't seen too often. One type is a leather hood that completely encloses the hammer and nipple area. Its purpose is to keep rain, snow, and dust or dirt off that part of the gun. If you're hunting in lousy weather, such a cover can prevent misfires. It is made as shown in the accompanying drawings. Pulling the securing thong allows it to open up and fall clear of the lock instantly.

The traditional wood ramrod (center) is preferred by traditionalists but is not nearly as durable or as reliable as the fiberglass loading rod at top, or the old-style steel rod at bottom. Ramrods to be carried on the gun must of necessity be rather small in diameter to avoid making the gun cumbersome; however, rods to be used purely for loading on the range should be only slightly under bore diameter.

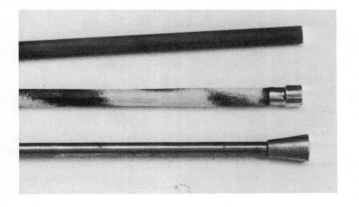

You'll never need a spring device until you try to remove or replace a mainspring—and then it will become very important. This is an original, made for military use, and models are still available from several suppliers.

The other type covers the barrel and stock in the vicinity of the nipple which sticks up through a hole. This cover's purpose is to prevent flame, cap fragments and powder fouling from scarring up the wood and metal near the nipple. This gadget is simply a strip of leather laced over barrel and stock, and with a hole through which the nipple protrudes.

Nipple protectors serve two purposes and a good one can be whipped into shape in a moment or two. A piece of fairly thick (not sole thickness, however) leather is shaped as shown—sort of a "dumbbell" shape. Punch a hole in one end to slip tightly over either the nipple itself or the hammer nose. To perform its function, the solid end of the leather strip is placed over the nipple and the hammer lowered fully upon it.

This protects the nipple in storage or carrying and also seals the nipple passage tightly as mentioned in the various loading instructions. Another type of protector can be made in the form of a snug-fitting brass or copper cup that fits over the nipple. It may be attached to a screw or staple in stock or lock plate by a length of small chain.

A **hunting bag** somehow seems to make you feel better equipped for muzzle loading afield. It isn't that all the shooting paraphernalia can't be carried on your person or in your pockets, it's just that the bag "fits" with the gun. There are several places you can buy a ready-made bag, but the one shown in the accompanying drawing can be put together in a single evening. The front, bottom and cover are a single piece; the two ends are separate.

The most commonly used bag material is buckskin, but calf tanned with the hair on also looks rather nice. The choice is yours; even canvas isn't bad. Simply cut the pieces as shown in the drawing and sew them together. If you want to be real frontiersy, punch holes with an awl (which was a vital part of every mountain

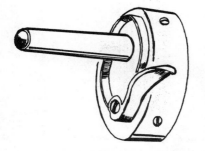
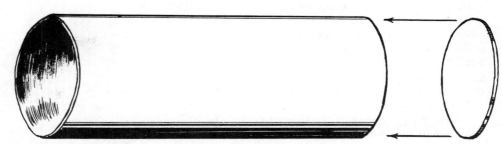

This modern-style tubular powder flask is easily made in a couple of hours. Only sheet brass or tubing and a ready-made head are needed.

man's gear) and do the job with thin thongs. A more practical approach is to have your local shoe repair shop do the job on a sewing machine. Don't try it on your wife's machine or you'll break a needle and upset her. Attach a closing strap and a shoulder strap—the basic job is done.

The hunting bag must be plentifully supplied with pockets. You can carry everything loose inside if you like, but fumbling for just the item you want will add new words to your profane vocabulary. All this can be avoided by sewing loops and pockets on the inside for nipple wrench, nipple prick, patch knife, can of extra patches, balls, capper or can of caps, and whatever else you use. When you're finished, there'll be a place for every item and you can grab what you need in an instant.

Hunting bags can wind up as fancy as you like. We've seen some that were completely covered with beadwork in Indian style and enough fringe to dress a belly dancer—representing a year's spare-time work. They were pretty, but even so, the simple buckskin outfit you put together in a single evening will be quite as convenient.

Should you become interested in bench-rest shooting with either slug gun or round-ball rifle, you'll get highly irritated the first time the gun tumbles to the ground as it's being cleaned or loaded. If the gun gets damaged or the sights are knocked out of line, you'll really scream. If you simply lean the gun against the bench, sooner or later you'll be picking it up off the ground. Then, too, such a gun is heavy enough to smash your toes.

Yet this is easily avoided. If you use a portable bench and carry it to range and matches, it can be notched or pegged to provide a secure place for the rifle. But even this won't *ensure* that the gun won't skid away and fall while being cleaned or loaded. I much prefer a **loading clamp** which grips the barrel tightly enough to keep the gun in place even if some clod kicks it as he walks by.

Such a loading clamp is shown in the drawings. It can be permanently installed on your portable bench or clamped to permanent ones found at some ranges. Either way, make it from hardwood. Make the jaws to

fit the barrel and use an oversized wing nut to pull the jaws together. It's easy to turn out in a single evening, even with no more than a jackknife, saw, and hand drill. Pad the jaws with felt or leather if you like. Top-notch guns are vitually irreplaceable, so don't take a chance on a fall ruining one of yours.

The caplock revolver, too, can be a lot easier to handle if provided with a **loading stand.** The one shown is a basic design that can be adapted to almost any revolver or single-shot pistol with minor changes. Basically, it provides a socket for the gun butt, and a clamp for the barrel. Slip the gun in place, tighten the barrel clamp and the gun can't possibly get away from you nor does it matter much if you're interrupted

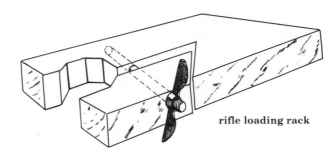

rifle loading rack

during loading. The gun will stay right there until you finish and no powder will be spilled.

This loading stand can be screwed permanently to your own portable or private bench, but we prefer to fit it with a broad plywood base and use a heavy C-clamp to tie it firmly to whatever bench is being used. Properly built and fitted to the gun(s), it won't budge, even when you are ramming oversized balls or conical bullets.

Patch cutters are a big convenience for the round-ball rifle. They are also quite simple to make. The easiest way to turn one out is to get a three- or four-inch piece of pipe with an inside diameter the same as the patch you want. File or grind one end from the outside only to produce a sharp edge. Finish by stoning or polishing and *keep it sharp.* A **wadcutter** for scatterguns or felt revolver wads is made in exactly the same manner.

In use, simply place several layers of patch material over a piece of cardboard on the end grain of a 4 x 4 or similar timber set on a solid rest. Bring the cutter against the patch material, and then give it a good whack with a wood or plastic mallet. It will cut cleanly through. The material and the patches may be pushed out with a dowel or rod. Standard shotshell wadcutters work very well for cutting small round patches and are used in the same way.

Paper cross patches are made with the same type of cutter, but there's no ready-made pipe for the job. You'll have to take a large-diameter piece of steel bar and laboriously saw, file and drill to produce cutting edges of the proper size and shape. There's no short cut for this job, so have at it. Personally, I don't own one. I save the trouble by using simple two- or

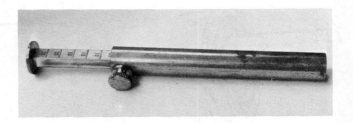

A simple, adjustable brass-powder measure such as this is a great convenience. It offers greater versatility than the one-charge spout of most powder flasks, and is the choice of many shooters for use with a powder horn.

Magazine cappers come in many forms, the most massive and durable of which is this model made only for the large, flanged "top-hat" musket caps.

A tompion is strictly a military device, originally supplied with each musket and intended to be used as a plug to keep out dirt. It's a handy gadget and costs little.

three-strip patches which are easily cut with knife and straightedge or metal template.

The dyed-in-the-wool muzzle-loading buff will eventually envision himself decked out in moccasins, fringed buckskins and coonskin cap. And, if it makes him happy, there's no really valid reason he shouldn't have them. Of course, I don't recommend that you wear them when going to the bank to apply for a loan, but at other times . . .

Many black powder shooters do have full mountain-man regalia, while others settle for a fringed hunting shirt and a battered wide-brimmed hat. Any seamstress can put a shirt together for you since it's a simple, basic tunic cut from soft buckskin. Periodically someone will offer in a magazine advertisement to make such garments to order. Frankly, I recommend getting your shirt that way instead of trying to make it yourself.

A fringed and beaded buckskin carrying case for your rifle will dress up the den a lot. In basic form, nothing could be more simple to make. Fold over a length of skin into a long, slender envelope that will just accept the rifle. Sew across one end and up the side, leaving the case long enough so that the rifle butt protrudes just a few inches.

Traditionally this type case was slipped over the rifle to protect it from moisture and dirt. It wasn't used in the manner of today's case or saddle scabbard. The cased rifle was carried in the hand, not slung over one's back or saddle.

The case furnishes lots of room to display your skill at bead work and fringing. Boy scout and similar manuals go into such decorative techniques in detail, so there's little reason for exploring them here.

I don't pretend that this has been a complete list of muzzle-loading accessories—or that the instructions for their fabrication couldn't be more detailed. I could have written a full book on powder horns and flasks alone, but then there wouldn't be room for all the other things of even greater interest.

Nevertheless, accessories are essential to the enjoyment, if not the bare operation, of muzzle-loading arms. Give some of the foregoing suggestions a try and I think you'll agree.

13/So You Want to Build Your Own Black Powder Gun

It might be said, I suppose, that there are roughly three types of black powder shooters wandering loose (sometimes much to the chagrin and embarrassment of wives and other close relatives) around the country. We've got the purist—the fellow who seeks only to shoot exactly the same equipment carried by his forefathers and to copy their methods precisely. This fellow would rather not shoot at all than to use anything less than a genuine Hawken or other fine original piece, Curtis and Harvey "Diamond Grain" powder, genuine split buckskin patches and everything else just exactly as it might have been found on the frontier. The individual who does this will certainly spend one hell of a lot of money for original pieces in fine shooting condition and, frankly, he will depreciate their value by shooting them. And, if the truth be known, his results on target may very well turn out to be less satisfactory than those obtained by the individual who is willing to take some advantage of present-day technology. This shooter may even go so far as to cast his bullets in the fireplace, read by candlelight and demand that his wife chew buckskin and serve Indian pudding on feast days.

Then we have the fellow who will spend hundreds and hundreds of dollars to make or have made the finest *modern* muzzle-loading arm that today's technology can produce. He cares not one whit what the resulting gun looks like and, in fact, it may resemble a piece of sewer pipe bolted to a railroad tie. But its bore and other critical components will be produced to unbelievably fine tolerances from the finest materials that money can buy. This type of shooter is a "perfectionist," as opposed to the "purist" mentioned above. His interest is purely in accuracy and nothing whatsoever may be allowed to stand in the way of achieving the smallest group. He particularly delights in producing a modern muzzle loader that will exceed the highest degrees of performance ever obtained by original arms of the muzzle-loading period. Buckskin and powder horn mean nothing to this fellow.

The purist and the perfectionist are more often than not monied professional men who can afford to take their preferred approaches to this grand game. Unfortunately, most of us do not fall into their income brackets. We make up the third class of front-loading shooters that must get the most shooting pleasure from every dollar we can scrounge out of the grocery money. I guess you might call us the "fun" shooters. We are neither purists nor perfectionists, nor do we get so deadly serious about the game that it starts giving us ulcers instead of curing them.

Handsome, accurate and durable muzzle loaders can be had for as little as $100 today. It is a matter of record that Hopkins and Allen Under-striker Caplock Rifles, manufactured by Numrich Arms and sold in this price range, have repeatedly wiped the eyes of shooters using custom-made or original arms worth the price of a new Volkswagen. This doesn't mean that the Hopkins and Allen is the best gun available, or the only one in this class, but is stated simply to show that there are low-priced guns that will allow the black powder buff of moderate means to compete with the Eldorado and Continental drivers. Black powder buffs, like most other gun enthusiasts, usually take pride in improvising and in being able to make what they can't or don't wish to buy. Consequently, you'll find many a Kentucky or Match rifle proudly displayed as the handiwork of its owner-shooter. Some of these lads are machinists or toolmakers and they've made every cotton-pickin' piece of that gun with their own two hands—just as did the frontier riflesmith of the 18th century.

Producing a gun by this means demonstrates a remarkable degree of skill, patience and perseverance that I, for one, do not possess. It also requires a fairly extensive shop setup most of us don't have and can't afford. The average shooter simply does not have the time, skill or patience to sit down with files, chisels, drill and hammer—nothing more, mind you—and carve the individual parts of a complete lock out of bar steel.

However, this doesn't mean that you or I cannot "make" a rifle (or pistol or shotgun, for that matter) from parts and materials that are readily available at reasonable prices. If you are reasonably handy with tools and fairly well supplied with patience—not to mention an understanding wife who will sit idly by while you ignore her for hours on end—you can put together in a single winter's long evenings a brand, spanking new rifle with which to start the spring shooting season.

How? Well, you can buy a lock, finished or as a semi-finished kit, from one supplier; a rifled, but otherwise unfinished, barrel from another; a maple plank from somewhere else; and miscellaneous pins, screws, hardware and sheet brass from the local hardware store. Then you can set about finishing each of these individual components and fitting them together into a complete gun. But there's an easier way. And, frankly, I strongly recommend it for your first gunmaking project. In this day and age, we are besieged with kits from which we can make almost everything from a picture frame to a 36-foot cabin cruiser. The black powder buff hasn't been ignored. Various kits are available, containing all the essential components to produce a comely and accurate cap-lock or flintlock rifle. Probably the major supplier of this type of kit is Dixie Gun Works, under the tutelage of Turner Kirkland, a gentleman and a scholar who searches the world over to stock his warehouses with virtually every black powder shooting item one can imagine.

To illustrate the manner in which you may make your own "Kentucky" rifle, I've selected the Dixie

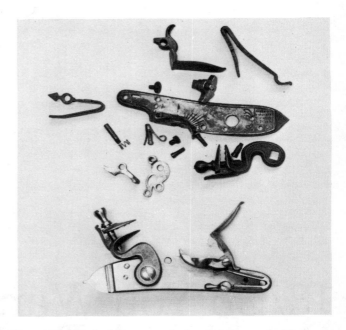

You may take the kit approach about as far as you like. Here is the complete lock supplied with the Dixie Kentucky Rifle Kit and alongside it is a lock kit also supplied by Dixie Gun Works for those who want to do a bit more of the work themselves. The lock kit is composed of all the completed parts necessary for the entire assembly, but does require some cleaning-up, tuning and fitting for best performance.

Gun Works Kentucky Rifle Kit, patterned after the flintlock rifles produced by early 18th century German gunsmiths in Pennsylvania. It is worth mentioning here that this kit may be had in either flintlock form or the simpler percussion type of a century later. The two are identical except for the ignition system.

The Dixie Kentucky kit arrives in a box somewhat longer than my red-headed secretary is tall. Opening it, you'll find that it contains the following:

    rifled octagonal barrel threaded for breech plug
    breech plug
    semi-finished maple stock
    complete lock
    trigger and trigger plate
    cast brass trigger guard and butt plate
    ramrod with fittings and thimbles
    sights
    miscellaneous pins, screws and small parts
    a complete set of illustrated instructions

This is everything you need to finish—with hand tools only—a complete Kentucky rifle that is capable of shooting fully as well as those turned out by the frontier smiths of yore. Assuming, of course, that you do your job properly.

Where do you begin? Simply examine all parts carefully and refer to your books and references until you are completely familiar with each and every part, its location and relationship with the others and its

As received, the barrel inletting is just very slightly too narrow for the barrel. It may appear that the barrel can be forced into its channel, and it probably can; but if this is done without first widening the channel properly, the stock will surely split.

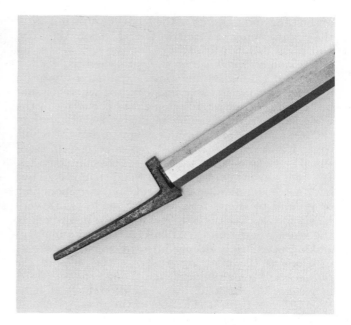

When the breech plug and its integral tang are screwed into the barrel, you'll notice the upper surface of the tang extends well beyond the top flat of the barrel. Eventually the excess must be dressed off, but this need not be done until inletting is completed or at least well under way. However, the sides of the tang should be filed smooth and tapered slightly inward before inletting begins.

function in the completed arm. The one thing you *cannot* afford to do is to rush madly in with mallet and chisel and expect to complete the job in an evening or two. Even if you are an expert with tools, remember that this is an unfamiliar job, and you'd best take it easy if you want to be able to brag about the results.

First comes inletting the barrel into the stock. The stock is already roughly shaped to the proper external configuration and has a very slightly undersized groove machined to accept the octagonal barrel. Drop the barrel into the slot and push it as far to the rear as it will go without riding up out of the slot. At this point, you will begin to get an idea of the amount of wood that must be removed.

Back up a bit now and take the rough breech plug and screw it fully home into the threaded end of the barrel. This is best done by clamping the barrel in padded vise jaws and fitting a smooth-jawed adjustable wrench on the widest portion of the breech plug. Actually, a breech plug wrench is best for the job, but with care you can get by without it. If the plug appears to be too tight in the barrel, a bit of white lead applied to the threads will ease its passage. Screwed all the way in, the flat upper surface of the breech plug should be parallel with one of the barrel flats. While with a flintlock it doesn't really matter which flat, a more workmanlike job will result if it is the one bearing the trademark and caliber marking. If the

plug does not draw up into proper alignment with a flat, very carefully file a minute amount of metal off either the barrel or the breech plug until proper alignment is achieved when the plug is turned in very tightly. Leave the plug in place.

However, if your project is percussion lock, the plug must draw up so that the bolster extends to the right horizontally and parallel to the top of the breech plug and tang.

At this point, take your files and true up the two sides of the plug and its tang. At the same time, shape the rear of the tang to your liking, using the illustrations or pictures in your references as a guide. If at this point you taper the sides of the plug and tang *very* slightly inward toward the bottom, it will be easier to get a good fit in the stock.

Now lay the barrel tang uppermost in the stock and slide it fully to the rear. Take a sharp pencil and mark around the tang. With a sharp-pointed knife, cut about 1/16-inch deep just inside the pencil mark you have made. Using a narrow (1/4-inch) chisel, remove the wood about 1/16-inch deep inside your incised line.

Before proceeding further, you'll have to have some means of knowing just where further wood must be removed to allow the metal to seat properly. So, emulate your forefathers by firing up a smoky candle and applying a coat of soot on the bottom and sides of the tang and as much of the barrel as does not enter the channel snugly. Place the barrel back in the wood and press it down firmly so that the soot leaves an impression on the wood at all contact points.

Lift out the barrel and slowly and carefully begin peeling off very thin shavings of wood wherever soot has clung. Take care you don't mar the edges of the wood as you work, making gaps that will show up in the completed job. Right now, you can ruin the whole thing by being in a hurry. Keep your chisels razor sharp and remove only the thinnest possible shavings. It's a lot easier to cut out more wood than it is to put back some you didn't mean to take out. Scrapers filed or ground to shape from old saw blades work very nicely for this. After the barrel has been in and out of the stock a few times, you will see that the metal is sinking perceptibly deeper into the wood. A word of caution—as the inletting proceeds, the sides of the recesses will remain black, even though the metal fits in easily. *Do not* tear away additional wood here. Wood-to-metal fit at the sides of the tang and barrel should be as snug as you can possibly keep them. Remove wood only from the bottom of the recesses. Under no circumstances attempt to pry wood out by levering the chisel against the edges of the recess. This will certainly spoil the much-desired close fit. Continue this process until sufficient wood has been removed under the tang and rear of the barrel to allow the entire length of the bottom flat of the barrel to lie smoothly against the precut channel.

As inletting progresses, you will encounter no difficulty with the flintlock gun. However, if you are using the percussion version, the bolster will eventually contact the wood. When it does, you will have to begin smoking it and inletting for it right along with the rest. If this is overlooked, the bolster bearing against the wood will throw the barrel out of alignment and louse up your entire inletting job.

The reinforced portion of the breech plug should make full, firm contact with the wood. If you've been sloppy and it doesn't, fill in with bedding compound as outlined in the chapter dealing with repairs.

When the barrel and tang appear to be inletted uniformly to one half of the barrel diameter, very carefully smooth up all inletting cuts and remove all soot from both wood and metal. Scrapers work best for this. Sandpaper will tend to spoil the clean, sharp wood-to-metal contact you've worked for so hard.

You may discover that the tang is seated only very shallowly into the wood at its rear end. If this is the case, then very carefully bend the rear of the tang down and deepen the inletting to match. The tang should be at least 1/16-inch deep in the wood, but 1/8 inch is much better.

Even after this is accomplished, a fair amount of tang will protrude above both wood and barrel. With files or grinder remove the bulk of this surplus, keeping the top of the tang flat and parallel with the

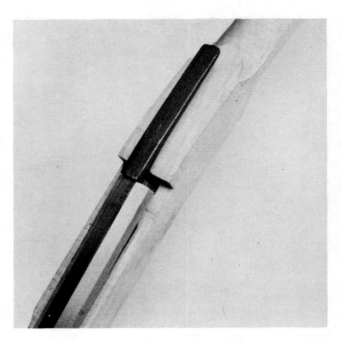

The barrel is laid in its groove and pressed as far rearward as it will go to show the approximate location of the tang recess. As inletting progresses, the barrel will move backward until its rear face is flush against the vertical wood surface.

top barrel flat at their junction, at the same time curving the rest gradually to match the curve of the stock. Leave about 1/64 inch of tang metal flush with the wood of the stock for careful finishing later.

We now need something to tie stock and barrel together while the lock and trigger are fitted which *must be done* before the tang screw (which is the most important fastening) can be fitted. Tenons (in the case of the Dixie kit, three) must be fitted to the bottom flat of the barrel. These tenons are rough castings which must be trued up with files, being careful to insure that their flat bases form straight male dovetails. Measure back 3 inches, 16 inches and 30 inches, respectively, from the muzzle and mark the bottom barrel flat. Using a scratch-awl, mark around each tenon at these positions, outlining a notch the width of the *smaller* end of the dovetail. Make vertical cuts with a hacksaw inside the outlined notches. Remove the excess metal with files, hand grinder or small cold chisel, and then clean up with files. Next, using a very small triangular file, undercut the edges of the notches so that the dovetail base of the tenon can be driven securely in place. The best file for this is a special dovetail file available from Brownell's. This is slow and exasperating work, and I know of no short-cuts. It is simply "cut and try" until the tenons fit the notches. Smoke the tenon bases to show where metal must come off. Should you inadvertently cut a notch a bit too large, its edges may be peened to close it up

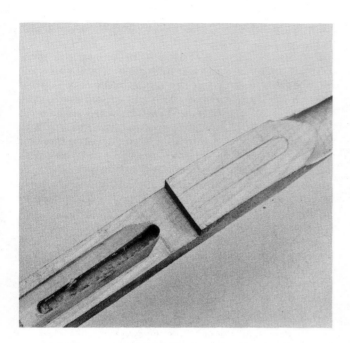

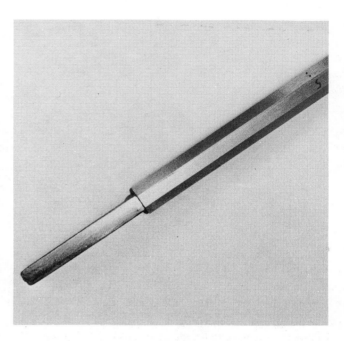

Before beginning any barrel and tang inletting, trace around the tang with the barrel held as far rearward in its channel as possible. This gives initial width and direction for the tang recess which must be cut as the barrel moves back and downward into the wood.

The tang has been filed down rather roughly until it is *nearly* flush with the top flat of the barrel. In this form, inletting may be completed; then the tang's upper surface is filed flush with the wood.

Where the inletting in the kit stock is nearly complete, it is simpler to sink the tang and breech plug first, then work the balance of the barrel down, more or less rotating about the tang position, until the barrel is half its depth into the stock full length. Note here that the protruding part of the breech plug has been filed flush with all eight barrel flats to avoid the necessity for any additional inletting cuts.

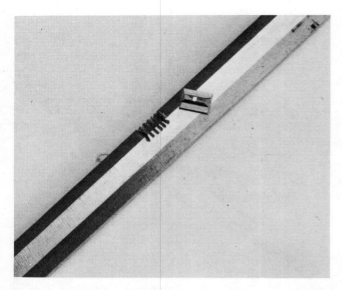

After marking the location of the barrel tenon dovetail, the first step in forming a hand-filed dovetail to accept the tenon is to make shallow, vertical saw cuts as shown. You *can* do the entire job with files, but the saw cuts greatly ease the job.

After the saw cuts have been made, hog out the excess metal with a coarse file; then use a dovetail file to clean up the edges and form the angled undercut at each end.

slightly, or solder may be used to help hold the tenon in place.

Personally, I consider this to be one of the most difficult operations in assembling the rifle. If you want to cheat just a little bit, the tenon bases may be filed smooth and flat, then carefully silver soldered to the bottom flat of the barrel. However, you will have to cut dovetails for the sights on top of the barrel, and without the practice gained in fitting the tenons, you will probably do a lousy job here. And it will be out in the open where everyone can see it. In the long run, it is best to go ahead and dovetail the tenons in place, gaining practice so you can do a workmanlike job in fitting the sights.

The sights can be fitted at this time or the job may be left for later. Take your pick. The upright portion of the rear sight should be 11-inches forward of the rear face of the barrel, and the forward edge of the front sight should be one inch back from the muzzle. Carefully cut and file the dovetail bases of the sights

Don't make the mistake of filing the dovetail too wide at first. As filing progresses, make the notch a bit wider on one side than the other and keep trying the tenon in the wider end. When the tenon will begin to enter, you may start straightening the edges so that the tenon may be driven in and held tightly. If by chance it does not appear completely solid, take a sharp-pointed punch and stake the barrel metal at either end of the dovetail.

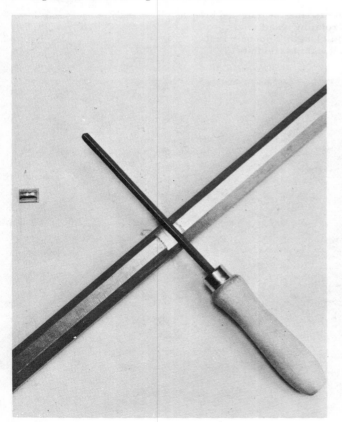

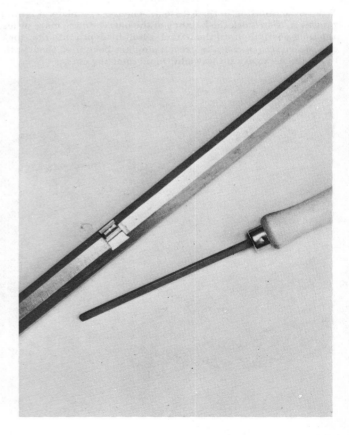

true, just as you did with the tenon. Mark the sight locations and very carefully saw and file the dovetails to shape. Take particular care to keep the bottom of the dovetails parallel with the barrel flat. Drive the sights into place; then file off the protruding portions of the bases to provide a neat appearance.

Now, to tie the barrel into the stock—carefully locate the tenon positions in the bottom of the barrel channel. Candle soot will help, so will careful measurement. Using a very narrow chisel, perhaps in conjunction with a small-diameter drill, inlet the tenons snugly into the bottom of the channel. They must be inletted deeply enough so that the barrel can rest solidly on the bottom of its channel.

Mark the approximate center of each tenon and by measuring from muzzle and top flat of barrel, locate drilling point on the stock. Seat the barrel in the stock, and secure it tightly in place with C-clamps or with wrappings of reinforced tape or strong cord.

If you will be using a drill press, align and clamp the

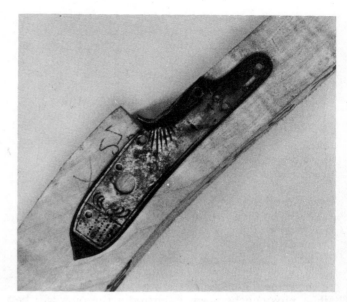

Initial positioning, outlining and inletting of the lock should be done with the stripped lock plate. This applies whether flint or percussion, for the internal parts will hold the plate too far away from the wood for proper fitting.

The inner side of the lock and the factory-machined, rough inletting in the stock. Note rough edges and splinters which must be cleaned up.

barrel and stock securely in place on its table so that the drill bit will pass squarely through stock and tenons. If the job is to be done by hand, then get someone else to stand off to the side and "eyeball" drill alignment as you proceed. The hole should be parallel to the top barrel flat and at right angles to the barrel's length. In any event, first drill through with a 1/16-inch diameter bit. The hole *must* pass through the tenon, though it need not cut the exact center. Drill all three holes, and then pull the barrel out and check to make certain each did pass through the tenon at an acceptable location. If you missed, you'll simply have to carefully plug the holes in the stock and start all over. Assuming the holes did pass through the tenons, take a 3/32-inch drill and open them up to finished size. Some slight correction can be made with the larger drill bit.

Barrel pins may be made from 6-penny finishing nails, or from brass wire or bronze or brass welding rod of the same diameter. If you want to be really fancy, silver pins can be used. Eventually the pins will be filed flush with the surface of the stock, but it isn't necessary to do that now. Simply drive the pins into place, thus securing the barrel solidly to the stock.

Next comes the inletting of the lock. First of all, check the outside edge of the lock plate to be certain that it is smooth and even. If it is not, or if there are burrs on it, clean up the entire perimeter with a smooth-cut file. A slight inward taper given the edges will facilitate inletting, but is not absolutely necessary.

The lock must be carefully aligned with the barrel. This really can't be accomplished properly unless you strip all internal parts from the lock plate. Do this

The sideplate may take many forms, from a single straight bar of brass to angular shapes such as this, or even a very ornate, serpentine form. The slotted bolt head seen at the center is that of the lock bolt; the other two are simply screws to secure the plate firmly in place. Normally, when there are two lock bolts, no additional fastening is needed.

carefully, and make certain you know which part goes back where, and in what order. An exploded view from one of your references can be a big help here.

If the gun is to be a flintlock, use a cleaning rod to measure the distance from the muzzle to the face of the breech plug. At this point, midway between upper and lower edges of the right vertical barrel flat, centerpunch for the vent hole. Now, lay the lock plate, with flash pan attached, on the side of the stock, positioning it so that the punch mark lies just above the bottom center of the pan. Maintaining this reference, position the lock plate so that its lines flow smoothly with those of the stock. Looking at a few pictures of original flintlocks will give you a feel for this positioning. Outline the lock plate on the wood with a sharp pointed pencil or scriber.

Inlet for the lock plate just as you did for the breech plug tang and rear part of the barrel. Work carefully and slowly until the plate is seated at least one half its thickness into the wood. At this point, assemble the internal parts to the lock plate and begin removing wood to allow them to seat in the stock as well. While a certain amount of clearance must be provided around the moving parts, removal of wood should be kept to the absolute minimum. Simply hogging out a huge hole—which is by far the easiest way of doing it—will seriously weaken the stock at a point not too strong at best. The lockwork recesses can be cut with nothing more than knives and chisels, but various-sized drill bits, even a hand grinder with rotary files, will speed up the work considerably. When room has been made for all of the internal lock parts, continue deepening the recesses until the outer surface of the flash pan seats solidly against the barrel flat at the vent center-punch mark.

During this final inletting, care should be taken to insure that the outer surface of the lock plate is parallel, both vertically and horizontally, with the right vertical flat of the barrel.

If you are working on a percussion gun, then lock alignment requires somewhat different treatment. Misfires, at best imperfect ignition, will result unless the hammer face strikes centrally and squarely upon the nipple. Strip the lock as before, but leave the hammer in place. Place the lock plate on the stock, and you will see that a half-round notch must be cut in the lock plate to clear the bolster. This is easily done with a round file or a hand grinder. As this notch is being cut, adjust its position so that the hammer face is aligned correctly with the nipple. The hammer face must meet the top of the nipple squarely. Once correct alignment is obtained, then outline the lock plate and proceed with the inletting as outlined above.

The lock is to be held in place by a screw entering from the *left* side of the stock. Some lock plates are drilled for this screw, others are not. If a drill press is available, drilling this screw hole properly is relatively easy. Remove the hammer and centerpunch the lock plate centrally in the reinforced portion between hammer and rear fence of flash pan. Level the lock plate on the drill press table, and drill through it squarely with a No. 21 drill. If no drill press is available, use a friend or two to eyeball the drill bit as squarely as possible.

Now replace the lock plate in the stock and either clamp or tape it solidly in place. Using the hole already drilled as a guide, drill through the stock with that same No. 21 drill. If the lock plate was inletted squarely into the stock and if the hole was drilled squarely in the lock plate, this hole will emerge on the left side of the stock at the proper location. Take the brass side plate and place it on the left side of the stock so that the round boss on its upper edge is centered over the hole just drilled. If this places the plate in roughly the location shown, everything is all right. If not, the hole should be plugged and redrilled at the proper angle. Centerpunch the boss on the side plate and drill through it with the No. 21 drill.

Next, take your files and very carefully clean up the edges of the side plate. If you feel like exercising your individuality by reshaping the outline of the plate somewhat, please feel free to do so. Pass that same No. 21 drill through the lock plate, stock and side plate next for a last check to make certain the hole is properly located and the side plate falls where it should. Remove both plates, and open up the hole in the stock with a No. 9 drill. Open up the hole in the side plate to the same diameter. If slight shifting of the side plate is necessary, it can be accomplished at this point by shifting hole location by filing it to the larger size.

Beg, borrow, steal or—as a last resort—buy a standard 10-32 tap and die set. Tap the hole in the lock plate full depth. Thread the end of the bolt blank with the 10-32 die. Make the threaded portion about 3/4-inch long. (Note: Some kits may be set up for a different thread size, so check.)

Replace the lock plate in the stock, and pass the threaded bolt through the side plate and the stock. Turn it into the lock plate sufficiently to draw the side plate up snugly against the stock. Adjust the position of the side plate on the stock, and then carefully outline and inlet it as you did the lock plate. Use the lock screw to draw the plate in as inletting progresses.

Since the brass is fairly soft, care must be exercised to insure that the ends of the side plate do not bend outward instead of seating evenly in the stock. The side plate may be inletted its full depth and filed flush with the wood of the stock, or it may be inletted only about one half its thickness and the edges filed to a pleasing bevel.

When the side plate has been fully inletted, cut off the excess of the bolt where it protrudes from the lock plate.

Now that the lock is fully inletted and secured solidly in place, recheck alignment of the vent hole

As final inletting progresses, the barrel moves downward into the stock while the lock moves inward from the right. In the case of a flintlock, the inner edge of the pan must butt up snugly against the right flat of the barrel as shown here. Drilling the vent should not take place until barrel and lock are matched up; then it should be drilled just above the bottom surface of the pan and centered therein.

punch mark with the flash pan. If any corrections are necessary, repunch properly. Drill into the barrel at the punch mark with a 3/32-inch bit. The hole should run parallel to the top and bottom barrel flats, but drift slightly forward at its inner end so that the full diameter of the hole is just barely forward of the breech plug face.

The trigger and tang screw are installed next. Draw a center line on the underside of the stock extending from the rear of the ramrod groove well past the rear of the lock plate. Centered on this line and beginning about 1/4-inch behind the position of the hammer screw, cut a vertical slot into the stock sufficiently wide to accept the flat upper portion of the trigger. Cut this slot deep enough to intersect the sear recess cut earlier from the right side. Positioning the trigger in this slot so that it will engage the sear approximately 1/8 to 3/16 inch from its rear edge, mark the outline of the trigger plate and continue inletting until the plate is almost flush with the wood. As the inletting progresses, take extra care to insure that the trigger remains vertical. As further inletting transpires, the lock will have to be removed because the sear will otherwise block progress of the trigger.

When the trigger plate is about 1/64 inch from being flush with the wood, stop the inletting and file down the rear portion of the trigger so that with the hammer cocked and the trigger plate fully seated, the trigger will just barely contact the sear. At this point, drill and countersink a hole in the rear of the trigger plate to accept a wood screw. Drill a pilot hole in the stock for this screw and turn it in solidly to hold the trigger plate in place.

Centerpunch the upper surface of the tang approximately 3/4 inch behind the rear face of the barrel.

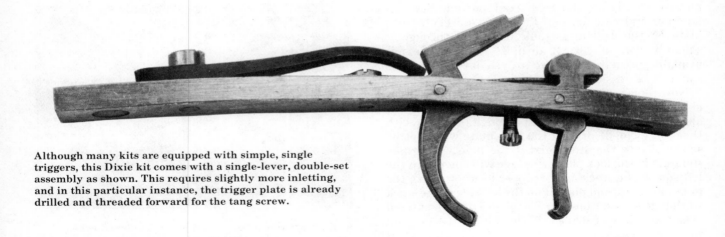

Although many kits are equipped with simple, single triggers, this Dixie kit comes with a single-lever, double-set assembly as shown. This requires slightly more inletting, and in this particular instance, the trigger plate is already drilled and threaded forward for the tang screw.

Once the lock has been inletted full depth, then the trigger plate is positioned on the underside of the stock, care being taken so that the trigger will make proper contact with the sear. This can be determined by viewing from the side; actually, there is usually a fair amount of latitude in trigger position, and 1/16 inch or so either way from the ideal will not affect the relationship noticeably.

Using eagle-eyed friends or a drill press, carefully run a No. 21 drill through the tang, stock and the reinforced forward portion of the trigger plate. Drill alignment is quite important here, for the trigger plate presents a rather small target. It is best to withdraw the drill as soon as you feel it touch the trigger plate. Then remove the plate and determine if the drill struck properly. If not, plug the hole in the stock and start over. If you go ahead and drill completely through the trigger plate and the hole is too far out of place, the plate must either be replaced or welded up. Once the hole is properly located through all three parts, tap the trigger plate for a 10-32 thread and thread the end of the blank tang screw the same for about three quarters of an inch. Open up the hole in the tang and stock with a No. 9 drill, insert the tang screw and turn it into the trigger plate securely. Assemble the lock to the stock, and make certain that the trigger will drop the hammer, yet is not bearing too heavily upon the sear. If all checks out properly, countersink the hole in the tang so that the head of the tang screw will be flush with its upper surface. Cut off the excess tang screw protruding from the trigger plate.

File the edges of the brass trigger guard that are to be inletted into the stock smooth and even. Also file the tenons of the trigger guard flat and straight. Position it over the trigger and trigger plate as shown, and then carefully mark around the tang portions to be inletted. Using the procedures already described, inlet both tenons and guard until tangs are very nearly flush with the surface of the wood. With the guard clamped or taped securely in place, drill through the stock and tenons, as was done on the barrel, and pin the guard in place.

At this stage of the game, you have a gun that will shoot! There is still one hell of a lot of work to be done to make it look and feel as a Kentucky should. But you have performed all of the operations necessary to convert that basketful of rough hardware into a shootable firearm. If you're like most do-it-yourself fans, you will not be able to resist dashing off to the range with powder horn and bullet pouch to see if everything works before putting in those many, many additional hours required to give the gun the polish and finish it now needs.

Actually, I can think of no single reason why you shouldn't shoot the gun at this stage; and, in fact, I feel it would be pretty hard to resist the temptations to do so. Keep in mind, however, that the raw, unprotected wood can easily be damaged (particularly at the toe of the stock) or badly stained by oil, grease or powder fouling. To avoid trouble in these areas, it is probably safer *not to* shoot the gun until it has been completely finished. Let your conscience be your guide.

The Dixie-kit stock is cut squarely across the butt and is not semi-inletted for the brass butt plate casting. Considerable wood must be removed, and the butt plate itself requires a lot of filing to shape.

The latter first. Carefully true up the plate where it will contact the wood. Keep all edges clean and square and both sides as identical as possible. While doing this, file or grind off the large casting "gate" on the side. This is simply superfluous metal formed there during the casting process.

With the face of the butt plate trued up, lay it in position on the butt of the stock and mark its position on the wood. Keep in mind that when installed and finished, the top line of the butt plate must be a smooth, clean continuation of the top line of the stock comb. With coping saw, band saw or what have you, hog off the bulk of the excess wood outside the marked position of the butt plate. Make the cuts perpendicular to the center line of the stock.

Get out your candle and your sharpest chisels again. Smoke the freshly filed surfaces of the butt plate, and begin spotting and inletting it just as you did the tang and breech plug. Probably the simplest method is to work the butt plate down and forward simultaneously until it is properly seated. Chisels must be kept *very* sharp as most of the cutting here is directly across the grain. While the wood may be cut straight across, a far more secure fit of the butt plate is obtained if wood is left to fill the hollows in the plate. As inletting progresses, tapping the plate with a rubber or rawhide mallet will produce better soot impressions. Throughout the operation, keep the wood in as intimate contact with the metal of the plate as possible. There is always the temptation to simply maintain firm, clean contact at the outer edge only, hogging out the rest of the wood. If this is done, then large gaps will show up when wood and metal are dressed down to their final shape.

Once the butt plate is fully inletted, clamp it securely in place and centerpunch a hole location 1/2-inch back from the front end of the top strap. Drill through the brass and at least an inch into the wood with a 3/32-inch drill. Obtain a solid brass countersink wood screw, preferably about 1-1/2 x 9 size. Open up the hole in the brass to accept the shank of the screw and countersink to accept the screwhead flush with the surface of the plate. If run slowly, a standard combination "screw drill" may be used to do the entire job in one operation—pilot hole in wood, clearance hole in plate and countersink. Turn the brass screw in tightly. If difficulty is encountered in turning it into the hard maple of the stock, apply a little soap to the threads or open the pilot hole slightly.

Centerpunch another screw hole slightly below center of the butt-plate arch. Drill and countersink here for a much larger, solid brass screw and turn it into place. With both screws turned in tightly, check wood-to-metal fit. If any gaps have developed, remove the plate and carefully trim the inletting until a perfect fit is obtained. After this is done, if you really want a first-class job, "regulate" the screws so that the slots in their heads run vertically. This can be done by very carefully deepening the countersink holes until the slots will come vertical as the screw is turned in tightly.

Brass furniture castings come in all forms, from almost-finished investment castings to rough sand castings such as this butt plate. Rough as this piece appears, finishing isn't really that difficult. Even with only an assortment of files, the excess may be cut away quickly to produce clean, smooth surfaces. If you happen to have access to a belt sander, the job will proceed considerably faster.

Get your files out again and carefully dress the excess brass down flush with the wood. Be very careful not to taper the brass backward but, rather, make it a straight continuation of the stock lines. It may be that at some points wood will overhang brass, but ignore this for the moment.

Using pictures of original guns as a guide, use files and fine-cut wood rasp to bring the stock and butt plate to the desired cross section. Having accomplished this, use files and coarse abrasive cloth wrapped around shaped pieces of hardwood to clean all casting marks from the rear face of the butt plate. Use care to insure that the flat edges of the plate are identical on both sides. Don't carry the arch deeper on one side than the other. This shaping operation is carried directly across the screwheads, dressing them flush with the surface of the plate. Try to produce a smooth, even surface free of waves and humps or hollows. Graceful curves are a characteristic of the Kentucky rifle and you don't want to louse them up at this stage of the game. Final polishing to a mirror-bright surface is best saved until later when the last finishing touches are being applied.

Careful trimming and shaping of the already-inletted trigger guard is next in order. Using small flat and half-round files, remove all mold parting lines inside and outside the guard. Then clean all mold roughness off the inside. A more attractive appearance will result if the cleaned surfaces are slightly rounded, not left flat. Take your skinniest three-cornered files and work carefully into all the notches and joint areas to produce clean, bright brass surfaces. With a fine-cut file, carefully shape the outer edges of the guard. Some trouble can be saved here if a template is made to insure that both sides of the guard will be shaped exactly. Keep the filed edges vertical. Again, use pictures or original guns to guide you.

Begin filing across the outer surfaces of the guard to remove all mold and casting marks and to arch the surface. Leave the guard as thick as practicable while producing a clean, bright surface. Be particularly careful that the smooth flowing curves are not distorted by this filing. Maintaining the arched cross section, thin out the outer edges of the guard, bringing them to a small radius, not a *sharp* edge. Along with this dressing of the guard, file down the front and rear tangs (the inletted portions) flush with the surface of the wood. If any difficulty is encountered in keeping the tangs seated solidly in the wood, install small, solid brass wood screws and give them the same treatment as those used to secure the butt plate.

This is as good a time as any to fit and finish the ramrod. The Dixie-kit stock has a predrilled ramrod channel. The rod blank is slightly oversized for the

Because it is so easy to work with files on brass, that rough casting can be converted rather quickly to the finished butt plate shown on this rifle.

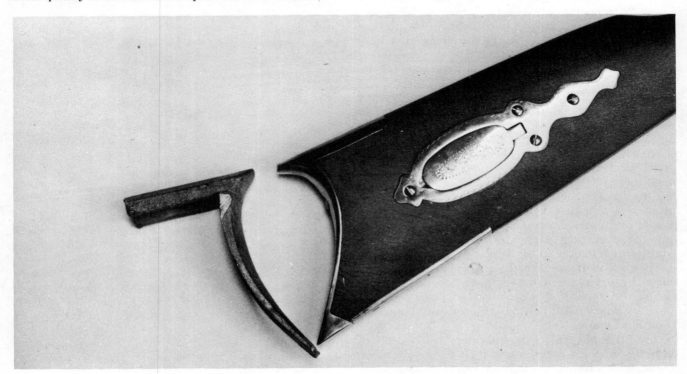

rear portion of the channel. Lightly sand the entire rod, applying a little effort on the end that is to fit into the hole at the rear of the channel. The inside of this hole may also be smoothed considerably by wrapping steel wool around a brass bore brush of the proper diameter and working it in and out of the hole vigorously on the end of a conventional cleaning rod. Having smoothed the rod well, carefully sand the channel full length so that the rod fits freely. A neater job can be done if fine-grit paper is wrapped around a smaller dowel and worked back and forth in the channel. This will avoid rounding the channel edges, as is sure to occur with hand sanding.

Three ramrod pipes formed from sheet brass are furnished. The two identical ones fit into the open groove with their front ends 4 inches and 14 inches, respectively, from the tip of the stock. The third one, with its extension piece, fits at the point where the groove becomes a hole. Carefully inlet the first two pipes until they are seated so that their bores form a continuation of the ramrod groove. The most work-manlike job results if the thimble flanges are soldered together and inletted to full wood-metal contact. However, the job can be simplified considerably by leaving the pipes as is, and simply cutting V-section notches as shown. Regardless of the method used, when the thimble is inletted to the proper depth, drill

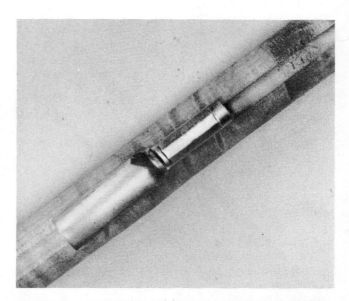

Here we have the rear ferrule or pipe for the ramrod loosely in the position it must occupy. The pipe portion is easily inletted just like the other pipes, but as it enters the wood, the thin, curved, rearward extension must also be fitted very carefully. In this Kentucky example, both the ramrod pipe and the sheet-brass nose cap are pinned into place.

The same guard after less than ten minutes of filing on the roughest parts—the bow and the front tang—which has cleaned up the surface and given it the proper shape. All the casting marks and roughness have been cleaned up, and relatively little effort will now be required to give it a polished surface.

Here we have a cast brass trigger guard as encountered in the kit. It looks rather rough and might give the impression that you'll never make it look right. However, the brass is soft and files quickly and easily.

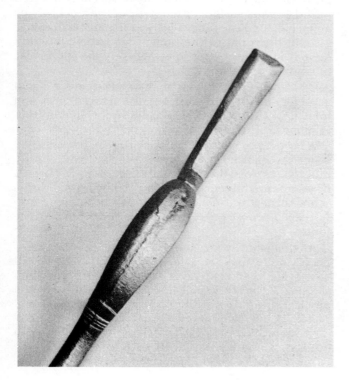

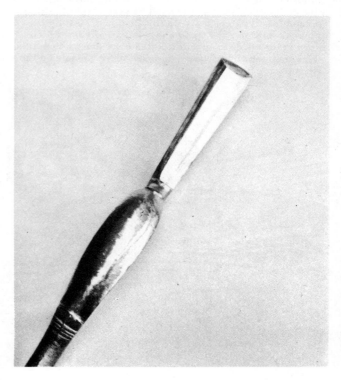

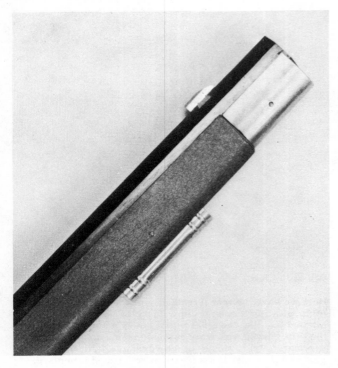

Old-time rifles often had the nose cap cast in place around a reduced portion of the stock from molten pewter or silver. If your fitting job leaves the cap a bit loose, add a few strategic dabs of glass bedding compound.

The rear ramrod pipe has a curved extension which reinforces the stock wood at its thinnest part over the ramrod hole. This extension must be very carefully fitted and not inletted too deeply. In this instance, most of its thickness is above the wood and it has simply been filed down at the edges to appear inletted more deeply than it is. The pin on the right secures the pipe, while the one on the left holds the barrel.

a 3/32-inch diameter hole through stock and pipe flange and drive in a pin identical to those used to secure the barrel.

The rear pipe presents a somewhat different inletting exercise. Its forward portion must first be inletted part way just as the others. As this inletting progresses, the thimble extension must be carefully bent and shaped to the same contour as the bulge of the stock. Once this is accomplished, then inletting is continued until the pipe bore is properly aligned with the ramrod and the extension is inletted its full depth into the wood. If the extension is reluctant to stay down in its recess, secure with a small brass screw and file the head flush.

At this point, try the ramrod blank in the thimbles to make certain that it may be easily pressed into place and withdrawn, yet is not so loose that it will slide out of its own weight when the muzzle of the completed gun is lowered. A threaded brass tip is supplied for the rod. Carefully file or carve a tenon on the tapered end of the rod to fit the recess in this tip. Secure a snug fit and make certain that the tip is properly in line with the rod; we don't want it pointing off toward the south forty. The traditionalist will want to pin or crimp this tip into place, but a simpler and equally effective method of securing it to the rod is the use of a small amount of epoxy cement. A steel worm threaded to fit the tip is furnished and other accessory tips may be purchased. Taper the rod carefully down to tip diameter.

A brass shield-shaped name or initial plate is supplied with the Dixie kit. This may be carefully inletted into the upper surface of the wrist of the stock, about an inch behind the tang. The traditionalist will solder a small brass pin to the underside of this plate and drive it into place after inletting. But the epoxy just mentioned works quite well.

On the other hand, you might want to order a gold or silver shield with your initials engraved on it and inlet it in the stock. Such shields are available from Hinman Outfitters.

A nose cap is not supplied with the kit, but one may be purchased from any of several sources and carefully inletted, as was the butt plate. Most do-it-yourself nose caps are intended to be secured by a small brass screw turned in from inside the barrel channel. Carefully file the nose cap metal flush with the wood of the forend.

At this point, your Kentucky has everything on it necessary to make it safe, durable and reliable. All that remains to be done is careful sanding and final shaping of the stock, polishing of the metal parts and application of an external finish to both wood and metal. It may be, however, that you wish to apply decorative inlays and/or a patch box that will be both decorative and utilitarian. If such is the case, these items should be carefully formed and inletted before

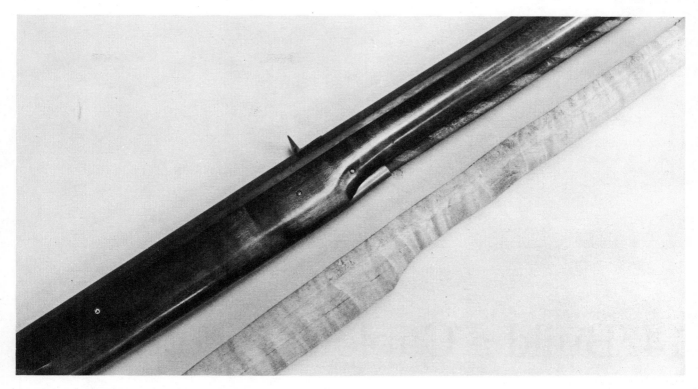

The kit stock below the completed stock easily takes on its appearance if you work slowly and patiently. There is very little wood to remove, the process being mainly one of smoothing and polishing.

final shaping and sanding of the stock. It is worthy of mention, however, that most people feel a Kentucky rifle is rather naked without at least some decoration of this type.

Bringing the stock to final shape requires very little effort in the case of the Dixie kit. In fact, leaving the existing contours as they are and simply sanding the stock carefully will produce a very nice-looking job. Even so, some shaping will be required in the area of the lock plate, trigger guard, and blending the machining marks on the butt and forend to produce smooth, flowing curves. Kits containing less well-finished stocks or working from a round blank is an entirely different matter.

The final polish to be applied to the butt plate and other brass parts is done in conjunction with finish sanding of the stock. Sandpaper should be backed with a solid block in order to prevent tapering or rounding off the edges of the brass. By sanding directly over wood and metal where they join, perfect matching of the two is obtained. Once the two have been sanded down with the finest grit paper you have, the exposed areas of the brass should be polished in boot-black fashion with strips of very fine abrasive cloth, and finished up with worn emery cloth. For that final high shine, red jewelers' rouge on a soft cloth or loose buffing wheel is by far the best. Polishing areas

inside the trigger guard is best done with very narrow strips of abrasive cloth and emery cloth or felt bobs in a hand grinder. Once the brass has been polished to the desired luster, the residue of all polishing material must be thoroughly washed off after which a coat of clear lacquer may be sprayed on to preserve the shine without frequent polishing.

In most kits, a fair number of burrs and machining marks will be found on the various parts of the lock. With small fine-cut files and abrasive stones, clean off all burrs and true up all edges. Make certain to keep all of the curves smooth and flowing, and avoid enlarging any holes. It may be that you would prefer a bevelled lock plate. If this is the case, then you will have originally inletted the lock plate only to one half its thickness. Then, at this point, very carefully file a smooth, uniform bevel that ends just at the surface of the wood. Give the trigger plate and trigger this same cleaning-up treatment with files and stones.

All that remains now is the application of an exterior finish to the metal parts of your Kentucky. The barrel can be blued by any one of several readily available home-use solutions. However, a proper "browning" job of the type originally used is much preferred. The procedures for this are covered in detail in the chapter devoted to finishing and refinishing of metal parts.

14/Build a Caplock Pistol

The caplock or flintlock pistol is virtually identical in every way to its rifle counterpart. It possesses all the same parts which are assembled in the same manner, and they perform the same functions. All of which is to say that if you hanker to build a single-shot muzzle-loading pistol, it may be done in exactly the same way already outlined for the rifle.

Assuming you'd like to do the job from a kit which contains all the necessary parts rather than start from scratch, check the Connecticut Valley Arms catalog. In it, you'll find a Kentucky-style .45 caliber pistol kit. It's offered in either percussion or flint persuasion and the two are identical otherwise; I'll use the flint version for my example here.

The kit contains an octagonal barrel with breech plug and tang already fitted and, in the percussion version, the bolster and nipple installed; fully assembled lock and side plate; trigger and trigger plate; brass trigger guard; finish-shaped maple stock; ramrod; and miscellaneous pins, screws, rod pipes, sights, barrel tenons, etc. All holes in wood or metal are drilled and tapped, and sight dovetails are cut in the barrel.

Assembly and fitting of the various parts and components is conducted exactly as for the rifle, except that the breech plug is furnished permanently installed on the barrel—one less step for you to worry about. There just isn't any point in repeating the whole procedure here. The one advantage obtained by the pistol is that there is much less wood work to do and no dovetails to be filed.

There are, however, a few points on which a bit of emphasis will not be out of order.

The breech plug is ground or polished flush with the top and side barrel flats—but it overlaps the bottom three flats. Inletting will be much easier if the overhang is filed off first, and careful filing around the tang/plug weld and all the edges will further simplify your work.

Even though the lock inletting appears complete, you should seat the *stripped* lock plate first, using the lock bolt as a guide pin. If you attempt to fit the assembled lock first, chances are the hole in the plate won't line up properly with the bolt hole in the stock. The same applies to the side plate; use the bolt to align it, or all the holes will likely be out of register when you are finished.

I've found it best to strip the lock plate, then inlet it and the side plate simultaneously, using the lock bolt to draw them both into the stock from opposite sides as work progresses. That way you'll be certain of proper alignment.

The one hole not drilled in this kit is the one for the tang screw. This hole passes the tang screw through the stock to engage the trigger plate. The best bet here is to inlet the tang first. Then inlet the trigger plate

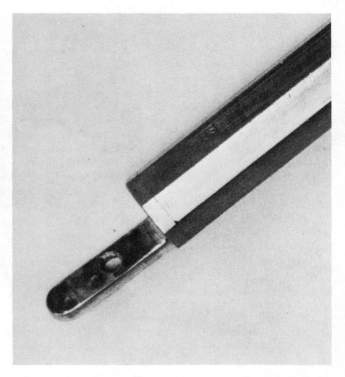

Although the barrel is fitted with a breech plug, there are very heavy burrs and other roughness on the plug and tang, and the plug overhangs the barrel at the bottom. Both the burrs and the overhang must be removed to simplify inletting.

The protruding flange of the CVA pistol kit breech plug has been filed flush with the barrel flats; the edges of the tang have also been beveled by filing for easier inletting.

The tang has been cleaned up, but the breech plug overhang is still present and prevents the barrel from entering full depth unless additional inletting is accomplished.

A complete flintlock is placed partially into the factory-inletted recess in the kit stock.
Note that the inletting for the edges of the lock plate is just a little too small;
although the rest of the lock enters freely, the plate rests on the surface.
The plate recess must be carefully pared along the edges until the lock seats snugly.

This simple sideplate is furnished with the CVA kit, and only a small amount
of inletting enlargement is required to seat it. Use both screws to pull
it evenly into place as the inletting is cleaned up.

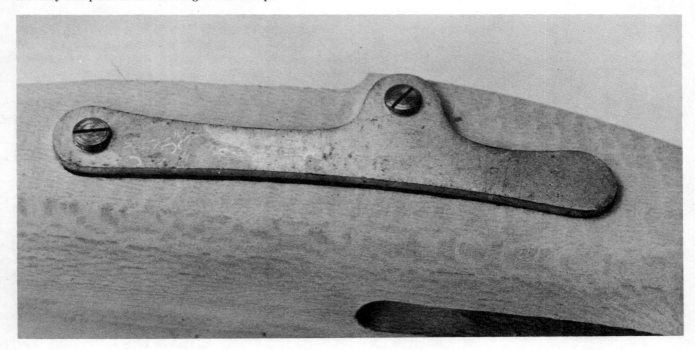

about halfway. Then, with both holes marked and center punched, drill a pilot hole of 3/32-inch diameter to connect them. The pilot hole may veer off a bit, but can then be trued up by enlarging it to finish up as a straight connection between tang and trigger plate. Another method of obtaining proper alignment is to drill halfway from each hole lining up by eye as well as possible and then cleaning up where the holes meet with a round file to produce a straight hole. If all your efforts are in vain, simply file the hole oversized so the screw will run straight between the tang and trigger plate—then wrap *one* layer of thin tape around the screw and fill in the gaps with glass bedding. The tape will produce enough clearance so that the screw can be easily removed.

This kit uses turned brass ramrod pipes held to the stock by short screws. In addition, the rear pipe (the long one) must be seated deeply into the ramrod channel; this requires very careful work.

Note also that in this kit the brass nose cap is secured to the barrel—not the stock—by two countersunk screws entering from the ramrod channel. *After* the barrel is fully fitted to the stock, attach the nose cap loosely to the barrel; then slide the barrel backward in its channel so the cap meets the wood; then it is easy to see what wood must be removed. A tenon to enter the rear of the nose cap must be left on the stock. After the cap is fully seated, it can be filed and polished flush with the wood.

Aside from these points, assembly of the pistol will proceed more rapidly than a rifle.

But, it may be that you'd just like to build a shootable, accurate pistol as cheaply as possible without any particular effort to make it a duplicate of an original type. This may sound like quite a chore on the surface, but it really isn't if you think things out beforehand.

What do we need? Of store-bought items, principally a lock and a barrel. Almost everything else can be made with hand tools, so let's try it that way, just to see how simple the job can be kept. The result won't be fancy, but it will shoot as well as a new gun from a top maker.

Scrounge around in the gunshops you know, looking in scrap boxes for 9 or 10 inches of usable rifled barrel of .35 caliber or over. It shouldn't be too hard to find a damaged 9mm (.35), .375, .44, or .45 barrel for next to nothing. If that doesn't work, write some of the big surplus dealers and ask for an 11mm or similar barrel. Some of them still have good U.S. .45-70 barrels which work beautifully. If you have much choice, I'd recommend a .45-70, 11mm Remington or 11mm Mauser barrel. As a last resort, buy an economical new .44 or .45 barrel from Numrich.

Saw off about a foot of the barrel near the breech, eliminating the chamber if present. Stick this in your pocket and go shopping for a breech plug. At the hardware store, look for a cap screw that is about the same diameter at the bottom of its threads as your barrel is at the bottom of its grooves. Get one screw this size and about 1 1/2-inches long. You'll only need a fraction of that length in the completed gun, but the extra length is for a purpose, so don't neglect it. Get another short screw that has a diameter about two thirds that of the bore. Get this one with a head as thick as possible.

Take all this home and lay out your files, drills and a hacksaw. Try to borrow taps to match the threads of the bolts you bought; but if this isn't possible, don't fret.

First, file the breech end (thickest, if there's any difference) of your barrel flat and square with the bore. If a tap is available to match the biggest screw, cut threads in the bore about 1/2-inch deep. The tap won't cut full threads clear to its end, so turn the screw in tightly, then back it off a bit. Keep it lubricated and repeat this until it deepens the threads to the full 1/2 inch. Two or three longitudinal grooves filed through the screw's threads will speed up this operation.

If no tap is available, file the end of the big screw to tap shape, tapering the threads down so it will start in the barrel. In short, make a tap from a bolt—it has been done many times before. The photos show what

The trigger plate is being inserted into its inletting cut in the kit stock. Note that a very large burr on the side of the plate is preventing its proper entry. Every part should be examined for burrs of this type, and they should be removed before attempting to place the plate into the stock.

The trigger-plate inletting is generally complete, but a bit tight in width, so that some scraping and trimming is necessary to seat the plate fully. Be sure to trim away burrs first, for they will interfere.

The ramrod pipe on the CVA pistol kit is held by a brass, metal screw entering from the barrel channel and turned into a threaded hole in the pipe.

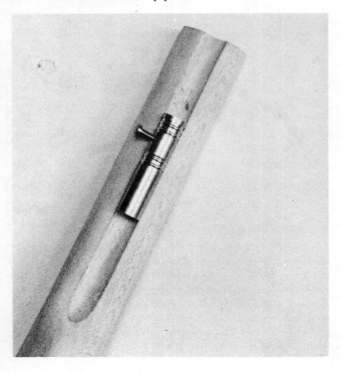

must be done. Stone the cutting edges a bit. Turn this improvised tap into the barrel 1/2 inch. Then, shorten it 1/8 inch and run it in again. Shorten further and turn in again, repeating until you've got a full thread 1/2-inch deep.

Now, shorten the cap screw to 1/2 inch of thread. This is your breech plug. File a piece of scrap steel to shape for a tang and have it either welded or brazed to the cap screw head as shown. If you own a bottled-gas torch, do the job yourself with silver solder and save the welder's fee. Turn this breech plug/tang assembly tightly into the barrel. If the latter is octagonal, align and fit the plug as outlined earlier to blend lines of barrel and breech plug together neatly.

The bolster or drum comes next. Just ahead of the face of the breech plug, centerpunch the barrel at right angles to the bore, also at right angles to the top of the tang. Drill a hole through the barrel wall very slightly larger than the other screw's diameter at the bottom of its threads. Tap threads into this hole as was done to fit the breech plug. Shorten the screw to the thickness of the barrel wall and turn it into the hole tightly. If necessary, file a flat on the barrel around the hole so the screw head will seat solidly.

Centerpunch the head of the screw and drill a 1/8-inch hole through it full length. Thread about the first 1/4 inch of this hole to take a convenient screw to form the clean-out plug.

Select a nipple size that the screw head will accommodate and drill and tap the nipple hole. This might best be saved until later so that the nipple and hammer locations can be matched up to get proper contacts and good ignition.

Now saw off the barrel at the muzzle to the length you want. To my way of thinking, 9 inches or 10 inches overall is plenty. True the muzzle up carefully; then chamfer the bore mouth lightly and break the sharp outer edge a bit with the file. For all practical purposes, that completes the barrel.

There's no point whatsoever in trying to make a lock. Sound new locks are available as inexpensively as $6.50. They will need polishing and a bit of tuning, but that's a lot less trouble than trying to make one, and a lot cheaper than buying a $40 unit. Be sure to order the pistol-sized lock. Get a back-action type if you like, but the typical bar lock is less trouble to fit and will allow you more leeway in stock shape.

You'll need to have a stock before the lock work can be done. Several styles are shown, laid out on 1-inch square grids to enable you to easily prepare a full-sized pattern. Select the one you want and make a pattern, scaling the forend to suit the length barrel you've chosen.

Pick out a piece of wood about 1 3/4-inches thick and big enough to fit the pattern. If you like things the easy way, a length of 2- by 6-inch pine or fir will make a usable stock. It won't be pretty, but it will be cheap. In fact, you can probably pick up an end cutoff at the lumberyard for free, and it's easy to whittle into shape. Personally, I prefer maple or walnut, but that's up to you. Maybe the best idea is to make the stock first from pine; then later if you decide upon some changes, make the new one from better wood.

Trace the pattern onto the wood. Either have the stock band sawed to shape or cut it out with a coping saw. Plane the top edge smooth and square, and then draw a center line down its full length. Place the stock blank in a vise and lay the barrel over the center line. Trace around the barrel, turning the pencil slightly inward so as not to make the outline too large. Use round gouges or rotary files in a hand grinder to rough out the barrel channel full length. Take care not to go outside the lines.

Smoke the barrel and tang and drop into the rough channel. Tap with a mallet to make a good impression and then lift out. Soot on the wood shows where more must be cut away. From this point onward, inlet the barrel and tang as described for the rifle. Go slow and easy and sink the barrel level—not high or low at one end—until it is one half its diameter into the wood.

Clamp the barrel tightly into the stock and drill a hole in the tang for a brass woodscrew of convenient size. Countersink and run the screw in tightly. Tie the barrel to the wood at the muzzle with soft wire or reinforced tape as a temporary measure.

Fitting the lock is next. Lay it on the side of the stock and carefully eyeball it into position. It must be aligned so that when inletted the hammer will line up with the nipple. The arc described by the *center* of the hammer face should pass through the center of the bolster, viewed directly from the side. Take care with this alignment, for once the lock is inletted, you'll play the devil shifting it without ruining the entire stock.

Clamp the stripped lock plate into place and trace around it. Cut just inside the lines with a sharp knife and start removing wood. This procedure, too, is covered in the rifle chapter, so I refer you there for details. Since we started inletting before the outside of the stock was shaped, the lock will have to be seated *below* the surface of the wood in order for the hammer to line up with the nipple.

If your lock is of conventional design, next inlet the side plate and fit the lock screw described for the Dixie rifle kit. If the attachment is different, make sure you understand it thoroughly before cutting into the stock.

Now is the time to carve away all the surplus stock wood. A model maker's plane, sharp knife and Stanley

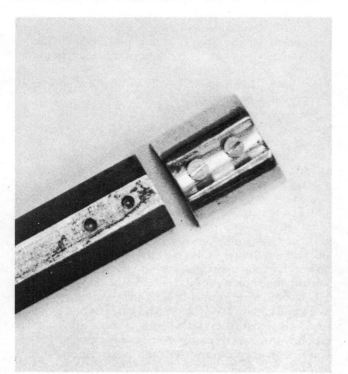

In the CVA pistol kit, the brass nose cap is attached directly to the bottom flat of the barrel by two screws. Cap, screws and the threaded holes in the barrel are visible here.

Fitting the ramrod tip is not a great task, but care should be exercised in trimming down the end of the rod so that it is not weakened at the shoulder. This tip is intended to be secured by a pin or screw, but the job is simpler and more durable when done with one of the modern "miracle" adhesives.

Even though the dovetail cuts have been machined in the CVA barrel, it is necessary to use a dovetail file to clean them up and carefully fit the rear sight.

"Sureform" rasp are all that's needed for this. Try the gun often while shaping the grip area or you may wind up with a shape you don't like. "Feel" is more important than looks in this area.

With the stock shaped nearly to final dimensions, the trigger must be fitted. You *can* make a trigger from a nickel's worth of steel—but a complete trigger and plate assembly costs only about $2.75, so you'll be money ahead to buy one. Inlet and regulate the trigger as already described for the Dixie rifle except that there won't be any tang bolt threaded into the plate. Use a single wood screw there instead.

Fancy trigger guards are for sale, but for a basic gun like this, you won't need one. Cut a strip of 1/16-inch thick brass and bend it as shown. Taper it toward both ends and bevel or round the edges for a more graceful appearance. Drill holes in both ends; then inlet them flush into the stock. Attach the guard with brass woodscrews and another job is done.

Disassemble lock and barrel from stock. Bend a rear sight from sheet metal as shown and lightly mark the center of its leaf. File a front sight from brass or coin silver and silver solder it into place. Silver solder the rear sight into place also, aligning it with the front blade. Don't cut the rear sight notch yet. Solder or

dovetail a tenon on the underside of the barrel, and then inlet, drill and pin it as outlined for the rifle.

Remove barrel and do the final shaping and sanding of the stock. Scrape and sand carefully to produce as smooth a surface as possible. Then whisker and apply your favorite stock finish.

Go over all steel parts now, polishing out file marks and carefully scraping away any excess silver solder. Polish all by hand, and then brown or blue as suits your fancy. For a gun of this type, I recommend quick-acting G-66 paste bluing compound. It produces a good blue finish in a minimum of time if used according to directions.

Bolt everything back together and it's ready to shoot. Snap a cap or two on the nipple and load up with, say, 20 grains powder in .45 caliber, 15 grains in .36, and a patched round ball. Remember that there's no notch in the rear sight yet, so as you shoot, file it in so that she shoots plumb center at 25 yards.

Once you've gotten this far, there really isn't much more you can do except learn the gun's habits and how to get the most from it. Of course, it may not look like much, but it was so inexpensive and easy to build that you'll probably do another one next winter—and it *will* be a beauty!

15/Cleaning and Preservation

Here and there in this book, I've touched on the cleaning of muzzle loaders as it applied in a particular instance. Now, we'll lump together all the cleaning information we've gleaned, and you can pick out that which suits your guns, circumstances and temperament best.

Black powder shooting is messy, any way you look at it. The large quantity of solid residue generated when the powder burns is black and sooty and clings to everything it touches. Over half of black powder remains behind as ash and other residue after firing. It makes the gun and shooter look as if they'd just crawled through a chimney. The residue is highly hygroscopic—it absorbs moisture from the air rapidly. Where the fouling lays on metal, this moisture will cause rust to begin in a matter of hours and it can encourage wood rot in damp climates. Black powder guns shot in a humid climate must be cleaned no later than the end of that same day. If they aren't, you can bet a bottle of your best Scotch whiskey they'll be red with rust by the next morning. Out in the desert country there is very little moisture in the air, so rust takes much longer to form. Guns have been found in the desert still in good condition after lying uncleaned in the sand for scores of years.

Avoiding the pitting effect of rust on bores and working parts is reason enough for prompt thorough cleaning. But there are other reasons. A dirty, fouled bore is less accurate than a clean one—primarily due to the solid particles clinging to its walls. Excessive fouling cuts patches, deforms bullets, and in some instances, makes loading virtually impossible. The bore isn't the only thing that suffers. Fouling that has collected in the nipple or bolster passage can spoil ignition, even cause misfires or hangfires.

Allowed to collect on lock parts, fouling can cause springs and screws to rust through. Accumulating in bolster, nipple, clean-out screw or breech plug threads, it can cause them to rust so badly the part may some day blow right out of its seat as a shot is fired. Working unnoticed down between stock and barrel, fouling will cause massive rusting of metal and rotting of wood. It can creep into a minute metal flaw, suck moisture from the air and eventually rust a hole right through the barrel.

If it seems I'm over-emphasizing the consequences of improper cleaning, it's for a reason. The finest black powder gun can be completely ruined in just a few days if fired and put away uncleaned. In the days when *all* guns had to be thoroughly and frequently cleaned, this wasn't likely to happen, for shooters trained themselves to clean often and thoroughly without even thinking about it. But with today's smokeless powder ammunition, modern rifles, pistols and shotguns are often shot for a whole season—even a year—without ever being cleaned. And they survive undamaged very well. With a few generations so conditioned to minimal cleaning, if any, it's too easy to think, "I'll clean it tomorrow." When tomorrow comes, something interferes; and by the time the job is remembered, a fine black powder arm is completely ruined by that red devil, rust.

How to clean? Simple. Black powder fouling is soluble in water. Plain hot water—the hotter the better—will dissolve black powder fouling as well and as quickly as the best expensive commercial cleaner available. A dash of soap or detergent helps remove grease, but isn't really necessary. For centuries it has been washed out or wiped off with a wet rag or patch. Old-timers used fibrous tow twisted around a "jag" on a "wiping stock" or into the worm on the ramrod. A slotted tip was also sometimes used to hold a piece of cloth for wiping the bore. I find wrapping a patch around a bore-sized bristle brush to be most convenient. The patch will often come off a jag or slotted tip and remain in the bore—a most frustrating occurrence—but the brush holds it better.

Today we have "black powder solvents" that can simply be sloshed on the fouled areas to provide rust protection for weeks or more. "Blacksolve" and "Gun Juice" are two common trade names. If you come in beat from a day of shooting and find yourself lined up for an immediate bridge or dinner commitment, these mixtures can be sluiced over the entire gun in a few seconds. They will protect it perfectly until the cleaning can be attended to properly. Some shooters just leave the gun like that until next shooting time, then swab it out and wipe it off. I've tried that a time or two, but it's too messy. Keep in mind that while these solutions prevent rust and keep the fouling soft and moist, they don't remove it—that comes only from *cleaning,* not just wetting down the gun.

Garden-variety (but thorough) cleaning of an assembled front-loading long gun is not difficult—just a bit more time consuming and messy than for a breech loader.

Lean the gun muzzle up against bench or table (better yet, clamp it somehow in that position). Cock the hammer and slip a piece of neoprene surgical tubing over the nipple. Run the tubing into bucket or basin or other drain—this keeps the mess off the floor, but its main purpose is to keep sooty water from soaking into the stock. Wrap an old towel around the barrel just below the muzzle to catch splashings and drippings. Take a bristle brush (not a *wire* brush) on a steel cleaning rod, dip it in hot water and swab the bore full length. Just a few strokes will loosen most of the fouling. Switch to a close-fitting patch or flannel mop and repeat with plenty of water.

Use a funnel to fill the bore with hot water which will slowly run out the nipple. Keep adding water until it comes out of the nipple clean and clear. Let

barrel drain, but not long enough for it to get cold. Swab the bore dry; then oil while the metal is still warm.

Next, remove the tubing and with a damp cloth wipe off any fouling around the breech area. Use an old toothbrush to get in around the base of the nipple, snail, etc. Don't overlook *any* crevices. Wipe everything dry. Lightly oil metal and, if needed, rub a bit of paste wax or your favorite linseed oil mixture on the stock to refresh its beauty.

When this method is used properly, not a drop of murky water will get on the stock or seep between metal and wood to cause rust.

A variation on this method is to remove the nipple or clean-out screw and replace it with a fitting, containing as large a passage as possible to which is attached a neoprene tube. The tube is placed in a bucket (or the bathtub) of hottest water. A tight-fitting patch or combination of patch and brush is then worked up and down in the barrel to pump water in and out. When all the fouling appears to be gone, clean water is used for a final rinse.

Another trick consists of the drain arrangement just mentioned combined with a hose slipped over the muzzle leading running hot water to the bore direct from the tap. The fouling is first loosened with a wet brush; then fast-running hot water does the rest.

Still another gimmick consists of a barrel-length metal or plastic tube of about half the bore diameter. The gun is held nearly level, but muzzle down and the tube is inserted up the barrel to the breech plug. The tube is connected by a hose to the hot-water tap. Water flows up the barrel tube, bounces off the breech plug and flows back out the muzzle, carrying the fouling with it. A nipple tube should be used to prevent water spurting out onto lock and stock. All of these running-water methods still require initial loosening of the fouling with a wet bristle brush.

No doubt there are other variations on the hot-water theme, but any of the foregoing will get a bore as clean as it can be gotten. I find it useful to add just a touch of nonsudsing detergent to the cleaning water, but I suspect its value is more psychological than real—except where the fouling has become solidly caked. Incidentally, should you suddenly discover that you *did* let a gun go uncleaned for several days, fill the bore with water and let it soak a few hours before getting panicky with rod and brush. The cleaning will be easier after the fouling is soaked soft.

Careful drying and oiling are essential after water cleaning. The main reason for using hot water is that it heats the metal which then speeds drying when the job is finished. Cold water will dissolve the residue nearly as fast but requires more careful drying of the gun. As noted elsewhere in this book, I usually dry revolvers in the kitchen oven after cleaning—then I *know* no water is trapped somewhere in a screwhole or recess. This isn't practical with long guns, so extra care should be taken to ensure everything is dry. Applying oil while the metal is hot from the water causes it to penetrate and provide maximum rust protection.

People have their favorite oils and greases to keep their guns fresh and bright from season to season. "Rig" is an old favorite, so is the old B.S.A. "Saftipaste." But the new aerosol cans of synthetic lubricants and preservatives are much handier to use and provide excellent protection. I've found the "Anderol," "Stoegerol" and "G-66" products reliable.

When using the patent cleaning mixtures, care should be taken to see they aren't slopped over the stock. Some will harm the finish, others won't. If used to excess, they'll seep into the wood at inletting cuts, weakening the stock. My only real objection to them is that they encourage hurried, sloppy cleaning because of their ability to prevent rusting even if the fouling hasn't been removed.

Of course, cleaning time is inspection time. Screws and pins must be checked for tightness. Nipple and bolster likewise, along with every other component

that is accessible without further disassembly. Repairs or replacements should be made as soon as discovered. Putting the work off only amplifies the defect. Occasionally, especially if the gun has been out in the wet, complete disassembly should be done. Clean and grease all parts covered by wood, and restore the wood sealer if necessary.

Stocks need occasional cleaning. Powder fouling must be wiped off after every shooting session or it will work into the wood and ruin the finish. When the stock is merely dirty, a soft bristle brush or coarse cloth and mild soap will clean it quickly. Use a "dry" lather with as little water as possible. Then a bit of paste wax rubbed on and buffed gently will restore that deep satin gleam. Check the chapter on stock making and repairs.

A gun properly cleaned and cared for will last through several lifetimes—but one neglected won't see you through a single season. The added effort of proper cleaning is more than offset by the sense of satisfaction you will obtain from doing well with an arm of an earlier century.

16/Competition and Games

Simply lining up on the range to fire a muzzle loader a few times at a conventional paper target is fun. But it's a rather prosaic test of skill among the thousands of black powder buffs from California to Maine and Mexico to Canada. They like more color and dash.

Someone showing up at a formal rifle or pistol club range clutching his long rifle and powder horn isn't going to get in much shooting. He'll get lots of conversation, interspersed with a few gibes, but a few demonstration shots are about all he'll be allowed. There simply aren't any recognized matches he can shoot in. "Britch-loadin" shooters all too often don't want their domain cluttered up with smoky, slow and dirty muzzle loaders. However, where his black powder brethren gather on their own ground, it's a hell of a lot different! There, if you've never seen it before, you'll observe some very interesting shooting—both for fun and for keeps.

The lone front-loader owner can get in his shooting only if he has access to spacious farm or woodland. If he's cooped up in a major city, there simply isn't any place to shoot. The real backbone of old-style shooting is the dozens of small clubs and the various state muzzle-loading associations. Wherever at least three shooters can get together, they can eventually form a club. Once that's done, assiduous digging will eventually produce a place where they can set up target boards and shoot, even though it be only some friendly farmer's creek bed. And a creek bed isn't bad at all—in fact, the neat, geometric, sophisticated ranges usually encountered make lots of muzzle loaders nervous. They prefer a more relaxed and woodsy shooting site where things can proceed informally and at leisure.

If you want to shoot and don't know of a club from which to get assistance, write to the National Muzzle Loading Rifle Association, P.O. Box 15, Friendship, Indiana 47021. First ask about joining that fine organization then ask about clubs and ranges in your vicinity. And just in case no club does exist, ask for instructions on forming your own clubk If it comes to that, don't despair. Just visit all the gun shops and ask for names of people who've bought muzzle-loading guns or are known there to be shooters of them. Armed with that information and a telephone, you're a damned poor salesman if you can't get a club started in a single evening. The outdoor columnist from the local newspaper can also be a help.

From then on, it's just a matter of setting up the club and affiliating with the NMLRA. As soon as you have an organization, you can start scouting for a suitable shooting site. Black powder shooting doesn't require a fancy setup. Just room for a few firing points, 50 yards clear range, a solid backstop and permission to shoot there. The rest, benches, target frames, etc., can be put up in a weekend or two. Incidentally, abandoned gravel pits and strip mines often make good range sites, even though not big enough to suit the breech-loader types. Old levees and embankments make good backstops, too. Just keep in mind that you don't need the fancy facilities demanded by modern-gun competition.

There's enough written elsewhere on range building that you will be able to find the information if you need it. Contact the NRA or NMLRA for help.

Now, let's get down to the type of competition you'll find among black powder shooters. There are many types of matches, each tailored to suit a particular type of gun or shooter.

Informal Sunday-afternoon (after church, of course) local shoots are usually confined to "shooting the mark" in the old-time way. Targets consist of an "X" on a board or paper. Traditionally, a piece of board or split log was charred in the fire, then an "X" scratched through the charred layer showed up sharp

and clear, white on black. Firing is from the prone position with rifle rested across a log or similar support. Matches can consist of a single shot from each competitor, the winner being the one who places his ball nearest the center of the "X." For the Fourth of July and similar occasions, meat shoots are held under somewhat different rules. Each shooter may fire as many shots as he likes, paying the entry fee for each one. His best shot goes for the record. Who cares if a fellow spends five bucks to win three dollars worth of bacon? I've seen it happen that way many times. A whole beef or hog carcass might be the prize, with different matches for each section.

Plain off-hand shooting is another mainstay of the game. It may be for score on ring targets, for group size or to "cut the X." Rapid-fire off-hand matches are great sport, both for shooters and spectators. Usually two shooters or two teams square off against a

Old-timers and their front-loading shotguns will surprise you with their performance over the traps. This gentleman has been shooting at the Nationals for years; broke 27 straight in '68 with his 12-gauge caplock scattergun. Who says muzzle loaders can't shoot?

The National Muzzle-Loading Matches now even have an official piper. This isn't unusual when one considers bagpipes were not uncommon on the frontier in the 18th century.

given number of breakable targets. The glory goes to the side breaking all its targets in the shortest time or breaking the most targets in a given time. Clay birds and small balloons are popular targets.

Spice is added to rapid-fire matches by using a long row of clay birds. The two competitors start at opposite ends and shoot successive targets toward the middle. The shooter can earn bonus points if he breaks all his targets. Then he gets into his opponent's share. Some pretty spirited competition can develop in this game. Speed isn't in the shooting as much as in loading, and more than one rushed competitor has shot his ramrod targetward to be forever reminded of the oversight by his companions.

When really experienced hotshots get together, a few more interesting games are played. Probably the most spectacular consists of "Shooting the Axe." Here, an axehead is secured to a suitable backstop—often a stump or log end into which one edge of a double-bitted axe is sunk. Two clay targets are placed straddling the axe. The object of the game is to hit the sharp axe edge with a bullet, causing the two bullet halves to splay out to hit and break the clay birds. Sure, it can be done, but even at close range, it's no piece of cake.

Another consists of "Cutting the Stock" or "Cutting the Stake," sometimes called a "Stake Shoot." A pair of wood uprights, which can be anything from a broom handle up to fence post, are set in the ground. A team or individual is assigned to each upright and on command starts shooting and continues until one or the other shoots his stake in half. Naturally, the winner is the first man or team to "cut the stake." With broomsticks or similar targets, this is fine practice for the individual shooter. However, it's more popular as a team event using rifled muskets. A four-gun team firing as fast as it can takes a while to cut a 4 x 6 timber with .58 caliber Minie balls, even with woodcutting-type bullets designed especially for the purpose.

Of course, pistol and shotgun fanciers all have their own pet games. Scattergunners shoot trap and handgunners shoot slow and rapid fire on standard paper targets. The latter also have speed and accuracy matches on rows of clay targets and balloons like the rifleman. Spectacular moving targets are also popular among pistoleros, such as an apple or grapefruit swinging on a string tied to a handy tree limb.

The bigger clubs will conduct more formal and extensive matches, often including virtually every game in the rule book. A couple I've heard of even have their own local version of the Seneca described later in this chapter.

The best of the local shoots is the state championship matches. Even if you don't figure you're good enough to compete at this level, you owe yourself the experience of attending and shooting a few of the simpler events. The knowledge of guns, equipment

Pistol matches seem fairly popular with the ladies, and this one doesn't do badly. Note modern, straight-line, speed-lock percussion pistol.

and techniques that can be picked up there is invaluable and will go a long way toward increasing your enjoyment of this grand game.

Two massive muzzle-loading events take place each year under the auspices and control of the NMRLA—they are the "Spring Shoot" and the "Fall National Championship Shoot." The latter is often referred to simply as "The Nationals." These events occur (as do others of lesser importance throughout the year) at the Association's official home and range just north of the friendly hamlet of Friendship, Indiana. This little community lies about 75 miles south of Indianapolis.

Twice each year, the area is innundated by hundreds of the finest people I've ever met—ranging from dirt farmers with an inherited "hawg rifle" to affluent professional men shooting modern guns costing thousands of dollars. Here gather the elite of the muzzle-loading clan; here can be seen the epitome of development of the muzzle-loading rifle (and pistol and shotgun). They come from coast to coast—even from Alaska and Hawaii—by airplane, camper, bus, car, motorcycle; you name it and somebody came in or on it. You might even find a few horses tied in one of the nearby thickets. The men don't come alone; wives, girl friends and children are there in droves. Many of them shoot, others tend the camp chores. Quite a few are in period dress to match "the mister's" outfit, and cook with gear you'd expect to see in a wagoncamp on

Heavy round-ball match rifles burn great quantities of powder and literally hide gun and marksman behind a thick white fog. This one, a flintlock, is really smoking things up at Friendship.

the Oregon Trail a century ago.

Proudly displayed or jealously guarded, depending upon the attitude of the owner, will be hundreds of thousands of dollars worth of the finest original and modern muzzle-loading arms one could hope to see. Modern-day artisans will be there, perhaps plying their tools on the tailgate of a pickup truck or in a tent.

Although conventional dress predominates, don't be surprised to see a lanky, bearded and moustachioed character in a long-fringed buckskin from head to toe, perhaps even draped with tartan sash, coonskin cap and bead-bedecked accoutrements. He might even be accompanied by a comely lass who looks as if she just stepped out of a tepee over the hill.

But in spite of all the sidelights—tomahawk throwing, knife throwing, trading and a little Taos Lightning (consolation for losers after dark)—shooting is their primary concern.

Every imaginable sort of shooting takes place. If I were to pick the three most interesting matches, I'd have to list the "Seneca" at the top because of its color and duplication of frontier situations; the Slug Gun Matches for the superb quality, precision and accuracy of the equipment used; and, last, the "Buffalo,"

where shooters rest their buffalo rifles on crossed sticks to duplicate the feats of early hide and meat hunters.

The Seneca is everyone's favorite, though few compete in it. Shooters must be in authentic frontier dress, which might be anything from breechclout and moccasins to broadcloth and boots with beaver hat. The match consists of much more than shooting and demands top physical condition. Regular competitors train all year for it.

The course is laid out along a rocky creek that twists up a draw. The shooter is poised at the starting line and at the "Go" signal moves out running. Up the creek a way he spots a partially hidden target, stops, loads his rifle, fires and runs on. Four more targets are up there somewhere, and he must locate and shoot all of them, then return down the creek to the starting line. It's a gruelling 300-yard run through water and gravel and over rough rocks, interspersed with five stops for loading and shooting. If you think it's easy, come on out and try it sometime.

Top Seneca runners complete the course in seven to eight minutes and shoot scores in the high 40's (possible 50). Highest score wins, but ties are broken by the fastest run. Its closest modern counterpart is the biathlon in which the hero has to ski and shoot his way across country against time. Many a Seneca runner would give anything for some of the biathloner's snow after his August run.

Occasionally, a Seneca runner will gallop off after his shot and drop or leave his ramrod behind. That's all, brother! The lady spectators cover their ears and the men listen sharply to see what new cusswords they can pick up.

The Seneca is intended to duplicate as nearly as possible the challenges a frontier rifleman faced in a running fight with hostile indians—or French or British, or Spanish or Mexican, depending on the time and place in history. It does this well, and probably more than one fight in Kentucky went exactly the same way.

The Slug Gun Matches are carried on at ranges out to 500 yards. The guns used weigh up to 60 pounds, shoot as much as 1-1/2 ounces of lead, and are marvels of mechanical precision. To watch a top shooter is fascinating. The cavernous bore is first carefully cleaned, and then a fresh cap or primer is placed on the nipple and fired to clear the innards. The bore is wiped again and the false muzzle is carefully fitted. After loading the powder, the shooter may then select a cast bullet, forge it with a hammer on a steel plate, and drop it into a swage which is further struck with precise, controlled hammer blows to shape the bullet. The bullet is next carefully centered on oiled paper strip patches in the false muzzle, started and seated carefully on the powder charge.

"Shooting the mark" is the oldest of marksmanship competitions. Here we have the traditional charred board upon which an "X" has been knifed to show white through the black char. Each of these target boards (shot at Friendship, Indiana in 1968) shows a bullet hole at or very near the center of the "X," illustrating the accuracy that can be obtained.

The big gun is now placed back in its rest and capped and the shooter carefully prepares to fire the shot. After reading mirage and checking wind and light, he'll touch off and a thumb-size slug will arc leisurely downrange to—he hopes—strike right in the group he's got going. All of this, cleaning, loading and shooting, may take nearly five minutes and the

Primitive match competitors at play. While killing time waiting for a match, they hold impromptu contests in knife throwing, tomahawk throwing and all other kinds of frontier games.

shooter is busy all the time. If you watch him for several shots, you'll see that every action is duplicated as carefully as possible from shot to shot; absolute uniformity is what the slug gun requires and what the shooter strives to achieve. And the accuracy that can be produced with a 45-minute ten-shot group will amaze you.

A slouch-hatted, bewhiskered figure sitting or squatting behind a heavy rifle rested over a pair of crossed sticks stuck in the ground conjures up visions of a squinting, odoriferous hide hunter leveling down on a herd of buffalo out on the Kansas prairie. And that's just what it is meant to do.

This is the "Buffalo" match. The guns allowed are comparable to those once used for taking the big American bison. The shooting position is prescribed to resemble the buffalo hunter's "stand" from which he might kill dozens of animals without ever moving. He needed the steadiest position possible, yet the waving buffalo grass was too high for him to shoot prone. So he shot sitting, kneeling or squatting, resting the long, heavy octagon rifle barrel across a pair of sticks. The barrel lay in the "V" of the crossed sticks and elevation could be varied by shifting the crossing point. Even the targets are buffalo silhouettes, with the aiming point right over the lungs where the old-timers usually shot.

Many other matches take place at Friendship, with events and classes for the ladies and youngsters as well.

Appealing to many as the shooting at Friendship is the vast "Commercial Row" where virtually every item even remotely associated with black powder shooting is on display. Want a quart of genuine bear's oil for patch lubricant? Or maybe some pure sperm oil? Someone there will have it. Need a new barrel or a new lock for your favorite smokepole? How about an authentic trade tomahawk, a peace pipe or a bag of Indian "Kinnikinik" tobacco? A new hunting shirt of finest fringed buckskin and a pair of knee-high beaded moccasins?

It's all there—all you can think of and more—and it's all for swappin' or sellin'. Some suppliers spend several thousand dollars just to display (and sell, of course) their wares at The Nationals.

The people, the guns, the shooting and all the rest combine to form an experience no muzzle-loading fan can afford to miss.

One of the most appealing facets of the muzzle-loading hobby is the opportunity it gives one for getting completely away from people and things—mainly the flurry and press of what so many people call "civilization."

The competent muzzle-loading buff who has proven his ability to make do and get along may eventually find himself invited to a "rendezvous." No, it's not what you think. The word "rendezvous" may mean one thing to the amorous and something else again to

the bearers of the long rifle.

In the days of the fur trade, factors and traders held a spring rendezvous for the trappers. Virtually overnight, a tent city, complete with saloons, stores, brothels and all the other essential elements would spring up hundreds of miles into the wilderness at some central, protected and well-watered location. The word would have gone out, and the mountain men and trappers would converge on the rendezvous from all directions laden with beaver pelts to trade. Invariably Indians gathered by the hundreds and more—partly to trade, partly to mooch and probably partly to see the ridiculous things white men would do to entertain themselves. Not the least of the rendezvous purposes was to provide the itinerant riflemen with the requisite whiskey and women for a monumental carouse which often ended only when his year's earnings were gone or he'd collected a knife or bullet in his ribs. They were hard men, and with only one fling a year available, they went at it full tilt, night and day. Many a buckskinned Lochinvar survived a year in the hostile wilderness only to pass from this vale of tears in a fog of Taos Lightning and flashing Green River steel at the rendezvous.

But the modern long rifleman's rendezvous isn't to catch up with civilization, but to get away from it. Not to carouse, but to relax. Not to die, but to live again.

Perhaps at one of the club shoots or at a big match you'll hear snatches of conversation from a group of three or four slouch-hatted, moccasined or booted figures under a shade tree.

"Early September good enough for you?"

"Good enough. Early enough to be comfortable, late enough to be no people around."

"Meet at the spring above Cooper's Bend. Primitive. One blanket, one horn of powder, salt, tobacco, little pemmican or jerky. Regular outfit otherwise."

"Fair. Walk in. All oughta be in by sundown the 5th. First one in clean the spring and shoot some supper meat. The rest get camp goin' as they come in."

"Done all around."

They shake and it's settled. What's settled? A fall rendezvous for three or four shooters who once or twice a year break clean with the business world and go back 200 years to spend a few days or a week or two, living by their guns, knives and wits in some isolated patch of forest. They'll walk in several miles, singly or together, carrying on their backs the bare minimum of supplies and equipment for survival—and a long, small-bore muzzle-loading rifle. Game and fish taken with primitive gear will constitute their entire diet. As a base camp, they'll have a fire and, maybe, a brush lean-to in case of bad weather. They'll sleep on the ground. If the weather turns bad or hunting is poor, they'll go hungry. They may be wet and cold, and

Not only the boys go all out in regard to period costume. There are quite a few other interesting sights, such as this warrior's delight perched alongside an isolated stream at the Nationals—maybe she's thinking about a swim; it was a hot day.

shot with a pea rifle, and handy enough with a snare and baited hook to feed yourself in the woods, and when you're woodsman enough to live in the woods off only the gear in your possible sack—then, and only then, you might get invited.

Less strenuous and of shorter duration are the "squirrel hunts" and "woods walks" often organized for small groups. They, too, are carried out with authentic equipment and dress. Participants expect to feed off game they kill and may be out two or three days. A woods walk may stretch for 30 miles or more and have certain tasks that must be performed at various stations along the way. And, they must be performed with primitive equipment. A meal may be prepared with improvised cooking gear; a fire may be started with flint and steel; a lean-to may be built; or a stream bridged; or a bee tree robbed.

A squirrel hunt may be just that—a dawn meeting in some hickory grove, followed by a day's hunting with flint or percussion squirrel rifles, fittingly ended around a campfire graced by squirrel carcasses cooking on greenwood sticks. Or it may be an extended affair approaching a rendezvous.

Hunting of all sorts plays a big part in today's use of muzzle-loading guns. Interest has grown to the point where many states have established special "primitive weapon" seasons for deer and similar game. A special season is set aside so that the primitive hunter won't have to compete with a horde of modern hunters equipped with scope-sighted long-range rifles and the urge to shoot at anything that moves. Over two-thirds of our states now either allow muzzle-loading hunting or set special seasons for it.

Range shooting is fine and a lot of fun, and it makes everyone better marksmen. The battered hat and the carefully smoked and fringed buckskins make us look pretty woodsy, especially if we don't shave for a few days.

But woods knowledge and marksmanship is put to the supreme test only when you're all alone in a hillside thicket and a cedar-tree buck works his way up the draw toward you. Can he see you? Can he wind you? Can you pick the right time and place, and can you kill him cleanly with the single ball in your front loader? The answers come quick and positive then. If they're all right, then you can take pride in being able to dredge up the latent skills that made those loose-walking mountain men able to conquer most of a continent.

Today we compete with our muzzle loaders for acclaim or maybe a side bet or two. And, if we don't like the gamble, we can walk away. The rifleman of yesteryear placed the biggest stake of all on his skill with the long rifle—his life. And he couldn't walk away if he didn't like the odds.

As I've mentioned before in an earlier chapter, muzzle-loading shooting has been going on all along—or, rather, I should say that it never stopped. In some

there won't be any guide or outfitter to take them by the hand if things get rough. Anything needing to be done, they'll do themselves or do without.

But, no matter what happens, they'll be living as did the trappers and scouts of the late 18th and early 19th century. For a time, they'll have cast the yoke of today aside—everything except their forest camp and the daily tasks of caring for themselves will have been wiped from their minds.

They may come back gaunt, unshaven and smelling a bit rank, and likely with indigestion and bruises, but they'll have gotten a fresh jump on the rest of the world, and it had better look out!

That's a rendezvous. When you're a good enough

This mountain man is off and running on the Seneca match. In a few yards he'll come upon a partially-hidden target which must first be identified, then hit with his long rifle. Five such targets and a 300-yard run constitute the match. It ain't easy.

parts of the country, notably the hilly South, percussion rifles never went out of fashion insofar as shooting for pure enjoyment is concerned. Men brought up on the caplock bought lever-action cartridge repeaters for mundane purposes like killing meat and convincing revenue agents to stay out. But for proving their skill in shooting the mark, they never forsook those fine long-barreled cap and flint rifles. Many of them have now been in the same families for well over a century and may have been freshed out two or three times.

Those guns were still in use in the hills of Ohio, Kentucky, Indiana and points south back in the early 1930's—casual use to please the owners, for there was no association or organization to tie shooters together and to set up competitions. Shooting was in the traditional manner when a few black powder fanciers gathered for a day or afternoon or for a more formal fall "Beef Shoot."

Slim Ackerman (who everyone in this game should know from his profuse writings) tells me that in February of 1931 a muzzle-loading match took place in Portsmouth, Ohio. It came about as a result of some earlier joshing E. M. "Red" Farris and a shooting buddy had taken by a black powder booster. The muzzle-loading clan had been invited to come on up

and show their prowess. Show, they did, from the hills of Ohio and Kentucky.

The match turned out so well that several people decided they'd like to try the muzzle loaders. Things looked promising, so the match was repeated the following year. New people and, undoubtedly, new guns showed up, and scores were higher. Interest was such that it seemed advisable to form an organization to promote, schedule and regulate matches and competition in general.

The upshot of all this was the formation of the National Muzzle Loading Rifle Association, with the genial Farris elected secretary and, as Slim put it, general factotum. The founding group also included Oscar Seth, who'd been a party to setting up that first match; Walter Cline; Bull Ramsey; Walter Grote; Boss Johnston; Clarence McNeer and a number of others. All had learned to love and appreciate the muzzle-loading rifle and recognized the common bond it already formed among many men.

An association bulletin was started and circulated, soon to be replaced by *"Muzzle Blasts,"* which remains today the official organ of the association. All members receive it and those who have had the foresight to save and have it bound over the years now own a valuable source of reference material on muzzle loading in all its forms. *"Muzzle Blasts"* has been put together for several years now by Maxine Moss, a delightful and dedicated lady.

Eventually the association purchased an attractive rolling, partly timbered tract of land just north of the village of Friendship, Indiana. The goal was a permanent range and association home. The result was a good one—it's a quiet area (except when a big match is in progress) and one can walk five minutes into the woods with long rifle in hand and feel he's left a lot of today's world behind.

The range was built—not much at first, but it grew and grew. It was named "The Walter Cline Range" after one of the founders and early association presidents. It lies along Laughery Creek and today rings to the crack of many a squirrel rifle all season long. And don't be surprised any day to see a figure there looking like a Sublette man just in with beaver pelts to trade. Full-period dress doesn't get you labeled "eccentric" there.

Additional land purchases have expanded the area considerably, and the ranges of today are well laid out, comfortable and roofed to provide protection from the elements. Matches are held frequently during good weather, but the highlight of the season is "The Nationals" already mentioned. Particularly impressive is the massive clubhouse with its stone fireplace and beamed ceilings where one and all can gather for bragging or explaining, whichever the scores dictate.

In the meantime, the association has functioned well. In addition to providing national championships, a permanent home for muzzle loading and a useful

At the matches, most scattergun shooters simply lay out all the necessaries in large open containers—rather than use flask, capper and shot and wad bags or pouches. An excellent reason for the no-smoking rule at the covered loading bench.

journal, it has promoted and fostered shooting throughout the country. There are well over 230 chartered muzzle-loading clubs in the United States affiliated with the association and subscribing to its codes, goals and ideals. Total membership is well over 18,000—all devoted shooters of yesterday's guns.

In accomplishing this the association has had to establish rules and regulations, though it appears they have been held to the minimum consistent with reasonable control—something that can't be said for many organizations.

As a result, competitive shooting is now based on classification. There are matches for tyros, youngsters, ladies and septuagenarians for revolver, pistol, shotgun, slug guns, round ball rifles and any other reasonable classification one might desire. Rules have been kept to the minimum consistent with ensuring everyone a fair chance at winning. Gun types are outlined loosely and so far this has worked well, without the bickering over minor points occasionally encountered among shooters of more modern firearms.

Through all this development, I'm certain Red Farris had a lot to do with keeping things practical and in preventing hidebound specialists groups from crowding fun shooters out. He's that kind of man. Still quite active in and for the association after more than 40 years, he is the only one remaining among the original founders. A big debt is owed him by all who enjoy muzzle-loading shooting today.

For the benefit of those who may want to make certain that new guns or equipment are adaptable to the competition at Friendship, I reproduce here excerpts from the latest edition of the NMLRA Range Rules. These rules and regulations apply in all competitions sanctioned by the association.

H. EQUIPMENT (RIFLES)

H-1: Metallic Sights—Any sight, including tube sights, not containing a lens or system of lenses, except a single lens may be attached to the rear sight as a substitute for prescription glasses.

H-2: Any Sights—Any sights without restriction as to material or construction, excluding scopes.

H-3: Open Sights—Rear open sight is one where the opening is a U, V or rectangular opening as wide at the top as at any part of the sight. Front sight may be a blade, pin-head, post or barleycorn, shaded or unshaded.

H-4: Telescopic Sights—Any sight or combination of sights containing lenses for the purpose of magnification.

H-5: Spotting Scopes—The use of a telescope to spot is permitted in all events.

H-6: Powder—It is an irrevocable rule that the propellent charge used in our muzzle-loading matches will be of BLACK POWDER AND BLACK POWDER ONLY.

H-7: Ignition—Ignition only by old-type percussion cap that fits on nipple or flint stone striking frizzen. NOTE TWO EXCEPTIONS:
(1) Wheel lock with original type of ignition.
(2) Slug Guns may use primers.

H-8: Flint-Locks—Safety shields must be used on all Flint Lock bench rifles.

H-9: Muzzle-Loading Gun—Any gun in which a black powder and patched ball or patched bullet is loaded in the muzzle of the rifle and ignition at the breech is by cap or flint. Exception—Revolver and Musket.

H-10: Musket as Issued—A musket as issued by States, National Government or Confederacy. Caliber .54 .58 or .69 only. Replicas permitted as approved by N-SSA.

H-11: Shooting Jackets may be used in any Muzzle-Loading Match up to and including a 10-X Large or Small Bore Jacket; standard weight will be allowed. No International type jackets allowed.

H-12: Gloves—See Q-1.

I. TYPES OF COMPETITION

I-1: Individual Match—An event in which the competitor reports to the Range Officer.

I-2: Re-Entry Match—An event in which the competitor is permitted to fire more than one score for record; one or more of the highest scores being considered to determine the relative rank of competitors. The number of scores which may be so fired, and the number of high scores to be considered in deciding the relative rank of competitors must be specified in the program.

J. POSITIONS

J-l: Offhand Position—This means extended arm supporting the rifle, no part of the supporting arm to touch the body; elbow to be at least six inches from the body. The rifle must rest in the palm of the hand and not on the fingertips except in Schuetzen Matches, where the palm or hip rest may be used or otherwise indicated on the match program.

J-2: Prone Position—In all prone matches, bench rests may be used when furnished by the shooter. In all prone matches when fired either in prone position or from a bench rest, no part of the rifle shall touch the ground or bench except that part which is supported by the muzzle rest. The butt of the rifle must be supported by some part of the body.

K. TARGETS

K-1: 6-Bull or 50-Yard Target Dimensions.
1 Sighting and 5 record bulls on tagboard or paper.

X ring— .39 in.	7 ring—3.89 in.
10 ring— .89 in.	6 ring—4.89 in.
9 ring—1.89 in.	5 ring—5.89 in.
8 ring—2.89 in.	

K-2: Single-Bull or 100-Yard Target Dimension.
1 sighting and 1 record bull on tagboard or paper in 5-shot events.
1 sighting and 2 record bulls on tagboard or paper in 10-shot events.

X ring—1 in.	7 ring— 8 in.
10 ring—2 in.	6 ring—10 in.
9 ring—4 in.	5 ring—12 in.

K-3: 200-Yard Target Dimensions.
1 sighting and 1 record bull on tagboard or paper in 5-shot event, 2 record bulls in 10-shot event.

X ring—2 in.	8 ring—12 in.
10 ring—4 in.	7 ring—16 in.
9 ring—8 in.	6 ring—20 in.

K-4: 300-Yard Target Dimensions.
The standard 200-Yard target is used on the 300-yard range.
K-5: Special and novelty targets shall be governed by the match in which they are used.

N. TYPES OF COMPETITION

N-1: Muzzle-loading Pistol and Revolver Match—Any match usually fired at ranges of twenty-five feet and over, indoors and out of doors, using one of these classes of arms:
(a) Any muzzle-loading revolver or multi-shot pistol using round ball or bullet and fired by percussion cap.
(b) Any single shot muzzle-loading pistol using round ball or bullet and fired by percussion cap.
(c) Any muzzle-loading flintlock pistol using round ball or bullet.
The sights on these arms must be entirely open and uncovered.
N-2: Re-Entry Match—An event in which the competitor is permitted to fire more than one score for record; one or more of the highest scores being considered to determine the relative rank of competitors. The number of scores which may be so fired and the number of high scores to be considered

in deciding the relative rank of competitors must be specified on the program.

O. TARGETS
P-1: Official Targets—In pistol matches, only targets approved by the National Muzzle-Loading Rifle Association will be used.
O-2: 50-Foot Rapid or Timed Fire Target (used for slow fire at 50 ft.) (9 and 10 rings blacked to form aiming bull.)

10 ring—1.80 in.	7 ring—6.14 in.
9 ring—3.06 in.	6 ring—8.32 in.
8 ring—4.46 in.	

O-3: 25-Yard Rapid or Timed Fire Target (used for 25-yard slow fire) (9 and 10 rings blacked to form aiming bull.)

10 ring—2.24 in.	7 ring— 7.46 in.
9 ring—3.76 in.	6 ring—10.08 in.
8 ring—5.44 in.	

O-4: 50-Yard Slow Fire Standard American Target (8, 9 and 10 rings blacked to form aiming bull.)

10 ring—3.39 in.	7 ring—11.00 in.
9 ring—5.54 in.	6 ring—14.80 in.
8 ring—8.00 in.	5 ring—19.68 in.

O-5: 25-Yard Rapid or Timed Fire Target. (Also used for 25-yard slow fire.)
Exactly the same target as the 50-yard slow fire Standard American, except that only the 9 and 10 rings are blacked to form aiming bull.

Q. ACCESSORIES
Q-1: Gloves—Gloves may not be worn which in any way form an artificial support.
Q-2: Spotting Scopes—The use of a telescope to spot shots is permitted competitors in all events. No part of the telescope or telescope stand may touch any part of the competitor's clothing or person.
Q-3: Shooting Kits—Shooting kits may be taken to the firing point when they are of such size and construction as to not interfere with shooters on the adjacent firing points.

17/Early Breech Loaders and Cartridge Guns

Man was more or less satisfied with muzzle loaders for the several centuries the flintlock reigned. The closest anyone had come to a successful breech loader with flint ignition was the Hall system, and it performed poorly. But with the coming of the percussion cap, it became evident he just *might* be able to produce reliable breech loaders. The "patent" percussion cap-ignited designs of before the Civil War aren't very common today. However, large purchases of Sharps, Burnside, etc., during that war make the later designs plentiful enough today that lots of people would like to shoot them. In the past couple years, we've even had limited production of reproductions of those Civil War breech-loading carbines. Best known and currently available is the Smith carbine.

Generally speaking, caplock breech loaders fall into two loading systems. In the first type, the rear of the barrel is uncovered by movement of either barrel or breech mechanism to allow some form of cartridge to be inserted into the barrel; the second type has a hinged breech section which raises or lowers at its front to be muzzle loaded with some form of cartridge, and then dropped back into alignment with the bore for firing. The Sharps is an excellent example of the first type, the Burnside of the second. Both types were intended to be loaded with loose powder and ball at the breech if the cartridge supply gave out, and could also be muzzle loaded if the breech mechanism failed

to open. The designers were coppering their bets in all directions to make their guns as attractive as possible.

All of the designs I'll mention here used the standard percussion cap on a nipple for ignition—the "cartridges" containing only powder and bullet and being provided with direct communication from nipple to powder for the cap flash.

Nearly all of these "separate ignition" guns can be fired today if one exercises some ingenuity. We'll go down the list in order of the quantities produced and describe how they can be loaded and shot today *without being altered.* All are primarily U. S. military arms, but civilian models will be encountered occasionally.

Sharps: The vertically sliding breech block is lowered by a lever, exposing the rear of the chamber. A *combustible* (nitrated) linen cartridge containing bullet and powder is inserted. Raising the lever lifts the breech block whose sharp upper edge shears off the rear of the linen cartridge, exposing the powder charge to flame from a percussion cap. The cap flash travels through a hole in the breech block into the powder.

Reproductions of the original cartridges are easily made from nitrated paper or linen as shown at the end of this chapter. In addition, if the gun breech is tight and not eroded, the breech block may be left closed and the gun loaded from the muzzle in the usual fashion. It may also be loaded by simply dropping a bullet into the chamber from the rear, with the muzzle down, and then pouring the chamber full of powder before closing the breech.

With any of the above methods, the Sharps has a habit of leaking at the breech. If parts are rusted or eroded badly, gas escapes in sufficient quantity to be dangerous to the shooter. In addition, loose powder gathers in the breech and is sometimes ignited by the cap flash, creating a secondary explosion there. *That* can be a real thriller if you're not expecting it.

Burnside: The chamber section of this gun tips up at its forward end to accept a tapered brass cartridge inserted rearward. The breech is closed and the cap flash reaches the powder charge through a hole in the rear of the case.

Lacking cartridges, the breech may be opened and a charge of powder poured into the chamber. This is followed by a bullet seated below the chamber mouth; the breech is closed and the piece fired. By leaving the breech closed, loading may be accomplished from the muzzle in the usual fashion. Since there is some gas leakage at chamber/barrel junction, a gas check is sold today to eliminate it when loading from the muzzle. This is a steel ring placed in the chamber

mouth; the force of the first firing wedges it forward to bridge the barrel/chamber gap. When firing is concluded, the ring is knocked back into the chamber with a rod so the breech may be opened for cleaning.

Best of all for the Burnsides are the polyethelene plastic cases currently sold. They approximate the original brass case and may be re-used many times.

Smith: The Smith breaks open somewhat like a shotgun and a *rubber* or paper and brass cartridge is inserted directly into the chamber. The rubber case can be duplicated by turning its likeness from Teflon rod and then loading with powder and bullet. If you'd prefer brass, cases can be made from brass tubing with a pierced plug soldered in the base. A flash hole in the center of the case head admits the percussion cap flash. This gun may be muzzle loaded if some form of obturating gas check case is used.

Maynard: This is a tipping-barrel design using an unprimed but otherwise fairly conventional rimmed brass cartridge case. A hole in the center of the case head admits the cap flash to the powder charge.

The cartridge case is necessary for firing this design since there is no other provision for sealing gas in the chamber. With a proper case, it may be loaded from

The Gallagher replica may be used as a breech loader with the brass cartridge shown protruding from the barrel breech or loaded from the muzzle (just like the original) with the chamber empty or with an empty cartridge case in place to provide a better gas seal.

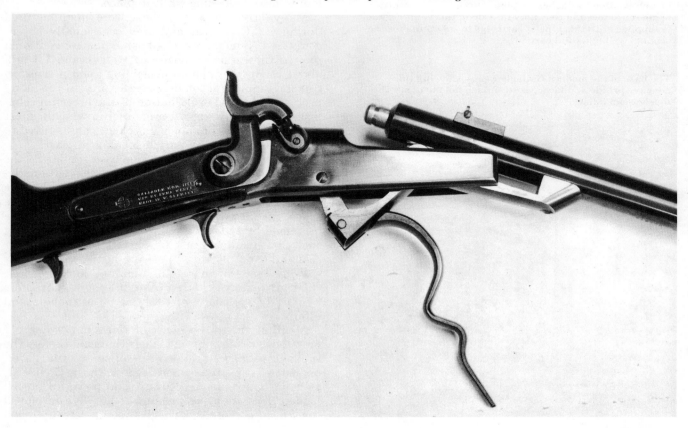

A modern turned-brass case, loaded with .535-inch round ball and powder, for use in the transition-period, breech-loading Gallagher carbine. This gun is currently being reproduced in Germany for sale in this country, and is supplied with this type of cartridge to substitute for the original Gallagher foil cartridge.

The base of the modern Gallagher case, showing the concave profile and large, central flash hole to admit the musket-cap flame.

the muzzle, or the case may be loaded with powder and bullet and used conventionally.

The Dixie Gun Works supplies a short, turned steel case which seals the chamber and allows muzzle loading *only*. A few small shops make up full-length brass cases for regular use. Typical methods of making Maynard cases are shown at the end of this chapter. No competent gunsmith or machinist will have any trouble making such cases. Since they last virtually forever, ten or twelve cases will keep a Maynard shooting for a long time, and their cost of a dollar or two each won't seem excessive at all.

Hall: The first standard U. S. breech loader and first made as a flintlock. It uses a separate chamber piece which pivots upward exposing the chamber mouth. It was originally intended for use with the standard paper musket cartridge. Bite off the end of the paper; pour in the powder; seat ball and rest of paper on powder; then close breech and fire. It was also meant to be loaded with loose powder and ball in the same manner as well as from the muzzle if the breech became inoperative for any reason.

The best you can do with this one is to load it just the way the designer intended (above). Since considerable gas escapes at the breech/barrel junction, one could fit a sliding gas check there. One similar to that described for the Burnside would certainly make shooting more pleasant, though it would restrict the gun to muzzle loading while in place.

Many other offbeat designs were manufactured during the Civil War and may occasionally be encountered. Some were chambered for conventional *primed* rimfire or centerfire cartridges, and I'll talk about them later. Those depending upon percussion cap and nipple ignition don't really present too many problems. A close examination of the breech mechanism will usually suggest a manner in which a short thin-walled brass or copper gas check can be fitted to allow safe shooting by muzzle loading at least.

In some instances a cartridge case similar to the Maynard can be made up and used conventionally. When this is done, care should be taken to see that the case fits the chamber snugly and that the rim fills the space intended. Some of those early cartridges were quite odd by today's standards. In making or having such cases made, it's best to work from a full chamber cast and carefully taken measurements.

While some of those old guns may look hopeless, there are few of them that can't at least be shot safely by muzzle loading. It just takes a bit of thought and effort.

Mention should be made of those many fine old metallic cartridge breech loaders that came before the smokeless era. The Golden Age of small arms development was spurred by and began with the Civil War. Reliable, convenient, accurate and powerful breech loaders of all the types we know today were developed toward the end of black powder's seven-century reign.

The repeating magazine rifle and shotgun were nurtured on black powder. The basic Mauser-type bolt-action rifle, destined in the following century to slaughter millions all over the globe, first barked with black powder. The lever, pump and automatic rifles were all first built around black-powder-loaded cartridges. That great destroyer, the machine gun, arose from man's genius fueled with black powder.

The Maxim machine gun, destined to arm both sides at Ypres, the Somme, Verdun and countless other blood-soaked arenas, won its spurs and acceptance piling up windrows of dead in Africa with black powder.

So with complete accuracy I say that virtually every type of gun we have today, with the possible exception of the automatic pistol, was first developed around black powder.

Uncounted millions of those black powder arms are still in shooting condition. And most of them seem to have wound up in this country by one means or another. They beg to be shot; with plenty of gun powder, lead and primers available, there's no reason for not using them.

Regardless of the caliber of the gun, it can, if in good mechanical condition, be fired with the proper bullet and all the FFg or FFFg powder the case will hold to the base of the seated bullet. Cases of those bygone days were designed to hold only the correct amount of powder, so can't be overcharged as often happens with smokeless powder.

Making paper cartridges of the Civil-War type is really quite simple. It begins with cutting blanks of the shape and size shown above from any tough but not too thick paper; the ones shown are cut from lightweight grocery bags. Lay the blank out as shown, place the cartridge stick in position.

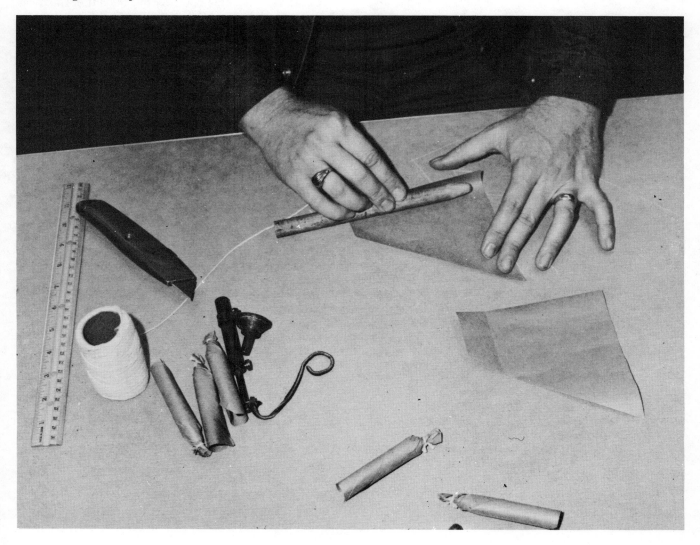

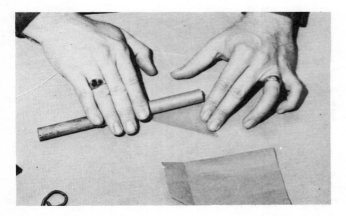

Roll the stick and paper forward, keeping the left edge straight.

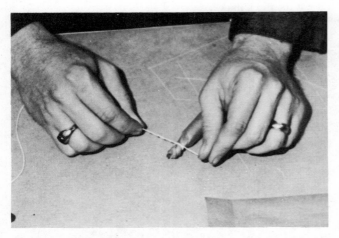

Twist the paper together where it extends beyond the end of the cartridge stick and then tie it off with heavy thread or light cord.

Take a Minie bullet which you have checked for size and roundness, and especially for perfection of base, and smear lubricant into its grooves.

Since factory black powder loads are no longer available in any caliber except as aged lots from dealers in obsolete ammunition, you'll have to reload; but this isn't a book on reloading. For that part of the story, I refer you to *Reloader's Guide,* by my friend R. A. Steindler.

However, some information may be in order. Reloading dies in virtually every black powder caliber can be obtained from RCBS, Inc., Box 729, Oroville, California 95965, as can all other loading equipment. But those who bought 1873 and 1886 Winchesters didn't have our modern reloading equipment, yet they got the job done. Cheap and simple sets of tools are available from Lee and Lyman. They aren't fast, but they are durable and reliable, and they will turn out perfectly-loaded cartridges.

But you can get by with nothing more than a bullet mold and a few scrap materials and household tools. Suppose you have an old Springfield or Remington .45-70-500 caliber rifle and a handful of empty cases.

First, wash the black powder fouling out of the cases as soon as they are fired. It will corrode and weaken the brass if not removed. Try each case in the chamber to make sure none over-expanded. Any that won't go in should be set aside for eventual full-length resizing.

Drill a 1/4-inch hole in a board or block of wood. Set the fired case over the hole, and with a 1/16-inch diameter nail or wire seated in the end of a piece of dowel, force out the fired primer. A little juggling will get the nail into the flash hole easily enough. This is simplified if the dowel just fits into the case and the nail is centered in it, providing automatic alignment as the dowel enters the case.

The case is now ready to be reprimed. Place a piece of dowel slightly longer (1/8 inch is enough) than the case in the case mouth and start a primer in the pocket by hand. Place this assembly squarely between the jaws of your vise with primer against one jaw, dowel against the other. Gently close the jaws to force the primer into its pocket. The primer must go in flush with the surface of the case head. A large C-clamp can also be used for the same purpose.

If you've an adjustable powder measure handy, set it to throw a charge of Fg or FFg that will come fully up to the base of the bullet when it is seated. Lacking a measure, don't fret; just pour in powder to fill the case to that point. If you have many rounds to load, cut a reject case off to hold exactly the right powder charge. Then use it as you would a charge cup for muzzle loading. A card or felt wad seated firmly on the powder makes handling more convenient while seating bullets, but isn't otherwise necessary.

Cast your bullets as outlined in Chapter 10, and when cool smear the grease grooves full of your favorite lubricant. Don't use too much and please keep the bases clean. Start a bullet by hand in a charged case. If the mouth seems pinched in and stops the bullet, flare it out a little with any hard conical object, even an old plumber's countersink rotated backward. Don't flare the mouth too much or it won't enter the chamber freely.

With bullet started straight, again place the cartridge-to-be in the vise and slowly close the jaws to press the bullet down on the powder.

A block of wood taped to one vise jaw as a stop will ensure reasonably uniform seating depth. If the bullet starts to lean, back off on the vise a bit and rotate the cartridge one-half turn. This will usually straighten out the bullet; but if it doesn't, do the job with your fingers.

Wipe any excess grease from the completed assembly, and you've got a loaded cartridge ready to fire.

Cartridges loaded in this fashion will do fine in single-shot rifles or when loaded directly into the chamber of repeating arms. In order to be used through tubular or box magazines, the case must be crimped on the bullet. Unless this is done, recoil will cause bullets to move in or out of the case mouth, resulting in failures to feed from the magazine. A bullet seat-crimp die is required for this, as is a tool or press in which to use it.

Eventually your cases will expand to the point they either won't enter the chamber or won't grip a bullet. To correct the former, they'll have to be resized and this means a resizing die. The old-style Lyman-Ideal type into which the case is driven or pressed is simplest and cheapest and entirely adequate for this type of loading. To merely tighten the case on the bullet the same operation must be performed but to a lesser degree. Use the same die, but run the case in only far enough to squeeze the mouth down enough to hold the bullet.

A handful of cases and the simple tools just outlined will enable you to keep any centerfire black powder breech loader talking for years to come. Of course, I chose only the .45-70 as an example. Exactly the same procedures and tools apply to any other caliber you might come up with from the .32-20 Winchester to the big .50 caliber 3 1/4-inch Sharps.

Often the old-timer will be encountered in a caliber for which it is very difficult to obtain even a few good cartridge cases. When that happens, look up the caliber in my book *Cartridge Conversions*. There you'll most likely find detailed instructions for making what you need from cases that are readily available by what we call "reforming."

Even after the fine breech-loading single-shot target rifles of the 1880's and 1890's came along, many a die-hard muzzle-loading fan was hard to convince. Even though the "cartridge guns" had proven themselves superior for hunting and war (which, to the true rifleman, is somewhat akin to hunting), accuracy purists were by no means ready to drop muzzle loading as a concept. To be sure, they liked the convenience of the brass cartridge case and easily operated breech, free of the bothersome details of

Place the bullet point-first in the open end of the cartridge tube and then press it down against powder charge with your cartridge stick.

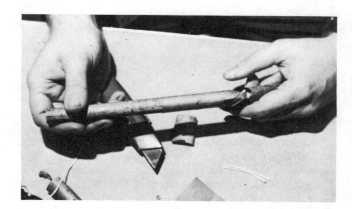

To copy the original U. S. military cartridge, form a second paper tube around the cartridge stick and insert it, closed-end first, into the first tube, snugly against the powder charge.

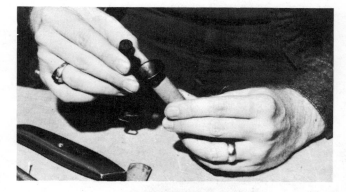

Using a flask or whatever type of powder measure you like, place the required powder charge in the paper cartridge tube. Unless you want to do only one cartridge at a time, you may want to supply yourself with a large loading block that will hold at least 10 or 20 tubes and their powder charges.

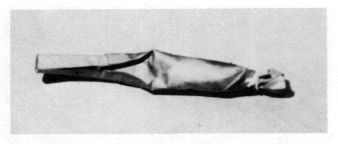

Pinch the cartridge paper off snugly behind the bullet; press the excess out flat, and iron it down with a thumb nail or cartridge stick; then fold the edges over as shown.

loose caps, powder flasks, etc. But to them, it just didn't seem likely that the bullet could be started from a new-fangled cartridge squeezed down to fit the rifling and still strike as close to dead center as the carefully front-loaded slug or ball.

They must have been right, at least during the transition period. In *The Breech-Loading Single-Shot Match Rifle,* the late Ned Roberts said, "Even as late as 1886, the best breech-loading match rifles in the hands of expert marksmen were not capable of making as high scores or small groups at 220 yards rest shooting, as those made with a muzzle-loading cap-lock rifle." He goes on to cite examples to prove his point, although Ken Waters points out that in at least one of the examples the muzzle loaders used the best available telescope sights and shot from machine rest, while the breech loaders used iron sights and were shot from muzzle rest only. In correspondence with Roberts, A. O. Niedner stated that the better shooters in this area all used muzzle loaders until around 1895. Even so, U. S. shooters beat the Irish and British teams at long-range shooting, The foreigners used muzzle-loading rifles, the Americans breech loaders.

To finish off the job, fold the tail of the paper forward over the cartridge body; if it won't lay snugly there on its own, use a dab of any quick-setting glue (I found the stick-type Pritt to be ideal for this purpose).

The end result of all this was that certain discerning gentlemen combined the two systems into what became known as "breech-muzzle-loading." The breech-loading rifle was used, along with a *bulletless* cartridge case containing the powder charge held in place by a thin wad. The bullet proper was loaded from the muzzle through a carefully fitted false muzzle in classic fashion.

Many top shooters asserted that only in this fashion could maximum accuracy be developed. They attributed the fine accuracy of muzzle-loading caplock rifles in part to the fact that no "fins" were produced on the bullet base. A bullet being driven forward into the rifling will have a small amount of metal displaced rearward as the lands cut into it. This displacement results in fins or tails of metal being dragged rearward of the base. Additional fins will be formed if the bullet is larger in diameter than the bore. On the other hand, a muzzle-loaded bullet is swaged down and cut by the lands toward its point, leaving the base free of distortion. Experts such as Dr. Mann and Harry Pope eventually proved to the satisfaction of themselves and many other shooters that breech-muzzle-loading kept bullet bases perfect and was worth the effort required, in terms of superior accuracy, if not speed and convenience.

Although some breech-muzzle-loading was done with paper patched bullets, the blunt cylindro-conoidal form with several annular grease grooves emerged as the best or at least the most popular. They were carefully cast to proper diameter, and then the grease grooves were filled by means of a lubricating pump without distorting the bullet in any way.

These lubricated lead bullets were then loaded through a false muzzle nearly identical to those used on caplock target rifles. Of course, the patch guides were not needed. To ease the human effort required to start the bullet, toggle-joint starters with considerable mechanical advantage were often used. The bullet was then seated to a predetermined point just ahead of the chamber by means of a stiff "loading rod." After all this, the primed powder-filled case was chambered, the breech closed and the gun was ready to shoot.

As with caplock target rifles, much depended upon the degree of perfection with which the bullet was made and seated. Special molds were often used, the Pope "nose-pour" type being deemed among the best, if not actually the very best. Perfection of base was sought by pouring and cutting off from the nose. Bullets were cast in two forms: tapered (stepped), with front bands of bore diameter and at least the base band groove diameter or slightly larger; straight, with all bands of bore diameter. Both had their staunch supporters, and both won matches.

Such guns were known to be highly temperamental, especially in regard to bullet lubricant and bullet hardness. Some shooters varied bullet lubricant-

Shown here are five different combustible cartridges: left to right—.31 round ball, .36 conical ball, .44 round ball, .44 conical bullet and .58 Minie-bullet.

hardness according to the seasons, having found that what produced best accuracy in hot weather was not adequate in cold—and vice versa. Bullet "temper," as it was called, might vary from one part tin to forty parts lead to as much as one part tin to twenty parts lead. Only extensive experimental shooting could tell the shooter what combination was best for a particular rifle. Two apparently identical rifles might have vastly different preferences.

As with the caplock muzzle loader, absolute uniformity of components and loading procedures were (and are) essential to match-winning accuracy.

In this manner, muzzle loading lived on as a concept essential to the production of maximum accuracy long after it was made obsolete from a practical standpoint by advancing technology. As late as the late 1940's and early 1950's, it was still believed by many that the modern breech loading rifle fired with self-contained cartridges loaded with metal jacketed bullets would never surpass the accuracy of the breech-muzzle-loading target rifle. Modern benchrest shooters have since proven otherwise, but it took them quite a while to do so.

As a matter of interest, one can use this breech-muzzle-loading system just for fun. There are thousands upon thousands of obsolete large-caliber black-powder single-shot rifles around the country. Most common are the Springfield Trapdoor models and the Remington Rolling Blocks. Simply load a patched ball or lubricated bullet from the muzzle using a ramrod stop to ensure that the bullet stops at the proper point in the barrel. Then chamber a primed and powdered case, and you're ready to shoot. Not very authentic perhaps, but lots of fun. The Remington also lends itself well to conversion to a true caplock muzzle loader, as outlined elsewhere in this volume.

Cartridges for muzzle-loading arms are a lot older than you might think; it isn't possible to say exactly

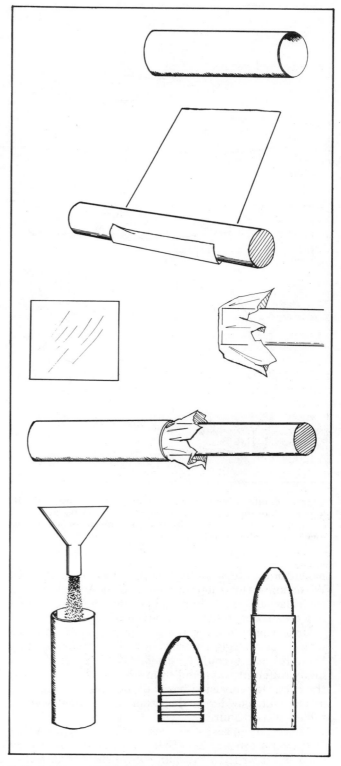

Cylindrical, combustible paper cartridges for Sharps and similar rifles are easily made as shown. After nitrating, roll paper into a tube that will enter the chamber; plug one end with a piece of tissue paper; charge with powder; seat bullet; and glue or tie case to bullet.

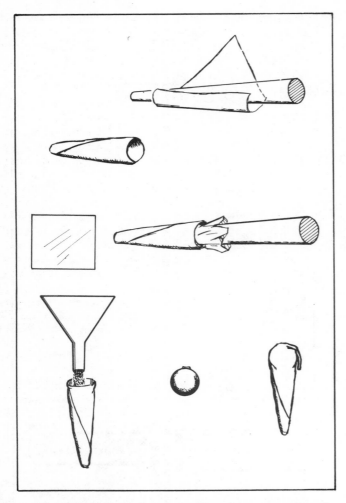

Tapered combustible-paper cartridges are no more difficult
to make than the straight kind. For revolvers they are
essential, but for that use, the case need not be brought
forward completely over the bullet as shown.

when they were actually used for the very first time.
We do know the troops of King Gustav Adolphus used
cartridges of a sort—ball and powder charge enclosed
in a twisted or rolled paper envelope.

Until the coming of the semi-rigid plastic tube or
vial, paper cartridges were about the only way loading
from the muzzle could be speeded up. Though made in
many different ways and from various sorts of paper,
the cartridge consisted basically of a paper tube: ball
in one end, powder in the other, both ends twisted,
folded or tied shut.

This type can easily be made today exactly as it was
well over a century ago. Select a piece of dowel very
slightly larger than the diameter of the ball or bullet
to be used. Make it long enough for convenient
handling and round off one end. Sand smooth, shellac
or varnish and then wax heavily. This is your cartridge stick, or form.

Wrap paper around it to determine the size sheet
needed to form a cartridge tube. Old cartridges were
not glued, the paper being overlapped sufficiently to
prevent powder leakage and you can cut your pattern
for this type. I prefer a glued tube; for it simply allow
1/4-inch or 3/8-inch overlap. Once the pattern is
made, make a template of it from cardboard or light
sheet metal. Then you'll be able to stack eight or ten
sheets of paper and cut that many blanks simultaneously with a razor blade or sharp knife. Don't use a
hard-finish glossy paper which will tear too easily. A
fairly soft, tough paper works best.

Roll a blank around the stick and brush the overlap
thinly with a quick-drying cement and press together.
Slip the resulting tube down so it overhangs the
rounded end of the stick. Twist the end of the tube
closed and secure it with a couple turns of heavy
thread tied securely. Slip the tube off the stick, set it
aside to dry and make some more. It pays to have
plenty on hand.

Drop the round ball or lubricated Minie bullet into
the paper tube to settle in the closed end. The Minie
must, of course, go in point first. Slip the stick in and
tap the ball to seat it solidly. With the stick still in
place, throw two turns of thread around the tube
directly behind the ball and tie it off. This prevents
powder from working down around the ball during
handling.

Draw out the stick and drop in the proper powder
charge. The remainder of the tube may be either tied
off tightly or closed by folding and creasing as shown.
Tying is the most secure method, but the folded tail is
easier to tear off when loading.

In use, this cartridge is torn open at the base,
powder is poured down the barrel and the ball and
attached paper are rammed down the bore.

Some shooters dip the bullet portion of such cartridges in melted tallow, but I find this too messy and
of little value.

**If you don't want to go to the trouble of making paper
cartridges and don't particularly care to bother with a
flask, make up plastic vials such as this from semi-rigid
tubing cut to length and capped on one end. Select tubing
that will be a snug fit on the bullet; pour in the powder
charge; then stopper the open end with the bullet. In use,
simply pluck the bullet out with fingers or teeth; dump the
powder down the bore; then seat the bullet in the usual
fashion.**

Modern shooters replace this type of musket cartridge with the plastic vial mentioned earlier. The powder charge is simply dumped into the vial. The bullet (Minie) is then forced into the vial mouth as a stopper. In use, the shooter grabs the protruding bullet in his teeth, twists off the vial and pours the powder down the bore. The bullet is then rammed in conventional fashion.

Combustible paper cartridges may be made for Sharps and similar breech-loading Civil War vintage arms. A flat-ended cartridge stick is made of a diameter that will produce a tube into which the bullet will fit snugly.

Good quality bond paper is best for this purpose. Some prefer onionskin because it is thin and light, but the cap flash will penetrate the heavier paper just as well if it is properly nitrated.

Paper is nitrated by soaking whole sheets in a saturated solution of potassium nitrate and hanging them up to drain and dry. This paper is then cut to a size that will roll around the stick and allow a substantial seam. Its length must be regulated so that when the assembled cartridge is fully forward in the chamber, its rear will reach the breech block, placing the powder close to the vent leading from the percussion cap. The nitrated paper will burn almost like gunpowder, leaving no significant residue in the chamber.

Roll the nitrated paper around the cartridge stick, glue the seam, slip the resulting tube off and let dry.

Nitrate onionskin paper and cut in squares that will fold back over the end of the cartridge stick as shown. Place on the end of the stick and press down into the cartridge tube flush with the end. Brush a bit of cement around the edge to secure it to the tube. Very little cement is required.

Drop the powder charge in the tube. Insert the bullet into the mouth of the tube. Brush glue around the mouth to secure bullet and case together. An alternate method is to tie the tube tightly around the bullet base or make the tube long enough that it may be tied shut over the nose of the bullet. In either case, dip the bullet portion of the completed cartridge in melted lubricant.

Combustible cartridges for revolvers are made in the manner just described except that a tapered forming stick is used with wedge-shaped blanks. Revolver cartridges must be tapered to the rear for easy insertion into the chambers. The drawings show this in detail.

Incidentally, I once met a fellow who made up this sort of tapered combustible cartridge for use in the .58 caliber rifled musket. It seemed to work well for him and did facilitate reloading. If you'd like to try it, just make an enlarged version of the revolver cartridge using a properly lubricated Minie bullet.

Paper cartridges are just another example of the things you can do to further enjoy muzzle-loading shooting. After a little practice, they won't be at all difficult to make.

18/Cannon

There are few more impressive sights—or experiences, for that matter—than a two-gun section of light artillery galloping into action. Blowing horses skid the limbered guns around so they point generally toward the enemy, throwing dirt and chunks of turf into the air as the big wooden wheels slue around; gunners and crew bail off the limber and horses, snatching away harness and separating gun and limber and manhandling the guns into line; each crewman races to his appointed place, grabbing implements; balls or shot and bagged powder charges are hurried from the limber.

The seemingly mindless rush of brightly uniformed figures shouting incoherently in the dust suddenly resolves itself into a fully-loaded brass Napoleon with its crew standing rigidly in their places while the gunner waits tensely, lanyard or linstock in hand, for the commander's "Fire!"

The lanyard is snapped—or the linstock flashes downward—and white smoke spurts upward from the vent. Roiling, churning clouds of white smoke spout from the muzzle, shot through with flashing tongues of yellow-orange flame, and the gun carriage leaps up and backward to the crashing roar known for centuries as "the voice of cannons to which men tremble."

That scene was common until barely a century ago—and it is particularly known for occurring in the American Civil War when the fabled horse artillery fathered by Alexander Hamilton galloped to the fore to crush the enemy's advance. Tales of gallantry and sacrifice among artillery men are legion, even in modern times, as the guns were thrust in to save the infantry. Artillery annals are filled with stories of batteries lost, at times sabered to the last man, as they covered the more mobile riflemen. "Redlegs," as the gunners were called (even today), were tied to their heavy guns and committed in the heat of battle; if the Gods of War frowned on them, they had but two choices: to die heroically feeding the hot muzzles of their brazen monsters or to flee in dishonor. Few ever chose the latter.

Such instances did not occur only in the dim and distant days of bright uniforms, golden guns and black powder. My old light battalion was shot off part of its guns in North Africa, but took them back viciously and continued the fight. In Korea, more than once the sun rose on a silent gun surrounded by its dead crew who had served their iron mistress to the last of breath and blood. Today there walk the streets young men who know firsthand of artillery gallantry in Asian jungles and swamps which equalled or surpassed any of the past.

Gunners have a fondness, affection, love and some mystical bond with their guns that surpasses understanding. Where the gun goes the gunners go, and if it cannot leave, then neither will they—though it may come back to mark their grave.

Perhaps this bond between blood and steel is partially explained by the nature of the earliest artillerymen, called then "Artillerist" or sometimes "Master Gunner." In the beginning, they were not of the military; no footmarches and lowly details for them. They were specialists, *civilian* specialists, with not-understood knowledge and skills with their charges that gave them stature with their liege lord comparable to that of his astrologer. An army didn't simply buy guns and service them with common soldiers. Instead it hired—for a high price plus a share of the spoils—a man *and* his guns and his crew. He often decided where, when, and how his guns would be used; he and his guns might be feared as much by the soldiers as the enemy's artillery. The Master Gunner earned his pay, as did his men, for they were as likely to be killed or maimed by their crudely cast charges as by the enemy. Artillerists guarded their secrets well, fearing to lose their exalted positions and fees if mere soldiers should learn how to handle artillery. In the end they lost, for soldiers did quickly learn to use the big guns.

Be that as it may, today muzzle-loading cannons play a significant part in the overall scheme of black powder shooting. In recent years, front-loading buffs who fancied muskets and uniforms have gone on to bigger things. A small cannon is obviously the next step up from a .75 caliber musket. While it's fun to just shoot any muzzle-loading cannon, many artillery fanciers go much farther than that, usually banding together in groups for both physical and economic support. In fact, some have gone so far as to assemble all the gear, including full period uniforms, to field a complete gun, crew and team of horses. In a few instances, this has been expanded to a two-gun *section* or a four-gun battery. These people are past the point of shooting just to please themselves and spend a lot of time performing before the public at all sorts of gatherings. Over 60 guns and crews took part in a recent large shoot in the East, though not all were equipped entirely as a Union or Confederate unit might have been in 1863.

Several such groups can and do gallop into view, re-creating exactly the scene described in this chapter's first paragraph, every item correct down to the last detail, even the harness and "US" rosettes on the gun team's bridles.

The people I am talking about love muzzle-loading cannons of the Civil–War period. Their ultimate ambition is usually to own a bronze Napoleon 12-pounder, complete with carriage, limber, chest and implements, and in shooting condition. Unfortunately, in their view, such guns are exceedingly rare today, most being in museums, at national parks and monuments, and worth thousands of dollars each.

Dixie Civil War Field Cannon with 43-inch tube and 2-3/16-inch bore. Mounted on a semi-modern carriage consisting of a welded trail and cheeks and old wooden wagon wheels. It's quite popular among cannon buffs.

Over the years, cannon enthusiasts have for those reasons made their own guns, ranging from half-inch bore miniatures up to full-sized 12-pounders and larger. There is sufficient demand for such items that today you can order from a reputable supplier a cast bronze or steel tube, either rough or finish-turned and bored, along with a set of authentic-looking wheels, and put your own 1200-pound artillery piece together in the garage. A full-scale 3 1/4-inch bore James-type tube only will weigh 800 pounds and cost from $400 upward—occasionally available from Dixie Gun Works. A complete full-sized replica with carriage can sometimes be had for around $2000. Considerably smaller and less costly is the 1/4-scale Napoleon, sold complete and ready to shoot for around $300. Its bronze tube is 16 1/2-inches long and the assembled gun measures 30 inches overall. Not as big or impressive as a full-sized Napoleon, but all parts work and the gun can be shot with round balls or blank charges. This gun isn't exactly a pocket-sized miniature and is big enough to tow along in a parade.

Up a notch in size is the Dixie "Little Mite," an all-iron, typical muzzle-loading smoothbore cannon of 1 1/4-inch bore. It has a 26-inch tube and measures 46 inches overall: Wheels are 18 inches in diameter. This may sound small, but the complete gun weighs in at 350 pounds. Smaller guns than this were actually used in warfare during the American–Revolutionary period, so don't get the idea it's just a toy. The 1 1/8-inch iron ball it hurls can punch through both sides of a house and keep on going.

Probably most representative of the cannon used by today's enthusiasts is the Dixie "Civil War Cannon" of 2 3/16-inch bore. It utilizes a 43-inch cast barrel and a built-up carriage with 40-inch wheels. It is generally loaded with a 4-ounce charge of special cannon

Fully-uniformed in 1870's style, this Indian War's crew readies its muzzle-loading Mountain Howitzer for firing in the desert outside Tucson, Arizona. Considering the period they represent, it is quite correct for these troops to be carrying metallic cartridges for Trapdoor Springfields in their belts and to be armed with single-action, cartridge revolvers, even though their artillery piece is of the earlier muzzle-loading type.

powder. Cast iron balls of proper size are available but baby food or juice cans filled with concrete are the most popular and economical projectiles. This little jewel will cost you around $400, ready to shoot. Not as pretty as a gleaming golden Napoleon, but a lot easier on the wallet.

A number of small makers produce a few cannons in their spare time, one of which is Bob Tingle of Shelbyville, Indiana. "Barney's Cannons" and the Erwin Brothers are larger makers which turn out hundreds of cannons. However, Dixie Gun Works is the best single source for a number of models, as well as for balls, accessories and parts. Turner Kirkland can produce almost any cannon you might want or be able to afford, though even he envies one friend of

mine who has five original bronze guns, complete with limbers and implements, in his barn.

Cannon gunnery is a bit different from regular muzzle-loading shooting. Reading contemporary accounts of artillery actions over a century ago will readily convince anyone that a cannoneer's lot was not a happy one. Accounts of burst guns and premature firings along with legs crushed by recoil and explosions of powder in limbers and in the gun pit seem to indicate the cannoneer wasn't a very good insurance risk.

All of those hazards can be eliminated in firing replica cannons and certainly this should be done. Only small powder charges should be used, mere fractions of the service charges used in comparable

The same crew firing a ceremonial round at the Three-Point Rifle and Pistol Range near Tucson; note positions of the individual crew members intended to keep them safe from the gun during recoil and also to minimize the effects of muzzle blast and retort. Gunner is at left and has just snapped the lanyard hard with his right hand to fire this load of canister which chewed up the 200-meter backstop on this range.

bore original guns. For example, a 6-pounder Civil War service charge was 1-1/4 pounds of powder—yet less than half a pound of cannon powder is more than enough to produce satisfactory results on today's cannon range. This reduction of powder charge eliminates the possibility of burst tubes and heavy recoil which were the bane of early-day cannoneers.

Careful servicing of the piece and rigid crew discipline will eliminate the other hazards. Here are things *not* to do:

Never place any part of your body in front of the muzzle of a loaded gun or while loading.

Never prime, cap or fuse the piece until you are *really* ready to fire.

Never leave the gun loaded—load only when in-

tending to fire immediately. If firing is delayed, draw the charge or isolate the gun.

Never insert a fresh powder charge after firing without first swabbing the bore *full length* with a *wet* sponge or mop.

Never fail to thumb the vent while loading.

Never stand directly behind any part of the piece as it is fired.

Never smoke or allow any high heat or open flame around the gun position, especially near the powder.

Never leave powder or powder charges exposed at the gun position.

Never overload.

Never use oversized projectiles.

Never use smokeless powder or fine-granulation

black powder.

Never joke around or indulge in horseplay.

Never use a cannon not known to be in perfect condition.

Never experiment with explosive or elongated projectiles.

Never fail to use plain, ordinary common sense in everything you do around the cannon.

Assuming that you or a group have somehow acquired a serviceable muzzle-loading cannon, how is it to be handled?

Most current models are intended to be ignited by time fuses—quite like the common dynamite fuse, although a percussion firing mechanism available from Dixie can be used. The fuse burns at the rate of about 30 feet per minute and each new batch should be tested against a stop watch. Do this before ever attempting to load the cannon.

Clean the bore and vent of grease or oil. I'll assume you've had the good judgment to retire with your artillery to a place where neither sound nor shot will create any hard feelings or injury to persons or property.

While a powder ladle can be used, it is sloppy, slow and far less safe than properly bagged powder charges. In fact, in the olden days artillery men used a ladle only as a last resort when bagged charges ran out.

Although plain paper and nitrated paper containers were once used for modern cannon shooting, they are less safe than *foiled* powder charges. Foiled charges are actually easier to make and use and have been required as a safety measure since the early 1960's. A properly foiled powder charge is fully enclosed by *two* layers of heavy aluminum foil—the heavy-duty broiler foil is best. Ideally, the charge is in cylindrical form, just small enough in diameter to slide easily down the bore.

Roll the powder charge in two layers of foil and fold the ends over snugly. Alternatively, for a neater job form two layers of foil into a cup using the inside of a can or plastic cup as a female mold; pour in the powder; then fold the top closed.

Place the bagged charge in the tube; then use the rammer to seat it solidly against the bore breech face. The foil bag may burst once it reaches the breech, although this is not actually necessary for proper ignition.

Follow the powder charge with wads equal in thickness to the bore diameter, rammed down tightly. Wads should be snug in the bore. Best are wads cut from composition board such as Celotex, but similar lightweight material can be used. Some cannoneers simply use crumpled newspapers rammed tightly, but this requires a lot of work.

Excellent wads can be made from newspaper beforehand. Make a mold from a length of pipe which is capped at one end. Soak newspapers in water, and then tamp solidly into the mold to the proper depth.

Old British naval gun on Dixie Civil-War style carriage.

Let dry or heat in an oven to speed things along. When the wad is dry, unscrew the pipe cap and push the wad out with a stick. The wad will be precompressed and will hold its shape. It will be much easier to load and ram than loose newspaper and it costs next to nothing.

Powder charge and wad are all that is necessary to fire a blank. No projectile is needed to produce a satisfying report. For demonstrations and saluting, certainly no projectile should be used. I'll talk about projectiles later.

With charge and wad in place, give attention to the vent. If ramming hasn't pushed loose powder up so as to be visible in the vent, thrust a probe down into the charge. Then dribble fine powder (FFFg) until visible in the vent. Take your length of fuse (remember the burning time) and thrust one end of it through the vent into the powder charge. Some gunners then like to dribble a bit more fine powder into the vent around the fuse, but it isn't at all necessary. However, it does make more smoke when the gun fires—certainly more impressive for spectators and photographers.

Split or fray the free end of the fuse and the gun is ready to fire. The splitting makes the fuse ignite much easier and may be done ahead of time.

Double check to make certain no one is near the muzzle or directly behind the gun. Then from the side, reach over and light the fuse. You must stand clear in the event of the million-to-one chance that the fuse will "flash through" rather than burn slowly. If it did flash through and you were standing behind the gun, it *could* run over you in recoil. Mangled feet and legs were common on shipboard in the days of muzzle-loaders—a rolling deck making it difficult for a man to keep clear of recoiling guns.

A match or taper is fine in perfectly calm weather, but a smoldering slow-match held in a linstock is best for lighting the fuse under normal circumstances.

The fuse burns down into the vent and your cannon

goes off with a hell of a roar. The powder charge you probably thought too small will surprise you with its violence. The blast will hurl chunks of wadding several yards, some of them smoldering and likely to start a grass fire. You'll do well to have a wet piece of old blanket or soaked burlap bags handy with which to beat out any flames that start. If this is your first time, take note of the distance chunks of wadding are hurled. They constitute *dangerous* missiles.

You can, of course, dispense with the fuse. To do that, dribble the vent full of priming powder; then apply the glowing end of the slow-match to the exposed powder. This provides more instantaneous firing—there being no fuse delay—and is a necessity for smooth volley firing if a percussion lock or friction primer is not being used.

Do it again. But reloading brings up a new problem—premature discharge due to embers smoldering down in the tube. The very first step after firing is to swab the bore full length with a snug-fitting sponge or sheepskin mop well soaked with water. Two or three passes are necessary to make certain all embers are extinguished.

"Thumb the vent," blocking the vent with your thumb, to keep water from carrying debris into the vent. A thumbstall or old leather glove finger will prevent blisters on your thumb and also makes the job easier. Follow by a dry swab down the bore if you like, though it isn't actually necessary. Heat from the previous shot will dry the tube quickly enough unless you've left the tube elevated so water collects at the breech.

Blow through the vent to clear it of water and use a small brush if necessary to clear it completely. Stopper it firmly with your thumb while the next powder charge is being rammed. This is just additional insurance that an ember still smoldering after swabbing

isn't fanned into life by air forced through the vent as the charge is rammed. *Any* glowing ember in the tube will cause the charge to explode while being rammed. Such an occurrence not only spoils the rammer staff, it can also spoil the fellow doing the ramming. Proceed as already described from this point; but rapid firing will make the tube very hot and when that happens, you'd best cool it down before loading up again.

What to do if the gun misfires? First leave the gun alone for a half-hour. You may only have a delayed-fire and it could go off disconcertingly while you are trying to correct it. There could be a tiny ember still alive in the end of the fuse. Then pull any fuse remnants out of the vent and brush away any loose powder or ash. Plunge the vent probe deep into the charge and work it around to loosen the powder. Dribble fine powder into the vent, insert new fuse and try again. Make certain the fuse sticks down well into the charge. It's wise to do all this while standing to the *side* of the gun, clear of its recoil path—just in case.

If all this fails, prepare to draw the charge. Use the cannon worm to pull out wadding. The worm will also usually serve to pull out a round ball; but if you're using the popular concrete-filled can projectiles, difficulty may be encountered. Try a small powerful magnet on the end of a rammer staff. If that doesn't work, try a sharp-edged right-angle hook which can be forced through the metal of the can to give purchase to draw it out.

Once the projectile is out, use the worm on the rest of the wadding, and then flush the powder out with water. Pour water into the elevated tube and loosen the charge with a sharp stick. Then lower the muzzle to let the slush run out. Finish by cleaning tube and vent thoroughly.

Let's get back to loading and projectiles. Iron balls about 1/4-inch less than bore diameter are available in

Typical of small-scale muzzle-loading cannons that have become popular is the "Little Mite" all metal rig sold by Dixie Gun Works. No lightweight, it weighs in at about 350 pounds, has a 26-inch tube and is 20 inches high. Bore is 1-1/4 inches and it makes one hell of a noise.

A full-scale reproduction of the Civil War James gun, weighing nearly half a ton. Steel tube-lined bore measures 3-1/4 inches. Can be purchased from Dixie Gun Works for about $500.

some sizes but are costly. Metal, baby-food and juice cans can be found which fit loosely into the more standard bores. Filled with concrete, they make entirely satisfactory *cheap* projectiles. Cans may also be filled with sand if they've not had their tops completely removed. A sand-filled projectile is easier to pierce and withdraw than one of concrete in the event of a misfire.

Once powder and wadding are in place, the projectile is seated on the wadding with the rammer. If you're shooting at relatively high angles of elevation, the gun may then be fired without a top wad. Personally, I prefer a tight-fitting wad over the projectile. This can be a single fiber disc or a pressed newspaper wad of the type already described. Don't make it too thick—one half to one inch is plenty. Don't get the idea that such projectiles are harmless. Either will punch through both sides of a barn as one individual who shall remain nameless found out. Even the very light powder charges give projectiles a most respectable amount of energy. Loaded with blanks, these cannons are still not toys. A quarter-sized chunk of wadding can cause serious injury if it strikes a person. I've seen wad fragments breeze right on through 1/4-inch plywood 10 feet from the muzzle. Muzzle-loading cannons are true firearms, just as deadly as a machine gun if improperly handled. Keep that in mind and they can be lots of fun.

19/Restoration and Refinishing

You'll probably start shooting with a modern re-production and might even eventually *build* your own battery. And a dozen guns later, although you'll still be shooting the modern pieces, there's no doubt that one day you'll just *have* to have an original gun or two. Collecting proper is far too involved a subject to go into here, but as a shooter/enthusiast you *will* find it very useful to be able to put an old, badly worn original gun back into some semblance of its original condition *without* spoiling its authenticity or reducing its value.

New-condition originals are as scarce as WCTU members at a whiskey salesmen's convention and are currently priced as high as used economy autos. So it's likely you'll buy something needing a bit of restoration even if you don't intend to shoot it. The fellows who do this sort of work for a living command high wages; you'll probably want to do the job yourself.

This is all fine except that more basically sound pieces than you can count have been spoiled by uninformed attempts at restoration.

"Restoration" means just that—*restoring* the piece as nearly as possible to its original condition. It *doesn't* mean varnishing the stock, gold-plating the trigger and giving the barrel a high-polish blue job.

Honest restoration consists of cleaning wood and metal without changing contours and without removing markings or evidence of genuine wear. It includes replacing *only* small parts such as pins, screws, springs, etc., to place the piece in operating condition, and repairing cracks, splits and serious dents or deformation. In instances where the original finish *can* be duplicated without otherwise spoiling the piece, it may also be part of legitimate restoration.

Recutting or relining a barrel to clean up a rusted-out bore is restoration, while installing a brand new barrel is *rebuilding* and, in my view, decreases the value of the piece even if the replacement is made identical to the original barrel.

So you've made a good buy and now have a muzzle loader that needs some work to make it look and function right!

First it must be carefully cleaned and disassembled. If not too dirty, disassembly comes first, but it may be so dirty that it can't be taken apart until cleaned. Either way, disassembly is covered in chapter 4 on repair and maintenance. About all that can be added here is that hurried or improper disassembly can easily ruin a good piece. This is particularly true of stocks. Never under any circumstances try to separate wood from metal by brute force. If they do not come apart with moderate effort, *something* is holding them together. It might be a concealed pin or screw, an undercut, or simply thick rust or old oxidized oil and grease. Nevertheless, find out and take care of it *first*. Then the parts will separate without damage.

After everything is apart, cleaning begins—before repair is attempted. Dirt and grease come off metal first. Use soap or detergent and water. Scrub with a stiff-bristled brush and take your time. Don't be tempted to scrape with a steel knife blade or similar instrument; remember that *only* the dirt and grease is to come off. Areas where a brush can't reach can be cleaned with small scrapers filed from hard plastic, brass—never steel—or copper. Flattened cartridge cases are good for this. Don't overlook recesses, screw and pin holes. An assortment of bore brushes will clean out almost any screw hole. A tight-fitting brush rotated in a hole will dig out all the dirt, even from threads. In a real stubborn case, use a brass bore brush. Ultrasonic cleaning is great for those holes and recesses, but dig out all the loose stuff first.

Often a gun that is horribly encrusted with dirt and oxidized grease and oil will turn out to have been beautifully preserved—simply because the dirt protected it. If that's the case, you're in luck.

More likely, though, you'll find varying degrees of rust, some of which will have come off with the soap and water scrubbing. Internal parts, having never been browned or blued, can be de-rusted very quickly. Simply coat them with "Naval Jelly" and wipe it and the rust off at the end of the prescribed period. Repeat the application if necessary. Other parts so heavily rusted that the original finish has obviously been eaten away may be given precisely the same treatment. The Naval Jelly will lift off every bit of rust, leaving bare metal. It will also remove original finish, which is a form of rust itself, so can be used only when you're sure there is none left.

More often than not, however, some finish will still be present and should be preserved. In such cases, rust removal is more a matter of patience and effort than of technique. Large coarse rust flakes are best flicked off with a probe made by fitting a large needle in a wooden handle. Relatively fine rust should first be soaked in light oil for a time—at least a few hours, and if you're not in a rush, longer certainly won't do any harm. Then take the finest steel wool you can find and gently rub off the rust. Keep adding oil and replace the steel wool as it becomes clogged with abrasive rust flakes. Flush the surface clean frequently to avoid forming an abrasive paste that will wear away the remaining finish. Use the steel wool in uniform strokes along the length of the part—the direction in which original polishing was done. Don't rub it round and round, and don't apply much pressure. Fine steel wool, properly used, will remove rust *without* spoiling the remaining finish.

Once all rust has been removed, it's time to appraise the situation and decide what else needs to be done. If the entire finish is gone and the surface is deeply pitted, it should be left as it is. Simply preserve it with a coat of oil or, if you prefer, a sprayed coat of clear lacquer. If a significant amount of old finish is present,

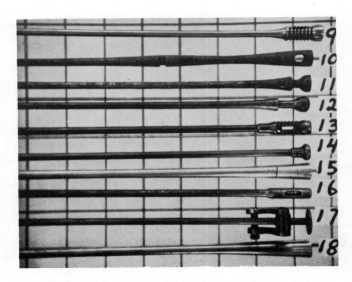

Replacement parts such as these triggers and ramrods are readily available, as are most other component parts. Many are of new manufacture, usually lost-wax casting technique, but hundreds of thousands of original parts are stocked by several firms such as the Dixie Gun Works.

the same procedure is in order. If most of the finish is gone, with only light to moderate pitting, refinishing *may* be in order. A browning solution can be applied directly over the metal without further treatment. The roughened surface won't reproduce the original smooth finish, but will take on color and will be somewhat protected by the new finish. Then treated areas will blend in with the remaining original finish.

On the other hand, light pitting can be polished off and the original finish duplicated. The advisability of this depends upon whether the polishing can be done without destroying any markings—and on whether you are competent to do a proper polishing job. Polishing is neither easy nor fast. Years ago I knew a man who did a masterful job of polishing and refinishing old guns. He used no power tools whatsoever. An octagon barrel, for example, was polished by thousands upon thousands of full-length strokes of *flat* Arkansas stones. The end result, which might have consumed weeks of his spare time, was a perfectly polished barrel with all edges as sharp and clean as new.

If you are willing to take the time to use similar methods, polishing by hand with shaped stones or abrasive cloth glued to shaped blocks, you *can* do the job. But there are no shortcuts and the process simply cannot be rushed. Every edge must be preserved and the original profiles and angles must not be changed. A proper job cannot be done on powered wheels by anyone but a *professional* gun polisher.

Application of a new finish depends upon the solution used. Browning is the most common and several solutions are available from the suppliers listed in the

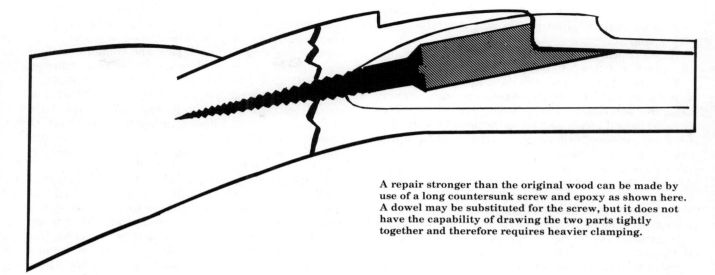

A repair stronger than the original wood can be made by use of a long countersunk screw and epoxy as shown here. A dowel may be substituted for the screw, but it does not have the capability of drawing the two parts tightly together and therefore requires heavier clamping.

Directory, Appendix 8. Many home-brewed solutions are listed in Angier's *Firearms Bluing and Browning*. Most important is to follow the maker's instructions. Once you've loused up the job is no time to read the fine print. Generally speaking, allow more coats and more time for the job than the instructions specify.

However, we still have the matter of repair or replacement of metal parts to consider. It's generally agreed that pins, screws, and springs can be replaced without detracting from the value of the piece. Pins and screws should be of the same type and dimensions as the original. A roll pin or a Phillips-head screw would certainly be frowned upon in a Kentucky rifle. Replacement screws and screw blanks are available in a wide variety of sizes to meet most needs. For example, complete sets of screws are sold for Colt percussion revolvers. The same applies to springs. Exact replacements are often available, some of original manufacture, and blank springs can be filed to fit. Nipples, being highly perishable, can be replaced without harming the piece. Some modern replacements are identical with the originals.

The more obvious parts are another matter. A missing hammer should be replaced if the gun is to look complete. But the replacement *must* be a duplicate of the original. The parts dealers can often supply an original hammer, frizzen, etc. If they can't, the problem still isn't too serious. Dozens of styles of hammers, triggers, top jaws, etc., are currently produced by the lost-wax casting process. More often than not, the proper size can be obtained. However, if the style or profile isn't exactly right, the careful workman can change it by filing, grinding or welding. Once this is done, though, the part should be marked in an inconspicuous place so that it is identifiable as a modern replacement. No matter how good it looks or how hard you worked on it, the part is not original to the gun. It is dishonest to claim or imply that it is.

This same general rule is applied to any replacement part other than pins, screws, springs and nipples.

Hammers worn loose on the tumbler or badly eroded on the face may be welded up and restored to original functioning and shape without losing their originality. The same applies to a refaced frizzen. These operations constitute a *repair,* not a *replacement.*

Stocks will often be in worse shape than metal parts. Splits and cracks in the lock and wrist area are common. Of course, cleaning is the first step in restoring any stock. Mild soap and lukewarm water applied sparingly with a bristle brush will get rid of the dirt. Don't soak the stock. Work up a dry lather on the brush and use that. Go over the entire stock, inside and out, and use scrapers in holes and recesses where the brush won't reach. Wipe with a cloth moistened with solvent.

The wood may turn out to be heavily oil soaked. Repairs and refinishing aren't practicable until the oil is removed. The traditional method is to heat the wood until the grease bubbles to the surface and can be wiped off. A great deal can be removed this way, but some will always remain just under the surface. Be careful, however; the stock can be warped by heat.

Far better is the use of carbon tetrachloride. This material gives off toxic fumes so must be used with care. In fact, I'm sure someone will write and chastise me for even suggesting its use—but with care you *can* use it safely, and it does a better job than anything else I've tried. First scrub all surfaces. This will remove grease to some depth, depending upon hardness and density of the wood. Further treatment is to immerse the stock in the solution. If the entire stock needs treatment, get a piece of lightweight pipe a little more than half as long as the stock and large enough to accept the widest part of the stock. Cap one end and fill with carbon tet. Immerse the stock, half at a time, and let it soak for a couple of hours. Then take it out and let the carbon tet evaporate, wiping off the grease left behind.

Repeat until the wood is free of grease deep enough to allow a new finish to be applied.

This treatment will bleach dark wood slightly, but only on the surface. It will also raise the grain, making extensive sanding necessary. Take particular care to ensure that all grease and oil are removed thoroughly from any areas requiring repair. In the case of a split or crack, wedge it slightly open and squirt carbon tet in through a hypodermic syringe and needle. Repeat until grease and dirt are flushed out and the fluid comes out clean.

Cracks and splits are easily repaired if they can be forced open enough to insert a hypo needle. Force epoxy cement in through the needle, and then clamp the parts together tightly. Use shaped blocks of soft wood to apply pressure with C-clamps, rod clamps or a vise. Do not clamp so tightly that the wood will be crushed or dented.

A complete break at the wrist is not uncommon and calls for drastic treatment. An almost-complete break is easier to repair if broken all the way and given the same treatment. First make sure the break surfaces are clean and free from oil or grease. Salvage all the pieces and splinters and make certain by trial assembly that they'll fit back in place.

Clamp carefully together snugly, but not too tightly, and check alignment. Select a long wood screw that will reach at least 1 1/2-inches past the break when run through the center of the wrist from the tang inletting recess. Carefully drill a pilot hole for this screw. The portion of the hole past the break should be large enough to avoid having the screw split the wood, yet small enough to allow the threads a good bite. The hole must be larger in very hard wood than in soft. The balance of the hole should allow free passage of the screw and, of course, the head must be countersunk to prevent it from interfering with the tang inletting.

Try to insert the screw and if everything works, separate the parts and apply a modest coat of epoxy cement on the mating surfaces. Fit them together and turn the screw in tightly to draw them together. Make sure the screw doesn't twist the parts out of alignment. A bit of soap wiped on the threads will help avoid this and will make driving the screw easier. Carefully epoxy back in place any exterior fragments of wood; then set aside for the epoxy to cure. A break repaired this way will be stronger than the wood surrounding it.

Even when carefully done, such a repair may show. If there are pieces of wood missing, matching scrap material must be carved to shape and glued in place. Once this is done, the joint must be carefully filed, scraped or sanded flush. Any minor gaps can then be filled with matching color-stick shellac rubbed in place

with a heated knife blade or small spatula.

Wood missing from other visible areas should be replaced. Often pieces will be broken or burned away around the nipple or flash pan, and sometimes along the edges of the barrel channel. The edges of the area must be carefully trimmed smooth with knife or chisel. Fit a new piece of matching wood in place; coat mating surfaces of the patch piece lightly with chalk; then press in place. Chalk smudges will show the high points to be trimmed down. Use epoxy cement and clamp in place. Once the joint is cured, file and sand the repair flush with original wood.

Minor gouges in the wood can be filled with stick shellac as described. Dents, where the wood fibers are not badly crushed or broken, can be raised by steaming. Shallow dents should be covered with a few layers of wet cloth and then a hot iron or soldering iron applied directly over the dent. Steam is formed, penetrating the wood fibers and expanding them back to original shape. Deep or very large dents may require more drastic treatment. A jet of steam applied directly to the wood is more effective. A hose can be clamped over the valve stem of a pressure cooker and used to direct steam into the dent. In either method, several treatments are often necessary to raise the dent. Patience and perseverance will pay off, however, so don't give up with the job half done.

Once all repairs are completed, consideration can be given to renewing the finish. If substantial original finish remains, you won't want to spoil it. In this case, use very fine steel wool to smooth the bare wood areas, feathering into the existing finish smoothly. Since the original finish was probably oxidized linseed oil, use a good grade of "boiled" linseed oil applied sparingly and rubbed in well with a lint-free cloth or the heel of the hand. Both stock and oil should be warm to facilitate penetration. This should be repeated at intervals of several days until the new finish matches and blends in with the old. If the relative humidity is high, the linseed oil may never harden completely; a "drying cabinet" will help, a box containing a light bulb to heat and dry the air.

If a completely new finish is required, sanding is the most important step. Just getting the wood smooth isn't enough—all the original edges and contours must be preserved. This will often require the use of hardwood sanding blocks shaped to fit specific areas of the stock. Glue sandpaper to these blocks to insure against buckling and stripping; rubber cement is best since it allows easy removal and replacement.

"Gritcloth" is the best sanding medium I've found, since its open mesh does not load up. Sand only with the grain of the wood. Work through progressively finer grades until the wood feels glass-smooth. At this point, many fibers will be bent over and compressed into the wood.

They need to be raised and cut off flush with the surface. This is accomplished by wetting the surface and then holding the stock near a source of high heat to turn the water to steam which will lift the offending fibers. This is called "whiskering." Wet, heat and sand lightly to cut off the whiskers. Use fresh, clean paper. Then repeat two or three times or until further wetting and heating does not raise any more whiskers. Next finish by polishing with well-worn, fine sandpaper. Only when this point is reached can a finish be safely applied.

While linseed oil was the traditional finish, modern oil-type, quick-drying finishes approximate it very closely when properly used. "Lin-Speed" has given good results when used sparingly and rubbed in well. If applied in accordance with the instructions and rubbed down with fine steel wool, it produces an excellent finish. Several other makes produce equally good finishes. Once the finish is completely dry and has been rubbed down, a coat or two of good paste wax will help keep it looking fresh.

Thus far, we've treated the stock as if there were no decorative inlays, patch boxes, etc. Often, though, there will be brass or silver stars and other decorations inletted flush with the surface of the wood. Unless they are quite loose, don't try to remove them. Those that are solidly in place should be left alone. Those slightly loose can be tied down by injecting epoxy cement under them through a fine hypo needle, then clamping or weighting them down until the cement cures. Those that are very loose can be carefully lifted out. Scrape the stock recess and back of the inlay clean, coat with epoxy and clamp in place. If the recess is too deep, causing the inlay to sink below the surface, glue a thin piece of wood in the bottom; then re-inlet.

This should all be done before sanding the stock in the vicinity of the inlay. Rough sanding can be carried right over a smooth inlay, but if engraving is present this will ruin it. Instead, sand *very* carefully right up to the edge of the inlay. If this leaves it protruding above the surface, you will be stuck with removing it and deepening the recess in the stock, then replacing it.

When sanding is finished the inlay should be flush with the wood, and the sanding marks can be buffed out with jeweler's rouge.

With all parts cleaned, repaired and otherwise refurbished, the gun can be re-assembled. Careful attention should be paid to fit of metal to wood, particularly in the breech plug/tang area. If wood has rotted or chipped away so that the metal is not fully supported, glass bedding compound should be used to fill the gaps. The same applies to any significant gaps elsewhere, but is especially important there because the breech plug and tang transfer all recoil loads to the stock. Any good grade of glass bedding material may be used, and all come with complete instructions for their use.

You may spend six months of your spare time in the manner just outlined to put a worn Hawken or Zouave back into original working condition. But the result will be a source of pride well worth the effort.

20/Echoes of the Past

All the world has its many historical societies. Their activities range from keeping mountains of musty, dusty documents in order, to living, breathing *people,* who actually *live* history instead of just studying or writing about it. The unknown, unheard-of researcher and librarian is essential, of course, if the records of history are to be available to generations yet to be born. After all, it was the actions of just such people, then and now, that make it possible for us to know what the past was like. Without the serious, sober student and his archives, we wouldn't even know that our Revolutionary forefathers wore their uniform trousers "very tight in the crotch, but very baggy in the seat" or that when leather was in short supply, soldiers' cartridge boxes were made of canvas. Nor would we know that during our Revolution the British enemy musketeers used the same yellow French flints in the cocks of their Brown Besses as the Continentals did in their Charleville muskets.

In the end, all historical activities depend upon those who seek out, store and eventually make it possible for us to retrieve knowledge of the past. Often to do so they must research and reconstruct, for the records are sometimes unclear or missing entirely. The matter of the French flints, for example, comes not from carefully kept old quartermaster records, but from recent work by modern archeologists. Ex-cavations at Revolutionary camp and battle sites by U.S. Park Service archeologists generated this knowledge through classification and identification of lost and discarded flints and flint fragments.

The *visible* historians are those who act out history, either now and then or as a matter of daily life. The entire Colonial Williamsburg complex is a classic example of this, and in particular it houses the Gun Shop where a regular crew demonstrates 18th century arms making.

On the other hand, there are active and very visible historians throughout the land; people who have banded together because of a common interest in arms, military history and the history of our nation. Such groups take many forms, but the most common are those pseudo-military organizations which copy the name, arms, dress and manner of specific military units of the U.S. Army at some point in history.

Apparently most numerous of this type of organization are those of the American Civil War; next come those of the Revolutionary War; and least numerous are those apeing U.S. Cavalry units of the Indian Wars period. The War of 1812, the Mexican War and the Spanish-American War seem to have been passed over; our 20th century conflicts are not yet far enough in the past to generate that sort of interest.

These organizations are not widely separated, single

The 5th Battery, Michigan Light Artillery of Lansing, scores a direct hit with its original bronze 12-pounder.
North-South Skirmish Association

units. Although certainly autonomous and generally independent, they are under some degree of regulation. The Brigade of the American Revolution sets standards for equipment and rides herd over the Revolutionary units; the North-South Skirmish Association handles the Civil War units similarly.

The Brigade of the American Revolution is a loosely structured organization formed in 1962 as a nonprofit organization to preserve the customs, dress and equipment of the Revolutionary War. Although formed by a small group of historians, it now enlists people from all walks of life. While professional status as a historian is not required for membership, one can hardly be active in the organization without becoming an active seeker of knowledge of the period.

The Brigade is commanded by George Woodbridge, who is also Major of the New England Corps of Light Infantry. This is one of the 80-odd units that comprise the Brigade and account for its approximately 2000 individual members. Although it is incorporated in New Jersey, the Brigade is headquartered in New York at the New Windsor Cantonment. This is a reconstruction of the last encampment occupied by the Continental Army under General George Washington before its formal demobilization in 1783.

Brigade members march back into time on weekends and holidays. They make public appearances and have monthly drills. Although their schedules are usually quite casual, the Bicentennial has created a great demand for them. Schedules have become hectic.

Be that as it may, members meet in small groups and immediately become individually indistinguishable from Revolutionary period soldiers, noncoms and officers. They don complete, authentic uniforms, arms and accouterments—breeches, leggings or boots, waistcoat, coat, stock, cocked hat, sword belt and more. Even shoes are often hand-lasted to 1770-ish patterns and worn over home-knit stockings. Uniforms may be of modern fabrics, but patterns and construction are as authentic as one can make them from detailed examination of surviving original items.

Members are especially meticulous about their arms. Not only are their smoothbore flintlock muskets exact copies of the originals, but so must be the innumerable crossbelts, buckles, pouches, bayonet frogs and scabbards, and other items pertinent to the main weapon. Even the ammunition they fire, ball or blank, consists of handmade paper cartridges as they were two centuries ago.

The groups meet as detachments representing original Revolutionary War military units of *both* sides of the conflict. When a detachment is formed, as were the 82 already in existence, it takes the name of an

**Looking as though they had just stepped out of the pages of history, members of
Lamb's Artillery demonstrate the art of 18th-century cannoneering with a 3-pounder.**
Brigade of the American Revolution

original unit. Today's roster includes the more famous regiments of the past: among them the 1st, 2nd, 3rd and 4th New York Continental Rifles; the famous "Black Watch" 42nd Highland Regiment; Lamb's Artillery; Hamilton's 5th Artillery; Morgan's Virginia Riflemen; Tryon County Militia; Continental Marine Corps; Tarleton's Dragoons; Knowlton's Connecticut Rangers and many others. A new detachment might select any as-yet-unused original unit name, as long as it is intended to be the same type unit—i.e., infantry, artillery, etc. Usually, though, regionalism prevails and other unit characteristics are also matched up.

Detachments normally meet monthly for drills, but the word "drill" often means little for many detachments are quite small. Even the larger detachments are often spread over hundreds of miles and cannot field a full roster most of the time. If only a few members can be present, the two-day drill may be mainly a family outing, with members working to-

gether on equipment or plans. When numbers are great enough, however, a full military encampment springs up overnight—complete with stacked arms, tents, cookfires and all that goes with it. Members may even be found eating hardtack and other 18th century field rations. With enough members present, there may be demonstrations of musketry and of field drill right out of Von Steuben's original manual written for the Continental Army. On festive occasions, a unit (or more than one) may grace a ball or dinner with both men and their ladies in full-period uniform and costume. And if a unit is sponsoring a social event itself, the menu might be right out of the Mount Vernon kitchen or a Philadelphia public house, circa 1776.

However, the greatest service of the Brigade and its detachments arises from the many public displays and demonstrations supplied at the request of cities and organizations. In this Bicentennial period, most de-

Soldiers of Colonel Billop's Corps of Staten Island Militia (Loyalist) fire a volley.
The drummer stands behind the unit, relaying commands by his drumbeats so that
they can be heard over the sounds of battle.
Brigade of the American Revolution

tachments are in constant demand to liven up one celebration or another.

From my viewpoint, the most important activity of the Brigade is its study and preservation of the arms and equipment of the late 18th century. By then, the flintlock smoothbore musket had reached the peak of its development in the Brown Bess and Charleville, and military tactics had reached definitive form based on the capabilities of those arms. Were it not for the Brigade and its activities, it's unlikely that fine hand-made Brown Bess copies would be available today; without the Brigade it might be impossible to know exactly what equipment the Revolutionary soldier carried and used. and how to duplicate it today. Without the Brigade, it's unlikely any of us would ever have a chance to see white-breeched Continentals at musketry practice or bayonet drill. The image of the Continental soldier to generations still unborn might forever be that which is portrayed in poor art

and film and television presentations, were it not for the Brigade.

Today millions of people have opportunities to see the Revolutionary soldier as he really was in equipment and arms authenticated down to the last stitch and the last screw and wisp of tow.

Civil War buffs play the same game as the Continentals, and in even larger numbers. There are over 3000 members spread throughout more than 175 units.

The North-South Skirmish Association is the regulating body for Civil War units. It, too, is a loose organization, which provides accreditation and establishes rules for uniforms and equipment and coordinates activities of all sorts. The N-SSA has its home range and headquarters in Gainsboro, Virginia. Twice each year this range resounds to the thunder and smoke of a three-day National Skirmish. These being the big national events, Skirmish units and individual

A corporal of the 3rd New Jersey Regiment fires a flintlock Brown Bess musket. Members of the Brigade of the American Revolution use only original weapons or those made to 18th-century specifications.
Brigade of the American Revolution

Colonel Knowlton's buckskin-clad Connecticut Rangers advance on a formation of the 23rd Regiment of Foot, Royal Welsh Fusiliers.
Brigade of the American Revolution

skirmishers from all over the country gather to participate.

Although national competitions hold the most status, it is the activities of local units in their own areas that are most popular in the public eye. Even though these units have long been noted for their colorful displays and demonstrations, they have been even more active since the beginning of the Civil War centennial. Because there are more units and because they are more widely distributed than Revolutionary units, Skirmish units may be seen almost every weekend at countless bicentennial activities. Local groups, formed to promote bicentennial activities find N-SSA units not only a natural crowd pleaser, but just about the most colorful activity to be had.

Recently I attended a two-day celebration in the little Illinois town of Knoxville—which any pistol shooter will recognize as the home of Gil Hebard Guns. Skirmishers from far and wide came to help,

some even trucking cavalry mounts all that distance. Their encampment occupied a large open area near the town square, complete with picketed horses, cookfires, Sibley tents, a blacksmith working his forge, red flannels on the wash line, straw pallets, obstacles, stacked arms, 12-pounder field guns and nearly anything else that might have been found in a Civil War camp—including some clear-glass, cork-stoppered bottles of liquid corn.

In some respects the Civil War units of the N-SSA are less formal and military-like than the Revolutionary detachments. For example, while the dress of the typical 1776 unit is sharp as a razor, quite a few Confederate units take pride in the fact that their original parent units were very poorly equipped and clothed during the 1860-1865 conflict. They demonstrate this with tattered—but authentic homespun—trousers and jackets, ragged blanket rolls, rope belts and bottles for canteens. That they look rough doesn't

A well-uniformed Confederate unit, the 27th North Carolina Troops of Oakridge, North Carolina.
North-South Skirmish Association

make them less authentic—eating and cooking gear, spectacles, and certainly their arms are meticulously correct original items or copies thereof.

The N-SSA prescribes the arms that may be carried and, of course, the artillery pieces that may be used. Safety is the first concern and authenticity follows next. Naturally any original arm proven to be in first-class, safe condition may be used for general activities. However, for competitions the rules change a bit and only arms of certain categories may be used in certain matches. Obviously, a light cavalry carbine can't compete with a full-length, big-bore rifle mus-

ket—so in matches they are separated.

Safety is of particular concern in the case of artillery pieces. Original guns are carefully tested and inspected before they may be fired publicly. Reproductions must be of an approved type. Civil War artillery buffs are more fortunate than their Revolutionary brothers. Although by no means cheap or plentiful, original Civil War artillery pieces and related equipment are far more numerous. This is due partly to greater numbers used originally, less time passed and more concern early in their life for their survival. To assemble a full battery of Revolutionary

Two soldiers of the only Hessian unit, the Fusilier Regiment von Ditfurth, fire in the direction of a line of Americans.
Brigade of the American Revolution

cannons would be difficult indeed, yet it is not uncommon in Civil War activities.

Few spectacles are more colorful and exciting than a Civil War battle reenactment or a lineup of artillery pieces throwing forth sheets of flame and clouds of white smoke as brightly uniformed canonneers rapidly serve their guns. The shouted commands and the ordered confusion of artillery drill always please the crowd.

Cavalry charging across the field, sabers flashing in the sun, horses snorting, harnesses jingling, troopers hoarsely screaming a strident battle cry—many of us

have heard our grandfathers describe this scene in years not long gone by. In my youth, many Civil War veterans were still alive and telling their experiences. If some of their tales grew or changed over the years as war stories do, it didn't lessen their effect. It is surely this close personal contact so many of us have had with the Civil War, its nearness in time, its broad geographical scope, the prevalence of well-identified battle sites and encampments and the profusion of artifacts of the period that brings about such wide participation and interest in the North-South Skirmish Association activities. There are over twice as many Civil War as Revolutionary units, and N-SSA membership is far greater than that of the Brigade of the American Revolution. The N-SSA is a bit older than the Brigade, dating back to the 1950's.

Detachments or units such as those of the N-SSA and the Brigade are not entirely unique to this country. They have direct counterparts in both private and governmental, ceremonial, military and quasi-military units all over the world. Within many military establishments will be found purely ceremonial units which have the dress, arms and other caparisons of a particular period or event in the nation's history. A classic example might well be the celebrated Horse Guards which almost every tourist visitor to London must see or perhaps the old Papal Guard which went so far back in history that its weapons were pole arms rather than muskets.

At present, neither the Brigade of the American Revolution nor the North-South Skirmish Association have any form of governmental sponsorship or support, even though they are recognized by some branches as highly beneficial. It is, in fact, amazing that such loose, private organizations can accomplish so much with so little; so much toward not only preserving history, but presenting it in living, breathing blood and flesh people from all walks of life. Funding for activities and equipment is nonexistent. In both organizations, individuals are entirely responsible for outfitting themselves to meet basic requirements. Uniforms, arms and accoutrements are paid for out of their own pockets. This, of course, insures that most members are genuine working enthusiasts and seek to participate rather than simply associate for reasons of status, exposure or ego.

Actually, membership in a unit is not always costly. To be reasonably and properly equipped as a member of a Confederate unit such as the Co. G, 15th Tennessee Volunteer Infantry, the largest single expenditure would be for a good reproduction Enfield, Springfield or Mississippi rifled musket. By careful shopping, that shouldn't cost over $75 in good, used condition. A bayonet, cartridge box, cap box and a shoulder belt complete the weaponry for only a few dollars. A Confederate uniform of the late war period can be approximated with brogans, almost any inexpensive serge trousers and jacket, a slouch hat or reproduction kepi and a checkered shirt. Field equipment could consist of a blanket rolled and tied with a rope, a small ground sheet, a bottle or tin canteen, a canvas knapsack, a tin cup and tin plate and a set of cheap 1920-ish eating tools. No big cash outlay at all.

On the other hand, someone wishing to outfit himself fully with both field and dress uniform of the Continental Army, as well as appropriate arms and field gear, might well invest over $1000. A custom-made, Artillery Sergeant's dress uniform (you can't buy that at Robert Hall's) will easily cost several hundred dollars. A pair of hand-lasted shoes or boots made from late 18th century patterns can cost nearly as much, and a best-quality Brown Bess musket reproduction will cost nearly $300.

In between those examples one can spend as little or as much as he likes in outfitting himself as a piece of living history.

Of course, when one gets into cavalry and artillery units, there are other factors. The prospective cavalryman will probably already own his mount, so will need only period horse gear. On the other hand, few recruits are likely to have a Revolutionary or Civil War field gun among the family artifacts. Good original guns bring many thousands of dollars, and all the related gear—limber, trailer, chests and implements, harness, etc.—are nearly as dear. Good, reproduction guns may be obtained for quite a bit less, but are still costly. The solution for artillery is found in a group effort in which several people pool their resources to finance the major items of equipment, while still taking care of their own individual needs.

However, as Ralph Hubbard, a member of the 15th Tennessee, pointed out to me, "It's not a matter of money, but a state of mind." Money alone, even enough to outfit a full regiment, won't make a man (or a woman) living history unless he possesses the state of mind that enables him to study, research, sleep on the ground, give up his weekends and *enjoy* what he's doing. If he possesses that state of mind, money won't present an insuperable obstacle.

I must commend the Brigade of the American Revolution and the North-South Skirmish Association, not to mention others that are less well known, for their tremendous efforts to preserve the military history of our nation. Let us hope they continue to do so and that others will follow their lead.

21/Cartridge Gun Replicas

Any muzzle-loading buff or gunshop operator knows quite well that an entirely new industry—called the "Replica Industry"—has sprung up since the middle 1950's to supply *new* muzzle-loading guns. It consists of a loose grouping of relatively large foreign manufacturers and some smaller domestic makers devoted to producing the guns, a large number of scattered companies making accessories and several large and a few small importers who tie the whole thing together.

The industry's main output is muzzle-loading guns ranging from 12-pounder cannons down through smoothbore Revolutionary muskets, Kentucky and Hawken rifles, shotguns, and a wide variety of pistols and revolvers.

Yet few take cognizance of the fact that we now have replicas of many black powder cartridge guns. By this, I mean guns originally designed around self-contained metallic cartridges, not the separately primed transition types. Most of these replicas are chambered for center-fire calibers, but a few are made for the ubiquitous .22 rimfire. The latter is the only black powder rimfire to survive although numerous center-fires are still with us.

In most instances, these cartridge replicas are line-for-line copies of designs that originated during the period 1855-1892. At most, they incorporate minor changes to adapt them to modern production meth-ods, such as investment casting. In fact, without investment casting, it is doubtful that it would be economically feasible to produce some of today's complex designs. The hundreds of machining operations originally required simply would be too costly. The same applies, of course, to the muzzle-loading replicas.

In addition, modern cartridge replicas contain much improved and stronger materials. Frames, breech blocks and receivers originally made from cast or wrought iron or from soft steel are today made from very strong steel alloys such as No. 4140. Today's Remington Rolling Block replica has a receiver several times stronger than originals made in the 1860's and 1870's. The same applies to Winchester M1873 copies, Martini actions and, in fact, to all cartridge replicas except those intended only for low-power cartridges using brass or bronze for major structural components. The Navy Arms "Yellow Boy" replica of the Winchester M1866 is the most prominent example of the latter.

So, with the exceptions noted, modern cartridge replicas are far superior in strength to their antecedents. In fact, some replicas are factory-chambered for cartridges developing three times the chamber pressure intended for the originals. Some single-shot rifle replicas of black powder designs are quite safe with magnum cartridges developing over 50,000 CUP (psi)

The British Martini-Henry, immortalized by Kipling, is copied today by Service Armament-Navy Arms in .444 Marlin and .45-70 with several barrel styles available.

chamber pressure. Most notable among these are the copies of the Winchester 1885 High Wall single shot and the Sharps Borchardt of 1878.

What we really have in modern cartridge replicas are guns far superior to the originals in strength and durability. We can have our cake and eat it too, in that we can shoot the "old" guns without being handicapped by their original weaknesses, and without the limitations of black powder ammunition.

Although mechanically superior to the originals, cartridge replicas do suffer somewhat in one area of comparison. Octagonal barrels and receivers of the 1880's were slowly and carefully polished by hand, then given a velvety-blue finish in the old way. The finish of today's guns is more black than blue, and the polishing is inferior. Much the same may be said of color-hardening, and also today's wood is generally of lower quality. There are other subtle differences such as visible casting marks and metal checkering cast-in instead of being hand-filed. We'd like these things done the old way, but costs don't allow it.

In spite of the obvious improvements, these guns remain 19th-century black powder designs and are at their best in the old black powder calibers. After all, a new Rolling Block in .30-40 or .444 Marlin can hardly have the appeal of the same gun in .45/120/550/3¼-inch Sharps caliber. Certainly a reproduction Remington Frontier revolver has more historic appeal in .44-40 than in .357 Magnum. So, though some of these guns are available in modern calibers, we include them here for their appeal and utility to the black powder buff who likes breech loaders.

Such cartridge replicas are offered by several manufacturers and importers—the bulk of them being produced abroad and sold principally in this country.

The largest supplier by far is Service Armament—Navy Arms Co.—who offers more types and models than all other sources combined.

Pricewise the better cartridge replicas are bargains. Though over-counter prices range from around $150 to nearly $300, one cannot evaluate them except by comparison with the cost of the originals. For example, in the 1880's a standard .45-70 Remington Rolling Block cost around $16 to $17 at a time when a prospective purchaser might be receiving 50 cents to a dollar for a long, hard day's work. Today's Rolling Block replica costs $165.

This means that today's buyer must work less than one-third as long as did his 1880 counterpart to earn the price of a new Rolling Block rifle. That makes it a bargain as far as I am concerned and the same may be said of the other cartridge replicas.

Cartridge replicas originated for the same reasons as did muzzle loaders. Original guns in safe shooting condition became scarce and prohibitively costly as collectors removed them from circulation. Thirty years ago I paid $7 for a very clean, shootable .45-70 Remington Rolling Block carbine. No replica could have been made to compete with that price, but today that old gun is worth far more than the $165 price of a new Navy Rolling Block. Thus, today's replicas are not only a bargain, but highly desirable to shooters.

So much for background. The subject of most interest is the cartridge reproductions that are actually available, and what it will cost to own them. For this purpose, here are modest descriptions and photos, shown under the original name applied to the item.

Browning Single Shot: Before selling his design to Winchester that became the M1885 single shot, John

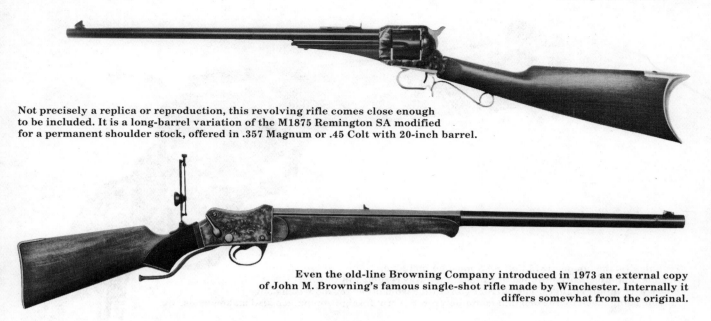

Not precisely a replica or reproduction, this revolving rifle comes close enough
to be included. It is a long-barrel variation of the M1875 Remington SA modified
for a permanent shoulder stock, offered in .357 Magnum or .45 Colt with 20-inch barrel.

Even the old-line Browning Company introduced in 1973 an external copy
of John M. Browning's famous single-shot rifle made by Winchester. Internally it
differs somewhat from the original.

Browning produced the same gun in Ogden, Utah.
Browning of today is again producing a modified copy
of this gun designated "Browning '78 Single-Shot
Rifle." It differs somewhat internally, but the appearance is the same as the original and functioning
remains essentially unchanged. It is offered in classic
style with 26-inch light, tapered octagonal barrel;
medium-weight round; and heavy round form. The
pistol-grip buttstock is checkered and the forend
carries a traditional schnabel.

Colt Single-Action Army: Made by Colt today more
or less just as the original SAA was produced from
1873 to 1941. Although not considered by some to be a
replica, it still falls into that category by my definition. It differs from other cartridge replicas only in
that it is made by its original manufacturer. Offered
by Colt in many short-run variations, it is basically
available in .45 Colt, .357 Magnum and .44-40 with 5½
and 7½-inch barrels in blue or nickel finish; blued guns
have color-hardening on the receiver. Standard grips
are checkered black plastic.

Martini Rifle: An accurate British-made copy of the
old Peabody/Martini-Henry action produced and
marked for Navy Arms. Originally dimensioned for
the .577 case, the action will accept the very largest
cartridges and carries the long "monkey-tail" operating lever. This replica is stronger than the original,
which had an enviable reputation for strength. Both
Standard and Creedmoor models are available in
.45-70 and .444 Marlin calibers. Receiver is color-hardened with cast-in ornamentation and bright-polished
breech block; barrel is blued; walnut PG stock with
checkered grip and schnabel forend.

Standard Rifle: 26″ or 24″, half-octagon or octagon
   barrel; .45-70 or .444 Marlin; open sights.
Creedmoor Rifle: 28″ or 30″ barrel; half-octagon or
   octagon bbl; .45-70 or .444 Marlin; Creedmoor-
   style tang sight.

Remington "Baby" Rolling Block Carbine: This
is a copy of the small 1901 Remington action with a
light 20-inch barrel and overall weight of 4¾ pounds.
Offered by Navy Arms in calibers .22 LR, .22 Hornet
or .357 Magnum. Action is color-hardened; barrel is
blued; butt plate and trigger guard are polished brass.

Remington M1875 Frontier Revolver: This is an
exceedingly good copy of the original Remington that
was intended to compete with the SAA Colt of 1873.
The design was superior to the Colt, and still is. This
copy has been modified by the internal addition of a
hammer safety, a considerable improvement over the
original that does not detract from its appearance or
performance in the least. Manufactured exclusively
for Navy Arms with smooth walnut grips in calibers
.357 Magnum, .45 Colt and .44-40 Winchester. The
first two calibers come with 7½-inch barrel, blue or
full-nickel finish. Blued guns have color-hardened
frame and polished brass trigger guard. Caliber .44-40
comes in 7¼-inch barrel, nickel finish only.

Remington Revolving Rifle: Not a genuine copy of
an original model, this is a carbine adaptation of the
Navy Arms M1875 Remington revolver patterned
after the old Remington percussion revolving carbine.
It follows the pattern set in muzzle-loading replicas in
which modern adaptations of one or more originals are
made in traditional style and form. In short, it isn't

Technically, the famous 1873 Colt SAA must be included.
Original manufacture continued until 1941, then was resumed in the mid-
1950's with minor changes. The current guns differ from other reproductions only
in their being made by the original manufacturer. Several foreign companies also make copies.

Outstanding among handguns is this Uberti (Italy) copy
of the 1875 Remington SA revolver made for and sold by
Service Armament-Navy Arms. Offered in .44-40 caliber, with
nickeled, 7 1/4-inch barrel; also in .45 Colt and .357 Magnum, 7 1/2-inch
barrel. In the 1870's this design was superior to the SA Colt, and it still is.

A variation of the "Baby" Remington action is the basis for this Service
Armament-Navy Arms rolling-block pistol in .22 LR, .22 WRFM or .357 Magnum.

This Navy Arms copy of the "Baby" Remington Rolling Block is a light carbine
at 4 3/4 pounds with 20-inch barrel. Calibers are .22 LR, .22 Hornet and .357 Magnum.

Navy offers several barrel variations in this copy of the full-sized Remington
Rolling Block in calibers .444 Marlin and .45-70.

One of the most famous U.S. arms, the "Trapdoor Springfield" has been reproduced
by Harrington & Richardson in both infantry-rifle and cavalry-carbine form,
chambered for the original .45-70 cartridge. Plain and commemorative variations have
been made, the Custer and Little Big Horn models being the most ornate and quite costly.

really a replica, yet it falls more into the replica class
than anywhere else. Navy Arms offers this model in
.357 Magnum or .45 Colt caliber with a 20-inch barrel,
sculptured trigger guard and smooth walnut buttstock with polished brass crescent butt plate. Finish is
blue with color-hardened frame.

Remington Rolling Block Pistol: An adaptation of
the small rolling block action originally called "Baby"
and made mainly for rimfire calibers. Marketed by
Navy Arms with 8-inch barrel in calibers .22 RF, .22
Magnum or .357 Magnum. Barrel is half-octagon,
fitted with modern open sights; smooth walnut grip
and forend; color-hardened receiver, blued barrel.

Remington Rolling Block Rifle: Manufactured in
Italy exclusively for Navy Arms and so marked. The
action copies the basic big-frame Remington of 1901
with a barrel shank and receiver large enough for
cartridges up to .50 caliber. Two barrel styles, full-oc-
tagon and half-octagon, are offered in calibers .45-70
and .444 Marlin. A few are also being chambered for
the long RCBS .45 basic case (3⅛ inches long). Open
sights of modern style are standard, and the upper
tang is drilled and tapped for an accessory long-range
tang sight. Actions are color- hardened and barrels are
blued; trigger guard, butt plates and stock bands are
polished brass.

These guns have demonstrated exceptional accuracy with factory-loaded .45-70 cartridges as well as
with handloads. Blow-up tests prove them to be many
times stronger than the original, and they accept
magnum-class loads without any sign of trouble.
Standard Rifle: 22″ octagon barrel; 24″ or 26″ octagon
    or half-octagon barrel; .45-70 or .444 Marlin.
Creedmoor Rifle: 28″ or 30″ half-octagon barrel;
    .45-70 or .444 Marlin.

Springfield Trap Door M1873: Famous for being
the first breech-loading rifle adopted by the U.S.
Army and for the part it played in the Indian Wars,
this rifle has been copied very accurately by Harrington & Richardson. Conceived originally as a commemorative item in carbine form, it has been continued in the H&R line as a plain standard item in .45-70
caliber. The "Little Big Horn" and "Custer" commemorative carbines are the most ornate and costly
commemorative guns produced in this country. The
standard models are perfectly ordinary in appearance,
almost indistinguishable from the originals.
Cavalry Carbine: 22″ barrel; .45-70; blue finish; sling
    ring and bridle.
Officers Model: 26″ barrel; .45-70; blue finish; en-
    graved action; metal forend cap; checkered grip;
    vernier tang sight.
Infantry Rifle: 32″ barrel; .45-70; blue finish.

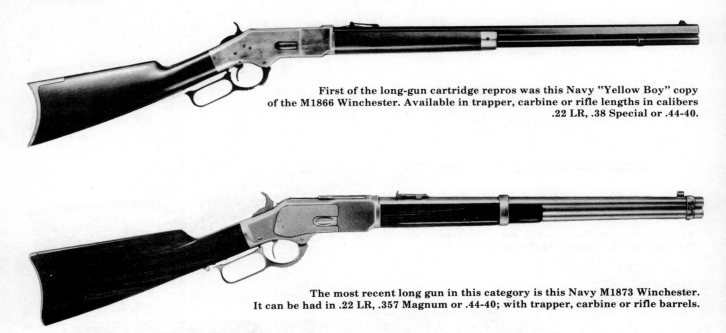

First of the long-gun cartridge repros was this Navy "Yellow Boy" copy of the M1866 Winchester. Available in trapper, carbine or rifle lengths in calibers .22 LR, .38 Special or .44-40.

The most recent long gun in this category is this Navy M1873 Winchester. It can be had in .22 LR, .357 Magnum or .44-40; with trapper, carbine or rifle barrels.

Winchester M1866 "Yellow Boy": An Italian-made copy of the '66 Winchester with some minor modifications. Made with a brass frame, it does not have the greater strength of other cartridge replicas. Receiver, forend tip and butt plate are polished brass; balance is blued. Offered by Navy Arms in several variations and calibers including ornate engraving on special order.

Trapper Model: 16½″ round barrel; open sights; calibers .22 LR, .38 Spl., .44-40.

Carbine Model: 19″ round barrel; open sights; calibers .22 LR, .38 Spl., .44-40.

Rifle Model: 24″ octagonal barrel; open sights; calibers .38 Spl., .44-40.

Winchester M1873: A modern copy of the famous '73 Winchester for Navy Arms by Uberti of Italy. All-steel construction, dimensionally correct. Stronger than the original but still somewhat limited in strength by the slender links locking the bolt. Offered by Navy Arms in several calibers and variations with smooth walnut stocks.

Trapper Model: 16½″ round barrel; blue finish; calibers .22 LR, .357 Mag., .44-40; open sights.

Carbine Model: 19″ round barrel; blue finish; calibers .22 LR, .357 Mag., .44-40; open sights.

Rifle Model: 24″ octagonal barrel; blued barrel, color-hardened receiver; calibers .357 Mag., .44-40; open sights.

Winchester Single-Shot M1885: Manufactured domestically by Clerke Recreation Products, this replica is designated the "Clerke High Wall." It is a slightly modified copy of the original Winchester high-wall action. Modifications adapt it to modern production methods, but appearance and functioning remain unchanged. There are numerous variations of stocking, caliber, barrel length and weight—ranging from a plain classic style to modern. Stronger than the original Winchester, the Clerke High Wall action is regularly used with chamber pressures in the 50,000 CUP range.

22/Performance of Modern Black Powder

It has been said here, and in many other references, that *black powder is black powder*. Since the advent of powder in its present form, one has been considered generally equal in performance to another, given the same granulation. Variations in quality have existed, and still do occasionally. Aside from that, though, no one felt there was any significant difference in the pressures and velocities produced by different powders available to shooters.

This may be due in part to the fact that for many years only Du Pont Powder was generally available. Small batches of other makes might crop up now and then—mainly British (Scottish, actually), for example, Curtis & Harvey. With essentially only one powder available there was a tendency to forget the performance differences that might exist. The few comments that were voiced were mainly lightly supported opinion about greater or lesser velocity, uniformity, and cleaner or dirtier burning of one or the other.

Apparently no one saw any particular need to conduct valid, controlled pressure and velocity tests with black powders, though a few did conduct pure velocity tests to determine the effects of charge weight and barrel length. The most notable compilation of such tests was published at the back of Turner Kirkland's Dixie Gun Works Catalog. Parts of that compilation are included in this book and were re-produced in their entirety in the first edition.

Then, with the destruction of the old Du Pont black powder mill, an influx of foreign powders replaced the old standby. Although sold under several different labels, these powders were mainly Curtis & Harvey from Scotland, with some coming from Canada. Following that, Gearhart-Owen resurrected the Du Pont plant to produce its own brand of powder, and there were reports of at least a couple new powder mills to be built.

All this prompted a great deal of interest in performance differences. Furthermore, as experience with several powders grew, it became obvious that they did *not* all produce the same pressure and velocity levels under the same conditions. It also became apparent to shooters that the new Gearhart-Owen product was by no means identical in performance with the old Du Pont powder it replaced—even though made by the same crew in the reconstructed Du Pont mill—and it differed widely from Curtis & Harvey.

Ed Yard, a well-known ballistician, took note of the apparent differences and also had previously voiced disagreement with such black powder legends as "you can't put in enough black to produce excessive pressures."

Under the sponsorship of Thompson/Center Arms, Yard undertook to conduct extensive pressure and velocity tests in rifle barrels. Using specially designed fixtures and pressure-measuring equipment (mostly developed by himself and using the crusher method with *lead* crushers) a series of tests was begun. Following Yard's lead, the Lyman Products for Shooters also conducted extensive pressure and velocity tests with various powders, primarily for publication in its "Black Powder Handbook," companion volume to its various reloading handbooks. However, let me first go back to Yard's tests, their raw results and his conclusions—much of which has been previously published in *Guns Magazine* and *Muzzle Blasts,* journal of the National Muzzle Loading Rifle Association.

Yard postulates that in the past there may have been ballistic variations of 15 to 25 percent among the various powders available. Since adequate samples of all the old powders weren't or aren't available for testing, this estimate is based upon variations that showed up in tests of the more recent powders and a few older ones.

It was also determined by tests that generally in round-ball rifles, increasing powder charge weight beyond ball weight produces considerable increase in pressure with little increase in velocity. In short, when charge weight exceeds ball weight, efficiency drops drastically. On the surface this may appear unreasonable, but it is not; the residue (ash, commonly called fouling) of black powder combustion constitutes 57 percent of its original weight. Thus, much of the powder's energy is consumed merely in driving its own residue out of the bore; as the amount of this residue increases in a given bore size, the force required to eject it rises at an increasing rate.

As an example, consider a .45 caliber rifle whose ball weighs 130 grains. A 130-grain powder charge produces 78 grains of residue which must be ejected along with the ball; thus, the powder is required to eject 208 grains of material from the bore. A further powder charge increase to 150 grains raises the total "ejecta" (residue plus ball) weight to 215.5 grains.

In reality, then (though seldom realized by shooters), increasing the powder charge actually increases the amount of work the charge must do; it is not simply a matter of applying more powder to do the same amount of work. Because of this, a point is reached at equal weights of powder and ball where powder efficiency begins to drop very rapidly. From that point onward, as Yard's tests established, little velocity increase can be had, though pressures continue to rise. It's simply a matter of ejecta weight-increase outrunning the increase in powder energy actually available to accelerate the ball.

In specific tests of a T/C .50 Hawken barrel, Yard established that increasing the powder charge beyond 170 grains actually *reduced* muzzle velocity. The same result was obtained in .45 caliber at the 130-grain level, which represents approximately equal weights of powder and ball.

Old-timers didn't know all this—there was no way they could have since neither chronographs nor pressure-testing equipment was available to them. They reasoned that if some powder was good, more was better. Large charges weren't especially common in the East with Kentucky rifles, but out West a .50 or .55 Hawken might be loaded with as much as 200 to 250 grains of powder. Mountain men knew that a good rifle could withstand such charges without damage, and when going up against Indians or grizzlies, they wanted all the power possible; efficiency concerned them not at all. Quite probably the larger smoke cloud, brighter muzzle flash and greater recoil of the larger charges were all the proof they needed that a rifle so charged "shot harder."

It has been said that eastern users of Kentucky rifles sometimes fired their guns over fresh snow with successively larger powder charges until unburned powder granules could be found on the snow. The greatest amount of powder that could be burned *without* showing unburned grains in the snow was considered the *maximum* usable charge. It was not *necessarily* the most desirable charge. I've never checked this against Yard's tests, so I can't say whether there is any direct relationship.

In running velocity tests, Yard also checked properly patched balls against the same ball used naked, as in the hurried loading reportedly used in battle and sometimes in hunting buffalo from horseback. Generally, when the loose naked ball was simply spat into the bore (having been carried in the mouth) to fall against the powder, velocity was about 250 fps less than when patched and rammed conventionally.

Velocity tests also established that velocity gain per inch of barrel beyond 28 inches is normally about 8 fps per inch, declining gradually with length until at 42 inches of barrel there is no further gain. In fact, in longer barrels, velocity may be expected to drop as bore friction overrides residual energy of expanding powder gases.

For this reason, the shorter barrels of plains or mountain rifles did not produce significantly less velocity (and consequently energy) than their long-tubed Kentucky/Pennsylvania counterparts. It is likely, other factors being equal, that the heavier powder charges generally used in the West more than compensated for any small difference.

Yard's tests also gave the lie to often-repeated claims that excessive black powder charges do not produce excessive pressures.

First, the old statements about black powder pressures must be viewed in the proper context. They are true if made in reference to *metallic* cartridges loaded with black powder, and it is my belief that such statements were originally made in that context. This makes sense, because original black powder cartridges were designed to hold a normal charge, and only a slight amount more could be crammed into the case, even by compression and/or varying bullet type and seating depth. Therefore, no amount of powder that could be contained in the case could produce excessive pressures. On the other hand, there is no such mechanical limit on the amount of powder that can be placed in a muzzle loader, except in the instance of revolvers or screw-barrel designs.

This same type of statement about black powder pressures has also been made *in comparison with smokeless propellants.* That is, the speaker means that pressures of abnormally large black powder charges cannot be excessive *by smokeless standards.* That statement is true, but it has no validity regarding muzzle-loading guns which are in no way intended for smokeless pressure levels. This is clearly evident when we consider that modern high-intensity rifle cartridges operate at around 50,000 CUP while normal full-charge muzzle-loader charges generate less than 20 per cent of that pressure.

What we really have here is gross distortion of essentially true statements about black powder behavior. Had they not been distorted over the years by being repeated out of context, there would have been no need for Yard's tests to refute them.

In any event, with *some* powders (of which more later), pressures with patched round balls can easily race well past 10,000 LUP very quickly as normal maximum (equal weights of powder and ball) loads are exceeded. Certainly the centuries-old design of muzzle loading rifles and shotguns was never intended for higher pressures. Even when made of superior modern materials of much greater strength, the inherent design weaknesses present the probability of failure under heavy pressures.

In .45 caliber, good working loads range from 70 to 100 grains of powder and produce (with FFg ICI powder) 4400 and 7500 LUP respectively. As charges go beyond that, pressures rise at an increasing rate. In .50 caliber the picture is much the same with charges of 80 and 130 grains. In the latter, going from 80 to 130 grains in ten-grain increments produces pressures of 4300, 4600, 4700, 5000 and 6000 LUP. Note that going from 120 to 130 grains increases pressure a full 1000 LUP, more than three times the increase brought about by 10 grains at any lower level.

Other factors also have an effect on pressure and velocity values. In one of Yard's tests, merely changing from a spit patch to the *same* patch lubricated with Crisco (vegetable shortening) increased pressure by 1500 LUP. Other lubricants probably have a similar effect, but test results are lacking at this time.

A fouled bore will increase pressure, as will greater patch thickness or greater ball diameter. Yard cites tests where patch thicknesses of .011 inch, .016 inch, .018 inch and .021 inch produced pressures of 3600, 3700, 4300 and 6000 LUP, respectively. Note that pressure does not increase arithmetically with patch thickness; the step of .003 inch from .018 to .021

produced a 1200 LUP increase, 17 times as much as the larger step up from .011 to .016 inch, and nearly three times the increase from .016 to .018 inch.

Keep in mind, then, that the effect on pressure of these variables can be, to a degree, cumulative. For example, let's say you have been shooting a heavy load (equal weight of powder and ball) with a thin spit patch and clean bore. If for some reason you might shoot this same load with a thicker patch lubed with Crisco in a fouled bore, the pressure could easily be *several thousand* LUP greater; velocity would not necessarily be much increased, but the gun could certainly be overstressed. An oversized nipple vent might cause the hammer to fly back and damage the lock; a loose or corroded nipple or drum might be blown out, etc.

Of course, such random variations *might* cancel out one another's effects on pressure—or they might accumulate in the opposite direction. The worst in this instance would be poor accuracy and/or reduced power, but the gun would not be strained, so there would be no danger to the shooter or to bystanders.

In the past there have been attempts to increase the performance of muzzle-loading rifles. Most common was the use of a "double-ball" load wherein a second patched ball (both of proper size for the bore) is rammed atop the first. Obviously doubling the projectile weight will increase both pressure and velocity. Yard conducted a test on this, using both .36 and .45 caliber barrels and normal full-charge loads for a single ball. In .36 caliber the single-ball load produced 6300 LUP, while two balls produced 12,300 LUP; the .45 barrel nearly duplicated this with 6400 and 12,600 LUP. Obviously the weight of the added ball produces a striking pressure increase.

Considering this, if one attempted a double-ball load with a maximum powder charge, the results might well be catastrophic. With the gun heavily overstressed, the slightest flaw or weakness could convert it to a veritable bomb. The shooter and bystanders alike could suffer greatly in such an instance.

With the pressures of double-ball loads in mind, one might expect heavier elongated bullets such as the traditional Minie and the recent Thompson/Center Maxi-Ball to also stress the gun highly. Though such bullets generally weigh about twice as much as a round ball of the same caliber, pressures are not as much greater as might be expected. In .45 caliber, the 230-grain Maxi-Ball and 100 grains of powder showed 7000 CUP, opposed to 3600 CUP for the round ball; in .50 caliber, the Maxi-Ball produced 7300 CUP, as to the round ball's 4200 CUP, both with 100 grains of powder. The pressure increase is substantial, but not as much as with double balls.

Incidentally, in both instances, the twice-as-heavy Maxi-Ball achieved a velocity roughly 80-85 percent of that of the round ball. In terms of projectile energy, then, elongated bullets make much more efficient use of powder. In .45 caliber the elongated bullet produced 11 fp of energy per grain of powder, while the patched ball produced only 8.6 fp per grain. This gives the long bullet a 28 percent edge, something certainly to be kept in mind when selecting a load for use on big game.

As was mentioned earlier in this chapter, Lyman Products for Shooters also conducted exhaustive tests in most of the areas of muzzle-loading interest. A portion of those tests relate very closely to Yard's conclusions about velocity and barrel length relationship.

One Lyman test involved 30-, 34-, and 43-inch .54 caliber barrels with patched balls and G-O FFFg powder. At one common charge, 160 grains, the 30-inch barrel produced 1972 fps; the 34-inch gave 1973 fps, and the 43-inch tube produced 2113 fps. Thus, from 30 to 43 inches (13 inches total), there was only 140 fps increase. That is barely over 10 fps per inch, quite comparable to Yard's value of 8 fps per inch.

Another Lyman test, in a 28-inch .50 caliber barrel, bears out Yard's contention that little increase in velocity but much in pressure is obtained by loading powder in excess of ball weight. Charges used ranged from 50 to 200 grains of G-O FFFg in 10-grain steps with a ball weight of 180 grains. Between 50 and 60 grains, velocity increased 100 fps; between 100 and 110 grains, the increase was down to 41 fps; from 150 to 160 grains only 12 fps was gained; the final jump from 190 to 200 grains produced only 10 fps increase, for a velocity of 2071 fps.

In the middle of the forgoing load range, pressure increased generally 150 to 450 LUP per 10-grain powder increase—but the last couple of 10-grain increases, leading to the final 200-grain load, produced nearly 1000 LUP increase each. Thus, in the beginning, velocity was gained at a rate of roughly 1 fps per 7 to 9 LUP, while at the top charges 1 fps was gained at the cost of 90-100 LUP.

It becomes obvious, then, that the last few dozen fps possible can be achieved only at a very high cost in pressure and, incidentally, equally high cost in powder consumed. Adding velocity at the rate of 1 fps per 1 grain of powder is a losing proposition any way you look at it.

Lyman tests in .50 caliber also very nearly duplicated Yard's results with elongated bullets. At a charge level of 100 grains, the bullet produced 22 percent more energy than the round ball; with 150 grains of powder, the superiority was a bit greater at just over 26 percent.

It is worth noting that Lyman offers its own solid-based, elongated conical bullet similar to the T/C Maxi-Ball used in Yard's tests. Lyman tests were run with bullets of this design—and for all practical purposes, the results with it relative to the round ball were identical to those obtained by Yard.

In Yard's test results available to me, there are no data on traditional hollow-based Minie bullets. On the other hand, Lyman ran extensive tests with this type in different styles and weights, and in calibers .58, .54 and .45. High-speed photos taken during these tests show quite clearly that the hollow skirt deforms as the bullet leaves the muzzle when an excessive powder charge is used. Depending upon the softness of the bullet alloy and upon the skirt thickness of the particular bullet, obvious deformation can begin to appear with any powder charge over 70-80 grains in .58 caliber. This deformation takes the form of a flaring out of the skirt under the influence of powder gases trapped temporarily inside it as the bullet is first deprived of the support of the barrel walls. As the powder charge and pressure go up, deformation increases.

As long as this deformation is concentric and uniform and not too great, accuracy will suffer little. However, the combination of very soft lead and massive powder charges can cause the skirt to open up on one side or even fragment—and then accuracy will be non-existent. This produces the strange-sounding "whistlers" musket shooters sometimes describe, the sound coming from the unbalanced, tumbling and gyrating bullet as it passes through the air.

The traditional .58 Minie weighing 505 grains is given only about 880 fps by the service charge of 70 grains of powder in a Zouave rifle with 32-inch barrel. At this level pressure is quite low—under 5,000 LUP. The charge may be increased, with Lyman's highest charge shown as 150 grains, producing nearly 1400 fps and 10,000 LUP.

At the higher levels the average soft Minie will deform badly and may shoot very poorly. This can be counteracted in two ways—by using a harder alloy (a heresy to the traditionalist) and by making the skirt walls thicker. Shiloh Products has made molds for me with skirt walls twice as thick as usual, and these tend to eliminate the problem. Such bullets have been used with good accuracy (in strong rifles) with 180-200 grains of powder without any evidence of deformation. In fact, in the hands of Val Forgett they have killed elephant, lion, buffalo, hippo and other African game.

In fact, while I have not done so, it would seem a simple enough matter to modify any Minie mold for thicker skirt walls. It would require only reducing the diameter of the appropriate part of the base plug—preferably by use of a toolpost grinder in a lathe.

I have said already that there *are* performance differences between today's various black powders. This was mentioned by Yard and is quite evident when one examines the Lyman test results carefully. It is particularly evident in the .54 caliber tests of round balls and the 410-grain Minie in 28-inch barrels.

Using Crisco-lubed .015-inch patching with the 220-grain ball, 100 grains of G-O FFFg produces 1605 fps and 10,890 LUP; 120 grains produces 13,890 LUP; 150 grains, 14,840. On the other hand, Curtis and

Harvey FFg produces nearly one-third less pressure and about 50 to 100 fps less velocity. At 100 grains pressure is 6550 LUP; at 120 grains, 8060 LUP; and at 150 grains, 9180 LUP. Even increasing the charge to 190 grains raises pressure to only 11,200 LUP, still over 3500 LUP less than the 150-grain charge of G-O powder under the same conditions.

With Minie bullet No. 533476, the situation is similar; 70 grains of G-O produces 5160 LUP and 993 fps while the same charge of C & H develops only 3710 LUP and 868 fps. At 100 grains, G-O produces 11,090 LUP while C & H generates 5600 LUP, hardly half the pressure. At 120 grains (the highest G-O charge published) pressure is 14,720 while C & H registers a mere 5600 LUP. In fact, Lyman's testers increased the C & H charge to 190 grains, producing 12,480 CUP and 1583 fps. That is 78 fps more velocity with 2240 CUP *less* pressure than the lesser G-O charge.

At this point it should be stated that the previous quotes from Lyman test results are not meant to condemn or praise either powder. Both are satisfactory, but they are by no means identical in performance—so loading data may not safely be interchanged with them.

If one desires maximum velocity at lowest pressure in a rifle but doesn't mind using a lot of powder toward that end, then Curtis and Harvey is the best choice. On the other hand, if maximum velocity from minimum powder is desired at the expense of increased pressure, then Gearhart-Owen is the logical choice.

Regardless of what I might choose, there is no doubt about what a Hawken-armed mountain man would have done 150 years ago—he'd have opted for G-O powder because of its higher energy output, regardless of the other factors.

With a round ball, 150 grains of G-O gives us 2008 fps and 1967 fp of energy at the muzzle. That is 13.11 foot pounds of energy per single grain of powder. At the same charge level, C & H powder delivers 1873 fps and 1711 fp. That is 11.41 foot pounds per grain of powder, roughly 13 percent less.

Do not assume that significant performance differences show up in different powders only in heavy big-bore rifle loads. Lyman's extensive tests of a wide variety of percussion revolvers proves otherwise.

Even in the smallest caliber, the .31, with its 50-grain round ball and limited powder capacity, the difference already noted between G-O and C & H powder is clearly evident. In a Replica Arms Baby Dragoon with 5 3/4-inch barrel, 10 grains of G-O FFFFg produced 694 fps (pressure not measured) while the same charge of C & H developed 665 fps. At 13 grains, the velocities were 795 and 749 fps, respectively—in essence, then, a velocity advantage of about 5 percent.

In a .36 caliber reproduction Colt Navy revolver with 7 1/2-inch barrel, a maximum charge of 29 grains

(all that the chambers will hold) of G-O FFFg drove the 81-grain round ball at 1097 fps with 9440 LUP. Of C & H the chambers hold only 26 grains, and it produced 899 fps and 6340 LUP. That is a velocity advantage in G-O's favor of 22 percent. With conical bullets, the advantage remains, but drops to only 11 percent.

In a .44 caliber 1860 Army the maximum charge of G-O FFFg is 37 grains and produces 1032 fps and 7940 LUP. The same charge applies to C & H, with a velocity of 852 fps and 5360 LUP. G-O's advantage here is 21 percent. With a 155-grain conical bullet, a chamber full of G-O produces 861 fps; of C & H, 785—still an advantage of nearly 10 percent.

While the larger-capacity Dragoon & Walker revolvers appear not to have been tested, there is no reason to expect the powder relationship to change when used in them.

Even though the pressures indicated with G-O powder are substantially higher than what many of us believed to be normal for percussion revolvers, they have been in use long enough to convince me that they are safe in modern reproduction guns. Original guns are another matter entirely and it was not uncommon for them to burst cylinders with powder we know must have been a lot less potent than the Gearhart-Owen product of today. I don't recommend its use in them.

It is obvious that if one wants maximum velocity and power in a percussion revolver (as for hunting) he must use G-O powder. Powder space is restricted; therefore, there is no way to use *more* C & H or other powder to equal the velocity with less pressure. That option is open only in rifles where powder capacity is, for practical purposes, unlimited.

As can be seen from the forgoing, even today's black powder differs a lot in its ballistic performance. At the beginning of this chapter, I quoted Ed Yard as saying the old-timers of this country may have encountered powder variations up to 25 percent. It may have been even more, since the two makes I've just been talking about differ that much, and they are produced with the advantages of a much more advanced technology. Some may wonder why we don't hear of complaints in the old days. Well, the complaints were there, and a good many of them were passed on in one way or another—maybe we just didn't recognize them. Contemporary writings often mention preferences for a particular powder—and we can only assume such preferences existed because the writer knew one to be better than others. Then, too, earlier in this volume I stated that E. I. Du Pont established his first powder mill near the Brandywine because of the *poor quality* of the product of other American mills.

The real reason we don't have specific information on powder differences in frontier times is that there were no instruments by which performance could be accurately measured. The crude "eprouvette," or powder tester, was little better than nothing, but its mere existence shows that the need for determining differences was known. Actually a good rifleman shooting from a rest at 40 rods could have made a far better determination of powder quality than an armorer with an eprouvette. He would have needed only to shoot like charges of different powders at a target to learn which was the "stronger" and more uniform. But those simple methods known so well to today's riflemen are based on knowledge of drop, trajectory, velocity loss and other factors that were not known to even the most erudite frontier marksman of the 18th and early 19th centuries.

In any event, we do have such knowledge today, as well as the instruments and methods to evaluate black powder performance precisely. That is what Yard and Lyman have been doing. We don't have more information on more powders simply because such test projects are lengthy and costly. Mainly because of the Lyman program, we have a wealth of data on Gearhart-Owen and Curtis and Harvey powder of current manufacture. Other makes will undoubtedly be tested fully in time.

As has been touched on briefly earlier, we now have more makes of black powder available than at any time since World War I. First and foremost is Gearhart-Owen, replacing Du Pont which terminated manufacture after its disastrous mill explosion in 1971. This powder is of excellent uniformity, corresponds to the old Du Pont granulation sizes and is the "strongest" of the available powders extensively tested to date. In short, grain for grain it appears to possess greater energy than the others—sufficiently so, that it should not be used as a charge-for-charge substitute in heavy loads developed with other powders. It would be best to back off on charge weight and work back up when very heavy loads are concerned. Gearhart-Owen powder is available only under the G-O name and label—unless some entrepreneur should repackage and relabel some for his own purposes.

Second is Curtis and Harvey powder made in the ICI (Imperial Chemical Industries) mill not far from Glasgow, Scotland. Once Du Pont was removed and before G-O began operations (a period of several years), C & H became the principal powder available in the U. S. A. It was imported and distributed under several labels, mainly its own and Hodgdon, but also "Austin" and "Meteor," not to mention some repacked in paper bags and similar improvised containers without any proper label late in 1971. Cans with Hodgdon and C & H labels were packed in Scotland, while Austin was imported in bulk and packaged here.

C & H powder under whatever label does not conform to the Du Pont and G-O granulation sizes, and it is not identical to either in performance. That

has been clearly established by the tests I've quoted earlier in this chapter. It is *good* powder, with a very high reputation throughout the world. Having become well established in distribution here when no other powder was available, it remains plentiful and widely used. Some shooters prefer it because it *is* less potent than G-O.

Third, we have powder produced by the Canadian Industries, Ltd., mill. What I have obtained thus far is in yellow cans labeled "Shurr-Shot" and distributed by C & M Gun Works. According to some tests made by Ed Yard, this CIL powder is very much like the old Du Pont product in both performance and granulation size. It is definitely not as "hot" or as potent as G-O powder, but is stronger than Curtis & Harvey. When more tests are completed and the results are available, we'll be able to place it properly between the two for meaningful comparison. Because it does lie between the two mentioned, it should not be used as a grain-for-grain replacement for C & H in very heavy loads—nor should it be replaced by G-O under the same conditions.

Another powder mill has been reported as being prepared for operation in Oklahoma, and while I have not obtained samples, I do have a red, white and blue cylindrical can labeled "Western." This is the label under which the powder is to be distributed once production begins. I don't know what the performance of this powder will be, but would expect it to fall somewhere between G-O and C & H. This is a reasonable expectation, for to be hotter than G-O might be hazardous, and to be weaker than C & H would probably reduce its market appeal.

According to latest reports, this mill is still in process of being constructed and equipped, so production won't begin until sometime in the future.

Another domestic powder existed for a short period of time, deliveries having begun in early 1974 and terminated in early November the same year. At that time the plant, located near Roosevelt, Utah, was partially destroyed by an explosion that resulted in two fatalities.

This was "Green River" powder, similar to Du Pont, and manufactured by a firm called Western Technology. There is no indication that production will be resumed, so at the moment, only small quantities of this powder are likely to be encountered. We do not have any specific test data available on Green River powder. Should it again become available in the future, such data will doubtless be circulated.

This is generally the complete picture of modern black powder, with one exception. That exception is a unique, newly developed propellant called "Pyrodex" which is intended for use in muzzle loaders. It is so unusual that I have devoted an entire separate chapter to a detailed presentation of it.

23/At Last,
a Black Powder Substitute

For many years there had been talk and efforts aimed at producing a "safer" substitute for black powder, but there was no really urgent need for it until restrictive legislation became a fact during the 1960's. That prompted much discussion on the subject but not a great deal of productive effort. Propellent and explosives makers were of the opinion that a substitute for black powder was not feasible.

Efforts to make black powder safer to produce, store and use began long before smokeless propellants were ever perfected; indeed, the quest for safety probably inspired much of the early work in substitute propellants which led to smokeless powder. But even after smokeless propellants came into general use, there continued to be a need for the unique characteristics of black powder. In essence, the burning rate of nitrocellulose or nitrocellulose-nitroglycerin-based smokeless propellants increases as chamber pressure increases. Black powder shares this characteristic technically but under the conditions of its use in muzzle-loading guns, this factor is not significant. Still talking in generalities, this means that if an overcharge of black powder is used in a firearm, the pressure will rise almost proportionately with the increase in powder—but only up to a point where most of the excess powder will merely be blown out of the barrel. Pressures will seldom exceed 20,000 psi even with an overload.

By contrast, the normal working pressures of modern rifles with smokeless powders is around 50,000 psi or greater, but even a 10 percent increase in powder may radically increase pressures, destroying the gun and maybe even the shooter.

Although high working pressures are desirable in modern smokeless-powder guns since they make high velocities possible, black powder guns are not designed for such high pressures; neither will they tolerate them without bursting. That is why smokeless powder can never be used safely in muzzle-loading arms.

Although it is possible to produce low-pressure, smokeless-powder loads for cartridge arms designed for black powder, such as the early Colt Single Action or the Springfield Trapdoor, it isn't feasible to attempt such loads in a muzzle loader. For one thing, if pressures are held to safe black powder limits, velocities and performance are apt to be inferior to those obtained with black powder. So a powder was needed which would produce good velocities at low pressures, as does black powder, but which would be safer to make, transport and use, and which would not send pressures beyond the safety limits with a minimal variation in the charge. The propellent companies did a lot of research in this area, but they never found a practical solution. Some of the researchers claimed that it couldn't be done; others said it could, but not at prices shooters would be willing to pay.

However, those opinions that "it can't be done" did not deter a brilliant young man Dan Pawlak from the state of Washington. Although his schooling was in other fields, Pawlak had taught himself the intricacies of explosives and pyrotechnic engineering. He holds several patents in this specialized area, many with an emphasis upon safety, such as a blasting cap for Primacord which may be fired while held in the hand—it's even been declared mailable! He has also served as a manufacturing engineer for Explosives Corporation of America and has done consulting, design and ballistic work for the firearms industry, including development of extremely effective emergency flares for rifles and pistols.

While working in the fireworks, motion-picture and demonstration/special-effects fields with black powder, Pawlak became dissatisfied with its performance and safety and felt that he could design a better substance to do the same job. He was also an active shooter and handloader and although he had done little muzzle-loading shooting, he was well aware of the special problems that black powder shooters were having with restrictive laws.

Pawlak knew of the previous failures, but his calculations showed that "in theory" a propellant could be formulated which would produce characteristics substantially identical to black powder in firearms, including identical pressure-velocity ratios, comparable bulk and density, similar appearance, smoke and smell, but with less sensitivity to heat, shock and sparks, and no tendency to explode—and at a price shooters could afford.

He was relatively confident that he could develop a propellant with those characteristics which would pass the Bureau of Explosives/Department of Transportation "blasting agent" tests—primarily firing a No. 8 blasting cap in a quantity of the substance without detonation—which would remove it from the "Class A High Explosive" category, in which black powder is included due to its ease of ignition. However, he hoped that the eventual product would also pass the far more rigorous flammable solid tests, which would put the product in the same category as smokeless propellants, allowing it to be shipped, stored and sold under the same less-burdensome restrictions of propellants sold to handloaders.

To get started, he teamed up with Mike Levenson, another young man experienced in explosives research and manufacture. But once the possible formulas had been worked out on paper and methods of laboratory "manufacture" developed, it was necessary to form and equip a complete ballistics laboratory—no simple or cheap task. For this Pawlak went to another friend for guidance, firearms designer and ballistician Pat Yates, an engineer with China Lake Weapons Center. Eventually the lab was established and equipped with chronographs, pressure guns and test barrels, pressure transducers, oscilloscopes, cameras and all the atten-

dant gear necessary to learn exactly how a propellant is performing in a good barrel. Thompson/Center, one of the leading black powder gun manufacturers, was strongly interested in the project and provided the muzzle-loading barrels and locks used in the pressure guns.

Some two years after beginning with the project—working on his own time and using his own money—Pawlak had developed a light grey propellant of much less bulk than black powder and lacking many of the desired features. Nevertheless, it served as a starting point and did prove that the approach being taken was a practical one—for that propellant exhibited essentially the same pressure/time curve characteristics as black powder. About this time, the name "Pyrodex" was chosen and Mike Levenson was named the coinventor. Later Levenson moved on to other projects and his minority ownership of the invention was purchased by Linn Emrich, another friend of Pawlak who provided much-needed financial support.

At this point, feeling he'd proven the validity of his approach and the feasibility of manufacturing a successful black powder substitute, Pawlak began seeking financial backing and assistance within the arms industry. Although considerable interest was shown by several firms, nothing developed and Pawlak had reached the limit of his resources. Neal Knox, editor and publisher of both *Handloader* magazine and *Rifle* magazine, attempted to help Pawlak interest a backer in Pyrodex. Knox became concerned that the search for a black powder substitute would be ended so he and Dave Wolfe, president and founder of the two magazines, invested in the process and the refinement of Pyrodex continued.

At that time, during the fall of 1974, Pyrodex was a grey propellant with black powder burning characteristics and density and extremely consistent pressure/time curves; but fouling was excessive, causing ignition difficulties unless the guns were cleaned after each shot.

In the following months, with the addition of more laboratory equipment and further modifications in the formula, the propellant neared its final form. Fouling was reduced well below that of black powder, allowing more shots and more consistent shot-to-shot pressure and velocity values without cleaning. Smoke characteristics were adjusted to approximate the smoke produced by black powder, and ingredients were added to give the sulphurous aroma characteristic of black powder combustion. No muzzle-loading buff could be expected to accept a propellant which didn't smell right or give off clouds of white smoke.

During these evolutionary changes, the color of Pyrodex was changed from grey to shiny black, thus giving it more similarity of appearance to black powder. However, close inspection, particularly under magnification, will show that individual granules have a more rounded, pebbly appearance, while black powder kernels have planes and facets. Actually, the appearance of Pyrodex is much like spherical powder, even though the propellants are made by dissimilar processes.

After many variations had produced a propellant with all the desired characteristics as exhibited in both laboratory and field tests, the big question was whether it would pass the "flammable solid" tests allowing it to be transported and stored in the same classification as similar-sized quantities of smokeless propellant and sold by firearms dealers licensed to handle smokeless but not black powder (which requires a special license and magazines).

Although there are several tests in the series which must be performed or witnessed by a Bureau of Explosives (BOE) official, perhaps the most crucial test is one in which an electric igniter is placed in one can in a case of powder such as the manufacturer uses to transport. The case, usually a carton containing ten one-pound containers of powder, is surrounded on four sides and on top by cartons of the same size, containing an equal weight (10 pounds) of inert material, usually sand. When ignited, the powder must not detonate, as would be evidenced by a hole in the ground. This is a severe test and some smokeless propellants have failed it.

In preparation for the BOE tests, Pawlak ran his own preliminary test set up exactly as prescribed by the U.S. Department of Transportation (DOT) regulations, *but with an igniter in every can in the case.* There was a mighty surge of flame as all that powder burned simultaneously, but there was no detonation (no hole in the ground).

A few weeks later, the igniter test and all other prescribed tests were passed with flying colors. The official laboratory report concluded: "If anything, it (Pyrodex) is probably a little safer than the conventional 'smokeless powder' because the ignition temperature is considerably higher."

For the first time in history, a propellant duplicating black powder performance in firearms had been given the same legal classification as nitrocellulose-based smokeless powders. Dan Pawlak, a stubborn young man working with a minimum of equipment and even fewer dollars, had done what generations of experts had claimed could not be done!

With DOT approval on the powder, all that remained in the area of research was scaling up from laboratory to plant production—no major problem, for all the final test powder had been made in miniatures of production machinery. So Pawlak and his associates turned off all other industry interest in favor of the foremost powder distributor: Hodgdon Powder Company, Incorporated. As a result of those discussions, Hodgdon will be the exclusive U.S. distributor of Pyrodex in the sporting arms field, in which all initial efforts will be concentrated. Manufacture will be by Pawlak and his associates at a new plant near Seattle, Washington, which was completed in late 1975. Powder is now available at some dealers.

Hodgdon is marketing Pyrodex through normal channels as "Replica Black Powder." This term was suggested by Maxine Moss, editor of *Muzzle Blasts,* the official publication of the National Muzzle Loading Rifle Association (NMLRA). Maxine had been aware of, and quite interested in, the project due to her concern with the safety aspects of black powder and the difficulty of NMLRA members obtaining it in many parts of the United States (for instance, Hawaii, where *no* black powder is available). As Maxine pointed out when suggesting the term, when NMLRA was first established only original muzzle-loading arms were used but because of their short supply, shooters quickly accepted the necessity of using replica muzzle-loading guns. As in the case of replica firearms, the use of Replica Black Powder in NMLRA matches would require a rule change, but hopefully this will be done as soon as NMLRA officers have tested Pyrodex and are aware that it safely duplicates black powder performance in caplock rifles.

Commercial Pyrodex is now standardized in two Replica Black Powder versions: No. 2F, which can be used in most of the same applications as FFg black powder; and No. 3F, suitable as a substitute for FFFg. Both of the Pyrodex powders are loaded on a volume-for-volume basis with the appropriate black powder grade (not weight for weight). The bulk density of Pyrodex is 52 to 55 pounds per cubic foot, as opposed to approximately 65 pcf of black powder; stated another way, a volumetric charge measure which throws 100 grains of black powder will throw 80 to 85 grains of Pyrodex.

However, when the same charge *volume* of Pyrodex is used in place of black powder, both pressure and velocity are almost identical to black powder with either ball or Minie-bullet loads.

The price of Pyrodex will vary in relationship to black powder according to the differences in transportation charges primarily, but it is anticipated that in most areas the prices will be similar; probably, the initial retail price of Pyrodex will be about $4 per pound. Because more shots can be fired from a pound of Pyrodex, it may be cheaper to shoot than black powder.

Proper ignition of Pyrodex requires that the bullet or ball be seated firmly against the powder charge, preferably with about 80 pounds of pressure. Failure to do so can result in reduced pressure and velocity. (While black powder isn't usually compressed this much by most shooters, it should be, for pressure transducer P/T curves show that it gives more erratic performance if the projectile is not firmly seated.)

Firing with the ball separated from the charge also reduces pressure and velocity. When a black powder load is fired with the ball separated from the charge, ringing or bulging of the barrel is possible—this *has not* occurred with Pyrodex loads, though pressure and velocity will be greatly reduced. Thus, Pyrodex eliminates the bulged-barrel hazard that sometimes occurs when a shooter loads black powder hurriedly or carelessly, or when excessive fouling interferes with proper ramming.

While Pyrodex *does* produce fouling similar to black powder, there is much less of it and it interferes less with loading. In tests, patched-ball rifles have been loaded and fired with Pyrodex as many as 100 *consecutive* shots *without cleaning,* yet ramming effort remained normal. This is not possible with black powder.

Interestingly, this fouling seems to have a self-lubricating quality, for in some guns best accuracy is obtained without lubricant on either patched balls or bullets such as the Thompson/Center Maxi-Ball. Of course in revolvers, grease should be applied to the mouth of the chamber to eliminate multiple discharges due to flashover.

This reduced and somewhat different fouling produces another distinct advantage in ballistic consistency. With black powder, consecutive shots *without* cleaning will display rapid shot-to-shot increases in pressure and velocity, with a resultant decrease in accuracy. Pressure not only increases, but becomes erratic with a very wide, extreme spread as fouling accumulates. Even for no-cleaning strings as long as 50 or more shots, with Pyrodex pressure and velocity values remain constant after the initial fouling shot. In effect, *without any cleaning,* Pyrodex produces ballistic consistency superior to the ballistic consistency obtained with black powder by thorough cleaning after every shot. With either propellant, the fouling left by the initial shot after cleaning causes an increase in pressure and velocity on the second shot—the increase is usually about the same for both. However, as the P/T curve shows, subsequent shots with black powder continue to increase in peak pressure, then become erratic, as varying amounts of the cumulative, residual fouling remain in the barrel. With Pyrodex, after the fouling shot, the P/T curves superimpose on each other for shot after shot; the amount of fouling obviously remains constant.

Cleaning is as simple, or simpler, than black powder because water or any of the various commercial products will leave the bore shining. Although Pyrodex contains corrosive salts similar to black powder, it also contains a rust inhibitor; therefore, although the fouling is hygroscopic and cleaning is mandatory after use, there is a little more margin for forgetfulness. While either propellant will rust a bore that is left uncleaned, Pyrodex is somewhat slower to rust the steel. But an uncleaned bore *will* rust!

On the opposite side of the fence, no propellant ignites as easily as black powder. An undersized or partially clogged nipple and/or drum vent that performs normally with black powder may cause detectable hangfires or even misfires with Pyrodex. In an effort to reduce hammer lift, many of the new or replacement nipples in caplock guns have orifices too small for consistent ignition with black powder and much too small for Pyrodex.

Furthermore, "weak" caps designed to touch off black powder may not light Pyrodex's fire in some applications, particularly if the nipple is small or the powder is not firmly compressed by the ball. In tests to date, Navy Arms' caps, made by RWS, appear to be the "hottest" available, and have given consistently excellent results with Pyrodex. If you run into ignition problems, first try switching caps; if that doesn't solve it, try a nipple with a slightly larger vent. Generally speaking, caps sealed with metallic foil are less suitable for Pyrodex than those containing lacquered paper. It would appear from this that the recent practice of using musket-sized nipples and caps on sporting rifles might be especially desirable with Replica Black Powder.

These same ignition characteristics cause the existing form of Pyrodex to be less than ideal, if not unuseable, in flintlocks. While it can be fired, particularly if black powder is used in the pan, there is a considerably longer "whoosh" of flame and gases from the vent hole as the Pyrodex gets up to the pressure at which it burns consistently. Ignition time of flintlocks is long enough without aggravating the situation.

In caplock revolvers, except those with unusually small nipple vents, there are no ignition difficulties provided the ball is firmly seated against the powder. If a reduced load is used (how many use them?), the levered rammer may not push the ball or bullet far enough into the cylinder to give the necessary seating pressure. No. 2F works very well in most revolvers.

Although tests have shown no significant difference between the performance of Pyrodex and the related grades of black powder, both Hodgdon and the manufacturer stress that Pyrodex Replica Black Powder is intended for use only in modern-made replica muzzle-loading caplock rifles and pistols. If you use Pyrodex in anything else, such as grandpappy's fowling piece—which may or may not be safe with black powder—you're strictly on your own.

Hopefully, Pawlak will put his inventive genius to the task of solving the problems of the flintlock shooter; but in discussing it with him and the other parties involved, it doesn't seem likely that it will happen anytime soon, primarily because of the difficulty in designing a powder with the "instantaneous" ignition characteristics of unconfined black powder while staying within the confines of the DOT flammable solid requirements.

Of course some of the traditionalists, most of whom use flintlocks, will insist on "genuine" black powder. Examples of this might be the heavy bench-rest, slug-gun shooters, although the superior ballistic consistency of Pyrodex would be expected to produce tighter groups. However, the traditionalists might be hard-pressed to define a "genuine" black powder, for a little historical research will reveal considerable differences between today's black powder and that of a century ago, much less the black powder of the flintlock era.

Although patents have been applied for both the formula and the manufacturing techniques for Pyrodex, they remain highly proprietary. But analysis shows that Pyrodex Replica Black Powder has some of the same key charcoal-sulphur-saltpeter ingredients as the "genuine" black powder. Therefore, it might properly be called a "modified black powder," a propellant with added substances which tame the less-pleasant aspects of black powder's nature.

But if he didn't know that Pyrodex isn't black powder, the average shooter wouldn't even realize it—for Pawlak came *that close* to achieving his "impossible" goal. From the performance standpoint, the only changes that the black powder shooter will see in Pyrodex are improvements. For these reasons, plus its greater safety and the fewer restrictions upon its shipment and possession, we expect to see wide use of Pyrodex Replica Black Powder in the very near future. Surely, every muzzle-loading buff will want to try it and make up his own mind.

It won't completely replace black powder, at least not with the present grades, but it should be a great shot in the arm for a shooting sport that is attempting to grow, and is growing, despite a tangle of federal, state and local restrictions.

Appendix 1/Bore, Ball and Bullet Dimensions

Much confusion exists as to standard bore and bullet or ball size of many of the muzzle loading arms available today. From several sources we've assembled here as much bore/bullet information as we could lay our hands on. Due to manufacturing tolerances, wear, and other factors we can't control, any particular gun may differ somewhat from the values given here. When that happens, some deviation will be required. In general, though, these figures are accurate and correct.

BALL SIZES FOR DIXIE RIFLES BARRELED BY DOUGLAS

Caliber	Bore Diameter	Ball Diameter
.32	.321″	.315″
.36	.363″	.355″
.40	.403″	.395″
.45	.451″	.445″
.50	.501″	.495″

BALL SIZES FOR DIXIE BARRELS MADE BY NUMRICH

.36	.347″	.340″
.45	.443″	.435″

DIXIE RIFLE BARREL WITH FITTED BREECH PLUG

.40	.400″	.395″

BALL DIAMETER FOR REPRODUCTION REVOLVERS

Make, Model and Caliber	Chamber Diameter	Ball Diameter
Replica, 1860 Army, .44 caliber	.446″	.450″
Sheriff's Model, .36 caliber	.372″	.376″

BALL DIAMETERS FOR REPRODUCTION REVOLVERS (cont'd)

Make, Model and Caliber	Chamber Diameter	Ball Diameter
Walker, .44 caliber	.440″	.441″
Wells Fargo, .31 caliber	.315″	.320″
Yank, .36 caliber	.372″	.376″
Army, Model 60 .44	.447″	.451″
Centennial, 1860 Army .44	.446″	.450″
Colt, M1851 Navy .36	.372″	.380″
Colt, 1861 Navy .36	.375″	.380″
Colt, 3rd Model Dragoon .44	.450″	.454″
Dragoon .44	.440″	.441″
Dragoon, Baby .31	.316″	.321″
Leech & Rigdon .36	.371″	.376″
Navy, 1861 .36	.371″	.376″
Navy, 1861 .36	.371″	.376″
Navy, 1st & 2nd Model Dragoon .44	.448″	.452″
Paterson .36	.378″	.380″
Reb .36	.372″	.376″
Remington Army .44	.450″	.454″
Remington Navy .36	.371″	.376″
Remington Revolving Carbine .44	.450″	.454″
Ruger, Old Army .44	.452″	.457″

LEAD BALL SIZES

Western Size Buckshot	American Size Buckshot	Diameter (caliber)	Number Per Pound
No. 9	No. 3	.25″	280
No. 8		.26″	263
No. 7½	No. 2	.27″	238
No. 7		.28″	232
No. 6		.29″	186
No. 5	No. 1	.30″	152
No. 4	No. 0	.32″	144

LEAD BALL SIZES (cont'd)

Western Size Buckshot	American Size Buckshot	Diameter (caliber)	Number Per Pound
No. 3	No. 00	.34''	128
No. 2	No. 000	.36''	112
No. 1		.38''	96
		.40''	70
		.44''	50
		.45''	48
		.52''	32
		.57''	24
		.61''	20
		.63''	18
		.66''	16
		.69''	14
		.72''	12
		1.00''	4
		1.67''	1

ROUND BALL WEIGHTS

Caliber	Weight	Caliber	Weight
.20	12.0 gr.	.56	263.4 gr.
.22	16.0 gr.	.58	292.6 gr.
.24	20.7 gr.	.60	324.0 gr.
.26	26.4 gr.	.62	357.4 gr.
.28	33.0 gr.	.64	393.2 gr.
.30	40.5 gr.	.66	431.2 gr.
.32	49.0 gr.	.68	471.6 gr.
.34	59.0 gr.	.70	514.4 gr.
.36	70.0 gr.	.72	559.8 gr.
.38	82.3 gr.	.74	607.8 gr.
.40	96.0 gr.	.76	658.4 gr.
.42	111.0 gr.	.78	711.7 gr.
.44	127.8 gr.	.80	767.9 gr.
.46	146.0 gr.	.82	826.9 gr.
.48	165.9 gr.	.84	888.9 gr.
.50	187.5 gr.	.86	934.0 gr.
.52	210.9 gr.	.88	1022.1 gr.
.54	236.2 gr.	.90	1093.4 gr.

ENGLISH SHOTGUN BORE SIZES

Following is the table of English small arms gauges as given in the Gun Barrel Proof Act of 1868:

Gauge No.	Bore Diameter	Gauge No.	Bore Diameter
A	2.000''	11	.751''
B	1.938''	12	.729''
C	1.875''	13	.710''
D	1.813''	14	.693''
E	1.750''	15	.677''
F	1.688''	16	.662''
1 (one)	1.669''	17	.649''
H	1.625''	18	.637''
J	1.563''	19	.626''
K	1.500''	20	.615''
L	1.438''	21	.605''
M	1.375''	22	.596''
2	1.325''	23	.587''
O	1.313''	24	.579''
P	1.250''	25	.571''
3	1.157''	26	.563''
4	1.052''	27	.556''

ENGLISH SHOTGUN BORE SIZES (cont'd)

Gauge No.	Bore Diameter	Gauge No.	Bore Diameter
5	.976''	28	.550''
6	.919''	29	.543''
7	.873''	30	.537''
8	.835''	31	.531''
9	.803''	32	.526''
10	.775''	33	.520''
34	.515''	43	.476''
35	.510''	44	.473''
36	.506''	45	.469''
37	.501''	46	.466''
38	.497''	47	.463''
39	.492''	48	.459''
40	.488''	49	.456''
41	.484''	50	.453''
42	.480''		

Note that the gauge system goes down only to No. 50, which was until comparatively recent times considered a small bore. Below that the actual bore diameter is used. Gauge sizes shown are reasonably standard throughout the world.

ROUND-BALL SIZES FOR FLINT AND PERCUSSION REPRODUCTION PISTOLS AND RIFLES

Gun	Bore Diameter	Ball Diameter
Brown Bess .75	.740''	.690''
Derringer Philadelphia .40	.410''	.395''
Dixie Halfstock Rifle .40	.400''	.395''
Dixie Flint Pistol .40	.400''	.395''
Dixie Flint Rifle .40	.400''	.395''
Dixie Percussion Pistol .40	.400''	.395''
Dixie Percussion Rifle .40	.400''	.395''
Dixie Target Pistol .36	.360''	.355''
Door Key Pistol .36	.373''	.350''
Enfield Rifle Musket .577	.577''	.570''
Flint Derringer .42	.420''	.410''
Gallager B-L Carbine .54		
Cartridge	.535''	.535''
Muzzle Loading		.530''
Harper's Ferry Flint Pistol .55	.562''	.555''
Hopkins & Allen Pistol .36	.347''	.340''
Hopkins & Allen Rifle .36	.347''	.340''
Hopkins & Allen Rifle .45	.443''	.435''
Hopkins & Allen Rifle .45	.443''	.435''
Mowery Allen & Thurber .54	.540''	.535''
Navy Buffalo Hunter .58	.580''	.575''
Navy Enfield Musketoon, smoothbore .58	.725''	.690''
Navy Harper's Ferry Rifle .58	.580''	.575''
Navy Mississippi Rifle .58	.580''	.575''
Navy M1861 Springfield .58	.580''	.575''
Overcoat Pistol .40	.410''	.400''
Percussion Brass Frame Derringer .40	.410''	.395''
Spanish Percussion Pistol .40	.410''	.400''
T/C Hawken .45	.450''	.445''
T/C Hawken .50	.500''	.495''
T/C Renegade .54	.540''	.535''
Tower Flint Pistol	.670''	.650''
Zouave, Remington Carbine .58	.580''	.575''
Zouave, Remington Rifle	.580''	.575''

Appendix 2/Powder Charge and Load Tables

There are more powder charge recommendations for muzzle loaders than one cares to consider, along with several rules of thumb concocted by various individuals. We can't say that one chart or rule is right and the others are wrong. Actually, they are all pretty much right. Some shooters load conservatively; others love loud noises and large charges of powder. We can say, however, that the charge data given in this appendix is *safe* in guns in good mechanical condition.

I acknowledge that some of the information here conflicts with, or at least differs from, that contained elsewhere in the book. This isn't serious since black powder is a forgiving propellant. You'll eventually want to adjust charges for best results in your particular gun anyway, so these are good to start with.

STANDARD MUZZLE LOADING CHARGES
(for Original Guns)

Type and Caliber	Ball Diameter	Powder Charge
.69 U.S. Muskets Models 1808-1812-1821-1831-1840-1842	.680″	80 gr. FFg
.69 U.S. Musket Models 1821-1840-1842, rerifled from smooth bore	.680″	75 gr. FFg
.69 Whitneyville Plymouth Navy Rifle	.680″	70 gr. FFg
.58 Remington Zouave	.570″ to .575″	60 gr. FFg
.58 U.S. Civil War Rifles Models 1855-61-63	.570″ to .575″	60 gr. FFg
.58 U.S. Springfield Pistols Model 1855	.570 ″ to .575″	40 gr. FFg

STANDARD MUZZLE LOADING CHARGES (cont'd)
(for Original Guns)

Type and Caliber	Ball Diameter	Powder Charge
.58 Fayetteville, Richmond, Cook Bros., Columbus and other Confederate Civil War Muskets	.570″ to .575″	60 gr. FFg
.577 English Enfield Rifle	.570″ to .575″	60 gr. FFg
.56 Colt Root Rifle	.562″	70 gr. FFg
.54 1804-1814-1817 U.S. Rifles	.535″	75 gr. FFFg
.54 U.S. Mississippi Rifle	.535″	75 gr. FFFg
.54 U.S. Pistol Models 1819-21-26-36-42	.535″	35 gr. FFg
.54 Halls Carbine	.535″	85 gr. FFg
.54 Halls Rifle	.535″	100 gr. FFFg
.54 Burnside	.558″	60 gr. FFFg
.54 Gallagher	.535″	55 gr. FFFg
.54 Green Carbine	.565″ to .569″	68 gr. FFFg
.54 Starr	.560″	60 gr. FFFg
.52 Sharp's Carbines & Rifles	.535″ to .555″	60 gr. FFFg
.50 Smith Carbine	.515″	50 gr. FFFg
.50 Maynard U.S. Issue	.517″	50 gr. FFFg
.44 Colt Dragoon	.453″	40 gr. FFFg
.44 Colt & Remington Army	.453″	28 gr. FFFg
.44 Modern made Remington and Colt Revolver	.450″	28 gr. FFFg
.44 Modern made Colt Dragoon	.451″	40 gr. FFFg
.41 Dixie brass framed Derringer	.395″	10 gr. FFFg
.40 Dixie Flint & Percussion Rifles	.395″	65 gr. FFFg
.40 Dixie Flint & Percussion Pistols	.395″	25 gr. FFFg
.40 Dixie Half Stock Target Rifle	.395″	55 gr. FFFg

STANDARD MUZZLE LOADING CHARGES (cont'd)
(for Original Guns)

Type and Caliber	Ball Diameter	Powder Charge
.36 Modern made Remington & Colt Rev.	.376″	22 gr. FFFg
.36 Colt & Remington Navy, Whitney, Pettingill, Savage, Cooper, Bacon and most .36 Revolvers	.376″	22 gr. FFFg
.31 Colt & Remington Pocket Revolver & other .31 American Revolvers	.321″	15 gr. FFFg
Pepperboxes—no standard caliber	.30′ to .38″	15 gr. to 20 gr.

POWDER CHARGE RULES

Kentucky Rifles: One grain weight of powder for each caliber, i.e.: .41 caliber rifle will use about 41 grains of black powder.

Single Shot Pistols: For most accurate shooting, use the lightest load possible and still get the ball to the target without a big drop in trajectory.

Percussion Rifles: Same directions as the single shot pistol.

BELGIAN SHOTGUN PROOF CHARGES

Every Belgian percussion shotgun goes through a thorough proof testing. In addition the barrel is stamped underneath with the true size in millimeters. On a double this is sometimes different on left and right barrels. This number is normally about 1-1/2 inches from the breech on the underside of the barrel. This chart shows the gauge of the gun, which is not marked on the barrel, and the diameter in millimeters. Also shown is the Belgian proof charge using black powder and one lead ball that is 6/10 millimeters less in diameter than the bore. Do not attempt to use these loads in hand-held firearms!

Gauge	Size in Millimeters	Black Powder Proof Charge in Grams	Weight of Lead Ball in Grams
1	35.0	156	236
	34.0	143	223
2	33.0	131	195
	32.0	119	177
	31.0	108	163
	30.0	98	148
3	29.0	88	132
	28.0	80	120
4	27.0	71	110
	26.0	64	96
5	25.0	56	86
	24.0	50	74
	23.8	48	72
	23.6	47	70
6	23.4	45	68

BELGIAN SHOTGUN PROOF CHARGES (cont'd)

Gauge	Size in Millimeters	Black Powder Proof Charge in Grams	Weight of Lead Ball in Grams
6	23.2	44	66
	23.0	43	64
	22.8	42	62
	22.6	41	60
	22.4	40	58
7	22.2	38	56
	22.0	37	55
	21.8	36	54
	21.6	35	53
	21.4	34	52
8	21.2	33	50
	21.0	32	49
	20.8	31	47
	20.6	29	45
9	20.4	27	44
	20.2	27	43
	20.0	27	42
	19.8	27	40
10	19.6	24	39
	19.4	24	38
	19.2	24	37
11	19.0	23	35
	18.8	23	34
	18.6	23	33
12	18.4	20	32
	18.2	20	31
13	18.0	20	30
	17.8	20	29
14	17.6	17	28
	17.4	17	27
15	17.2	17	26
	17.0	17	25
16	16.8	15	24
	16.6	15	23
17	16.4	15	23
18	16.2	15	22
	16.0	13.5	21
19	15.8	13.5	20
20	15.6	13.5	19
21	15.4	12	18.5
	15.2	12	18
22	15.0	12	17
23	14.8	10.5	16.5
24	14.6	10.5	16
25	14.4	10.5	15
26	14.2	9	14.5
27	14.8	9	14
28	13.8	9	13.5
30	13.6	9	13
31	13.4	8	12
32	13.2	8	11.5
34	13.0	7	11
36	12.8	7	10.5
38	12.6	7	10
40	12.4	7	9.5
42	12.2	6	9.5
44	12.0	6	8.5
46	11.8	6	8.5
48	11.6	5	7.5
50	11.4	5	7

BELGIAN SHOTGUN PROOF CHARGES (cont'd)

Gauge	Size in Millimeters	Black Powder Proof Charge in Grams	Weight of Lead Ball in Grams
54	11.2	5	6.8
58	11.0	4	6.5
	10.8	4	6
	10.6	4	5.5
	10.4	4	5.5
	10.2	4	5
	10.0	4	5

CAUTION: The above charges are for *proof* loads only. Do not attempt to use them for hand-held shooting.

SHOTGUN LOADS
(Convert Drams to Grains from Weight Tables)

	Drams Powder	Oz. Shot	Type Load
4 Ga.	8-10	3	Medium
10 Ga.	5	1-3/4	Heavy
10 Ga.	4-1/2	1-1/2	Medium
10 Ga.	4	1-1/2	Light
12 Ga.	4-1/8	1-3/8	Heavy
12 Ga.	3-3/4	1-1/4	Medium
12 Ga.	3-1/4	1-1/8	Light
16 Ga.	3-1/8	1-1/8	Heavy
16 Ga.	3	1	Medium
16 Ga.	2-1/2	1	Light
20 Ga.	2-3/4	1	Heavy
20 Ga.	2-3/8	1	Medium
20 Ga.	2	3/4	Light
28 Ga.	2	5/8	Medium
32 Ga.	1-3/4	1/2	Medium
410 Ga.	1-1/2	1/2	Medium

BRITISH SERVICE LOADS FOR MUZZLE LOADING GUNS

Established in 1896 by the Gunmakers Company and the Guardians of the Birmingham Proof House under the authority of the Gun Barrel Proof Act, 1868.

	Powder		Ball	Shot
Gauge	Grains	Drams	Grains	Ozs.
4	273	10	1531	3-1/2
5	213	7-25/32	1217	2-25/32
6	179	6-17/32	1025	2-11/32
7	154	5-5/8	889	2-1/32
8	135	4-15/16	793	1-13/16
9	122	4-15/32	725	1-21/32
10	109	4	656	1-1/2
11	96	3-1/2	574	1-5/16
12-13	89	3-1/4	547	1-1/4
14-15	82	3	492	1-1/8
16-18	75	2-3/4	437	1
19-21	68	2-1/2	383	7/8
22-30	55	2	328	3/4
31-40	41	1-1/2	246	9/16
41-50	27	1	164	3/8

WEIGHT MARKINGS OF FLASKS

Whether a flask is for a pistol, rifle or fowling piece can be determined by its size and by the markings on the chargers. Some, but not all adjustable chargers have numerical markings at the different positions.

American or English flasks are marked in drams, except for Colt who used grains avoirdupois. European flasks are marked in grains apothecaries weight.

Black powder is sold by avoirdupois weight; 16 ounces or 7000 grains to the pound. A pound contains 256 drams.

Apothecaries weight is 12 ounces to the pound and contains 5760 grains.

Dixon flasks measure the drama at 27-1/2 grains apothecaries weight.

The following table of converting drams to grains avoirdupois in round numbers may be helpful.

1	Dram equals	27-1/2	grains
1-1/4	Drams equals	34	grains
1-1/2	Drams equals	41	grains
1-3/4	Drams equals	48	grains
2	Drams equals	55	grains
2-1/4	Drams equals	61	grains
2-1/2	Drams equals	68	grains
2-3/4	Drams equal	75	grains
3	Drams equals	82	grains
3-1/4	Drams equals	89	grains
3-1/2	Drams equals	96	grains
3-3/4	Drams equals	102	grains
4	Drams equals	109	grains

GRANULATION SIZES OF DU PONT BLACK POWDER

Granulation	Passes Opening	Not Pass
Fg	.0689″	.0582″
FFg	.0582″	.0376″
FFFg	.0376″	.0170″
FFFFg	.0170″	.0111″

The following load data have been developed and acquired since the initial publication of this book and represents the most up-to-date information available at the time of publication.

.36 CALIBER RIFLED BARREL, ROUND BALL

For any .36 caliber rifled barrel with patched round ball. Barrel used below had bore diameter of .365″ and groove diameter of .384″. Nearly all makers today use a bore diameter suitable for .360 to .365″ or very slightly smaller balls. Larger barrels do occur, however, requiring either a slightly larger ball or thicker patching.

Note that balls for .36 caliber revolvers are properly of .375 to .380″ diameter; therefore, balls are not interchangeable between rifle and revolver.

Velocities below were obtained with .360″ balls, weighing 70 to 71 grains; .015″ patch lubed with Crisco and G-O FFFg powder.

Conical or Minie-type bullets are not available in this caliber; however, hollow-base .38 Special wadcutter bullets perform well with light charges at short range, while other .38 Special or .357 Magnum bullets do well with stiff powder charges.

.36 CALIBER RIFLED BARREL, ROUND BALL

Powder Charge (Grain)	20″	24″	28″	32″	36″	40″
25	1375 fps	1340 fps	1330 fps	1335 fps	1385 fps	1590 fps
30	1475 fps	1460 fps	1455 fps	1460 fps	1515 fps	1650 fps
35	1580 fps	1585 fps	1580 fps	1580 fps	1645 fps	1785 fps
40	1680 fps	1700 fps	1710 fps	1700 fps	1775 fps	1915 fps
45	1780 fps	1805 fps	1831 fps	1825 fps	1905 fps	2045 fps
50	1890 fps	1925 fps	1960 fps	1945 fps	2030 fps	2170 fps
55	1950 fps	1985 fps	2020 fps	2030 fps	2110 fps	2230 fps
60	2010 fps	2060 fps	2090 fps	2110 fps	2190 fps	2290 fps
65	2060 fps	2125 fps	2157 fps	2190 fps	2270 fps	2400 fps
70	2130 fps	2180 fps	2224 fps	2270 fps		2505 fps

.40 CALIBER RIFLED BARREL, ROUND BALL

For any .40 caliber rifle with patched ball. Velocities below were obtained with a .395″ ball, .015″ patch greased with Crisco and G-O FFFg powder.

Powder Charge (Grain)	28″	32″	36″	40″
30	1255 fps	1270 fps	1310 fps	1330 fps
40	1490 fps	1515 fps	1540 fps	1595 fps
50	1590 fps	1650 fps	1780 fps	1860 fps
60	1740 fps	1830 fps	1890 fps	2000 fps
70	1930 fps	2030 fps	2060 fps	2150 fps
80	2010 fps	2080 fps	2170 fps	2240 fps
90	2090 fps	2160 fps	2175 fps	2280 fps
100	2135 fps	2195 fps	2270 fps	2305 fps

Barrels used above were of .403″ bore diameter, thus required a .395″ ball. However, some barrels of .40 caliber are larger, intended for use with a .400″ ball. Most modern makers designate barrel caliber by nominal bore diameter; some have been designated by the diameter of the ball proper for use in them. Consequently, most .40's are of nominally .400″ bore diameter and require a .395″ or smaller ball; however, some are made to use a .400″ ball and are thus of .405 to .410″ bore diameter. It will always pay, especially with older barrels, to ascertain the actual bore diameter rather than go purely by caliber designation or marking when selecting ball diameter.

As of this writing, there are no standard, conical or Minie-type bullets available in this caliber (.40), so only round balls are practical. However, one may use conical bullets intended for the .38-40 Winchester cartridge, provided they are not too large to be rammed easily down the bore. Though of solid-base design, they will upset to fill the grooves if cast soft and loaded ahead of a stiff charge of FFFg powder.

44 CALIBER RIFLED BARREL, ROUND BALL

For any .44 caliber rifle barrel with patched ball.

This is another caliber generally designated by ball diameter rather than barrel bore diameter. Bores usually run about .447 to .448″, with grooves about .010″ deep or less, making groove diameter .462 to .467″. Proper ball diameter is nominally .437″, though

with thin linen patching, balls up to full-bore diameter may be used at the cost of greater loading effort.

Velocities below were obtained with 127-grain balls .437″ in diameter, with .015″ patch lubed with Crisco and G-O FFFg powder.

Powder Charge (Grains)	20″	28″	32″
30	1075 fps	940 fps	1210 fps
40	1195 fps	1160 fps	1385 fps
50	1315 fps	1380 fps	1560 fps
60	1440 fps	1605 fps	1735 fps
70	1540 fps	1730 fps	1880 fps
80	1650 fps	1860 fps	2025 fps
90	1770 fps	1965 fps	2160 fps
100	1885 fps	2070 fps	2260 fps
110	1940 fps	2120 fps	2310 fps
120	1985 fps	2160 fps	2360 fps
130	2000 fps	2165 fps	2390 fps

Inasmuch as we have both the .44 and .45, one of them is really superfluous for round-ball use. Both will drive patched balls at essentially the same velocity (within 50 to 100 fps of one another) with the same amounts of powder. The .44 ball weighs 127 grains, the .45 a mere 5 or 6 grains more. In theory, the .45 is the more lethal of the two, but as a practical matter, it would be hard to tell the difference.

Incidentally, note that balls for .44 rifle and .44 revolver are not interchangeable. The revolver requires a larger ball, some .454 to .457″ in diameter, so it really should be designated ".45."

.45 CALIBER RIFLED BARREL, ROUND BALL

For any rifle barrel of nominally .45 caliber with patched round ball. Bore diameter of modern barrels is fairly well standardized at .450 to 453″, accompanied by .010″ deep grooves. With normal .010 to .016″ patching, .445″ ball diameter is considered correct. However, some shooters prefer a thicker patch and so use the .437″ .44 ball. An unusually tight barrel may also require the smaller ball. Occasionally a barrel will be found designated .45 caliber but rifled for .450″ balls, thus having a bore diameter up near .460″. I've mentioned this sort of confusion before, barrels occasionally designated as to caliber by proper *ball* diameter instead of bore diameter. When in doubt, measure the bore diameter, regardless of what the caliber marking might be.

The following velocities were obtained in a bore diameter of .452″ with 133 grain, .445″ balls, .015″ patching, Crisco lubricant, and G-O FFFg powder.

.45 CALIBER RIFLED BARREL, ROUND BALL

Powder Charge (Grains)	28″	32″	36″	40″	43″
30	1065 fps	1240 fps	1295 fps	1330 fps	1331 fps
40	1240 fps	1435 fps	1470 fps	1470 fps	1498 fps
50	1420 fps	1630 fps	1640 fps	1615 fps	1665 fps
60	1595 fps	1820 fps	1815 fps	1755 fps	1831 fps
70	1760 fps	1980 fps	1975 fps	1925 fps	1969 fps
80	1920 fps	2135 fps	2135 fps	2095 fps	2106 fps
90	1980 fps	2215 fps	2230 fps	2190 fps	2237 fps
100	2040 fps	2275 fps	2255 fps	2290 fps	2367 fps
110	2040 fps	2300 fps			
120	2045 fps	2315 fps			
130	2050 fps	2360 fps			
140	2060 fps				
150	2095 fps				
160	2135 fps				
170	2175 fps				

Note in the 28″ column how little velocity is gained as weight of powder charge approaches weight of ball.

.50 CALIBER RIFLED BARREL, ROUND BALL

For any rifle barrel of nominally .50 caliber.

The .50 is a caliber normally designated by bore diameter which runs .500 to .503″ with grooves .010 to .012″ deep. Correct ball diameter is usually considered to be .498″, but .495″ is needed by many barrels unless a very thin patch and hard ramming is acceptable.

The .50 ball weighs 180 grains and, all things considered, is regarded by many to be the minimum for use on big game. It not only has 23 percent more cross-sectional area than the .45—which means it destroys more tissue—at 2000 fps, the .50 possesses over 35 percent more energy.

The velocities below were obtained with 180 grain .498″ balls with Crisco-lubed .015″ patching in .503″ bore barrels, with G-O FFFg powder.

Powder Charge (Grains)	26″	28″	32″	43″
50	1350 fps	1335 fps	1445 fps	1505 fps
60	1460 fps	1460 fps	1555 fps	1640 fps
70	1575 fps	1590 fps	1665 fps	1725 fps
80	1690 fps	1690 fps	1780 fps	1855 fps
90	1805 fps	1795 fps	1890 fps	2000 fps
100	1880 fps	1875 fps	1980 fps	2095 fps
110	1960 fps	1955 fps	2065 fps	2190 fps
120	2040 fps	2010 fps	2100 fps	2245 fps
130	2125 fps	2065 fps	2140 fps	2295 fps
140		2080 fps	2150 fps	

.50 CALIBER RIFLED BARREL, ROUND BALL (cont'd)

Powder Charge (Grains)	26″	28″	32″	43″
150		2100 fps	2170 fps	
160		2120 fps	2180 fps	

.54 CALIBER RIFLED BARREL, ROUND BALL

For any rifled .54 caliber barrel with patched round ball.

Calibers of .50 to .60 were popular in the early 19th century, but only recently have modern shooters opted for anything above .50 except the .58 rifle musket. The .54 fits nicely in the middle and is the only standardized "modern" caliber falling into this range. Almost all barrels are of recent manufacture and have a bore diameter of .540″ and groove diameter just over .560″. Standard ball diameter is considered to be .535″ with medium (.015″) patching.

One exception is the German-made barrel of the reproduction .54 Gallager carbine, circa 1861. This barrel has a bore diameter of .535″ and a groove diameter of .540″. Unusual for a gun of the muzzle-loading era, it possesses 16 very shallow (.025″ deep) grooves.

The velocities shown below were obtained from a barrel with .540″ groove diameter using .535″ 220 grain balls, Criscoed .015″ patching and G-O FFFg powder.

.54 CALIBER RIFLED BARREL, ROUND BALL

Powder Charge (Grains)	28″	30″	34″	38″	42″
40	1060 fps	1110 fps	1135 fps	1150 fps	1160 fps
50	1125 fps	1165 fps	1250 fps	1275 fps	1295 fps

.54 CALIBER RIFLED BARREL, ROUND BALL (cont'd)

Powder Charge (Grains)	28″	30″	34″	38″	42″
60	1250 fps	1275 fps	1360 fps	1390 fps	1415 fps
70	1375 fps	1385 fps	1440 fps	1480 fps	1520 fps
80	1450 fps	1465 fps	1520 fps	1470 fps	1625 fps
90	1530 fps	1545 fps	1590 fps	1630 fps	1670 fps
100	1605 fps	1640 fps	1660 fps	1690 fps	1730 fps
110	1680 fps	1730 fps	1760 fps	1795 fps	1815 fps
120	1730 fps	1825 fps	1850 fps	1885 fps	1900 fps
130	1780 fps	1920 fps	1910 fps	1965 fps	2010 fps
140	1895 fps	1970 fps	1970 fps	2050 fps	2110 fps
150	2010 fps	2020 fps	2030 fps	2090 fps	2120 fps
160	2020 fps	2070 fps	2095 fps	2140 fps	2150 fps

Note from the above:

1. Adding 14″ of barrel at the 40-grain powder charge increases velocity only 100 fps; at 160 grains, only 130 fps is gained.
2. In the 28″ barrel, the complete velocity range is only 940 fps, from 1060 to 2020 fps; in the longest barrel it is only 990 fps, very nearly the same.
3. Generally speaking, doubling the powder charge produces only about 35 percent velocity increase; quadrupling powder charge produces about 85 to 90 percent velocity increase.
4. In medium-length barrels (34″ here) the minimum powder charge produces about 28 fps per grain of powder; the heaviest charge (160 grains) produces only 13 fps per grain of powder.

.58 CALIBER RIFLED BARREL, ROUND BALL

For any rifled barrel of nominal .58 or .577 caliber with patched round ball.

In early days, rifles of .50 to .60 caliber were not uncommon in the west, usually in the heavy short-coupled Plains Rifle or Mountain Rifle of Hawken style. Even then, the .58 was probably less popular than .52, .54, .55, and other bores. The .58's popularity is a recent thing generated mainly by the wide availability since about 1960 of fine reproductions of Civil War .58 caliber rifled muskets. Doubtless the .58 musket would have generated popularity for the same size round-ball rifle in its own day, had it been around long enough—but the rifled musket was replaced by breech loaders immediately following the Civil War.

In any event, the .58 is popular today mainly in rifled musket reproductions as well as the Hopkins & Allen underhammer rifle. With the exception of musket reproductions, most modern .58 guns are rifled mainly for round balls with eight or so deep grooves (.010″ or more). On the other hand, the muskets are usually rifled with 2, 3 or 4 very wide, shallow grooves and relatively wide lands. As a practical matter, both types perform well with patched round balls loaded conventionally.

Standard bore diameter for the .58 runs .575 to .580″. Ball diameter is properly .005″ under bore diameter, but most commonly used is .575″ diameter, a bit tight for the smaller bores even with very thin patching. I've owned several tight-bored muskets which simply couldn't be loaded with a .575″ ball without using a hammer.

Velocities shown below were obtained in barrels of musket type .575″ bore diameter, .585″ groove diameter—with 260 grain .575″ balls, .010″ patching, Crisco lube and G-O FFg powder.

Powder Charge (Grains)	22″	24″	32″
50	865 fps	905 fps	945 fps
60	935 fps	990 fps	1030 fps
70	1005 fps	1080 fps	1115 fps
80	1075 fps	1165 fps	1180 fps
90	1160 fps	1225 fps	1240 fps
100	1270 fps	1285 fps	1295 fps
110	1315 fps	1330 fps	1350 fps
120	1380 fps	1370 fps	1400 fps
130	1420 fps	1445 fps	1450 fps
140	1460 fps	1520 fps	1505 fps
150	1520 fps	1585 fps	1560 fps
160	1585 fps	1650 fps	1615 fps
170	1650 fps	1730 fps	1670 fps
180		1786 fps	1740 fps
190		1810 fps	1775 fps

The above charges do not approach ball weight for the simple reason that musket-barrel walls are much thinner than those of the typical round-ball rifle barrel and so are not as strong. Thick-walled modern *rifle* barrels will safely handle powder charges equal to ball weight, producing about the same velocities such charges produce in .50 and .54 caliber, that is, well over 2000 fps.

In any event, the above charges should *not* be exceeded in musket-type barrels found in Zouave, Enfield, Springfield and Mississippi Rifle reproductions.

.75 CALIBER (SMOOTHBORE ONLY) ROUND BALL

For Brown Bess and Charleville replicas and similar flintlock smoothbore muskets. Bore dimensions may vary, requiring balls ranging from .715″ diameter (545 grains wt.) to .690″ or smaller. Ball diameter should be chosen as large as possible and still ram smoothly and easily down the bore when encased in greased .020″-thick patching or wrapped in cartridge paper. If the ball is smaller than this, velocities will be reduced and accuracy will suffer.

Following loads were fired in a Japanese-made Brown Bess replica with 42″ barrel. Powder is G-O FFg; substitution of C&H will produce *about* 10 percent less velocity, charge-for-charge.

Powder Charge (Grain)	Velocity	Increase over previous charge
20	335 fps	
30	455 fps	+ 120 fps
40	570 fps	+ 115 fps
50	660 fps	+ 90 fps
60	750 fps	+ 90 fps
70	820 fps	+ 70 fps
80	880 fps	+ 60 fps
90	940 fps	+ 60 fps
100	1010 fps	+ 70 fps
110	1050 fps	+ 40 fps
120	1090 fps	+ 40 fps
130	1135 fps	+ 45 fps
140	1185 fps	+ 50 fps
150	1210 fps	+ 25 fps
160	1220 fps	+ 10 fps

Note fairly consistent decline in velocity increase produced by the charge increase. Further increases in powder charge might be safe enough, but would produce too little additional velocity to be worthwhile.

When bore diameter is such that a plastic one-piece 12-gauge shotshell wad will enter freely without too much play, performance (and sometimes accuracy) may be improved. Charge with loose powder in the usual fashion; then ram a prepared wad/ball combination on top of it. Prepare the wad by placing a generous blob of lubricant in the shot cup; then press a ball into the cup. Add more lubricant over the ball in the cup.

Ball diameter and shot-cup wall thickness must be matched to the bore so that the combination is snug in the barrel, yet not too tight to be rammed easily. When the three are properly matched, no wad is needed to hold the ball down against the powder.

Ball/wad units may be made up beforehand, complete with lubricant, then sealed in Saran wrap or similar plastic film. They may then be carried in your pocket or pouch without mess. Leave the plastic wrap on when ramming; it won't cause any harm or even any visible effect.

Use of a close-fitting plastic shotshell virtually eliminates windage and increases powder efficiency. Its cushioning effect also produces some reduction in recoil.

.44 CALIBER MINNIE BULLETS

If you own a .45, the .44 is really superfluous; .44 bullet diameter is only about .010″ less than the .45, and weight of comparable bullets is only about 15 grains. Minie-type .44 bullets have been available about as long as in .45 and are a recent development. Traditionally the .44 was a round-ball caliber. Today Lyman offers two .44 Minie bullets of more or less traditional design; No. 445599 weighs 250 grains and the longer No. 445369 weighs 290 grains.

Velocities shown were obtained in barrels of .447″ bore diameter with .464″ groove diameter, with G-O FFFg powder and Crisco lubricant.

250 GRAIN LYMAN BULLET # 445599

Powder Charge (Grains)	20″	28″	32″
30	630 fps	755 fps	950 fps
40	850 fps	973 fps	1125 fps
50	1070 fps	1190 fps	1305 fps
60	1285 fps	1410 fps	1480 fps
70	1390 fps	1520 fps	1565 fps
80	1495 fps	1625 fps	
90	1560 fps		
100	1620 fps		

290 GRAIN LYMAN BULLET # 445369

Powder Charge (Grains)	20″	28″	32″
30	570 fps	770 fps	865 fps
40	780 fps	965 fps	1040 fps
50	995 fps	1160 fps	1215 fps
60	1210 fps	1355 fps	1390 fps
70	1300 fps	1450 fps	1485 fps
80	1390 fps	1540 fps	1565 fps
90	1455 fps	1605 fps	1620 fps
100	1520 fps	1645 fps	1665 fps

.45 CALIBER MINI AND CONICAL BULLETS

During the heyday of the muzzle loader, .45 caliber was purely a round-ball proposition except, perhaps, in those few "picket-ball" guns that were made. In the past decade, however, mold makers have supplied Minie-type hollow-base bullets in this caliber—probably prompted by the popularity of the type in military calibers. More recently the Thompson/Center "Maxi-Ball" solid-base bullet has been offered, and a similar bullet is now available from Lyman as No. 454616. This modern solid-base bullet is superior to the Minie, offering better velocity retention and penetration, and is not subject to skirt deformation with heavy powder charges.

The following velocities were obtained in barrels of .452 to .453″ bore diameter, .473″ nominal groove diameter. G-O FFFg powder was used throughout, with Crisco lubrication of the bullet.

LYMAN BULLET #454616, SOLID-BASE, 230 GRAIN

Powder Charge (Grains)	28″	32″	36″	40″
30	940 fps	1020 fps	930 fps	1065 fps
40	1140 fps	1185 fps	1130 fps	1235 fps
50	1335 fps	1355 fps	1330 fps	1400 fps
60	1530 fps	1520 fps	1530 fps	1570 fps
70	1640 fps	1635 fps	1630 fps	1685 fps
80		1745 fps	1735 fps	1800 fps
90		1805 fps	1795 fps	1860 fps

MINIE BULLET, LYMAN #454613, 265 GRAIN

Powder Charge (Grains)	28″	32″	36″	40″
30	780 fps	715 fps	1040 fps	825 fps
40	1000 fps	960 fps	1180 fps	1050 fps
50	1210 fps	1200 fps	1315 fps	1270 fps
60	1430 fps	1440 fps	1455 fps	1490 fps
70	1510 fps	1515 fps	1550 fps	1600 fps
80	1550 fps	1560 fps	1590 fps	1710 fps
90	1575	1600 fps	1635 fps	1795 fps

SOLID BULLET, LYMAN #454612, 300 GRAIN

Powder Charge (Grains)	28″	32″	36″	40″
30	940 fps	940 fps	895 fps	950 fps
40	1085 fps	1100 fps	1070 fps	1100 fps
50	1230 fps	1260 fps	1240 fps	1250 fps
60	1380 fps	1420 fps	1410 fps	1405 fps
70	1450 fps	1490 fps	1520 fps	1505 fps
80			1610 fps	1510 fps
90			1660 fps	1680 fps

Overall, the .45 is probably the most popular caliber for muzzle-loading rifles. It strikes a happy compromise in that it is considered by many to be adequate for big game, yet isn't too large for small game. Recoil is light, and powder and lead costs are low compared to the bigger bores.

.50 CALIBER, MINIE AND CONICAL BULLETS

Traditionally the .50 has been a round-ball caliber. Minie bullets have not generally been available in this caliber, but in recent years, Thompson/Center has introduced its excellent "Maxi-Ball" grooved, solid-base .50 bullet. This design combines the Minie's ease of loading with solid-bullet casting ease, yet performs as well as the Minie. It possesses extremely good velocity retention and penetrates better in game than either round ball or Minie. It does, however, require stiffish powder charges for best accuracy. More recently Lyman has produced a similar bullet, No. 504617.

The following velocities were obtained from barrels with .503″ bore and .525″ groove diameter, using the Lyman bullet No. 504617, 370 grains, greased with Crisco and G-O FFFg powder.

Powder Charge (Grains)	26″	28″	32″
45	1035 fps	1000 fps	1060 fps
50	1085 fps	1070 fps	1115 fps
55	1135 fps	1130 fps	1170 fps
60	1185 fps	1200 fps	1230 fps
65	1235 fps	1260 fps	1280 fps
70	1285 fps	1330 fps	1340 fps
75		1365 fps	1370 fps
80		1405 fps	1400 fps
85		1440 fps	1435 fps
90		1480 fps	1470 fps

.54 CALIBER MINIE & CONICAL BULLETS

The .54 caliber got its biggest boost when adopted for a short time by the U.S. Army, before the Civil War, in a rifled musket. Though used by civilians in round-ball rifles, the Minie bullet never saw much use except, perhaps, in a few liberated rifled muskets. The form and principle of the hollow-base Minie bullet were too new for civilians. Before military use could prove the Minie to the sportsman and trapper, breech loaders were on the way. Then, too, round balls were easily cast, even in a home-made mold; on the other hand, Minie molds were hard to make and to use.

Minies and conicals of .54 caliber are best cast .533 to .535″ diameter for the .540″ bore diameter. Only one such bullet is widely available, Lyman's No. 533476, weighing nominally 410 grains. It's an excellent game bullet with good velocity retention and a flat nose which helps destroy tissue.

The following velocities were obtained in barrels of .540″ bore and .560″ groove diameter, bullets of .533″ diameter, Crisco lube and G-O FFFg powder.

410 GRAIN BULLET, LYMAN #533476

Powder Charge (Grains)	28″	30″	34″
50	740 fps	725 fps	940 fps
60	865 fps	900 fps	1070 fps
70	995 fps	1070 fps	1190 fps
80	1135 fps	1175 fps	1300 fps
90	1280 fps	1280 fps	1405 fps
100	1365 fps	1375 fps	1475 fps
110	1450 fps	1470 fps	1545 fps
120	1505 fps	1545 fps	1615 fps
130		1620 fps	
140		1656 fps	

.58 CALIBER CONICAL AND MINIE BULLETS

The .58 rifled musket was originally made for

hollow-base Minie bullets. This caliber had not been particularly popular among round-ball rifles. The U.S. Army first replaced its smoothbore muskets with the rifled musket in .54 caliber, but then increased the caliber to .58. Most modern .58 rifles are reproductions of Civil War rifled muskets and so are rifled specifically for the Minie-type bullet with three or four wide, shallow grooves (.004 to .005" deep) and wide lands. Having relatively thin barrel walls, these guns should not be fired with powder charges exceeding one-fourth the bullet weight. On the other hand, thick-walled rifle barrels can be safely used with charges of well over 200 grains of powder. Take note that Minie bullets of old style with thin-skirted walls will distort and lose accuracy with the heavier powder charges. The heavier charges should only be used with modern thick-skirted Minies such as Lyman's No. 577611 or the Shiloh "Stake-buster." Such bullets will withstand charges of 150 grains or more of powder. The Shiloh bullet has been fired by this author with 200 grains of DuPont FFFg without base distortion—in a thick-walled rifle barrel, of course.

Although standard .58 Minie bullet diameter is considered to be .575", the bullet should be .003 to .005" smaller than actual bore diameter for easy ramming, especially in a fouled barrel. Bullets may be sized down in a ring die or reduced by rolling them between two smooth steel bars.

The following velocities were obtained in a barrel

of .575" bore diameter, .584 groove diameter; bullets lubricated with Crisco, bullet diameter .575", G-O FFg powder.

505 GRAIN BULLET, LYMAN # 575213

Powder Charge (Grains)	22"	26"	28"	32"
50	610 fps	630 fps	600 fps	725 fps
60	700 fps	715 fps	685 fps	810 fps
70	795 fps	800 fps	770 fps	890 fps
80	890 fps	890 fps	850 fps	970 fps
90	980 fps	980 fps	930 fps	1050 fps
100	1075 fps	1070 fps	1010 fps	1130 fps
110	1135 fps	1125 fps	1065 fps	1190 fps
120	1195 fps	1180 fps	1120 fps	1240 fps
130	1235 fps	1220 fps	1180 fps	1300 fps
140	1260 fps	1265 fps	1230 fps	1350 fps
150	1275 fps	1300 fps	1270 fps	1395 fps

570 GRAIN BULLET, LYMAN # 57730

Powder Charge (Grains)	22"	24"	26"	32"
50	730 fps	730 fps	685 fps	668 fps
60	800 fps	810 fps	760 fps	740 fps
70	870 fps	885 fps	840 fps	815 fps
80	940 fps	960 fps	920 fps	885 fps
90	1000 fps	1030 fps	990 fps	955 fps
100			1060 fps	1020 fps
110			1110 fps	1080 fps
120				1140 fps
130				1195 fps
140				1250 fps

400 GRAIN BULLET, LYMAN # 575602

Powder Charge (Grains)	22"	24"	26"	28"	32"
50	640 fps	655 fps	680 fps	570 fps	560 fps
60	740 fps	750 fps	745 fps	670 fps	660 fps
70	840 fps	850 fps	810 fps	770 fps	765 fps
80	940 fps	945 fps	875 fps	870 fps	870 fps
90	1035 fps	1045 fps	1010 fps	960 fps	980 fps
100	1130 fps	1140 fps	1140 fps	1050 fps	1090 fps
110	1200 fps	1220 fps	1225 fps	1105 fps	1140 fps
120		1300 fps	1310 fps	1160 fps	1185 fps
130				1200 fps	1230 fps
140				1235 fps	1280 fps
150				1311 fps	1330 fps
160					1380 fps
170					1420 fps
180					1460 fps

SINGLE-CHARGE VELOCITY/CALIBER/BARREL LENGTH TABLE
G-O FFFg POWDER; NORMAL BALL DIAMETER; .015" PATCH WITH CRISCO LUBE.

70 gr., G-O FFFg	.36 cal.	.40 cal.	.44 cal.	.45 cal.	.50 cal.	.54 cal.	*.58 cal.
20" bbl.	2128 fps	1760 fps	1544 fps				975 fps
28" bbl.	2225 fps	1940 fps	1735 fps	1995 fps	1590 fps	1375 fps	1000 fps
32" bbl.	2270 fps	2000 fps	1885 fps	1980 fps	1665 fps	1415 fps	1115 fps
36-37" bbl.	2300 fps	2050 fps	1900 fps	1975 fps	1715 fps	1460 fps	1160 fps
42-44" bbl.	2505 fps	2100 fps	1945 fps	1970 fps	1725 fps	1525 fps	1125 fps

*All .58 caliber with G-O FFg powder.

Single-charge comparison: Everyone has a favorite powder charge, it seems, for each caliber and length

gun they use. Considering other data available, I wondered what would happen if a single medium-weight charge was compared in a variety of calibers and barrel lengths.

Shown are results of my tests, computation and research. Beneath each caliber heading will be found velocity values for the firing of 70 grains of G-O FFFg (except in .58 caliber) in several different barrel lengths. Note that in each barrel length, velocity goes down as caliber increases. In a 28″ barrel, the same powder charge produces 122.5 percent more velocity in .36 caliber than in .58; in 36 to 37″ barrels, the .36 caliber is 101.3 percent faster than the .58.

Keep in mind, however, that this relationship is valid only for the one powder charge shown. Changing the charge will cause the relationship to shift in a manner that can't be predicted accurately. My choice of a 70-grain charge was made simply because it is maximum for the .36 caliber and still adequate for the .58.

Velocity per grain of powder (G-O FFFg, except as noted) in medium-length rifle barrels (32 to 34″) with standard round balls and normal (.015″) greased (Crisco) patch. Values shown beneath each caliber charge shown in the left-hand column.

Powder Charge (grains)	.36 (71 gr. ball)	.40 (92 gr. ball)	.44 (127 gr. ball)	.45 (133 gr. ball)	.50 (180 gr. ball)	.54 (220 gr. ball)	.58 (260 gr. ball) (FFg powder)
30	49	45	40	41			
40	43	40	35	39			
50	39	37	31	33	29	26	19
60	35	34	29	30	26	23	17
70	32	31	27	28	24	21	16
80		28	25	27	22	19	15
90		26	24	25	21	14	14
100		23	23	23	20	17	13
110			21	21	19	16	12
120			20	19	18	15	12
130			18	18	16	15	11
140				17	15	14	11
150					14	14	10
160					14	13	10
170					13	13	10
180					12	12	10
190							9

Above values are calculated on the basis of tests and observations by the author and other test data that has been published from time to time. Velocity averages of several reports were divided by powder charge weights to obtain the "fps per grain" value shown. These are only approximate for any given gun and are applicable only to Gearhart-Owen powder. Values will normally be less when other powders and/or coarser granulations are used.

Under no circumstances is it safe or practical to use this table in reverse to calculate a charge to produce a desired velocity.

The principal use of this table is to estimate velocity when barrel length and powder charge are known.

Velocity per grain of powder (G-O FFFg, except in .58 caliber as noted) in medium-length barrels (32 to 34″) with Minie-type bullets of the weights indicated. All bullets greased with Crisco, no patch.

Powder Charge (grains)	.44, 250 gr.	.45, 265 gr.	.50, 370 gr.	.54, 410 gr.	.58, 505 gr.
30	32	24			
40	28	24			
50	26	24	22	19	14
60	25	24	20	18	13
70	22	22	19	17	13
80	21	20	18	16	12
90	19	19	16	16	12
100	17	18	16	15	11
110			15	14	11
120				13	10
130					10
140					10
150					9
160					9

The remarks appended to the similar table for round-ball loads apply here as well.

.44 PERCUSSION REVOLVER

Although the .36 caliber was the more popular in the middle 19th century, the .44 is the one most often associated with the westward expansion after the Civil War. Today replicas and semi-replicas of original guns are available in two basic designs, Colt and Remington, with a half-dozen variations on the former. In addition, there is the thoroughly modern Ruger design made only in .44/.45 caliber.

The .44 is the most forgiving of sloppy loading and is the only percussion revolver caliber for which modern-design bullets are available. It almost invariably wins high-level revolver competitions over the smaller calibers.

Our loads shown below were tested in a Centennial Arms Colt .44 1960 Army with 8″ barrel, .442″ bore diameter, .446″ groove diameter and .443″ chamber diameters. Swaged round balls of .451–.452″ diameter, 139 grains weight were used with Hodgdon's Spit Ball lubricant and G-O FFFg powder.

ROUND BALL, SWAGED, .451″, 139 GRAINS, G-O FFFg

Powder Charge (Grains)	8″ bbl.
16	660 fps
18	695 fps
20	720 fps
22	250 fps
24	785 fps
26	830 fps
28	880 fps
30	915 fps
32	955 fps
34	990 fps
36	1020 fps

CONICAL BULLET, LYMAN # 450229, 155 GRAIN, G-O FFFg

Powder Charge (Grains)	8″ bbl.
18	690 fps
20	725 fps
22	770 fps
24	845 fps
26	870 fps
28	860 fps

Top loads with both bullets fill all the available powder space. If greased, felt wads should be used over the powder and charge volume must be reduced accordingly.

.36 CALIBER PERCUSSION REVOLVER

If we go by the quantities produced by major manufacturers during the percussion era, the .36 or "Navy" caliber was substantially the favorite, trailed not too far by the .44, with the .31 in last place by a considerable margin. By today's standards, even the stiffest possible round-ball .36 load is rather weak for serious use, delivering only about 220 fp of energy with about 1100 fps from a 7 1/2-inch barrel. Even the pip-squeak .38 Special lead RN load exceeds that a good bit. Going to heavier conical bullets didn't help much, for they reduced powder capacity so that the maximum energy that could be developed remained about the same. Even today most shooters use round balls in .36 caliber for that reason, plus they are much easier to load.

A wider variety of models, makes and barrel lengths is available in .36 than in any other caliber today. All but the Remington Belt Pistols are merely minor variations of the original Colt M1851 .36 Navy. The sights of the Remington are by far the most practical.

The loads listed below were tested in a Navy Arms Remington Belt Pistol Target Model, 6 1/2-inch barrel, .374″ chamber diameter, .362″ bore diameter, .375″ groove diameter. Cast .380 balls, Hodgdon's Spit Ball lubricant and G-O FFFg powder were used.

ROUND BALL, .380″, 83 GRAINS, G-O FFFg

Powder Charge (Grains)	6-1/2″ bbl.
10	640 fps
12	685 fps
14	740 fps
16	805 fps
18	875 fps
20	950 fps
24	1005 fps
26	1060 fps
28	1100 fps

CONICAL BULLET, LYMAN # 37583, 150 GRAIN, G-O FFFg

Powder Charge (Grains)	6-1/2″ bbl.
8	450 fps
9	470 fps
10	500 fps
11	530 fps
12	550 fps
14	610 fps
15	650 fps

Top charges with both bullets fill all the available powder space. If greased, felt wads should be used over the powder and charge weight must be reduced accordingly.

.31 CALIBER PERCUSSION REVOLVER

Although caplock revolvers were made in smaller calibers during their heyday, .31 is the smallest available in reproduction guns. Bore diameter is nominally .300″ and chamber diameter is .310″. Chamber diameter determines ball size insofar as round balls must be *larger* than the chamber so they will fit tightly and seal the chamber. Thus, .320″ diameter balls are standard for the .31. This corresponds to number 0 buckshot. 0 buck is a perfect substitute for cast .320″ balls—being swaged, rather than cast, the balls are more homogeneous and more uniform in density and weight. Further, they have no sprue to be trimmed or oriented in loading.

The .31 is a great plinking gun and not bad for small game when bettter sights, other than the original Colt style, are installed. It becomes the "Kit Gun" of muzzle loading and is the most economical to shoot of all calibers. A bag of 0 buck, a flask of powder and a can of caps will suffice for a weekend of fun shooting.

The following loads were worked up in a Navy Arms Wells Fargo Model replica with 5 3/4-inch barrel with .310″ chamber diameter, .300″ bore diameter and .318″ groove diameter. Swaged 0 buckshot (50 grains weight) was used in round-ball loads; G-O powder and Hodgdon's Spit Ball lubricant over the bullet were used in all loads.

ROUND BALL, #0 BUCK, 50 GRAINS, G-O FFFg

Powder Charge (Grains)	5-3/4″ bbl.
10	595 fps
12	660 fps
14	740 fps
15	760 fps

ROUND BALL, #0 BUCK, 50 GRAINS, G-O FFFFg

Powder Charge (Grains)	5-3/4″ bbl.
10	690 fps
12	745 fps
14	830 fps
15	160 fps

Conical bullets can be used in the .31 as in other caplock revolvers but very little space is left in the chamber for powder; consequently velocities that may be obtained are quite low. For this reason I don't recommend their use.

Appendix 3/
Black Powder Velocities

Many factors influence the velocities of muzzle-loading guns other than the mere ratio of weights of powder to lead. Patched round balls are the most common projectiles. From tests that have been conducted with modern black powder in guns of conventional design, the data in the following table has been generated. Obviously, conical bullets and other deviations will invalidate the table. Also, pistols, shotguns and slug rifles obtain quite different velocities than patched ball rifles and must be treated separately.

Any factor which alters breech pressure has a direct influence on muzzle velocity as well. Such considerations as fit of the ball, tightness after patching, roughness of the bore, whether the bore is clean or dry, fouled or oiled—all have measurable effects on velocity. Another important factor is efficiency of ignition, and some foreign percussion caps are much hotter than any manufactured in this country.

American black powder of today is far more uniform than that of Civil War days; thus, velocities will be consistent if all other factors are kept reasonably uniform.

The following chart indicates velocities produced by various ratios of bullet to powder weight.

Ball weight	Powder weight	Velocity
1	1	2570 fps
1-1/2	1	2325 fps
2	1	2135 fps
2-1/2	1	1975 fps
3	1	1850 fps
3-1/2	1	1750 fps
4	1	1670 fps
4-1/2	1	1600 fps
5	1	1535 fps

Ball weight	Powder weight	Velocity
5-1/2	1	1480 fps
6	1	1425 fps
6-1/2	1	1375 fps
7	1	1325 fps
7-1/2	1	1280 fps
8	1	1235 fps
8-1/2	1	1200 fps
9	1	1155 fps
9-1/2	1	1120 fps
10	1	1035 fps

The following velocities and corresponding energies for the cal. .69 flintlock musket (smoothbore) and cal. .58 percussion rifle were the results of U.S. Army tests of the mid-19th century. Velocities of comparable guns and loads may be estimated with reasonable accuracy from these values.

Cal.	Powder	Bullet	Velocity	Energy
.69	110 grs.*	412-gr. rd. ball	1500 fps	2060 fp
.58	60 grs.	510-gr. Minie	963 fps	1050 fp

*Including priming. A lighter charge is required in present-day black powders.

Extensive velocity measurements were made with ballistic pendulums by Capt. Alfred Mordecai of the Ordnance Department and given in his "Report of Experiments on Gunpowder Made at Washington Arsenal in 1843 and 1844." The averages shown in the following chart were tabulated by him as typical velocities. The corresponding energies have been computed and added. A5 rifle powder and 219-gr. round balls of 32 to the pound were used throughout.

For the cadet's musket the balls were wrapped in cartridge paper and for the common rifle in greased patches. The Hall's and Jenk's arms were shot breech loaded, with the balls naked. Capt. Mordecai commented that the velocity loss from the leaking joint of the Hall's breech was serious. Among incidental findings of the small arms portion of these tests was the importance of effective wadding or patching to attainment of full velocity.

Arm	Bore dia.	Bbl. length	Powder	Velocity	Energy
1. Cadet's musket, old pattern (flintlock Common rifle)	.57″	35.5″	70 gr.	1690 fps	1390 fp
2. 1841 (percussion)	.54″	32.5″	100 gr.	2018 fps	1980 fp
3. Same			70 gr.	1755 fps	1500 fp
4. Hall's rifle, 1826 (flintlock breech loader)	.52″	35.1″	70 gr.	1490 fps	1080 fp
5. Hall's carbine, 1840 (percussion breech loader)	.525″	23.38″	70 gr.	1240 fps	750 fp
6. Jenk's carbine 1844 (percussion breech loader)	.52″	24.25″	70 gr.	1687 fps	1385 fp

A .45 caliber (.451″) flintlock rifle of new manufacture has been chronographed. The 135-grain round ball was shot with a greased patch in a 44″ barrel. The charge of FFFg black powder shown gave the following velocities. Striking energies at muzzle have been computed and added. FFFg granulation Du Pont powder was used throughout.

Charge	Velocity	Energy
30 gr.	1180 fps	420 fp
40 gr.	1560 fps	730 fp
50 gr.	1700 fps	865 fp
60 gr.	1800 fps	970 fp
70 gr.	1940 fps	1130 fp
90 gr.	2100 fps	1325 fp
100 gr.	2140 fps	1375 fp

The following table gives the velocities and corresponding energies of round balls of approximate size suitable for firing with a patch from cylinder bores of the gauges shown. These combinations are the ones in which standard shot charges are approximated by the weights of round ball. The velocities are of standard shotgun loads, with small corrections where weights of shot charges and round balls are not exactly the same.

Gauge	Std. bore dia.	Undersize ball	Powder	Velocity	Energy
10	.775″	670 gr.	130 gr.	1370 fps	2790 fp
12	.729″	560 gr.	102 gr.	1330 fps	2200 fp
16	.662″	420 gr.	68 gr.	1225 fps	1400 fp
20	.615″	335 gr.	61 gr.	1275 fps	1210 fp

PISTOL VELOCITY

A .40 caliber Dixie percussion pistol with 9″ barrel has been chronographed with the following results. FFFg and cloth-patched round ball were used.

Powder	Velocity	Maximum Variation
20 gr.	816 fps	49 fps
30 gr.	872 fps	86 fps
35 gr.	1145 fps	110 fps
40 gr.	1178 fps	50 fps

A .40 caliber Dixie percussion rifle was tested extensively on modern chronograph equipment. Patched round balls of proper diameter were used. Beginning with the barrel 40″ in length, 5-shot strings were fired with the charges shown across the top of the following chart. The barrel was then shortened 2″ and the test was repeated. The barrel was successively shortened in 2″ steps until at 20″ muzzle blast became objectionable and the tests were terminated. The heavier charges were eliminated in the shorter barrel lengths for the same reason.

The results are charted below. Read right from barrel length then down from powder charge. Velocity is shown where the two columns intersect.

CHARGE WEIGHTS IN GRAINS OF DU PONT FFFg

Barrel Length	38	47	56	65	75	84	94	104	114	120
40″	1551	1770	1884	1987	2059	2178	2260	2356	2437	2463
38″	1567	1747	1879	1992	2099	2216	2306	2347	2359	2398
36″	1543	1735	1836	1994	2079	2189	2194	2301	2274	
34″	1493	1610	1828	1966	2063	2186	2272	2246		
32″	1527	1654	1819	1913	2017	2098	2199	2233		
30″	1460	1642	1796	1932	1984	2052	2088	2064		
28″	1492	1623	1742	1903	1973	2095	2089			
26″	1445	1596	1734	1838	1902	1944	1952			
24″	1449	1593	1710	1784	1894	2019	2092			
22″	1468	1553	1668	1733	1844	1879	1937			
20″	1420	1509	1631	1703	1818	1863	1976			

Appendix 4/Useful Data

CONDITION STANDARDS FOR ANTIQUE FIREARMS

FACTORY NEW—All original parts; 100 percent original finish; in perfect condition in every respect, inside and out.

EXCELLENT—All original parts; over 80 percent original finish; sharp lettering, numerals and design on metal and wood; unmarred wood; fine bore.

FINE—All original parts; over 30 percent original finish; sharp lettering, numerals and design on metal and wood; minor marks in wood; good bore.

VERY GOOD—All original parts; zero to 30 percent original finish; original metal surfaces smooth with all edges sharp; clear lettering, numerals and design on metal; wood slightly scratched or bruised; bore condition disregarded for collectors' firearms.

GOOD—Some minor replacement parts; metal smoothly rusted or lightly pitted in places, cleaned or reblued; principal lettering, numerals and design on metal legible; wood refinished; scratches, bruises or minor cracks repaired; in good working order.

FAIR—Some major parts replaced; minor replacement parts may be required; metal rusted, may be lightly pitted all over, vigorously cleaned or reblued; rounded edges of metal and wood; principal lettering, numerals and design on metal partly obliterated; wood scratched, bruised, cracked or repaired where broken; in fair working order or can be easily repaired and placed in working order.

POOR—Major and minor parts replaced; major replacement parts required and extensive restoration needed; metal deeply pitted; principal lettering, numerals and design obliterated; wood badly scratched, bruised, cracked or broken; mechanically inoperative; generally undesirable as a collectors' firearm.

DECIMAL EQUIVALENTS OF FRACTIONS OF AN INCH

1/64	0.015625	17/64	0.265625	33/64	0.515625
1/32	0.03125	9/32	0.28125	17/32	0.53125
3/64	0.046875	19/64	0.296875	35/64	0.546875
1/16	0.0625	5/16	0.3125	9/16	0.5625
5/64	0.078125	21/64	0.328125	37/64	0.578125
3/32	0.09375	11/32	0.34375	19/32	0.59375
7/64	0.109375	23/64	0.359375	39/64	0.609375
1/8	0.125	3/8	0.375	5/8	0.625
9/64	0.140625	25/64	0.390625	41/64	0.640625
5/32	0.15625	13/32	0.40625	21/32	0.65625
11/64	0.171875	27/64	0.421875	43/64	0.671875
3/16	0.1875	7/16	0.4375	11/16	0.6875
13/64	0.203125	29/64	0.453125	45/64	0.703125

DECIMAL EQUIVALENTS OF FRACTIONS OF AN INCH (cont'd)

7/32	0.21875	15/32	0.46875	23/32	0.71875
15/64	0.23475	31/64	0.484375	47/64	0.734375
1/4	0.250	1/2	0.500	3/4	0.750
49/64	0.765625	27/32	0.84375	59/64	0.921875
25/32	0.78125	55/64	0.859375	15/16	0.9375
51/64	0.796875	7/8	0.875	61/64	0.953125
13/16	0.8125	57/64	0.890625	31/32	0.96875
53/64	0.828125	29/32	0.90625	63/64	0.984375

CONVERSION TABLE MILLIMETERS TO INCHES

MM	.0	.1	.2	.3	.4	.5	.6	.7	.8	.9
0	——	.003937	.007874	.01181	.015748	.019685	.023622	.027559	.031496	.035433
1	.03937	.043307	.047244	.051181	.055118	.059055	.062992	.066929	.070866	.074803
2	.07874	.082677	.086614	.090551	.094488	.098425	.102362	.106299	.110236	.114173
3	.11811	.122047	.125984	.129921	.133858	.137795	.141732	.145669	.149606	.153543
4	.157480	.161417	.165354	.169291	.173228	.177165	.181102	.185039	.188976	.192913
5	.196850	.200787	.204724	.208661	.212598	.216535	.220472	.224409	.228346	.232283
6	.236220	.240157	.244094	.248031	.251968	.255905	.259842	.263779	.267716	.271653
7	.275590	.279527	.283464	.287401	.291338	.295275	.299212	.303149	.307086	.311023
8	.314960	.318897	.322834	.326771	.330708	.334645	.338582	.342519	.346456	.350393
9	.354330	.358267	.362204	.366141	.370078	.374015	.377952	.381889	.385826	.389763
10	.393700	.397637	.401574	.405511	.409448	.413385	.417322	.421259	.425196	.429133
11	.433070	.437007	.440944	.444881	.448818	.452755	.456692	.460629	.464566	.468503
12	.472440	.476377	.480314	.484251	.488188	.492125	.496062	.499999	.503936	.507873
13	.511810	.515747	.519684	.523621	.527558	.531495	.535432	.539369	.543306	.547243
14	.551180	.555117	.559054	.562991	.566928	.570865	.574902	.578739	.582676	.586613
15	.590550	.594487	.598424	.602361	.606298	.610235	.614172	.618109	.622046	.625983
16	.629920	.633857	.637794	.641731	.645668	.649605	.653542	.657479	.661416	.665353
17	.669290	.673227	.677164	.681101	.685038	.688975	.692912	.696849	.700786	.704723
18	.708660	.712597	.716534	.720471	.724408	.728345	.732282	.736219	.740156	.744093
19	.748030	.751967	.755904	.759841	.763778	.767715	.771652	.775589	.779526	.783463
20	.787400	.791337	.795274	.799211	.803148	.807085	.811022	.814959	.818896	.822833
21	.826770	.830707	.834644	.838581	.842518	.846455	.850392	.854329	.858266	.862203
22	.866140	.870077	.874014	.877951	.881888	.885825	.889762	.893699	.897636	.901573
23	.905510	.909447	.913384	.917321	.921258	.925195	.929132	.933069	.937006	.940943
24	.944880	.948817	.952754	.956691	.960628	.964565	.968502	.972439	.976376	.980313
25	.984250	.988187	.992124	.996061	.999998	1.003935	1.007872	1.011809	1.015746	1.019683
26	1.023620	1.027557	1.031494	1.035431	1.039368	1.043305	1.047242	1.051179	1.055116	1.059053
27	1.062990	1.066927	1.070864	1.074801	1.078738	1.082675	1.086612	1.090549	1.094486	1.098423
28	1.102360	1.106797	1.110234	1.114171	1.118108	1.122045	1.125982	1.129919	1.133856	1.137793
29	1.141730	1.145667	1.149604	1.11535	1.157478	1.161415	1.165352	1.169289	1.173226	1.177163
30	1.181100	——		——		——		——		——

It's often convenient to know how much energy your bullet is developing as it leaves the muzzle. When velocity and bullet weight are known this can be computed, but the table (right) is more easily used. Having determined the velocity from Appendix 3 or from your own tests, simply lay a straightedge across the table under the correct velocity reading. Opposite will be seen the energy *per grain of weight* for any bullet. Simply multiply this figure by the bullet weight in grains to get energy in foot-pounds.

For example, you're shooting a 100-grain ball at 1850 fps. Read off 1850 in the left column and opposite you'll see the value 7.60. Multiply 7.60 by bullet weight, 100, and the result is 760 fps. This is the energy of that bullet at the muzzle.

TABLE OF BULLET ENERGY

Velocity in fps	Energy per Grain of Bullet Weight	Velocity in fps	Energy per Grain of Bullet Weight
600	.80	640	.91
610	.82	650	.94
620	.85	660	.96
630	.88	670	.99
680	1.02	930	1.92
690	1.05	940	1.96
700	1.08	950	2.00
710	1.11	960	2.04
720	1.15	970	2.08
730	1.18	980	2.13
740	1.21	990	2.17
750	1.24	1000	2.22
760	1.28	1010	2.26

TABLE OF BULLET ENERGY (cont'd)

Velocity in fps	Energy per Grain of Bullet Weight	Velocity in fps	Energy per Grain of Bullet Weight	Velocity in fps	Energy per Grain of Bullet Weight	Velocity in fps	Energy per Grain of Bullet Weight
770	1.31	1020	2.31	1900	8.01	2150	10.26
780	1.34	1030	2.35	1910	8.10	2160	10.36
790	1.38	1040	2.40	1920	8.18	2170	10.45
800	1.42	1050	2.45	1930	8.35	2180	10.55
810	1.45	1060	2.49	1940	8.37	2190	10.65
820	1.49	1070	2.54	1950	8.44	2200	10.74
830	1.53	1080	2.59	1960	8.53	2210	10.84
840	1.56	1090	2.63	1970	8.61	2220	10.94
850	1.60	1100	2.68	1980	8.70	2230	11.04
860	1.64	1110	2.73	2240	11.14	2420	13.00
870	1.68	1120	2.78	2250	11.24	2430	13.11
880	1.72	1130	2.83	2260	11.34	2440	13.22
890	1.76	1140	2.88	2270	11.44	2450	13.33
900	1.79	1150	2.93	2280	11.54	2460	13.44
910	1.83	1160	2.99	2290	11.64	2470	13.55
920	1.87	1170	3.04	2300	11.74	2480	13.66
1180	3.09	1460	4.73	2310	11.83	2490	13.77
1190	3.14	1470	4.79	2320	11.95	2500	13.88
1200	3.19	1480	4.86	2330	12.05	2510	13.99
1210	3.25	1490	4.93	2340	12.16	2520	14.10
1220	3.30	1500	5.00	2350	12.26	2530	14.20
1230	3.36	1510	5.06	2360	12.37	2540	14.32
1240	3.41	1520	5.13	2370	12.47	2550	14.44
1250	3.47	1530	5.19	2380	12.58	2560	14.55
1260	3.52	1540	5.26	2390	12.68	2570	14.67
1270	3.58	1550	5.33	2400	12.78	2580	14.78
1280	3.63	1560	5.40	2410	12.90	2590	14.89
1290	3.69	1570	5.47			2600	15.01
1300	3.75	1580	5.54				
1310	3.81	1590	5.61				
1320	3.86	1600	5.68				
1330	3.92	1610	5.75				
1340	3.98	1620	5.82				
1350	4.04	1630	5.90				
1360	4.10	1640	5.97				
1370	4.16	1650	6.04				
1380	4.22	1660	6.12				
1390	4.29	1670	6.19				
1400	4.35	1680	6.26				
1410	4.41	1690	6.34				
1420	4.47	1700	6.41				
1430	4.54	1710	6.49				
1440	4.60	1720	6.57				
1450	4.66	1730	6.64				
1740	6.72	1990	8.79				
1750	6.80	2000	8.88				
1760	6.88	2010	8.97				
1770	6.95	2020	9.06				
1780	7.03	2030	9.15				
1790	7.11	2040	9.24				
1800	7.19	2050	9.33				
1810	7.27	2060	9.42				
1820	7.35	2070	9.50				
1830	7.43	2080	9.60				
1840	7.51	2090	9.70				
1850	7.60	2100	9.80				
1860	7.68	2110	9.90				
1870	7.76	2120	9.98				
1880	7.84	2130	10.07				
1890	7.93	2140	10.17				

There is considerable interest in muzzle-loading artillery. While most of the shooting done these days is with new-production replica or look-alike guns, information on Civil-War period guns is always of interest. Having it at hand, we can compare the results of modern cannon shoots. Listed below are the essential characteristics of the more widely-used Civil War artillery pieces.

HOW TO LOAD BLANK SHOTSHELLS

Black powder is used in factory-loaded blank shotshells and should be used in handloaded blanks. FFg granulation is recommended.

Either paper, plastic or brass shells may be used. The inside diameter of brass shells is greater than that of paper shells, requiring special over-sized wads which are readily available. Brass cases should be scrubbed in soapy water with a bristle brush immediately after firing to remove residue which would eventually corrode them. Paper or plastic cases must be resized, just as for shot loadings.

10-gauge shells are loaded with 6 to 8 drams of powder, 12-gauge with 6 drams, 16-gauge with about 4 drams and 20-gauge with about 3 drams. Smaller charges work equally well if the report is loud enough to suit you.

It is essential that you use an extra heavy wad over the powder. Place a nitro card over the powder; then use commercial wads or newspaper carefully packed in tightly to fill the case, leaving just enough room for a solid crimp.

Keep in mind that the wads constitute a substantial projectile. At close range they are nearly as dangerous as a bullet. Don't under any circumstances fire a blank directly at a person or animal.

FIELD ARTILLERY OF THE CIVIL WAR

	Bore Diam.	Material	Length of tube	Weight of tube	Weight of projectile	Powder Charge	Range at 5 degree elev.
6 Pounder	3.65''	bronze	60''	884 lbs.	6.10 lbs.	1.25 lbs.	1,523 yds.
6 pdr. Wiard	2.56''	steel	56''	600 lbs.	6.00 lbs.	0.60 lbs.	1,800 yds.
6 pdr. Whitworth	2.15''	steel	70''	700 lbs.	6.00 lbs.	1.00 lbs.	2,750 yds.
10 pdr. Parr.	3.00''	iron	74''	890 lbs.	9.50 lbs.	1.00 lbs.	1,850 yds.
10 pdr. Wiard	3.00''	steel	58''	790 lbs.	10.00 lbs.	1.00 lbs.	1,850 yds.
12 pdr. gun	4.62''	bronze	78''	1757 lbs.	12.30 lbs.	2.50 lbs.	1,663 yds.
12 pdr. How.	4.62''	bronze	53''	788 lbs.	8.90 lbs.	1.00 lbs.	1,072 yds.
12 pdr. Blakeley	3.40''	steel	59''	800 lbs.	10.00 lbs.	1.00 lbs.	1,850 yds.
12 pdr. James	3.67''	bronze	60''	875 lbs.	12.00 lbs.	0.75 lbs.	1,700 yds.
12 pdr. Nap. rifles	4.62''	bronze	66''	1227 lbs.	12.30 lbs.	2.50 lbs.	1,619 yds.
12 pdr. Whitworth	2.75''	steel	104''	1092 lbs.	12.00 lbs.	1.75 lbs.	2,800 yds.
12 pdr. Whitworth	2.72''	steel	84''	1000 lbs.	12.00 lbs.	2.00 lbs.	3,000 yds.
20 pdr. Parr.	3.67''	iron	84''	1750 lbs.	20.00 lbs.	2.00 lbs.	1,900 yds.
24 pdr. How.	5.90''	bronze	65''	1318 lbs.	18.40 lbs.	2.00 lbs.	1,322 yds.
24 pdr. James	4.62''	bronze	78''	1750 lbs.	24.00 lbs.	1.50 lbs.	1,800 yds.
32 pdr. How.	6.40''	bronze	75''	1920 lbs.	25.60 lbs.	2.50 lbs.	1,504 yds.
3'' Armstrong	3.00''	steel	76''	996 lbs.	12.00 lbs.	1.25 lbs.	2,200 yds.
3'' Armstrong	3.00''	steel	83''	918 lbs.	12.00 lbs.	1.25 lbs.	2,100 yds.
3'' Ord.	3.00''	iron	69''	816 lbs.	9.50 lbs.	1.00 lbs.	1,830 yds.

Pdr.—Pounder   Nap.—Napoleon   How.—Howitzer   Parr.—Parrot

When you are planning to build or have built a new rifle, calculating its weight can be a bit of a problem. The major proportion of the weight is concentrated in the barrel, and you can't weigh the barrel until it's at hand. Barrel weight needs to be known *before* ordering. By use of the tables below, the weight of a given length, size and caliber barrel can easily be determined. Or, on the other hand, a barrel can be selected to suit a previously chosen weight.

WEIGHTS OF 43'' OCTAGON BARRELS
Measured Across the Flats

Cal.	13/16''	7/8''	15/16''	1''	1-1/8''
.32	6-2/16 lbs.	6-2/16 lbs.	7-14/16 lbs.	9-8/16 lbs.	12 lbs.
.36	5-8/16 lbs.	6-8/16 lbs.	7-5/16 lbs.	9-3/16 lbs.	11-8/16 lbs.
.40	5 lbs.	6-5/16 lbs.	7 lbs.	8-9/16 lbs.	11-3/16 lbs.
.45	4-13/16 lbs.	5-12/16 lbs.	6-8/16 lbs.	8-4/16 lbs.	10-14/16 lbs.
.50	4-4/16 lbs.	5-4/16 lbs.	6-3/16 lbs.	7-10/16 lbs.	10-5/16 lbs.

WEIGHTS IN OUNCES PER INCH OF OCTAGON BARRELS
Measured Across the Flats

Cal.	7/8	15/16	1	1-1/16	1-1/8	Cal.	7/8	15/16	1	1-1/16	1-1/8
.22	2.7	3.2	3.6	4.1	4.5	.48	2.0	2.5	3.0	3.5	4.1
.24	2.7	3.2	3.6	4.0	4.5	.50	2.0	2.4	2.9	3.4	4.1
.26	2.6	3.1	3.6	4.0	4.5	.52	1.8	2.3	2.8	3.4	4.0
.28	2.6	3.1	3.5	4.0	4.4	.54	—	2.3	2.7	3.3	3.9
.30	2.6	3.1	3.5	4.0	4.4	.56	—	2.1	2.7	3.3	3.8
.32	2.5	3.0	3.4	3.9	4.4	.58	—	2.0	2.6	3.1	3.7
.34	2.5	2.9	3.4	3.9	4.4	.60	—	1.9	2.5	3.1	3.6
.36	2.4	2.9	3.4	3.9	4.4	.62	—	1.8	2.4	2.9	3.5
.38	2.4	2.8	3.3	3.8	4.3						
.40	2.3	2.8	3.2	3.8	4.3						
.42	2.3	2.7	3.2	3.7	4.3						
.44	2.2	2.7	3.1	3.7	4.2						
.46	2.1	2.6	3.1	3.6	4.2						

Screw-hole threads are often stripped or rusted out and must be recut to place the gun in good shooting condition. The tap sizes shown are suitable for freshing out or recutting threads for the screw sizes listed opposite. The fit is not always perfect, but acceptable new threads can be cut and matching screws are readily available.

> 3/16 x 24 tap: No. 2, 4, 7D, 55 and 54 screws.
> 10 x 24 tap: No. 1 screw.
> 6 x 40 tap: No. 24, 27, 60, 68, 66, 27, 24R, 83 and 85.
> 8 x 36 tap: No. 3, 23, 25, 26 and 84.
> 8 x 32 tap: No. 22, 58, 57P, 58P, 59 and 57.
> 12 x 24 tap: No. 34, 66, and 63.
> 10 x 32 tap: No. 82.
> 12 x 28 tap: No. 88 and Gate catch screw.

A percussion cap can be a bit of a problem to fit correctly on a nipple. The sizes are not entirely standardized. Modern nipples generally measure .163″ tapered to .168″, plus-or-minus .002″, from top to bottom. The .167-8″ caps will be a snug fit on some nipples; others will fit only by forcing. If the caps that you are using must be forced on your nipples, grind or polish the neck of the nipple to reduce the diameter and allow the cap to fit better. The following cap dimensions are averages and are sufficient to show why a perfect fit isn't always obtained.

	Inside Diameter	Length
No. 10 Alcan	.167″	.178″
No. 11 Italian	.168″	.153″
No. 1075 German	.170″	.170″
Eley No. F4-12	.170″	—
No. 1055 German	.170″	.220″
No. 11 Remington	.170″	.190″
No. 11 Belgium (Dixie)	.172″	.206″
Eley No. F4-21	.175″	—
No. 11 Winchester	.175″	.200″
Eley No. F4-25	.177″	—
No. 12 Alcan	.178″	.195″
No. 12 Remington	.178″	.190″

Handloaders know that some makes and models of primers produce greater velocity than others, all other factors being equal. The same is true, to a degree, with percussion caps. This is confirmed by the results of test firing tabulated below.

	Dixie Caps	German Caps	Italian Caps	Remington Caps
No. of shots	17	20	13	10
Lowest Velocity	2024	2041	1992	1976
Highest Velocity	2091	2100	2074	2128
Maximum Variation	67FPS	59FPS	82FPS	152FPS
Average Velocity	2062	2066	2035	2086

Appendix 5/Dos and Don'ts

Don't shoot an old gun until it has been disassembled, examined and found to be safe. That is, the breech plug must be tight, the drum tight and the nipple tight and clear. The barrel must be free and clean. For any accuracy at all, it probably will need to be freshed out or re-rifled.

Don't shoot any piece until it has been proven safe by proper proof testing.

Don't prime the pan of a flinter or cap a percussion arm until the arm is pointed at the target which you intend to shoot.

Don't smoke while handling black powder.

Don't rush on a misfire to examine the piece until sufficient time has elapsed to be reasonably assured that a latent spark is not active.

Don't pour powder directly from the flask or horn into a just-fired barrel—wipe it first; then use a measure.

Don't engage a target shooter in conversation when he is firing for record or while he is loading.

Don't handle the equipment of others without specific permission.

Don't as a matter of curiosity tinker or fool with another's sights at any time.

Don't allow a powder horn to remain in the sun for extended periods. It is liable to crack and split.

Don't place your finger in the muzzle of a barrel while examining the piece. Perspiration contains acids and salts which cause rust to form rapidly.

Don't buy an old gun, especially if the price is substantial, until it has been dismantled to permit an examination of its interior.

Don't buy a gun without a receipt stating the piece is authentic and is as represented.

Don't use smokeless powder in any amount in black powder guns.

Don't prime the clean-out or nipple hole to expel a bullet when the main powder charge has not been poured into the barrel without first ramming the ball flush against the priming load. If the priming charge does not expel the bullet, reprime with sufficient FFFFg. The first firing will have moved the ball up the barrel some unknown distance, thus permitting a sufficient additional priming charge to be inserted thru the clean-out hole. BUT, this time ram the ball back against the powder before firing.

A brand new rifle of modern steel components blew up at the Friendship Shoot 1959 because of the failure of its operator to heed advice akin to the foregoing.

Don't shoot any piece until you've ascertained there is no foreign matter in the barrel.

Don't believe the old Kentucky which belonged to Great Grandad drove a tack at any range every shot. Grandad was lucky if it drove *one* tack from the rest position at 25 yards.

Don't believe the saying "They don't put the stuff into them today that they did years ago." Actually the steels available to the old gun makers were of unknown and unascertainable quality and analysis. Steel-making techniques had not advanced to the point that impurities were removed nor could quality be controlled. For a detailed account of this premise, see *American Rifleman* of December, 1959.

Don't assume an old gun is unloaded—check it—many of them are loaded.

Don't point any gun, even though you know positively it is unloaded, at anything you don't intend to shoot. This is the cardinal rule for safety in gun handling—*NO* exceptions to this rule.

Don't store any gun for any period of time in a case, particularly a sheep-lined case, unless accompanied by VPI crystals or paper.

Don't store your guns in a basement. All basements are damp when artificial heat is absent. If you must so store your guns, wipe them inside and out at frequent intervals.

Don't store your mold or swage without a generously oiled bullet in it.

Don't store or carry your gun in an unlined canvas case if you value the finish on it. Canvas will deface finishes.

Don't permit your rifle or pistol to remain in the hot sun between relays or from one relay to a later one. The barrel will heat unevenly from the sun's rays, thus causing non-uniform expansion, which in turn will cause inconsistent points of impact on the target. When it is not in use, store it in the shade or cover with a canvas or blanket.

Don't bend your body over the muzzle when ramming a bullet into a charged barrel.

Don't pour powder into a barrel which has been oiled for storage. Clean it first with a patch or two; then snap a cap to burn oil out of the tube; then load for shooting.

Don't get careless at any point during the procedures of muzzle-loading shooting.

Don't drink intoxicants if you intend to shoot and don't shoot if you have been drinking. No booze or no shooting.

Appendix 6/Glossary

Ampco nipple—A modern type of percussion nipple, made of a special alloy which has the appearance of brass but is much harder, tougher and highly resistant to erosion of the flash hole from the heat of ignition.

aperture sight—A "peep" rear sight with a small hole through which the eye automatically centers the front sight. The most accurate type of metallic sight.

arquebus—A very early matchlock firearm, later including certain wheel locks. Usually refers to an arm of better workmanship rather than crude military pieces.

back-action lock—A later type of percussion side-lock in which the mainspring is to the rear of tumbler and hammer.

ball—The spherical lead projectile used in the major-ity of muzzle-loading rifles and pistols.

ball and swan drops—A combination load consist-ing of a ball over which were a number of the large shot used in swan hunting, approximately .27 caliber, followed by a wad. Used occasionally in warfare, in coach pistols against highwaymen and (in certain areas) in the earlier formal pistol duels.

ballistics—The science of a projectile's actions after the propellant's explosion and the various factors which influence its accuracy.

ball screw—An attachment for the threaded end of a ramrod to remove a lead projectile without firing the arm.

Baltic lock—A primitive, early version of the flint-lock in use about 1600.

band spring—A spring which is depressed to remove a barrel band from a musket.

bar-action—The more usual side-lock type in which the mainspring is in front of the tumbler and hammer.

barleycorn—A conventional early front sight of sim-ple bladed type, very low in height. So named because its shape often suggested a barley grain before thresh-ing.

barrel—The metal tube from which the projectile emerges upon firing.

barrel band—One of the several bands holding barrel and forend together on most military muskets.

barrel key—A flat key which holds barrel and forend together on many half-stock rifles and shotguns.

barrel pin—A round metal pin which fastens barrel to forend, usually on earlier full-stock arms.

belted ball—A lead ball cast with a single raised belt around its circumference to be mechanically fitted into the deep two-grooved rifling of certain muzzle-loading rifles, particularly British Smith, Purdeys, etc.

bench rifle—A type of target rifle, often quite heavy, designed especially for firing from a bench rest with the shooter seated.

black powder—The standard propellant of the muzzle loader. It is basically a mechanical mixture of potassium nitrate, charcoal and sulphur.

blunderbus—A firearm with a flared muzzle often used to repel boarders in naval warfare. It is erroneously pictured as the standard arm of the pilgrim fathers which it definitely was not.

bootleg—A slender muzzle-loading pistol, usually with a compact underhammer action, which could be carried inside a boot if desired.

bore—The hole in a tubular gun barrel through which the projectile passes.

bore gauge—An instrument for determining the exact diameter of a bore.

bore sighting—Adjusting of the sights to coincide exactly with a point upon which the bore is aligned at a given distance. With a muzzle loader, this may be done by removing barrel and breech plug.

box lock—A lock mechanism with the hammer inside of the lock plate and projecting above it.

breech—The rear end of the barrel.

breech plug—A threaded plug which provides a gas-tight seal for the rear of the barrel and to which the tang is usually attached.

breech pressure—The pressure exerted by the rapidly expanding gases of the ignited propellant, measured in psi (pounds per square inch).

breech seal—a metal or plastic seal which is designed to provide obturation to an arm such as a Civil War breech-loading carbine so that it may be used as a muzzle loader.

bridle—A plate that provides support for the inside end of those screws upon which the sear and tumbler pivot in a conventional lock.

Brown Bess—The smoothbore flintlock musket of the British forces during our colonial period.

browning—An oxidation process for finishing barrels and metal parts, which predated modern bluing.

buck and ball—A musket load as sometimes used in the Civil War, usually consisting of one spherical musket ball behind three buckshot. A deadly short-range load.

buckshot—Large round lead shot, usually ranging from .24 to .36 caliber. In multi-ball loads, these were used in riot control, combat and big-game hunting.

buggy rifle—A small light rifle, often in the form of a long-barreled single-shot pistol with rifle sights and a detachable shoulder stock. Popular around the 1870's for protection, small game and informal target shooting.

bullet—The projectile itself, not the entire cartridge as the term is often erroneously used.

bullet mold—A metal tool containing a cavity or cavities for the casting of lead balls or other firearm projectiles.

bullet patch—A patch of cloth, buckskin or similar material surrounding a ball in a muzzle-loader bore, which engages the rifling and serves as a gas seal.

butt mask—On earlier pistols, a metal butt cap representing a grotesque face.

butt plate—A protective metal plate on the rear of a buttstock.

buttstock—The widening portion of the wooden stock which goes against the shoulder.

caliber—The nominal diameter of the bore of a firearm expressed in thousandths of an inch.

cannelure—A shallow grease groove around the circumference of a conical bullet.

cap box—A hinged metal trap in the stock of a percussion shotgun, in the butt of a Deringer pistol, etc. Also, a leather belt-pouch for musket caps in the Civil War period or a small pocket container.

caplock—Another term for a percussion firearm.

cartridge box—For our purposes, the leather pouch in which musketeer carries paper or combustible cartridges.

case-hardening—A metal-heating process in conjunction with bone and leather scraps, or more recently, chemicals which impart a beautiful finish in mottled colors while making the metal surface quite hard.

cast-off—A variation to the right in a gun stock from alignment with the barrel to better fit a right-handed shooter. To the left for a southpaw is called cast-on.

chamber—An unrifled portion of the barrel at the

rear where the powder charge receives ignition. Seen in some muzzle loaders, but not usually.

charger—A powder measure for one exact charge. May be on a horn, a flask or a separate instrument. Fixed or adjustable.

checkering—The decorative roughening of a hand-grip. Seldom seen on muzzle loaders except for shotguns and some duelling pistols.

cheek piece—A raised portion behind the comb of a stock to align the eye with the sights.

cherry—A steel burr of precise shape to cut the cavity in a bullet mold blank.

choke—The varying constrictions near the muzzles of shotguns to control the range at which an ideal pattern occurs. Different chokes are desirable for different conditions. Fine custom-made muzzle-loading rifles are often given a touch of choke for superior accuracy.

cleaning patch—A cloth patch, usually flannel, for wiping the bore between shots or thorough cleaning after the day's firing.

coach pistol—Usually a smooth-bore, this was a pistol once carried by travelers for protection. Not recommended for target accuracy.

cock—The action of drawing back the hammer. Also an early term for the hammer of a flintlock.

comb—The raised top of a stock just back of the wrist or trigger-hand grip.

combustible cartridge—A muzzle-loading cartridge encased in nitrated paper or other material which is completely consumed by the flame of ignition. Most used in percussion revolvers.

cone—Early term for a percussion nipple.

corned powder—Crude early-type black powder, which was the first attempt at formation into grains.

corrosion—The deterioration of a bore or other metal surface from oxidation or other chemical reaction. See *erosion*.

creep—The erratic, rough pull of a trigger when sear and tumbler notches have not been properly stoned smooth.

culot—The iron wedge in the hollow base of a Minie bullet, per French Captain Minie's original design.

American ordnancemen later eliminated this expanding wedge.

curly maple—Favorite stock wood of the early American "Kentucky rifle" makers. They selected only certain kinds of maple and preferably from sparse rocky terrain for maximum figure in the grain.

cylinder—The revolving portion of a percussion revolver usually containing six chambers.

cylinder bore—A shotgun barrel which is not choked.

damascus—An early barrel steel made from strips of various steels welded together in a pleasing design. The harder metals resisted browning more than the milder ones, which accounted for the beautiful effect; but we vastly prefer a plainer and stronger barrel for actual shooting!

detent—A detent, or fly, should be added to the tumbler when a set trigger is installed. It cams the sear nose down during firing to miss the half-cock notch. It does not interfere with half-cocking otherwise.

detonating powders—Very powerful high explosives which are initiated by a blow, not requiring ignition. They made the percussion cap possible and modern primers. Alexander Forsythe developed the first practical detonator lock for firearms about 1805 and patented it in 1807, but it did not gain general acceptance for many years. Although mercury fulminate was already known, Forsythe refused to use it, preferring his mixture of potassium chlorate, charcoal and sulphur.

disc primer—used on many of the separate-primed Sharps rifles of the transition period. Hammer action caused a tiny magazine to place a disc primer over the nipple for each shot. This was the "Lawrence patent."

dog lock—A manually-operated catch which engaged the rear of the hammer on some early flintlocks.

double action—An arm in which one long pull of the trigger cocked the hammer, turned the cylinder if there was one and fired the piece.

double-neck hammer—Or reinforced hammer, was used on many later flintlocks, especially military arms. It was less graceful but stronger than the more standard "goose-neck" flint hammer. With improved steels, most percussion arms returned to the goose-neck style.

double rifle—There were several types of double rifles made in the U.S., both in flint and percussion.

The side-by-side double rifle was largely a British preference for the big game of Africa and India. Many top quality British percussion rifles found their way here with their sportsmen when our buffalo, elk and grizzly were plentiful.

drift—The lateral error in a bullet's flight due to its rotation from the rifling.

drop—The distance from the line of sight to the top of the comb and the top of the heel of a stock.

duelling pistol—A superb quality single-shot in either flint or percussion designed solely for aristocratic mayhem. Contrary to common belief, these were seldom covered with light-reflecting inlays and filagree. A small percentage of the "duellers" now around actually were for that purpose.

duplex load—One in which a tiny priming charge of "bulk" smokeless shotgun powder is loaded ahead of a reduced charge of black powder for cleaner shooting, etc. Only for the thoroughly experienced shooter. Currently outlawed in many larger matches across the nation.

elevation—Raising the rear sight raises the point of impact. Raising the front sight lowers it.

eprouvette—A device in either flint or percussion by which the comparative strength of powder samples may be tested, usually by a rotating gauge and stationary needle. Not too accurate, but a peachy conversation piece.

erosion—The enlargement of a bore, touchhole or nipple vent from the intense heat of ignition coupled with projectile wear. Reasonable loads increase barrel life.

escutcheon—A metal inlay strengthening the hole through which a barrel key or other fastening is inserted.

false muzzle—The accessory which is placed precisely upon the muzzle of the finer target rifles during loading, particularly bench rifles to aid in accurately starting the bullet without deforming it and to prevent damage to the rifling at the muzzle.

fence—A projection on the rear of the flintlock pan to divert the flash from the face of the shooter.

finial—The decorative end of a patch box, trigger-guard strap, lock plate or other metal gun part.

flash—Ignition of the priming powder in a flint-lock pan when the main charge fails to explode.

flash guard—See *fence.*

flintlock—Traditional arm of our colonial forefathers in which a flint strikes steel, dropping incandescent shavings into a pan of priming powder. The flash sets off the main charge through a touchhole. Generally considered the first fairly practical firearm.

forend—Or forearm. The portion of the wooden stock which lies under the barrel.

fouling shot—A first shot into the backstop to remove every vestige of oil before firing a match.

fowling piece—Generally accepted to mean an earlier shotgun—a light single barrel.

freshening—The rejuvenation of a worn bore by deepening each groove, then smoothing the tops of the lands. This will generally require a new mold or enlargement of the former one's cavity. Simpler than either re-rifling or sleeving, if your bore is not too far gone.

frizzen—Also hen, pan cover, steel, battery, etc. Various names for the steel part which the flint scrapes to fire a flintlock.

frizzen spring—The outside spring which controls the frizzen's position.

fulminating powders—Detonating agents such as fulminate of gold and of silver were discovered as early as 1600 but found no practical purpose. The discovery of fulminate of mercury was announced on March 13, 1800, leading to the invention of the percussion cap almost 20 years later.

furniture—All the minor metal trim on a muzzle loader which may be of brass, iron, German silver or sterling silver.

gain twist—A type of rifling in which the pitch or the degree of twist increases steadily as the bullet progresses from breech to muzzle.

gauge—Any measuring device. Also the size of a shotgun bore determined by the number of spherical balls of bore size which comprise one pound of lead. Example: one pound makes 12 balls that fit a cylinder-bored 12-gauge shotgun. Thus, larger numbers mean smaller bores, the opposite of rifle calibration.

German ring target—An early type of paper target, the popularity of which extended into the Schuetzen match era of the 1880's.

globe sight—A fine front sight like an erect small-headed pin, shaded by a short metal cylinder. Makers such as Norman Brockway sometimes used a hog bristle for the pin.

goose-neck hammer—The graceful single-necked hammer of the flint and the percussion eras.

grooves—The spiral cuts of rifling which cause a bullet to rotate in flight.

group—A good target group is a series of bullet holes in close proximity. Sight adjustments will then move future groups to the target's center.

gunflint—A hand-shaped piece of flint stone with a chisel edge for firing a flintlock.

gunpowder—The propellent explosive used in small arms.

hair trigger—The forward or firing trigger of a double-set trigger assembly. It may be adjusted to release at a very light touch.

hammer—The piece which holds the flint in a flint-lock or which strikes the capped nipple in a percussion arm.

hammer spur—The thumbpiece on the upper rear of a typical percussion hammer.

hand cannon—The earliest small arm in firearm history. More useful for scaring the enemy's horses than as a serious weapon.

hangfire—A dangerous condition when an apparent misfire goes off after a brief delay. Keep it pointed downrange!

heel—The corner of the buttstock at the top of the butt plate.

horse pistol—A large pistol, chiefly military, used by early horsemen and often carried in a pommel holster.

hunting pouch—The leather pouch, usually decorated, in which the early American rifleman carried patching, spare flints, priming horn and other accessories for his long rifle.

hydraulic bullet—A muzzle-loading projectile drilled to insert water after which the hole is plugged. This gives increased expansion on a solid target such as game.

ignition—The method by which the charge is fired, such as flintlock, percussion cap, slow match, fuse, pyrites, linstock, pill lock, etc.

incised—When a surface is cut to a given depth as on wood or leather; preparatory to relief carving, leather tooling, inlaying, etc.

inlays—Decorative shaped pieces of metal, ivory, contrasting wood, etc., let into the surface of a gun-stock and finished flush with that surface.

inletting—The precise woodworking which permits barrel, lock and other major parts to fit into recesses in the stock which exactly receive them.

iron pyrites—A common mineral, a yellowish metallic-looking sulfide. The "fool's gold" of the inexperienced prospector. Striking sparks from steel, it was the ignition agent of both the wheel lock and the pyrites lock.

Jaeger rifle—An early German arm from which our Kentucky rifle evolved, being drastically modified to suit New World conditions.

jag—A serrated, ridged or button-ended tip for a cleaning rod to grip the cloth patch.

Kentucky rifle—The traditional long flintlock rifle of our pioneer forefathers. One of the few purely American developments in firearm history, reaching its peak of excellence between 1775 and 1830.

knapper—A skilled workman who chips out gunflints using hand tools exclusively. Currently, the only remaining professional knappers operate in the village of Brandon, England.

lands—The raised spiral ridges between the grooves of the rifling.

lap—A precisely fitting plug, usually of lead and charged with abrasives, for smoothing out a bore.

linen—A cloth material woven from flax fiber, often preferred for ball patches.

loading block—A small strip of hardwood drilled with several holes which carry pre-patched balls to save time in loading a rifle.

lock plate—The flat metal plate upon which the firing mechanism of a conventional muzzle loader is mounted.

lock-screw—A long screw running laterally through the stock to hold the lock in place.

lock-screw plate—A metal plate opposite the lock plate which supports the heads of the lock-screws.

magazine capper—A convenient device for dispensing one percussion cap at a time directly onto the nipple.

mainspring—The heavy spring which actuates the hammer.

mainspring vise—A clamp to compress the mainspring for easier disassembly of the lock mechanism.

matchlock—The earliest firearm to include an actual mechanism. A smoldering, nitrated hemp cord (the "match") was levered into contact with the primed pan.

materiel—The equipment of the military. Not to be confused with the raw *material* from which it is made.

metallic sights—Gun sights which do not contain magnifying glass lenses, etc. A stipulation in the rules of many matches.

Minie bullet—The conical projectile of the Civil War infantry rifle and similar Minie rifles. The pressure of propellent gases expand its hollow base into the rifling grooves.

miquelet—Forerunner of the true flintlock, it had an outside mainspring. It differed from the snaphance in having frizzen and pan cover in one piece.

misfire—Failure of a loaded arm to fire when intended. See *hangfire*.

mule ear lock—A percussion system with a flat side hammer which pivoted laterally.

musket—Generally, the long full-stocked smoothbored shoulder arm of the early infantryman. The first issue rifles were sometimes termed "rifled muskets" and their outside appearance was little changed.

musketoon—A shorter shoulder arm of musket pattern between the infantry musket and cavalry carbine in length. Issued to artillery and sappers (military engineers).

muzzle—The front end of a barrel.

muzzle energy—The force exerted by the bullet, expressed in foot pounds, calculated at or near the muzzle. A better term is kinetic energy which more properly describes the same calculation at various distances.

muzzle loader—A firearm designed to be loaded from the muzzle or front end by means of a ramrod. Percussion revolvers are included, as their chambers are loaded from the front of the cylinder. Also may refer to a person who shoots muzzle-loading firearms.

muzzle velocity—Speed of the projectile, expressed in feet per second (fps), at the muzzle or at various measured distances.

nipple—The tiny tube of a percussion arm upon which the cap is placed. With its threaded base it is readily replaceable.

nipple wrench—A tool for removing or replacing nipples. Comes in various sizes.

nose cap—The metal cap on the front end of a muzzle loader forend, particularly on a full-stock arm.

octagonal barrel—Seen on many of the earlier muzzle loaders, this is the conventional 8-sided barrel.

open sights—The standard V-notch rear and plain blade front sight.

pan—The receptacle which holds the priming powder in the flintlock and previous ignition systems.

patch box—The lidded recess in the buttstock of some muzzle-loading rifles in which greased patches were carried, or else the tallow for greasing them as they were used.

patch cutter—An instrument for precutting bullet patches with the aid of a mallet.

patch knife—If you do not use precut patches, each is trimmed at the muzzle during loading with this extremely sharp knife.

patent breech—Or French breech. One in which the breech plug and nipple seat are cast in one block. This has an upturned hook on its rear which engages a slot in a separate upper tang. In a half-stock rifle, for example, one barrel key is pulled and the barrel lifts right out for convenience in cleaning or transporting.

patina—The mellow finish that comes with age on a fine gun or fine furniture. Usually it is a mistake to remove it.

pattern—The shot pattern obtained by a shotgun. Generally found by firing at a single spot in the middle of a 30-inch circle at 40 yards. The percentage of the total shot charge inside the circle is a guide to the degree of choke. Even distribution of the shot is essential. A pattern with large gaps in it is a "blown" pattern.

pepperbox—A repeating percussion pistol of the

1840's with a revolving chamber aligning with a single barrel in turn. Usually small caliber, rifled and double action.

percussion—The cap and ball, last type of muzzle loader before the advent of practical breech loaders.

percussion cap—A small copper or brass cup-shaped primer containing a tiny amount of detonating powder such as mercury fulminate. Often foil lined and waterproofed.

pick—Or picker. A fine steel wire to clean out a nipple vent or flintlock touchhole.

picket bullet—One of the first conical bullets developed in this country. Only the very base was bore size, tapering forward from there. Extreme care was required in loading to prevent it from tipping and losing all accuracy.

pill lock—A very early percussion system. An extremely tiny round pellet of fulminate was used instead of the later metal cap.

pipes—The short tubes on the underside of a muzzle loader for holding the ramrod.

pistol—A firearm to be held in one hand. Thought to have derived from Pistoia, an early Italian firearm center.

pitch—Or twist. The angle or speed of the rifling.

plains rifle—With the westward migration, a shorter rifle was needed for loading on horseback, and heavier calibers for buffalo, etc. The famous Hawken rifles were usually half-stock plains rifles.

powder flask—A container for gunpowder generally of copper, brass or zinc, typical of the percussion era. Normally has a measuring charger on top.

powder horn—From our colonial period comes the powder container of cow or buffalo horn, more often used with a separate non-adjustable charge measure. Proper accessory with a flintlock.

powder measure—A separate accessory with a graduated plunger, useful for experimenting with varying loads in the field.

primer—On some percussion bench rifles, a special attachment permits ignition by a modern primer instead of an ordinary cap.

priming—The finer powder in a flintlock's pan.

priming horn—A miniature horn for FFFFg priming powder.

projectile—The ball or bullet shot from a firearm.

proof marks—Tiny stampings in a barrel's surface to signify that it has been proof fired with a prescribed overload under government supervision as a safety measure.

propellant, propellent—Stumbling block of many a writer. The first is the noun; the second is the adjective. Example: For the propellant we use a propellent powder. A "low" explosive suitable for gunpowder.

pull—The measurement from the firing trigger to the center of the butt plate.

pyrites lock—An improvement over a matchlock, in which iron pyrites fell against a steel frizzen. It had the manually operated pan cover of the matchlock and the outside mechanism of the later miquelet.

Queen Anne pistol—A flintlock, usually without a forend, with a barrel that unscrews to accept the load in the breech end.

ramrod—The rod, generally of hickory, with which the ball is pushed down the bore against the powder charge.

reentry match—One in which the shooter is allowed to fire more than one score for record.

revolver—A handgun with a multichambered cylinder and a single barrel.

revolving rifle—A rifle with the above type of mechanism. In the 19th century, Colt and Remington were leading manufacturers of these arms.

rib—The strip of steel above the joint between the barrels in a side-by-side double gun or rifle.

rifle—A shoulder firearm designed to fire a single projectile and with grooves cut in its bore.

rifle saw—A short, file-like cutter at the end of a wooden rod. Drawn through a barrel and mechanically guided in a spiral motion, this cuts the rifling grooves one at a time.

rifling—The spiral grooves in a rifle's bore which improve accuracy by imparting a spin to the projectile.

saltpeter—Potassium nitrate.

sear—The lock part which engages the tumbler and hammer until released by trigger pressure.

sear spring—The small spring which actuates the sear.

serpentine powder—The first crude black gunpowder before corning was developed. A coarse non-uniform meal.

set trigger—A mechanism in which a rear trigger is "cocked" so that a slight touch on the front trigger fires the arm. This eliminates all "creep" or "drag." Switzerland even put them on some issue military rifles.

shooting bench—A solid bench for shooting a rifle from a rest.

shot dipper—A graduated measure on a wooden handle for measuring one charge of bird shot.

shot pouch or flask—A container, often of leather, for bird shot.

side plates—Plates on each side of a patch-box cover.

sighting shot—A nonscoring shot at the beginning of a match to "get the range" dope with wind, adjust sights, etc.

single-action—A revolver which must be manually cocked for each shot.

sizing—An additive to certain cloth materials to give them "body." Must be washed out before using as patching.

skin cartridge—A combustible cartridge for percussion revolvers encased in nitrated hog's intestine.

sling—The leather or web strap on a military musket or rifle. Now used as an aid in aiming but formerly only as a help in carrying the pieces on a long march.

sling swivels—Two metal loops on a shoulder arm to which a sling may be attached.

smooth-bore—Any small-arm or artillery piece, the bore of which is not rifled.

snail—The "water-drain" type of base for a percussion nipple often seen on higher-grade guns instead of a drum.

snaphance—Similar to its successor, the true flintlock, except that frizzen and pan cover were two separate pieces.

spanner—A wrench for cocking a wheel lock.

sperm oil—Oil from the sperm whale or cachalot. Once a favorite for lamps and for gun oil.

spotting scope—A small telescope, usually 20 power, used for examining the target from the firing point.

spring, flat or "kick"—The original type of spring used in early firearms.

spring, helical—A coil spring, not to be confused with a spiral spring.

sprue—The small flat on one side of a cast ball where excess lead was removed by the cut-off plate.

spur trigger guard—One with a hook on its lower side to support the second finger and give better control of a hair trigger.

starter—A short wooden rod for placing the ball partway down the bore before using the ramrod.

steady pin—The little knob on the edge of a flat mainspring which fits into a slot in the lock plate.

stirrup—The pivoting piece connecting mainspring to tumbler in some locks.

stock—The main wooden portion of a firearm, especially a shoulder arm.

striking a barrel—The lengthwise finish draw-filing of a barrel's exterior, especially an octagonal barrel, with a special double-handed striking file.

string measure—The pioneer-scoring method in which wooden plugs were inserted in each bullet hole, a string drawn around all and measured. The shortest string won. Through the years, there have been several variations of this, some involving the center and some only measuring group size. Today, "string measure" is done from the center with calipers and the distances totaled.

superposed rifles—Double-barreled rifles, one barrel over the other. The barrels of many early ones pivoted upon a longitudinal axis so that one lock would fire whichever barrel was uppermost.

swaging—Putting conical projectiles through a precise die under pressure to bring them to the exact diameter and shape desired.

tape primer—A roll of paper tape containing fulminate pellets at regular intervals. It furnished the ignition for specially-modified rifles, etc., during the Civil War era on the principle of a toy repeating-cap pistol.

tennon—A slip of metal dovetailed into the bottom of a barrel through which a barrel key or pin passes, holding the barrel in the stock.

thimble—A "pipe" or short tube for holding the ramrod.

tinder—A highly flammable substance, such as flax tow or charred linen, used to catch sparks to start a fire. The pioneer used the mechanism of his flintlock to ignite his tinder in camp.

toe—The corner of the buttstock at the bottom of the butt plate.

toe plate—The metal strip on the bottom of a Kentucky rifle butt next to the butt plate.

tompion—A plug inserted in a gun muzzle during storage to keep out dirt or moisture. Seldom used today. Do not use wood or other hygroscopic materials.

top jaw—The upper half of the clamp which holds a flintlock flint.

top jaw screw—The heavy screw which clamps the flint in position.

touchhole—The vent through which a flintlock pan transmits its flash to the main charge.

tow—Crude unspun flax used in pioneer days like a cleaning patch.

trajectory—The vertical curve of a bullet's flight.

trap—A shotgun contest on aerial targets, usually breakable "clay pigeons." Also the instrument which projects these targets into the air.

trigger—The small lever by which a firearm is fired. Originally "tricker" because it did the trick.

trigger guard—The metal bow which guards against accidental trippings of the trigger.

trigger plate—A metal strap set into the bottom of the stock to control lateral motion of the trigger. Sometimes trigger assembly is attached to it, sometimes not.

trigger spring—A small spring which returns the trigger to its forward position.

tube lock—A very early percussion system developed about 1815 in which the hammer crushed a fulminate-filled copper tube inserted directly into the vent.

tube sight—Ancestor of the telescope sight. A long, thin metal tube, often full length of the barrel, not containing optical lenses. With rear aperture and front pin-head, it allowed maximum definition of the sight picture.

tumbler—Central piece of the conventional lock, turning with the hammer. This contains the half-cock and full-cock notches plus the detent if there is one.

twist—The pitch or angle of spiral of the rifling grooves.

under rib—A metal rib on the underside of a half-stock's barrel supporting the ramrod thimbles.

under-striker lock—A percussion lock with the hammer underneath, often with the mainspring serving as the trigger guard.

upper tang—An extension of the breech plug which is held in the small of the stock by a screw.

V-spring—A flat V-shaped spring considered superior to an ordinary single-leaf spring.

vent—The small aperture of any muzzle loader through which the flame of ignition reaches the main charge.

vernier sight—A precise, adjustable rear aperture sight developed in the middle 1800's.

wad cutter—A steel tool for cutting out shotgun wads with a mallet. Also used for the smaller bullet patches.

wheel lock—A more complex mechanism following the matchlock, in which iron pyrites pressed against the serrated edge of a rotating wheel. Ronson still uses the idea.

windage—A lateral adjustment (or allowance) in sighting.

wiping rod—A cleaning rod used during firing to wipe the bore out between shots.

worm—A corkscrew tip for a rod to hold a cleaning patch or to remove one stuck in the bore.

wrist—The small of the stock grasped by the firing hand.

zero—The ideal sight setting at a given range from which adjustments will be made to meet varying conditions of light, wind, etc.

Appendix 7/Abbreviations

AE: automatic ejectors

AP: armor piercing in reference to bullets

API: armor piercing incendiary in reference to bullets

AR: automatic rifle; *American Rifleman* magazine

AS: automatic safety

BB: bevel base in reference to bullets; bull barrel in reference to a gun

BBL: barrel

BC: ballistic coefficient in reference to bullets

BC: battery cup primer

BL: blank, cartridge or stock

BN: bottle neck in reference to a cartridge case

BP: black powder

BPE: black powder express in a cartridge designation

BT: boat tail in reference to bullets; beaver tail in reference to stocks

C & H: Curtis & Harvey powder (Imperial Chemical Industries)

Car: carbine

CCI: CCI-Omark, ammunition maker

CF: centerfire

CI: center of impact

CIL: Canadian Industries, Ltd.

CL: Core-Lokt bullet (Remington)

CN: cannelure in a bullet or case

CT: copper tube in a bullet designation

DA: double action in a handgun

DB: double barrel in reference to a gun; double base in reference to powder

DC: double cavity in a bullet mold

Den: headstamp for Denver Ordnance Plant

DST: double set trigger

DT: double trigger

DWM: Deutsche Waffenundmunitions Fabrik, used as a headstamp and as a prefix to numerical cartridge designations

EB: expanding bullet

EC: headstamp for Evansville Chrysler Ammunition plant

ECS: headstamp for Evansville/Chrysler/Sunbeam ammunition plant

EK: Eley-Kynoch ammunition

ER: eye relief

Ex: excellent in NRA condition standards

F: fair in NRA condition standards; fire, in reference to a gun safety

FA: headstamp for Frankford Arsenal

FB: flat base in reference to bullets

FC: full choke in reference to shotguns; full charge in reference to ammunition

FC: Federal Cartridge Corporation headstamp (also FCC)

FL: flintlock

FMJ: full metal jacket in reference to bullets

FP: foot-pounds in reference to energy; full patch (FMJ) in reference to bullets
FPS: feet per second in reference to velocity
FS: full stock
FW: featherweight

G (Gew): *Gewehr,* German word for rifle
G: good in NRA condition standards
GC: gas check in reference to bullets
GO: Gearhart-Owen powder
GR: G. Roth, used as a headstamp and as a prefix to numerical cartridge designations

H: Hodgdon (B.E.) as a prefix in a powder
H & H: Holland & Holland, old-line British gun-making firm sometimes called "Holland's"
HA: Hopkins & Allen
HB: hollow base in reference to bullets; heavy barrel in reference to barrels
HE: hand ejector (ejection) in reference to a revolver
HJ: half jacket in reference to bullets
HMG: heavy machine gun
HP: hollow point in reference to bullets; high power in reference to cartridge or gun designations
HR: Harrington & Richardson
Hy: Hornady Manufacturing Company

IC: improved cylinder choke
IL: inside lubricated in reference to bullets
Imp: improved in a cartridge designation
IMR: improved military rifle powder as a prefix in a powder designation

JHP: jacketed hollow point in reference to bullets
JSP: jacketed soft point in reference to bullets

K (Kar): *Karabiner,* German word for carbine

L: lead in reference to bullets
LC: headstamp for Lake City Arsenal
LC: Long Colt in reference to handgun cartridges
LE: Lee Enfield rifle
LGS: Lyman Gun Sight Co. (Lyman Products for Shooters)
LMG: light machine gun
LP: large pistol primer
LR: large rifle primer
LW: lightweight

M: model, as M-16 rifle
M & P: Military & Police in reference to a Smith & Wesson revolver
Mag: magazine

MC: metal case in reference to bullets; Monte Carlo-style comb in reference to stocks
MC or Mod: Modified choke
ME: muzzle energy of a bullet in foot pounds
MH: Martini-Henry rifle or Merwin Hulbert revolver
MK: Mark, sometimes used instead of M or Model, as in Revolver .455, MKVI
MOA: minute of angle
MP: metal point or metal piercing in reference to bullets
MR: mean radius, average shot distance from center of impact
MRT: mid-range trajectory height
MS: Mannlicher-Schoenauer rifle
MV: muzzle velocity of a bullet in feet per second

N: Norma Projectilfabrik as a prefix in a powder designation
NC: non-corrosive in reference to primers
NE: nitro express in a cartridge designation
NE: non-ejector
NM: National Match in reference to guns, equipment or ammunition manufactured or selected specifically for the U. S. National Rifle & Pistol Matches
NMNC: non-mercuric, non-corrosive in reference to primers
NSE: non-selective ejectors

OAL: overall length, cartridge or gun
OL: outside lubricated in reference to bullets
OP: over powder wad; open point in reference to bullets; Official Police in reference to a Colt revolver
OS: over shot wad; open sight
OU: over-under, barrels placed one above the other; sometimes indicates "superposed"

PB: plain base in reference to bullets
PC or PCC: Peters Cartridge Co. in reference to a headstamp or ammunition label
PG: pistol grip
PL: percussion lock
PP: paper patch in reference to bullets; Police Positive in reference to Colt revolvers
PP: Power-Point (Winchester) or protected point in reference to bullets; Police Positive in reference to Colt revolvers; Pistole Polizei (Police Pistol) in reference to Walther pistols
PPC: Police Pistol Course, a course of fire used in training police in handgun marksmanship
PS: peep sight
PSP: pointed soft point in reference to bullets

QD: quick detachable

QR: quick release

R: Sturm, Ruger, Inc.
RB: Rolling Block (Remington) rifle or pistol
RE: recoil energy
Rem-UMC: Remington-Union Metallic Cartridge Co.
RF: rapid-fire in reference to target shooting; rim-fire in reference to ammunition
RGS: Redfield Gun Sight Co.
R-P: Remington-Peters
RPM: rounds per minute in reference to cyclic rate of fire of an automatic weapon
RV: recoil velocity

S: safe in reference to a gun safety
S & W: Smith & Wesson
S & W/F: Smith & Wesson Fiocci
SA: Savage Arms
SA: Sierra Products
SA: single action in a handgun; also Springfield Armory; sometimes semi-automatic
SAA: Single Action Army, a Colt revolver
SB: single base powder
SBS: side-by-side in reference to double barrel guns
SD: sectional density in reference to bullets
SF: slow fire
SJ: short jacket in reference to a bullet
SL: headstamp for St. Louis Ordnance Plant
SMG: submachine gun
SMLE: Short Magazine Lee Enfield rifle
SO: secant ogive, a term used by Hornady to describe a particular form of bullet ogive
Sp: Speer Products
SP: small pistol primer; also superposed gun
SP: spire point or soft point in reference to bullets
Spcl: Special, as in .44 Special, in a cartridge designation

Spitz: spitzer (pointed) bullet
SR: semi-rimmed in reference to a cartridge case
SR: small rifle primer
SRC: saddle ring carbine
SS: single shot; sometimes shotshell
SST: single selective trigger; also single set trigger
ST: set trigger or single trigger; Silvertip (Winchester-Western) in reference to bullets
SWC: Semi-Wadcutter in reference to bullets
SV: Super Vel Cartridge Corp.
SX: Super X (Winchester-Western) in cartridge designation; also designates a form of varmint bullet by Hornady

TD: take down
TF: timed fire
TH: taper heel (same as boat tail)
Tr: tracer in reference to bullets
TW: headstamp for Twin Cities Arsenal

UMC: Union Metallic Cartridge Co.

Var: variable, indicating variable magnification in a scope sight
VG: very good in NRA condition standards
VR: ventilated rib

WC: wad cutter in reference to bullets
WCC: headstamp for Western Cartridge Co.
WL: wheel lock; also the small tie-breaking scoring ring inside the ten-ring of a standard American target
WP: waterproof
WRA: Winchester Repeating Arms Co.
W-W: Winchester-Western

X: single-diameter magnification, i.e., 3X is magnification of 3 diameters

Appendix 8/
Directory of the Arms Trade

This directory may not be 100 percent complete, but it includes a wide variety of sources for muzzle-loading goods and services. Inclusion herein does not constitute a recommendation of a particular firm, nor does failure to be included constitute any lack of approval.

Antique Arms Dealers

Abels, Robert.   P. O. Box 428, Hopewell Junction, New York 12533

Agramonte, Inc., Ed.   41 Riverdale Ave., Yonkers, New York 10701

Bannerman Sons, Inc., F.   P.O. Box 126, Blue Point, New York 11715

Boggs, William.   1243 Grandview Ave., Columbus, Ohio 43212

Ed's Gun House.   1626 West 9th St., Winona, Minnesota 55987

Epps, Ltd., Ellwood.   Hwy. 11 North, Orillia, Ontario, Canada

Farris Muzzle Guns.   1610 Gallia St., Portsmouth, Ohio 45662

Fidd, A. A.   Diamond Point Rd., Diamond Point, New York 12824

Flayderman, N. & Co.   Squash Hollow, New Milford, Connecticut 06776

Fulmer's Antique Firearms.   P. O. Box 792, Detroit Lakes, Minnesota 56501

Glass, Herb.   Bullville, New York 10915

Goergen's Gun Shop.   P.O. Box 499, Austin, Minnesota 55912

Goodman's for Guns.   1101 Olive St., St. Louis, Missouri 63101

Griffin's Guns & Antiques.   R. R. 4, Peterboro, Ontario, Canada K9J 6X5

Gun Shop, The.   6497 Pearl Rd., Cleveland, Ohio 44130

Hansen & Company.   244 Old Post Rd., Southport, Connecticut 06490

Heritage Firearms Co.   R.R. 7, Box 69, Wilton, Connecticut 06897

Holbrook Arms Museum.   12953 Biscayne Blvd., North Miami, Florida 33161

Jackson Arms.   6209 Hillcrest Ave., Dallas, Texas 75205

Jerry's Gun Shop.   9220 Ogden Ave., Brookfield, Illinois 60513

Kenfix Co.   3500 East Hillsborough Ave., Tampa, Florida 33610

Lever Arms Service, Ltd.   771 Dunsmuir St., Vancouver, British Columbia, Canada V6C 1M9

Malloy, John J.   Briar Ridge Rd., Danbury, Connecticut 06810

Moore, Charles W.   R.R. 2, Schenevus, New York 12155

Museum of Historical Arms.   1038 Alton Rd., Miami Beach, Florida 33139

National Gun Traders, Inc.   225 S.W. 22nd Ave., Miami, Florida 33135

New Orleans Arms Co., Inc.   P.O. Box 26087, New Orleans, Louisana 70186

Old West Gun Room.   3509 Carlson Blvd., El Cerrito, California 94530

Outrider, Inc., The.   3288 LaVenture Dr., Chamblee, Georgia 30341

Pioneer Guns. 5228 Montgomery, Cincinnati, Ohio 45212

Powell & Clements Sporting Arms. 210 East 6th St., Cincinnati, Ohio 45202

Retting, Martin B., Inc. 11029 Washington, Culver City, California 90230

Ridge Guncraft, Inc. 234 North Tulane Ave., Oak Ridge, Tennessee 37830

S. G. International. P.O. Box 702, Hermosa Beach, California 90254

Safari Outfitters, Ltd. 71 Ethan Allen Hwy., Ridgefield, Connecticut 06877

San Francisco Gun Exchange. 124 Second St., San Francisco, California 94105

Santa Ana Gunroom. P.O. Box 1777, Santa Ana, California 92702

Ward & Van Valkenburg. 402 30th Ave. North, Fargo, North Dakota 58102

Wiest, M. C. 234 North Tulane Ave., Oak Ridge, Tennessee 37830

Yale's Gun Shop. 2618 Conowingo Rd., Bel Air, Maryland 21014

Yearout, Lewis. 308 Riverview Dr. East, Great Falls, Montana 59404

Yeck Antique Firearms. 579 Tecumseh, Dundee, Michigan 48131

Bullet and Patch Lubricants

Alpha-Molykote Corp. 65 Harvard, Stamford, Connecticut 06904

Bullet Pouch. Box 4285, Long Beach, California 90804

Chopie Mfg., Inc. 531 Copeland, LaCrosse, Wisconsin 54601

Cooper-Woodward. P.O. Box 972, Riverside, California 92502

Herter's, Inc. Waseca, Minnesota 56903

Hodgdon, Inc., B. E. 7710 West 50 Hwy., Shawnee Mission, Kansas 66202

Javelina Products. P.O. Box 337, San Bernardino, California 92402

Lenz-Product Co. P.O. Box 1226, Station C, Canton, Ohio 44708

Lyman Products for Shooters. Middlefield, Connecticut 06455

Micro Shooter's Supply. P.O. Box 213, Las Cruces, New Mexico 88001

Shur-X-Bullet Co. 1493 Dewey Ave., Rochester, New York 14615

Cartridges for Collectors

Belton, J. A. 52 Sauve Rd., Mercier, Chateauguay City, Quebec, Canada

Bigler, Peter. 291 Crestwood Dr., Milltown, New Jersey 08850

Blakeslee, George. 3135 West 28th, Denver, Colorado 80211

Bratton, C. W. P.O. Box 42, Joy, Illinois 61260

Duffy, Charles E. Williams Lane, West Hurley, New York 12419

Gussman, R. A. P.O. Box 38, Canton, Massachusetts 02021

Howe, Ed. 2 Main St., Coopers Mills, Maine 04341

Jackson Arms. 6209 Hillcrest Ave., Dallas, Texas 75205

Miller Bros. Rapid City, Michigan 49676

Oregon Ammo Service. P.O. Box 19341, Portland, Oregon 97219

Spangler, Perry. 513 South Lynch, Flint, Michigan 48503

Tichy, Ernest. 365 South Moore, Denver, Colorado 80226

Tillinghast, James C. P.O. Box 568, Marlow, New Hampshire 03456

Cleaning and Refinishing Supplies

Arms Research of Texas. P.O. Box 19435, Houston, Texas 77024

Agramonte, Ed. 41 Riverdale Ave., Yonkers, New York 10701

Birchwood-Casey Chemical Co. 7900 Fuller Rd., Eden Prairie, Minnesota 55343

Bisonite Co., Inc. P.O. Box 84, Buffalo, New York 14217

Blue & Gray Products, Inc. 817 East Main St., Bradford, Pennsylvania 16701

Brobst, Jim. 299 Poplar St., Hamburg, Pennsylvania 19526

Brothers, George. Great Barrington, Massachusetts 01230

Bucheimer, J. J.. Airport Rd., Frederick, Maryland 21701

Chopie Mfg., Inc. 531 Copeland, LaCrosse, Wisconsin 54601

Clenzoil Co. P.O. Box 1226, Station C, Canton, Ohio 44708

Gun-All Products. P.O. Box 244, Dowagiac, Michigan 49047

Hoppe, Frank C. P.O. Box 97, Parkesburg, Pennsylvania 19365

Jet-Aer Corp. 100 Sixth Ave., Paterson, New Jersey 07524

Lehigh Chemical Co. P.O. Box 120, Chestertown, Maryland 21620

Liquid Wrench. P.O. Box 10628, Charlotte, North Carolina 28201

Lynx-Line Gun Products. Div. Protective Coatings, Inc. 20626 Fenkel Ave., Detroit, Michigan 48223

Mill Run Products. 1360 West 9th, Cleveland, Ohio 44113

Mistic Metal Mover, Inc. R.R. 2, Box 336, Princeton, Illinois 61356

Mitchell Chemical Co. Wampus Lane, Milford, Connecticut 06460

New Method Mfg. Co. P.O. Box 175, Bradford, Pennsylvania 16701

Numrich Arms Co.   West Hurley, New York 12491

Outers Laboratories.   P.O. Box 37, Onalaska, Wisconsin 54650

Pemberton, Glenn A.   260 Macedon Center Rd., Fairport, New York 14450

Rice Gun Coatings.   1521 43rd St., West Palm Beach, Florida 33407

Riel & Fuller.   423 Woodrow Ave., Dunkirk, New York 14048

Rig Products Co.   P.O. Box 279, Oregon, Illinois 61061

Rocket Chemical Co., Inc.   5390 Napa St., San Diego, California 92110

Rusteprufe Labs.   605 Wolcott St., Sparta, Wisconsin 54656

Shooters Specialties.   P.O. Box 264, LaMirada, California 90638

Van Gorden, C. S.   120 Tenth Ave., Eau Claire, Wisconsin 54701

Williams Gun Sight.   7389 Lapeer Rd., Davison, Michigan 48423

Withrow, Arthur C.   Los Angeles, California 90022

Components

Division Lead.   7742 West 61 Pl., Summit, Illinois 60502

Du Pont.   Explosives Dept., Wilmington, Delaware 19898

Hercules Powder Co.   910 Market St., Wilmington, Delaware 19899

Lyman Products for Shooters.   Middlefield, Connecticut 06455

Meyer Brothers.   Wabasha, Minnesota 55981

Remington-Peters.   Bridgeport, Connecticut 06602

Tillinghast, James C.   P.O. Box 568, Marlow, New Hampshire 03456

Vitt & Boos.   Sugarloaf Dr., Wilton, Connecticut 06897

Winchester-Western.   New Haven, Connecticut 06504

Custom Gunsmithing and Custom Gun Work

Anderson's Guns.   706 South 23rd St., Laramie, Wyoming 82070

Ann Arbor Arms, Inc.   1340 North Main, Ann Arbor, Michigan 48106

Atkinson Gun Co.   P.O. Box 512, Prescott, Arizona 86301

Bacon Creek Gun Shop.   Cumberland Falls Rd., Corbin, Kentucky 40701

Bain & Davis Sporting Goods.   559 West Las Tunas Dr., San Gabriel, California 41776

Bankard, William G.   4211 Thorncliff Rd., Baltimore, Maryland 21236

Benson, Irvin L.   Saganaga Lake, Pine Island Camp, Ontario, Canada

Bess, Gordon.   708 River St., Canon City, Colorado 81212

Boone Mountain Trading Post.   Averyville Rd., St. Marys, Pennsylvania 15857

Carl's Powder Keg.   14331 Clark St., Riverdale, Illinois 60627

Chicago Gun Center.   3109 West Armitage, Chicago, Illinois 60647

Crouthamel, Philip R.   513 East Baltimore, East Lansdowne, Pennsylvania 19050

Dunlap, Roy.   2319 Fort Lowell Rd., Tuscon, Arizona 85719

Ernst Custom Guns.   Fort Atkinson, Wisconsin 53538

Fellowes, Ted.   Beaver Lodge 9245-16th Ave. S.W., Seattle, Washington 98106

Frederick Gun Shop.   10 Elson Dr., Riverside, Rhode Island 02915

Fuller Gunshop.   Cooper Landing, Alaska 99572

Hobaugh, William.   P.O. Box 657, Philipsburg, Montana 59858

Huckleberry Gun Shop.   10440 Kingsbury Rd., Delton, Michigan 49046

Johnson's Kenai Rifles.   P.O. Box 6208, Annex Branch, Anchorage, Alaska 99502

Koozer, Ward.   P.O. Box 18, Walterville, Oregon 97489

McCormick's Gun Bluing Service.   4936 East Rosecrans Ave., Compton, California 90221

MacFarland, Harold E.   Star Route, Cottonwood, Arizona 86326

Maurer Arms.   2366 Frederick Dr., Cuyahoga Falls, Ohio 44221

Milhoan, Robert U. & Son.   R.R. 3, Elizabeth, West Virginia 26143

Mills Custom Stocks.   401 North Ellsworth, San Mateo, California 94401

National Gun Traders, Inc.   225 S.W. 22nd Ave., Miami, Florida 33135

New Mfg. Rifle Co.   539 Hidden Valley Dr., Houston, Texas 77037

Pachmayr Gun Works.   1220 South Grand Ave., Los Angeles, California 90015

Peterson Gun Shop, A. W.   1693 Old Highway 441, N., Mt. Dora, Florida 32757

Rush's Old Colonial Forge.   106 Wiltshire Rd., Baltimore, Maryland 21221

Schielke, George.   Washington Crossing, Titusville, New Jersey 08560

Schuetzen Gun Works.   1226 Prairie Rd., Colorado Springs, Colorado 80909

Sharon, J. Hall.   P. O. Box 106, Kalispell, Montana 59901

Southgate, R.   R.R. 2, Franklin, Tennessee 37064

Suter's House of Guns.   332 North Tejon, Colorado Springs, Colorado 80902

Van Patten, J. W.   P.O. Box 145, Foster Hill, Milford, Pennsylvania 18337

Williams Gun Sight Co.   7389 Lapeer Rd., Davison, Michigan 48423

Wyatt's Custom Gunshop.   Kosciusko, Mississippi 39090

York County Gun Works.   R.R. 4, Tottenham, Ontario, Canada

Gun Cases, Cabinets and Racks

American Safety Gun Case Co.   Holland, Michigan 49424

Coladonato Bros.   P.O. Box 156, Hazleton, Pennsylvania 18201

Dutton's.   R.R. 8, Box 508, Jacksonville, Florida 32216

Hodgdon, Inc., B.E.   7710 West 50 Hwy., Shawnee Mission, Kansas 66202

Kolpin Mfg., Inc.   P.O. Box 231, Berlin, Wisconsin 54923

Lock, Stock & Barrel.   Woodland Rd., Carlisle, Massachusetts 01741

Mastra Co.   2104 Superior, Cleveland, Ohio 44114

National Sports Div.   19 East McWilliams St., Fond du Lac, Wisconsin 54935

Protecto Plastics, Inc.   201 Alpha Road, Wind Gap, Pennsylvania 18091

Saf-T-Case.   P.O. Box 10512, Dallas, Texas 75207

Schoellkopf, Buddy.   4100 Platinum Way, Dallas, Texas 75237

Gun Parts, Antique and Replica

American Import Co.   1167 Mission St., San Francisco, California 94103

Antique Gun Parts, Inc.   1118 South Braddock Ave., Pittsburgh, Pennsylvania 15218

Armoury Inc., The.   R.R. 25, New Preston, Connecticut 06777

Bannerman Sons, Inc., F.   P.O. Box 126, Blue Point, New York 11715

Braverman, Shelley.   Athens, New York 12015

Carter Gun Works.   2211 Jefferson Park Ave., Charlottesville, Virginia 22903

Century Arms Co.   3-5 Federal St., St. Albans, Vermont 05478

Cole, T. P.   457 Ella St., Wilkinsburg, Pennsylvania 15221

Cornwall Bridge Gun Shop.   P.O. Box 67, Cornwall Bridge, Connecticut 06754

Craig, W. H.   P.O. Box 927, Selma, Alabama 36702

Darr's Rifle Shop.   2309 Black Rd., Joliet, Illinois 60435

Dixie Gun Works, Inc.   Hwy. 51, Union City, Tennessee 38261

Federal Ordnance, Inc.   9643 Alpaca St., S., El Monte, California 91733

International Gunmakers.   12315 Newburgh, Livonia, Michigan 48150

Kindig's Log Cabin Sport Shop.   R.R. 1, Box 275, Lodi, Ohio 44254

Lever Arms Service, Ltd.   771 Dunsmuir, Vancouver, British Columbia, Canada V6C 1M9

Lucas, Edward E.   32 Garfield Ave., Old Bridge, New Jersey 08857

Lyman Products for Shooters.   Middlefield, Connecticut 06455

Marek, R. M.   R.R. 1, Box 1-A, Banks, Oregon 97106

Markwell Arms Co.   2413 West Devon, Chicago, Illinois 60645

Mazzola, Thomas I.   6937 54th Ave., Maspeth, New York 11378

Navy Arms Co.   689 Bergen Blvd., Ridgefield, New Jersey 07657

Numrich Arms Co.   West Hurley, New York 12491

Outrider, Inc., The.   3288 LaVenture Dr., Chamblee, Georgia 30341

Powder Horn.   330 Perrine St., Piscataway, New Jersey 08854

Replica Models, Inc.   610 Franklin St., Alexandria, Virginia 22314

Retting, Inc., Martin B.   11029 Washington, Culver City, California 90230

Riflemen's Headquarters.   R.R. 3, RD 550-E, Kendallville, Indiana 46755

Romig, Norman S.   910 Fairmont Ave., Trenton, New Jersey 08629

S&S Firearms.   88-21 Aubrey Ave., Glendale, New York 11227

Service Armament Co.   689 Bergen Blvd., Ridgefield, New Jersey 07657

Simmons Spec., Inc.   700 Rogers Rd., Olathe, Kansas 66061

Solingen Cutlery.   P.O. Box 306, Montrose, California 91020

Stoeger Industries.   55 Ruta Court, South Hackensack, New Jersey 07606

Verner, R. M.   263 Kurtz Rd. Marietta, Georgia 30060

Waffen-Frankonia.   P.O. Box 380, 87 Wurzburg, West Germany

Weisz, C. H.   P.O. Box 311, Arlington, Virginia 22210

Wescombe, W. H.   P.O. Box 488, Glencoe, California 95232

Guns, American Made and Foreign Imports

American Import.   1167 Mission St., San Francisco, California 94103

Armoury, Inc., The.   R.R. 25, New Preston, Connecticut 06777

Centennial Arms Corp.   3318 West Devon, Chicago, Illinois 60645

Century Arms.   5340 Ferrier St., Montreal 309, Quebec, Canada

Challenger Mfg. Corp., Inc.   118 Pearl St., Mt. Vernon, New York 10550

Colt Firearms, Inc.   150 Huyshope Ave., Hartford, Connecticut 06102

Connecticut Valley Arms, Inc.   Haddam, Connecticut 06438

Cumberland Arms.   1222 Oak Dr., Manchester, Tennessee 37355

Dixie Gun Works, Inc.   Union City, Tennessee 38261

Firearms Import & Export Corp.   2470 N.W. 21st St., Miami, Florida 33142

Frazier, Clark K.   R.R. 1, Rawson, Ohio 45881

Golden Age Arms Co.   14 West Winter St., Delaware, Ohio 43015

Green River.   4326 120th Ave., S.E., Bellevue, Washington 98007

Greyhawk Arms Corp.   1900 Tyler Ave., Unit 15, South El Monte, California 91733

Harrington & Richardson.   Industrial Row, Gardner, Massachusetts 01440

Hawes Firearms.   8224 Sunset Blvd., Los Angeles, California 90046

High Standard Mfg. Co.   1817 Dixwell Ave., Hamden, Connecticut 06514

Interarms.   10 Prince St., Alexandria, Virginia 22313

Jana International.   P.O. Box 1107, Denver, Colorado 80201

Lyman Products for Shooters.   Middlefield, Connecticut 06455

Markwell Arms.   2413 West Devon, Chicago, Illinois 60645

Mowrey Gun Works, Inc.   P.O. Box 28, Iowa Park, Texas 76367

Navy Arms Co.   689 Bergen Blvd., Ridgefield, New Jersey 07657

North American Arms Co.   3303 Old Conejo Rd., Newbury Park, California 91320

North-Star Arms.   R.R. 2, Box 74A, Ortonville, Minnesota 56278

Numrich Arms Co.   West Hurley, New York 12491

PJK, Inc.   1527 Royal Oak Dr., Bradbury, California 91010

Potomac Arms Corp.   P.O. Box 35, Alexandria, Virginia 22313

Richland Arms.   321 West Adrian St., Blissfield, Michigan 49228

Sturm, Ruger & Co.   Southport, Connecticut 06490

Thompson/Center Arms.   P.O. Box 2405, Rochester, New Hampshire 03867

Tingle, Bob.   1125 Smithland Pike, Shelbyville, Indiana 46176

Trail Guns Armory.   2115 Lexington, Houston, Texas 77006

Gunsmithing Schools

Colorado School of Trades.   1545 Hoyt, Denver, Colorado 80215

Lassen Community College.   P.O. Box 3000, Susanville, California 96130

Oregon Institute of Technology.   Klamath Falls, Oregon 97601

Pennsylvania Gunsmith School.   812 Ohio River Blvd., Pittsburgh, Pennsylvania 15202

Trinidad State Junior College.   Trinidad, Colorado 81082

Gunsmithing Supplies, Tools and Services

Alley Supply Co.   Carson Valley Industrial Park, Gardnerville, Nevada 88410

American Edelstaal, Inc.   350 Broadway, New York, New York 10013

Armite Labs.   1845 Randolph St., Los Angeles, California 90001

B-Square Co.   P.O. Box 11281, Fort Worth, Texas 76110

Benrite Co.   353 Covington, San Antonio, Texas 78220

Brownell's.   200 South Front Street, Montezuma, Iowa 50171

Chicago Wheel & Mfg. Co.   1101 West Monroe St., Chicago, Illinois 60607

Christy Gun Works.   857 57th St., Sacramento, California 95819

Clymer Mfg. Co.   14241 West 11 Mile Rd., Oak Park, Michigan 48237

Dremel Mfg. Co.   4915 21st St., Racine, Wisconsin 53406

Grace Metal Products.   115 Ames St., Elk Rapids, Michigan 49629

Kasenite Co., Inc.   3 King St., Mahwah, New Jersey 07430

Marker Machine Co.   P.O. Box 426, Charleston, Illinois 61920

Mittermeier.   3577 East Tremont, New York, New York 10465

Neise, Inc.   Karl A., 5602 Roosevelt Ave., Woodside, New York 11377

P&C Tool Co.   P.O. Box 22066, Portland, Oregon 97222

Richland Arms Co.   321 West Adrian St., Blissfield, Michigan 49228

Roderick Arms & Tool Corp.   110 2nd St., Monett, Missouri 65708

Shaw's.   Rt. 4, Box 407-L, Escondito, California 92025

Starrett, L. S.   Athol, Massachusetts 01331

T. D. C.   P.O. Box 42072, Portland, Oregon 97242

Turner, C. Hunt.   618 South Gore Ave., Webster Groves, Missouri 63119

Twin City Steel Treating Co., Inc.   1114 South 3rd, Minneapolis, Minnesota 55415

Williams Gun Sight Co.   7389 Lapeer Rd., Davison, Michigan 48423

Wilson Arms Co.   63 Leetes Island Rd., Branford, Connecticut 06405

Wilton Tool Corp.   9525 West Irving Park Rd., Schiller Park, Illinois 60176

Handgun Accessories
Bo-Mar.   P.O. Box 168, Carthage, Texas 75633
Dangelzer, John.   3056 Frontier Pl., N.E.,
Albuquerque, New Mexico 87106
Frielich, R. S.   396 Broome St., New York, New
York 10013
Pachmayr Gun Works.   1220 South Grand, Los
Angeles, California 90015
Reiver, Jules.   4104 Market St., Wilmington,
Delaware 29899
Sportsmen's Equipment Co.   415 West Washington,
San Diego, California 92103

Handgun Grips
Herrett's Stocks.   P.O. Box 741, Twin Falls, Idaho
83301
Sanderson Custom Pistol Stocks.   17695 Fenton,
Detroit, Michigan 48219
Southwest Cutlery & Mfg. Co.   1309 Olympic Blvd.,
Montebello, California 90640
Womack, John W.   3006 Bibb St., Shreveport,
Louisiana 71102

Holsters and Leather Goods
Bianchi Holster Co.   100 Calle Cortez, Temecula,
California 92390
Bohlin, Edward H.   931 North Highland Ave.,
Hollywood, California 90038
Heiser Saddlery Co., Herman H.   1024 Cherokee St.,
Denver, Colorado 80204
Hume, Don.   P.O. Box 351, Miami, Oklahoma 74354
Lawrence, George.   306 S.W. First Ave.,
Portland, Oregon 97221
Myres Saddle Co., S.D.   P.O. Box 9776, El Paso,
Texas 79988
Navy Arms Co.   689 Bergen Blvd., Ridgefield, New
Jersey 07657
Tandy Leather Co.   1001 Foch, Fort Worth, Texas
76107

Hunting Knives, Axes and Hatchets
Baker Forged Knives.   P.O. Box 514, Hinsdale,
Illinois 60521
Bean, L.L.   Freeport, Maine 04032
Bear Archery Co.   R.R. 1, Grayling, Michigan 49738
Biggs, Lee.   3816 Via LaSilva, Palo Verde,
California 92266
Bone Knife Co., Ralph.   806 Avenue J, Lubbock,
Texas 79401
Bourne, H. Gardner.   1252 Hope Ave., Columbus,
Ohio 43212
Bowen Knife Co.   P.O. Box 14028, Atlanta, Georgia
30324
Brown, L.E.   3202 Del Amo Blvd., Lakewood,
California 90712
Buck Knives, Inc.   P.O. Box 1267, El Cajon,
California 92022

Busch Custom Knives.   418 Depre St., Mandeville,
Louisiana 70448
Callan, Pete.   17 Sherline Ave., New Orleans,
Louisiana 70124
Camillus Cutlery Co.   Main St., Camillus, New
York 13031
Case Knives, W.R.   20 Russell Blvd., Bradford,
Pennsylvania 16701
Challanger Mfg. Co.   118 Pearl St., Mt. Vernon,
New York 10550
Collins, Michael.   R.R. 4, Batesville Rd.,
Woodstock, Georgia 30188
Cooper Knives.   P.O. Box 1423, Burbank, California
91505
Custom Cutlery.   907 Greenwood Pl., Dalton,
Georgia 30720
Dan-D Custom Knives.   P.O. Box 4479, Yuma,
Arizona 85364
Davis Custom Knives.   North 1405 Ash, Spokane,
Washington 99201
Day, Philip.   R.R. 1, Box 465T, Bay Minetter,
Alabama 36507
Dennard, J.R.   907 Greenwood Pl., Dalton, Georgia
30720
D'Holder Custom Knives.   6808 North 30th Dr.,
Phoenix, Arizona 85017
Dickey, Charles E.   803 N.E. A St., Bentonville,
Arkansas 72712
Dowell, T.M.   139 St. Helen's Pl., Bend, Oregon
97701
Dozier, Rob.   P.O. Box 58, Palmetto, Louisiana
71358
Ek, John.   547 N.W. 119th St., North Miami,
Florida 33167
Fischer Custom Knives.   R.R. 1, Box 170-M,
Victoria, Texas 77901
Frank, H.H.   R.R. 1, Mountain Meadows,
Whitefish, Montana 59937
Franklin Handmade Knives.   R.R. 2, Columbus,
Indiana 47201
Furlow, James.   2499 Brookdale Dr., N.E., Atlanta,
Georgia 30345
Garcia Sporting Arms Co.   329 Alfred Ave.,
Teaneck, New Jersey 07666
Gault Knives.   1626 Palma Plaza, Austin, Texas
78703
Gerber Legendary Blades.   14200 S.W. 72nd St.,
Portland, Oregon 99223
Gutman Cutlery Co., Inc.   900 South Columbus
Ave., Mt. Vernon, New York 10550
H&B Forge Co.   R.R. 2, Box 24, Shiloh, Ohio 44837
Hale Handmade Knives.   609 Henrietta St.,
Springdale, Arkansas 72764
Heath, C.M.   119 Grant St., Winnecone, Wisconsin
54986
Henckels Twinworks, J.A.   1 Westchester Plaza,
Elmsford, New York 10523

Heritage Custom Knives. 2895 Senaca St., Buffalo, New York 14224

Herron, G.H. 920 Murrah Ave., Aiken, South Carolina 29801

Hibben Knives. P.O. Box 207, Star Route A, Anchorage, Alaska 99502

Hueske, Chubby. 4808 Tamarisk Dr., Bellaire, Texas 77401

Imel Custom Knives. 945 Jameson Ct., New Castle, Indiana 47362

Imperial Knive Assn. Co., Inc. 1776 Broadway, New York, New York 10019

Indian Ridge Traders. P.O. Box X-50, Ferndale, Michigan 48220

Jet-Aer Corp. 100 Sixth Ave., Paterson, New Jersey 07524

Johnston, LaDow. 2322 West Country Club Parkway, Toledo, Ohio 43614

KA-BAR Cutlery, Inc. 5777 Grant Ave., Cleveland, Ohio 44105

Kirk, Jon W. 800 North Olive, Fayetteville, Arkansas 72701

Kneubuhler, W. P.O. Box 327, Pioneer, Ohio 43554

Kustom Made Knives. 418 Jolee, Richardson, Texas 75080

Lile Handmade Knives. R.R. 1, Box 56, Russellville, Arkansas 72801

LocKnife, Inc. 11717 East 23rd St., Independence, Missouri 64050

Loveless, R.W. P.O. Box 7836, Arlington Station, Riverside, California 92503

Ludwig, Bob. 1028 Pecos Ave., Port Arthur, Texas 77640

Marble Arms Corp. 420 Industrial Park, Gladstone, Michigan 49837

McBurnette, H.O. R.R. 4, Box 337, Piedmont, Alabama 36272

Mims, John T. 620 South 28th Ave., Apt. 327, Hattiesburg, Mississippi 39401

Mitchell Knives. 511 Ave. B., South Houston, Texas 77587

Moran, W.F. R.R. 5, Frederick, Maryland 21701

Morseth Sports Equip. Co. 1705 Hwy 71 N., Springdale, Arkansas 72764

Naifeh Knives. R.R. 13, Box 380, Tulsa, Oklahoma 74107

Nolen Knives. P.O. Box 6216, Corpus Christi, Texas 78411

Normark Corp. 1710 East 78th St., Minneapolis, Minnesota 55423

Ogg Custom Knives. R.R. 1, Box 230, Paris, Arkansas 72855

Olsen Knife Co., Inc. 7 Joy St., Howard City, Michigan 49329

Ramrod Knife & Gun Shop. R.R. 5, State Rd. 3 North, Newcastle, Indiana 47362

Randall-Made Knives. P.O. Box 1988, Orlando, Florida 32802

Richtig, F.J. Clarkson, Nebraska 68629

Rigid Knives. P.O. Box 460, Santee, California 92071

Ruana Knife Works. P.O. Box 574, Bonner, Montana 59823

Russell, A.G. 1705 Hwy. 71 N., Springdale, Arkansas 72764

Sanders. 2358 Tyler Lane, Louisville, Kentucky 40205

Schmier, Jack D. 16787 Mulberry Ct., Fountain Valley, California 92708

Schiffman Custom Knives, N.H. 963 Malibu, Pocatello, Idaho 83201

Schwarz, John J. 41 Fifteenth St., Wellsburg, West Virginia 26070

Sigman, C.R. Star Rte., Box 3, Red House, West Virginia 25168

Silver Fox Knives. 4714 44th St., Dickinson, Texas 77539

Smith & Wesson. 2100 Roosevelt Ave., Springfield, Massachusetts 01101

Smith, John T. 6048 Cedar Crest Dr., South Haven, Mississippi 38671

Sonneville, W.J. 1050 Chalet Dr. W., Mobile, Alabama 36608

Sparks, Bernard. P.O. Box 32, Dingle, Idaho 83233

Stone Knives. 703 Floyd Rd., Richardson, Texas 75080

Thompson/Center. P.O. Box 2405, Rochester, New Hampshire 03867

Towell, Dwight L. R.R. 1, Midvale, Idaho 83645

Track Knives. 1313 2nd St., Whitefish, Montana 59937

Tru-Balance Knife Co. 2115 Tremont Blvd., Grand Rapids, Michigan 49504

True-Temper. 1623 Euclid, Cleveland, Ohio 44100

Unique Inventions, Inc. 3727 West Alabama St., Houston, Texas 77027

W-K Knives. P.O. Box 327, Pioneer, Ohio 43554

Western Cutlery Co. 5311 Western Ave., Boulder, Colorado 80302

Wilber, W.C. 400 Lucerne Dr., Spartanburg, South Carolina 29302

Wilson, Ronnie. P.O. Box 2012, Weirton, West Virginia 26062

Zaccagnino, Don. P.O. Box Zack, Pahokee, Florida 33476

Metallic Sights

B-Square Eng. P.O. Box 11281, Fort Worth, Texas 76110

Bo-Mar Tool & Mfg. Co. Box 168, Carthage, Texas 75633

Buehler, Inc., Maynard P. 17 Orinda Hwy, Orinda, California 94563

Burton Arms Co. P.O. Box 524, Coshocton, Ohio 43812

Elliason, George. 2109 Carroll Pl., Tampa, Florida 33612

Hi-Lo Sights. P.O. Box 131, Lyndon Station, Wisconsin 53944

Lyman Products for Shooters. Middlefield, Connecticut 06455

Marble Arms Corp. 420 Industrial Park, Gladstone, Michigan 49837

Merit Gunsight Co. P.O. Box 995, Sequim, Washington 98382

Micro Sight Co. 242 Harbor Blvd., Belmont, California 94002

Original Sight Exchange Co. P.O. Box J, Paoli, Pennsylvania 19301

Redfield Gun Sight Co. 5800 East Jewell St., Denver, Colorado 80222

Simmons Gun Specialties, Inc. 700 Rodgers Rd., Olathe, Kansas 66061

Trius Products. P.O. Box 25, Cleves, Ohio 45002

Williams Gun Sight Co. 7389 Lapeer Rd., Davison, Michigan 48423

Miscellaneous

bedding kit; Bisonite Co. P.O. Box 84, Buffalo, New York 14217

bedding kit; Resin Systems Div., Fenwal, Inc. 400 Main St., Ashland, Massachusetts 01721

bore collimator; Alley Supply Co. P.O. Box 458, Sonora, California 95370

bore lamp; Spacetron, Inc. P.O. Box 84, Broadview, Illinois 60155

borescope; Eder Instrument Co. 2293 North Clybourn, Chicago, Illinois 60614

borescope; J.G. Mundy. 1008 MacDade Blvd., Collingdale, Pennsylvania 19023

breech plug wrench; Swaine Machine. 195 O'Connell, Providence, Rhode Island 02905

bullet trap; Sterling-Fleischman,Inc. Pennsylvania Ave., Malvern, Pennsylvania 19355

chrome barrel lining; Marker Machine Co. P.O. Box 426, Charleston, Illinois 61920

chronograph; American Craftsmen. 12645 LaCresta Dr., Los Altos Hills, California 94022

chronograph; Avtron. 10409 Meech, Cleveland, Ohio 44105

chronograph; B-Square Co. P.O. Box 11281, Fort Worth, Texas 76110

chronograph; Chrondek Electronics, Inc. 2125 D St., LaVerne, California 91750

chronograph; ITCC. 4117 Sherman, Riverside, California 92303

chronograph; Micro-Sight Co. 242 Harbor Blvd., Belmont, California 94002

contour gauge; Pennsylvania Industries. P.O. Box 8904, Philadelphia, Pennsylvania 19135

custom bluing; J.A. Wingert. 124 West 2nd St., Waynesboro, Pennsylvania 17268

distress flares; Marsh Coulter Co. P.O. Box 333, Tecumseh, Michigan 49286

Ear-Valv; Sigma Engineering Co. 11320 Burbank Blvd., North Hollywood, California 91601

epoxy kit; Ann Arbor,Inc. 13400 North Main, Ann Arbor, Michigan 48107

Firearm Identification Service; H.P. White Co. P.O. Box 331, Bel Air, Maryland 21014

gun bedding kit; Resin Div., Fenwal, Inc. 400 Main St., Ashland, Massachusetts 01721

hearing protector; American Optical Co. Southbridge, Massachusetts 01550

hearing protector; David Clark Co. 360 Franklin St., Worcester, Massachusetts 01601

hearing protector; Curtis Safety Products Co. P.O. Box 82, Webster Square Station, Worcester, Massachusetts 01601

hearing protector; Ray-O-Vac. 212 East Washington, Madison, Wisconsin 53703

hearing protector, Sanitizer Bath; Graco Pharmacy Co. 172 West Main St., Meriden, Connecticut 06450

leather rest-bags; B. Tuller. 29 Germania, Galeton, Pennsylvania 16922

magazine, powder; C&M Gun Works. 2603 41st St., Moline, Illinois 61265

miniature guns; C.H. Stoppler. 1426 Walton Ave., New York, New York 10459

nipple wrenches; Chopie Tool & Die Co. 531 Copeland Ave., LaCrosse, Wisconsin 54603

NRA targets; Wisler Western Target Co. 205 2nd St., San Francisco, California 94105

powder flasks; Jewell Powder Flask Co. Central Ave., East Bango, Pennsylvania 18013

powder flasks repair; G.S. Bunch. 7735 Garrison, Yattsville, Maryland 20784

recoil pads, etc.; Mershon Co., Inc. 1230 South Grand, Los Angeles, California 90025

recoil pads; Pachmayr Gun Works. 1220 South Grand Ave., Los Angeles, California 90015

recoil pads; Supreme Products. P.O. Box 4261, Glendale, California 91302

recoil reducer; J.B. Edwards. 269 Herbert St., Alton, Illinois 62002

restoration; J.J. Jenkins. 462 Stanford Pl., Santa Barbara, California 93105

rifle rests; The Gun Case. 11035 Maplefield, El Monte, California 91733

RIG, NRA scoring plug; Rig Product Co. P.O. Box 279, Oregon, Illinois 60262

Salute cannons; Naval C. Rt. 611, Doylestown, Pennsylvania 18901

shooting coats; 10-X Mfg. Co. 100 S.W. 3rd, Des Moines, Iowa 50309

shooting glasses; M.B. Dinsmore. P.O. Box 21, Wyomissing, Pennsylvania 19610

shooting glasses; Mitchell's. P.O. Box 539, Waynesville, Missouri 65583 shooting ranges; Shooting Equipment, Inc. 4616 West 20th St., Chicago, Illinois 60650

silver grip caps; Bill Dyer. P.O. Box 75255, Oklahoma City, Oklahoma 73107

silver grip caps; Katz & Prosser. 18401 Via Jose, San Lorenzo, California 94580

springs; W.C. Wolff Co. P.O. Box 232, Ardmore, Pennsylvania 19003

stones, Arkansas; A.G. Russell. 1705 Hwy. 71 N., Springdale, Arkansas 72764

target carrier; Tyrol Sports Arms. 7860 West Jewell, Lakewood, Colorado 80227

target, folding; Gopher Shooters Supply. P.O. Box 246, Faribault, Minnesota 55021

target holder; Product Masters Mfg. Co. 5013 Aldrich Ave., Minneapolis, Minnesota 55430

target patches; Time Products Co. 355 Burlington Rd., Riverside, Illinois 60546

target stamp; Amos. R.R. 1, Telegraph Rd., Brownsville, Pennsylvania 15417

taxidermy; Jack Atcheson. 2309 Hancock Ave., Butte, Montana 59701

taxidermy; Jonas Bros. 1037 Broadway, Denver, Colorado 80203

taxidermy; Knopp Bros. Spokane, Washington 99210

taxidermy; John Schneider. Clifton, New Jersey 07015

taxidermy; Mac's. 201 North Grand Ave., Waukesha, Wisconsin 53187

trophies; Blackinton & Co. 140 Commonwealth, Attleboro Falls, Massachusetts 02763

trophies; F. H. Noble & Co. 559 West 59th St., Chicago, Illinois 60621

Reboring and Rerifling

Ackely. P.O. 2235 Arbor Lane, Salt Lake City, Utah 84117

Atkinson Gun Co. P.O. Box 512, Prescott, Arizona 86301

Bain & Davis Sporting Goods. 559 West Las Tunas Dr., San Gabriel, California 91776

Carpenter's Gun Works. Gunshop Rd., Plattekill, New York 12568

Fuller Gun Shop. Cooper Landing, Alaska 99572

Kaufield Small Arms Engineering Co., John. P.O. Box 306, Des Plaines, Illinois 60018

Koozer, Ward. P.O. Box 18, Walterville, Oregon 97489

Les' Gun Shop. P.O. Box 511, Kalispell, Montana 59901

Morgan's Custom Reboring. 707 Union Ave., Grants Pass, Oregon 97526

Nu-Line Guns. 3727 Jennings Rd., St. Louis, Missouri 63121

Petersen, Al. P.O. Box 8, Riverhurst, Saskatchewan, Canada SOH 3P0

Schuetzen Gun Works. 1226 Prairie Rd., Colorado Springs, Colorado 80909

Siegrist Gun Shop. 2689 McLean Rd., Whittemore, Michigan 48770

Small Arms Engineering. P.O. Box 306, Des Plaines, Illinois 60018

Snapp's Gunshop. 6911 East Washington Rd., Clare, Michigan 48617

Southgate, R. R.R. 2, Franklin, Tennessee 37064

Van Patten, J.W. P.O. Box 145, Foster Hill, Milford, Pennsylvania 18337

West, Robert G. R.R. 1, P.O. Box 941, Eugene, Oregon 97402

Reloading Tools and Accessories

Alpha-Molykote Corp. 65 Harvard, Stamford, Connecticut 06904

Anchor Alloys, Inc. 966 Meeker Ave., Brooklyn, New York 11222

B-Square Engineering Co. P.O. Box 11281, Fort Worth, Texas 76110

Belding & Mull. P.O. Box 428, Philipsburg, Pennsylvania 16866

Bonanza Sports, Inc. 412 Western Ave., Faribault, Minnesota 55021

Cascade Cartridge, Inc. P.O. Box 660, Lewiston, Idaho 83501

Cooper Engineering. 612 East 20th, Houston, Texas 77008

Cooper-Woodward. P.O. Box 972, Riverside, California 92502

Division Lead Co. 7742 West 61st Pl. Summit, Illinois 60502

Dom Enterprises. 3985 Lucas, St. Louis, Missouri 63103

Fitz. P.O. Box 49697, Los Angeles, California 90049

Flambeau Plastics. 802 Lynn, Baraboo, Wisconsin 53913

Gun Clinic, The. 81 Kale St., Mahtomedi, Minnesota 55115

H&H Sealants. P.O. Box 448, Saugerties, New York 12477

Hensley & Gibbs. P.O. Box 10, Murphy, Oregon 97533

Hodgdon, Inc., B.E. 7710 West 50 Hwy., Shawnee Mission, Kansas 66202

Javelina Products. P.O. Box 337, San Bernardino, California 92402

Lee Engineering. 46 E. Jackson, Hartford, Wisconsin 53027

Lyman Products for Shooters. Middlefield, Connecticut 06455

National Lead Co. P.O. Box 831, Perth Amboy, New Jersey 08861

Ohaus Scale Corp. 29 Hanover Rd., Florham Park, New Jersey 07932

Powd-R-Horn. 3802 West Augusta, Phoenix, Arizona 85021

RCBS, Inc.   P.O. Box 1919, Oroville, California 95965

Redding,Inc.   114 Starr Rd., Corland, New York 13045

Rochester Lead Works.   Rochester, New York 14608

Rotex Mfg. Co.   8305 Sovereign Row, Dallas, Texas 75222

SAECO.   P.O. Box 778, Carpinteria, California 93013

Scientific Lubricants Co.   3753 Lawrence Ave., Chicago, Illinois 60625

Shooters Accessory Supply (SAS).   P.O. Box 250, North Bend, Oregon 97459

Rifle Barrel Manufacturers

Atkinson Gun Co.   P.O. Box 512, Prescott, Arizona 86301

Ackley, P.O.   2235 Arbor Lane, Salt Lake City, Utah 84117

Christy Gun Works.   875 57th St., Sacramento, California 95831

Douglas, G.R.   5504 Big Tyler Rd., Charleston, West Virginia 25312

Hobaugh, William H.   P.O. Box 657, Philipsburg, Montana 59858

International Gunmakers.   12315 Newburgh Rd., Livonia, Michigan 48150

Les' Gun Shop.   P.O. Box 511, Kalispell, Montana 59902

Nauman, L.E.   1048 South 5th, Douglas, Wyoming 82633

Numrich Arms.   West Hurley, New York 12491

Sharon Rifle Barrel Co.   P.O. Box 106, Kalispell, Montana 59901

Titus Barrel & Gun Co.   R.R. 1, Box 23, Heber, Utah 84032

Watts, M.G.   5627 Euclid, Kansas City, Missouri 64130

Wilson Arms.   63 Leetes Island Rd., Branford, Connecticut 06405

Scopes, Mounts, Accessories and Optical Equipment

Bausch & Lomb Optical Co.   635 St. Paul St., Rochester, New York 14602

Browning Arms.   Rt. 4, Box 624-B, Arnold, Missouri 63010

Buehler, Inc. Maynard P.   17 Orinda Hwy., Orinda, California 94563

Bushnell Optical Co.   2828 East Foothill Blvd., Pasadena, California 91107

Conetrol. Hwy. 123 South, Seguin, Texas 78155

Firearms International.   4837 Kerby Hill Rd., Washington, D.C. 20022

Flaig's.   Babcock Blvd., Millvale, Pennsylvania 15209

Kesselring Gun Shop.   R.R. 1, P.O. Box 350, Burlington, Washington 98233

Kuharsky Bros.   2425 West 12th St., Erie, Pennsylvania 16501

Leupold & Stevens Instruments.   P.O. Box 688, Beaverton, Oregon 97005

Marble Arms Co.   420 Industrial Park, Gladstone, Michigan 49837

Marlin Firearms Co.   100 Kenna Dr., New Haven, Connecticut 06473

Modern Industries, Inc.   613 West 11th, Erie, Pennsylvania 16501

Numrich Arms.   West Hurley, New York 12491

Premier Reticles.   Perry, West Virginia 26844

Redfield Gun Sight Co.   5800 East Jewel Ave., Denver, Clorado 80210

Unertl Optical Co., John.   3551-5 East St., Pittsburgh, Pennsylvania 15214

Weaver Co.,W.R.   7125 Industrial Ave., El Paso, Texas 79915

Targets and Bullet Traps

Detroit Bullet Trap Co.   2233 No. Palmer Dr., Schaumberg, Illinois 60172

National Target Co.   4960 Wyaconda Rd., Rockville, Maryland 20852

Product Masters.   5013 North Aldrich, Minneapolis, Minnesota 55430

Sheridan Products, Inc.   3205 Sheridan, Racine, Wisconsin 53403

X-Ring Prod. Co.   Outers Laboratory, Onalaska, Wisconsin 54650

Appendix 9/Books and Periodicals for the Black Powder Buff

Although not all of the books and magazines on the list that follows are directly related to muzzle loading, reading them will enhance your overall knowledge of guns. Those publications devoted to muzzle loading will be obvious from their titles; others contain information about shooting the old guns. The range of subjects is wide enough so that the information gleaned will be applicable to muzzle loaders as to other arms.

Books

Angier, R. H. **Firearms Bluing and Browning.** 1936. Stackpole.

Askins, Charles. **Texans, Guns and History.** 1970. Winchester Press.

Baird, John D. **Fifteen Years in the Hawken Lode.** 1971. Buckskin Press.

——**Hawken Rifles: The Mountain Man's Choice.** 1968. Buckskin Press.

Baker, Clyde. **Modern Gunsmithing.** 1963. Stackpole.

Blackmore, Howard L. **British Military Firearms, 1650-1850.** 1962. Arco.

——**Guns and Rifles of the World.** 1965. Viking Press.

Boothroyd, Geoffrey. **The Handgun.** 1970. Crown.

Bowman, Hank W. **Famous Guns from the Winchester Collection.** 1958. Arco.

——**Famous Guns from the Smithsonian Collection.** 1966. Arco.

Bridges, Toby, ed. **Black Powder Gun Digest.** 1972. D.B.I.

Buchele, William. **Recreating the American Long Rifle** (orig. title: **Recreating the Kentucky Rifle**) 1967. Shumway.

Butler, David F. **U.S. Firearms, The First Century, 1776-1875.** 1973. Winchester Press.

Carey, A. Merwyn. **English, Irish and Scottish Firearms Makers.** 1967. Arco.

Coggins, Jack. **Ships and Seamen of the American Revolution.** 1969. Stackpole.

Dillin, John G. **The Kentucky Rifle, 5th Ed.** 1967. Shumway.

Dunlap, Roy F. **Gunsmithing.** 1963. Stackpole.

Glendenning, Ian. **British Pistols and Guns, 1640-1840.** 1967. Arco.

Hicks, James E. **French Military Weapons, 1717-1938.** 1964. Flayderman.

Howe, Walter J. **Professional Gunsmithing.** 1946. Stackpole.

Kennedy, Monty. **Checkering and Carving of Gunstocks.** 1962. Stackpole.

Keogh, S.G. **Samuel Colt's New Model Pocket Pistols.** 1964. Keogh.

Kindig, Joe, Jr. **Thoughts on the Kentucky Rifle in its Golden Age.** 1971. Shumway.

Klinger, R. and R.A. Wilder. **Sketch Book '76: The American Soldier, 1775-1781.** 1967. Pioneer Press.

Lavin, James D. **History of Spanish Firearms.** 1965. Arco.

Lenk, Thorsten. **The Flintlock: Its Origin and Development.** 1969. Saifer.

Lewis, Berkeley R. **Small Arms and Ammunition in the United States Service, 1776-1865.** 1956. Smithsonian Institution Press.

Lindsay, Merrill. **The Kentucky Rifle.** 1972. Arms Press.

——**One Hundred Great Guns.** 1967. Walker and Co.

Moore, Warren E. **Weapons of the American Revolution.** 1967. Funk and Wagnalls.

MacFarland, Harold E. **Introduction to Modern Gunsmithing.** 1965. Stackpole.

National Muzzle Loading Rifle Association. **Muzzle Blasts: Early Years Plus Vols. I and II, 1939-41.** 1974. Shumway.

Nesmith, J.H. **The Soldier's Manual for Cavalry, Artillery, Light Infantry and Infantry** (first published in Philadelphia in 1824). 1963. Shumway.

Nonte, George C., Jr. **Firearms Encyclopedia.** 1973. Times-Mirror (Dist. by Harper and Row).

——**Home Guide to Muzzle Loaders.** 1974. Stackpole.

——**Pistol and Revolver Guide, 3rd Ed.** 1975. Stoeger.

——**Pistolsmithing.** 1974. Stackpole.

Peterson, Harold R. **Book of the Continental Soldier.** 1974. Stackpole.

——**Encyclopedia of Firearms.** 1964. Dutton.

——**Pageant of the Gun.** 1967. Doubleday.

——and Robert Elman. **Great Guns.** 1971. Grosset and Dunlap.

Pollard, Hugh B. **The History of Firearms.** 1974. B. Franklin.

Riling, Ray. **The Powder Flask Book.** 1953. Bonanza.

Rosebus, Waldo E. **American Firearms and the Changing Frontier.** 1962. Eastern Washington.

Russell, Carl. **Firearms, Traps and Tools of the Mountain Men.** 1967. Knopf.

Rywell, Martin. **American Antique Pistols.** Pioneer Press.

——**Confederate Guns.** Pioneer Press.

——**The Powder Flask.** Pioneer Press.

——**U.S. Muskets, Rifles and Carbines.** Pioneer Press.

Schon, J. **Rifled Infantry Arms.** (Facsimile reprint of book orig. pub. in Dresden, Germany, in 1855. Trans. by Capt. J. Gorgas, U.S.A.). 1965. W.E. Meuse.

Serven, James E. **Colt Firearms from 1836.** 1964. Foundation.

Shumway, George. **Arms Makers of Philadelphia.** Shumway.

——**Long Rifles of Note—Pennsylvania.** 1968. Shumway.

Steindler, R.A. **The Firearms Dictionary.** 1970. Stackpole.

——**Reloader's Guide, 3rd Ed.** 1975. Stoeger.

Steindler, R.A., ed. **Shooting the Muzzle Loaders.** 1975. Jolex, Inc.

Tout, Thomas F. **Firearms in England in the Fourteenth Century.** 1969. Shumway.

West, Bill. **Marlin and Ballard, Arms and History, 1861-1971.** 1972 B. West.

——**Remington Arms and History, 1816-1971.** 1972. B. West.

——**Savage and Stevens, Arms and History, 1849-1971.** 1971. B. West.

——**Winchester—Complete: All Wins and Forerunners, 1849-1970.** 1976. B. West.

Wilkinson, F. **Flintlock Guns and Rifles.** 1971. Stackpole.

Periodicals

American Field
American Field Publishing
 Company
222 West Adams Street
Chicago, Illinois 60606

American Firearms Industry
7001 North Clark Street
Chicago, Illinois 60626

The American Hunter
National Rifle Association
1600 Rhode Island Avenue, N.W.
Washington, D.C. 20036

The American Rifleman
National Rifle Association
1600 Rhode Island Avenue
Washington, D.C. 20036

The American Shotgunner
P.O. Box 3351
Reno, Nevada 89505

Argosy
Popular Publications, Inc.
420 Lexington Ave.
New York, N.Y. 10017

Arms Gazette
13222 Saticoy Street
North Hollywood, California 91605

Army
Association of the U.S. Army
1529 18th Street, N.W.
Washington, D.C. 20036

Ducks Unlimited
P.O. Box 66300
Chicago, Illinois 60666

Field & Stream
CBS Publications
383 Madison Avenue
New York, N.Y. 10017

Fishing and Hunting News
Fishing and Hunting News, Inc.
511 Eastlake E.
Seattle, Washington 98109

Fur-Fish-Game
(Harding's Magazine)
A. R. Harding Publishing Co.
2878 East Main Street
Columbus, Ohio 43209

Great Lakes Sportsman
Sportsman Publications, Inc.
26555 Evergreen Road, Suite 410
Southfield, Michigan 48076

The Gun Report
110 South College Avenue
Aledo, Illinois 61231

Gunsport and Gun Collector
Leisure Publishing Company
711 Penn Ave.
Pittsburgh, Pennsylvania 15222

Gun Week
911 Vandemark Road
Sidney, Ohio 45365

Gun World
Gallant Publishing Company, Inc.
P.O. Box 325
Brea, California 92621

Guns and Ammo
Petersen Publishing Company
8490 Sunset Boulevard
Los Angeles, California 90069

Guns Magazine
8150 North Central Park
   Boulevard
Skokie, Illinois 60076

The Handloader
Box 30-30
Prescott, Arizona 86301

Hunting
Petersen Publishing Company
8490 Sunset Boulevard
Los Angeles, California 90069

KaHagon
131 North Main Street
Pittston, Pennsylvania 18640

Muzzle Blasts
P.O. Box 67
Friendship, Indiana 47021

National Defense
American Defense Preparedness
   Association
819 Union Trust Building
Washington, D.C. 20005

Outdoor Life
Times Mirror Magazines, Inc.
380 Madison Avenue
New York, N.Y. 10017

Outdoor Press
N. 2012 Ruby Street
Spokane, Washington 99207

Point Blank
Citizens Committee for the Right
   to Keep and Bear Arms
1601 114th S.E.,
Bellevue, Washington 98004

Popular Mechanics
The Hearst Corporation
224 West 57th Street
New York, N.Y. 10019

Popular Science
Times Mirror Magazines, Inc.
380 Madison Avenue
New York, N.Y. 10017

Precision Shooting
Box 6
Athens, Pennsylvania 18810

The Rifle Magazine
Box 30-30
Prescott, Arizona 86301

Saga
Gambi Publishing Corporation
333 Johnson Avenue
Brooklyn, N.Y. 11026

The Shooting Industry
Publishers Development
   Corporation
8150 North Central Park Boulevard
Skokie, Illinois 60076

Shooting Times
P.S.J. Publications
News Plaza
Peoria, Illinois 61601

Shotgun News
Box 1147
Hastings, Nebraska 68901

Skeet Shooting Review
National Skeet Shooting Association
P.O. Box 28188
San Antonio, Texas 78228

Sports Afield
The Hearst Corporation
250 West 55th Street
New York, N.Y. 10019

Sports Illustrated
Time, Inc.
1271 Ave. of the Americas
New York, N.Y. 10020

Trap and Field
Curtis Publishing Company
1100 Waterway Boulevard
Indianapolis, Indiana 46202

True
Petersen Publishing Co., Inc.
8490 Sunset Boulevard
Los Angeles, California 90069

Canadian Periodicals

Alberta Sportsman
Railton Publications, Ltd.
125 Talisman Avenue
Vancouver, British Columbia

B.C. Outdoors
Northwest Digest, Ltd.
Box 900, Station A
Surrey, British Columbia V3S 4P4

Fish and Game Sportsman
Nimrod Publications, Ltd.
P.O. Box 1654
Regina, Saskatchewan

Northwest Sportsman
Railton Publications, Ltd.
125 Talisman Avenue
Vancouver, British Columbia

Quebec Chasse et Peche
Les Publications Plein Air, Inc.
3339 Desmartean Street
Montreal, Quebec

Western Fish and Wildlife
J.L. Grundle, Editor and Publisher
1591 Bowser Street
Vancouver, British Columbia

Wildlife Crusader
Manitoba Wildlife Federation
St. James and Notre Dame
Winnipeg, Manitoba